# Old Age from Antiquity to Post-Modernity

With the publication of *Old Age from Antiquity to Post-Modernity* historical gerontology takes a major step toward maturity. Focusing on three critical issues – participation, well-being and status – in defining continuities and changes in the elderly's place in society, this is the best collection of essays in this subfield published to date.

W. Andrew Achenbaum, Institute of Gerontology,
University of Michigan

Ageing is fast becoming the outstanding issue of our time. All students of the subject will find this volume illuminating, as will everyone concerned with social welfare.

Peter Laslett, Trinity College, Cambridge

Based upon interdisciplinary themes such as status and welfare, *Old Age from Antiquity to Post-Modernity* contains a collection of essays examining old age and the elderly in past societies, and the problems of a rapidly ageing population in its historical context.

From Ancient Greece to modern Germany and New Zealand, this book features both methodological and empirical studies, and includes essays on:

- ageing in antiquity
- old age in the high and late middle ages – image, expectation and status
- ageing and well-being in early modern England
- balancing social and cultural approaches to the history of old age and ageing in Europe
- old age in the new world – New Zealand's colonial welfare experiment

*Old Age from Antiquity to Post-Modernity* represents a substantial contribution to the historical understanding of old age in past societies as well as to the discussion about the application of different research methodologies to historical scholarship.

**Paul Johnson** is Reader in Economic History at the London School of Economics.
**Pat Thane** is Professor of Contemporary History at the University of Sussex.

# Old Age from Antiquity to Post-Modernity

Edited by Paul Johnson and Pat Thane

London and New York

First published 1998
by Routledge
11 New Fetter Lane, London EC4P 4EE

Simultaneously published in the USA and Canada
by Routledge
29 West 35th Street, New York, NY 10001

© 1998 Selection and editorial matter, Paul Johnson and Pat Thane;
individual chapters, the contributors

Typeset in Times by Routledge
Printed and bound in Great Britain by Biddles Ltd, Guildford and
King's Lynn

*British Library Cataloguing in Publication Data*
A catalogue record for this book is available from the British Library

*Library of Congress Cataloging in Publication Data*
Old age from Antiquity to post-modernity / edited by Paul Johnson
    and Pat Thane.
    (Routledge studies in cultural history; 1)
    1. Old age – History. 2. Old age – Social aspects. 3. Aged – History.
    I. Johnson, Paul, 1956– . II. Thane, Pat.
    III. Series
    HQ1061.0377  1998   98–20561
    305.26–dc21   CIP

ISBN  0–415–16464–8

# Contents

# Illustrations

## Figures

## Tables

# Contributors

**Patrice Bourdelais** is Professor at the Ecole des Hautes Etudes en Sciences Sociales in Paris. He is author of *Le nouvel âge de la vieillesse. Histoire du vieillissement de la population* (1993).

**Christoph Conrad** is Managing Director of the Centre for Comparative History of Europe, Free University of Berlin. His research interests include the history of welfare states, the development of opinion and market research, and current debates in historiography. His publications include *Vom Greis zum Rentner. Der Strukturwandel des Alters in Deutschland zwischen 1830 und 1930* (1994), and (with Paul Johnson and David Thomson) *Workers versus Pensioners: Intergenerational Justice in an Ageing World* (1989).

**Paul Johnson** is Reader in Economic History at the London School of Economics. He has written on various aspects of modern British social history, and on both the history and the economics of old age, including (with Jane Falkingham) *Ageing and Economic Welfare* (1992). He is currently working on the relationship between law and the economy in Victorian England.

**Tim G. Parkin** is Professor of Classics at the University of Canterbury, Christchurch, New Zealand. He completed a D.Phil. at the University of Oxford, and has published on various aspects of Roman social history, including *Demography and Roman Society* (1992). He has a book on Roman old age forthcoming, and is currently working on a study of methodological approaches to ancient social history.

**Shulamith Shahar** is Professor Emeritus of Medieval History at Tel Aviv University. She is author of *The Fourth Estate: A History of Women in the Middle Ages* (1983), *Childhood in the Middle Ages* (1990), and *Growing Old in the Middle Ages: 'Winter Clothes Us in Shadow and Pain'* (1997).

**Richard M. Smith** is Director of the Cambridge Group for the History of Population and Reader in Historical Demography, University of Cambridge. His books include *Land, Kinship and Life-Cycle* (1984) and (with Zvi Razi) *Medieval Society and the Manor Court* (1996). His current research focuses on the demographic correlates of welfare practices in England c.1550–1834.

**Pat Thane** is Professor of Contemporary History at the University of Sussex. Her publications include *The Foundations of the Welfare State* (1982, revised second edition 1996) and (with Gisela Bock) *Women and the Rise of the European Welfare State* (1991). She has just completed a study of the history of old age in England which will be published by Oxford University Press in 1999.

**David Thomson** is Professor in History, Massey University, Palmerston North, New Zealand, and Research Associate, Cambridge Group for the History of Population. His Cambridge Ph.D. on 'Provision for the Elderly in England, 1834–1908' began a long interest in how societies meet the income needs of their elderly. Recent major projects include *Selfish Generations? How Welfare States Grow Old* (1996) and *A World Without Welfare: New Zealand's Colonial Experiment* (1998).

**David G. Troyansky** is Associate Professor of History at Texas Tech University. He is author of *Old Age in the Old Regime: Image and Experience in Eighteenth-Century France* (1989) and co-editor of *The French Revolution in Culture and Society* (1991). He is currently writing a book on the retirement of French magistrates in the first half of the nineteenth century.

# Preface

A session on the history of old age and ageing at the 18th International Congress of Historical Sciences in Montreal was the starting point for the essays drawn together in this book. We would like to thank all those who contributed to the discussion at the Congress, and to other scholars who have read and commented on the essays contained in this book. Special thanks are due to Theo Barker, who first suggested that the history of old age would be an appropriate subject for the Montreal Congress, and to Heather McCallum at Routledge who has steered this project through from initial idea to publication.

# 1   Historical readings of old age and ageing

*Paul Johnson*

In 1977 Peter Stearns noted, with scarcely any degree of exaggeration, that 'only one article by a professional historian exists on any aspect of the history of ageing'.[1] In the past two decades considerable progress has been made in remedying this omission through the study of structures created for and by older people and by giving historical voice to older people in past societies. This interest of historians in old age and ageing parallels a more general concern in modern industrial societies with the rapid ageing of the population now under way, and its consequent medical, social service and financial effects. The work of historians has not, however, simply been derivative of modern concerns. Increasingly historians have challenged many of the assumptions in social and biomedical theories of ageing, and have shown that contemporary beliefs in some former 'golden age' of old age – in which older people were venerated in their community and cared for by their family – are largely untrue.[2]

The past two decades have also been a period of some intellectual ferment within the historical profession as positivism and empiricism have been challenged by philosophical relativism. This challenge has emphasised or re-emphasised the situatedness of historical texts within ambiguous and multiple constructions of meaning, and has encouraged historians to pay more attention to the silences and ambiguities of their sources. For historians of old age and ageing, these changes in intellectual fashion have been enormously beneficial in suggesting new ways of recovering and refashioning a largely absent past. Yet they also generate problems of coherence and consistency, since much of the historical investigation of old age and ageing has continued to pursue the more empiricist paradigms of demographic and economic history. There exists, therefore, a tension between relativistic and positivistic approaches to the history of old age, but there is no obvious reason to privilege one approach above the other.[3] The experience of old age in the past was not just the result of a 'social construction' of categories by regulatory agencies, nor was it simply a 'natural' response to physiological ageing.

The chapters gathered together in this volume review and reconsider the position of old age in the study of history, the role of historical evidence in informing contemporary public and policy debate, and the impact of evolving historical methodology in influencing the study of old age. The study of the actions of and reactions to older people in the past allows historians to unravel much of the hidden social dynamic which binds individuals into family, community and national groupings. Patterns of land ownership and rules of inheritance establish a legal framework within which the economic strength of older people can be analysed. Demographic analysis of household structures reveals much about the family networks of older people; charitable and Poor Law treatment of the dependent elderly tells us about social conceptions of need, desert and responsibility. Changing medical attitudes to the physical problems of the elderly, which have variously seen senescence as a natural and acceptable stage of life and as a fatal illness, say much about both medical practice and the social construction of sickness. The representation of the elderly in art, literature and popular culture – whether as witches or as sages – shows how different societies order, categorise and compartmentalise different social groups. The articulation by older people of beliefs about their rights, duties and status reveals the multiple manners in which they have ascribed meaning to their life course.

In order to provide an organising framework for chapters which range in chronological coverage from the ancient world to the twentieth century, authors have focused their chapters around three broad themes:

1   *Participation*   This covers not only the presence of older people in the labour market, but also their informal (household or communal) activities, relating both to production and consumption. It broadly relates to the active involvement of older persons in civil society.
2   *Well-being*   This covers economic well-being (or lack thereof) and the provision of welfare support by family and by formal and informal public systems, together with the physical well-being of older people and their care and treatment when ill. It broadly relates to the passive treatment of older persons by civil society.
3   *Status*   This covers the social position of older individuals and of the elderly as a group, as determined by political, legal, medical and cultural rules and customs. It broadly relates to the construction of categories about and by older people in civil society.

As will become clear, the historical accounts provide few simple linearities of development in any of these three themes, and these themes do not necessarily encompass the diversity of historical enquiry, either in scope or in method. In this introductory chapter I attempt to identify the areas of concord and discord in terms of evidence, interpretation and methodology. But before moving to a consideration of these separate contributions, it is important first to define and locate the terms 'old age' and 'ageing' in their historical, historiographical and contemporary settings.

## Definitions of 'old age' and 'ageing'

In contemporary discussion there frequently emerges confusion over the meanings of and interpretations placed upon the terms 'old age' and 'ageing' because of their interchangeable use to describe both conditions and processes which can be either individual or societal. Societies can become younger as well as older, depending on how fertility and mortality trends alter the age composition of the population. Individuals, on the other hand, age inexorably over their life course, though 'ageing' is a term frequently restricted to the later part of the life course, with the words 'growing' and 'maturing' used to describe the ageing from childhood to some point in adulthood. Exactly when the individual ageing process makes an adult 'aged' or 'elderly' is a matter of social convention and legal and administrative definition. As Paul Johnson shows in Chapter 10, the institutionalisation in the twentieth century of public and private pension systems which provide benefits at set ages, the associated development of formal retirement ages, and the establishment of a multitude of other age thresholds for inclusion or exclusion from certain groups, activities or entitlements had, by the 1970s, created a set of social conventions that old age began at 60 or 65.

Historical investigation of old age, particularly that focused on elements of public policy, has unsurprisingly also tended to adopt these same age definitions. For instance, in his analysis of pension provision under the Old Poor Law in England in Chapter 4, Richard Smith concentrates on people aged 61 years and over, though he recognises both the arbitrary and the relative nature of this age threshold by comparing the treatment of this population with that of people aged 50 or below. Smith's point is not that 60 was the key turning point in the life course when individuals moved from maturity to old age, but rather that this threshold can be used heuristically by the researcher to identify the shifting correlates of age and public policy implementation. This allows the effect of age to be examined separately from the effects of gender or marital status or income on the individual's entitlement to a Poor Law pension and so enables the historian to infer from the observed behaviour of Poor Law administrators something about their conception of the expected capacities or incapacities of persons of different ages.

Although the adoption of an age threshold of 60 or 65 in historical enquiry might appear to represent an uncritical use of twentieth-century definitions, we now know that formal age thresholds of this sort have remarkably deep historical roots. Shulamith Shahar notes in Chapter 3 that in medieval legislative texts the onset of old age was nearly always defined as being between 60 and 70, at which age males were granted exemption from military service, trial by battle, service on town watches and payment of taxes or obligatory work. Women were not generally liable for such duties, and so do not feature in these sources, but in regulations concerning the punishment of vagabonds and beggars, the attainment of age 60 entitled both females and males to more lenient treatment.

However, according to Patrice Bourdelais (Chapter 6) it was not until the later seventeenth century that such age thresholds began to be used in a more consciously analytical way to construct broad social categories – a consequence both of intellectual developments in political arithmetic and a growing desire by national governments to improve the efficiency of public administration and tax systems, especially in their newly acquired colonies. The bureaucratic construction of these statistical categories has had, says Bourdelais, a profound influence on the subsequent development of attitudes both to old age and to the process of population ageing, because age thresholds that had functional seventeenth-century origins have become increasingly dysfunctional as they have been transmitted unaltered to the twentieth century.

It is clear that the demographic and cultural significance of any specific chronological age threshold will change over time, and this can cause difficulties for historians working in both positivistic and relativistic modes. In his study of the role of old age in the health system in nineteenth- and twentieth-century Germany in Chapter 7, Christoph Conrad finesses this problem by explicitly analysing his quantitative data on medical services over the entire range of ages from birth to death. This focus on the distribution of services across the age spectrum allows him directly to relate the treatment of older people to that of younger adults and children, and so helps to place the study of old age within a broader context of the changing age-specific nature of medical services.

For cultural historians of old age the shifting meanings that may be ascribed to any particular chronological threshold become the focus of study rather than a methodological problem to be addressed or overcome. In his chapter on ageing in early modern Europe (Chapter 5), David Troyansky argues that the category of old age was constructed in moral ways both to laud and censure forms of behaviour deemed appropriate and inappropriate, just as the modern concept of retirement has, according to some sociologists, been constructed and reconstructed in the twentieth century to suit the shifting needs of capitalist labour markets.[4] In the nineteenth and twentieth centuries, the age structuring of the life course has been heavily determined by actions of institutions, particularly those of the central and local state, while in earlier times spiritual influences were of greater significance.

Yet while the multiple and often ambiguous use of the term 'old age' in historical texts can be highly revealing of attitudes, beliefs and value systems, it can also be perplexing. In Chapter 2 Tim Parkin shows that literary evidence from Ancient Rome may be adduced to 'show' that old age could be stated as beginning as early as the age of 42 years or as late as 77. This categorical flexibility was not restricted to the upper end of the age spectrum – the epitaph on a Roman tombstone describes a man of 50 as dying 'in the flower of his youth'. As Pat Thane has cautioned in a discussion of attitudes to ageing and the elderly,[5] conflicting and ambiguous representations of old age in art, literature, drama and poetry can be located in all time periods, and it is very difficult to evaluate their significance. Some may be descriptions of current reality – at least as perceived by the author – but others may be ironic, romantic or metaphysical, expressing fears or hopes or beliefs about what old age will or should be like. These sources indicate that at any one time there exist competing representations of old age from which individuals can construct their own expectation of the life course, but, says Thane, it is particularly difficult to evaluate whether one form of discourse is especially dominant at any one time.

Nevertheless it may be possible to identify periods when certain sets of ideas about old age undergo profound reassessment. Troyansky and Bourdelais both see such shift in eighteenth-century France, when old age moves from being the object of ridicule to the object of respect. Much depends, of course, upon what evidence is selected and how it is interpreted. Conrad argues that older people have moved from the margins to the very centre of health care systems since 1900. These twentieth-century trends may be indicative of increased social and political status for older people in general, but equally they may be read as responses to a growing social and economic exclusion of the elderly from civil society. It is clear that ideational changes can affect both the way people think about old age, and the way in which individuals and institutions define 'old age' in functional terms, even though we may not be able to draw direct links between thought worlds and social structures.

The terms 'old age' and 'ageing' have taken many different meanings in past societies, and the processes of change have been complex and non-linear. Historical research over the past two decades has become increasingly aware of and informed by the changing meanings of these terms. Yet there exists a tension between the work of historians who examine changing meanings through a close analysis of ideas and the self-representations of individuals, and those who look instead at the definitions implicit in the rules and actions of social institutions. Whether it is attitudes about old age in any country or period which have largely determined actions, or instead the material circumstances and actions that have been responsible for moulding attitudes, remains a central issue of debate in historical investigation of old age and ageing, and a key determining factor in the way different historians have defined the subject.

## Participation

What does a reading of historical evidence tell us about the active involvement of older persons in past societies? The discourse on the socio-economic position of older people in modern society embodies a strong belief that the twentieth century has witnessed a significant marginalisation of the aged. This is most clearly articulated in arguments about the declining economic standing of older workers in the labour market as retirement has become formalised as a key institution for exit from the labour force.[6] But similar views also emerge in discussion of modern consumer society – that its emphasis on youthful purchasers, products and images serves to denigrate the interests of older people with older bodies.[7]

Implicit in these late twentieth-century beliefs is a strong assumption that older people were in some ways more active and more valued participants in civil society in the past. The historical record is less clear cut. This is partly because very little evidence exists for the ancient, medieval or early modern periods about the participation of the majority of older persons who were neither literate, nor wealthy nor powerful. I will return in the final section of this chapter to the problem of partial evidence, because it raises important issues about the broader meanings that can be ascribed by cultural historians to the self-representations of narrow elites. Smith's study of English Poor Law pensions provides some rare examples of non-elite pension histories from the seventeenth century in which it is clear that even quite frail old women were expected to earn something through domestic work, even when in receipt of continual public assistance. But it is far from clear that this sort of labour force participation was a positive or liberating experience; the administrative presumption appears to have been that the elderly poor should continue to work until prevented by complete physical or mental incapacity.

This appears to have been an enduring attitude. Parkin notes that the extent to which old people in ancient society were an integral part of that society or were in some way excluded from full participation depended on the degree of capability of the individual. The older person would not be wholly marginalised so long as he or she was still capable of performing some useful function, be it as statesman or as childminder. To a large extent, therefore, people were defined as old not according to their chronological age but according to their individual capability to perform duties. Nevertheless, there were presumptions about appearance in old age (grey hair, bent back, tremulous voice) which cut across purely functional definitions of capacity and so served to prejudice attitudes towards older people. Furthermore, the culturally dominant norm – that of the adult male warrior – privileged a functionality based on physical strength and agility which particularly disfavoured older men. Parkin concludes that any rights held by elderly people in ancient society were far from automatic, and had to be won and maintained through continued performance and incessant pressure.

In medieval Europe, according to Shahar, it was also true that authority and role were not based on an ascriptive criterion of age, but rather on functional capacity. While there are rare examples of upper and lower age limits (people over 55 could not be elected to public office in Lucca, while in Venice it was rare for a man under 50 to be elected to any of the ruling councils), in general no preference was given to the elderly on the one hand, but nor were they obliged to retire as long as their functional capacity did not fail. Within the church hierarchy the practice was to favour age – the majority of popes were elected in their fifties or sixties, and many other prelates had distinguished late-life careers. Lanfranc was appointed Archbishop of Canterbury by William the Conqueror when he was 65, and died in office in 1089 aged 84; Hildegard of Bingen founded her new independent community of nuns when she was 67 years old, and remained at its head until her death in 1179 at the age of 81. Among the nobility there was a high rate of unnatural death, but of those who reached old age, some continued to render military service – John Howard, Duke of Norfolk, died in battle aged about 75. Such life histories demonstrate that for exceptional individuals, chronological age alone was of little importance in determining their participation in civil society.

In medieval peasant society, Shahar suggests, patterns may have been more diverse. In southern Europe, where the extended family was dominant, elderly peasants did not retire, but instead kept their status as heads of the household and cultivated their land together with one or more of their offspring. In northern Europe, where the nuclear family was dominant, the peasant handed over his farm to one of his offspring (or where necessary another relative or non-kin) by an agreement whereby the latter guaranteed to keep him and care for him until the end of his days. Here the retirement from control of (though not necessarily participation in) the farm was determined not simply by functional capacity but also by family circumstances and demographic pressure.

These important regional differences in the ways in which peasants responded to old age illustrate how attitudes to and behaviour in old age may be conditioned by underlying economic and social systems. They also show that retirement – the deliberate withdrawal from an active life before the onset of physical incapacity – is not an invention of the twentieth century. On the other hand, in medieval Europe retirement undoubtedly entailed a diminution of status, so its attractions were always ambivalent. According to Bourdelais and Troyansky, this began to change in eighteenth-century France with the construction of a pension system for public employees which legitimated a deliberate and anticipated withdrawal from work in old age. Here the argument runs in the opposite direction – from attitudes to systems. The shift from ridicule to respect for the elderly, the change of image, had a formative impact on actions by altering the way in which state officials viewed their careers and their ideas of proper ageing and retirement. This is the moment, suggests Troyansky, when civil servants began successfully, and habitually, to articulate a perceived right to a formal retirement and a formal pension, thus blazing a trail that all other citizens in western societies have followed. It marks the transition from retirement as an exceptional circumstance to retirement as a social norm, a transition completed, but certainly not created, in the twentieth century.

How far this normalisation of retirement from work marks either a substantial improvement or significant marginalisation in the economic and social standing of older people remains a matter of contention. Those who see power and authority exercised primarily through the labour market will read the evidence less favourably than those who place greater emphasis on the individual's power to construct his or her own social and cultural world through decisions about what and how to consume. But perhaps this is a less innovative outlook than at first appears. In the ancient world, just as in the modern, economic resources enabled some people to compensate for the physical frailty associated with old age, and to maintain a level of social and political participation that was denied to many who were younger and more economically active, but poorer. Mass retirement in the twentieth century reflects an expansion in the economic resources of older people which has enabled ever greater numbers to remain active in civil society without continued formal participation in the labour market.

## Well-being

Shahar notes that in the idealisation of the attitudes towards the elderly and of their condition in pre-industrial society, the fact that there was no legal age of obligatory retirement has often been singled out as one of the advantages enjoyed by older people in the past. But she also points out that the absence of obligatory retirement also meant the absence of pension schemes. This was good for older people whose physical and mental capacities did not fail, but it also exposed those whose strength did fail, and for whom there were no retirement settlements, nor assets, to dire poverty and humiliation. How did past societies treat those older people who were no longer economically or physically self-sufficient?

In antiquity, according to Parkin, there was never any institutionalised system of retirement or of pensions; old-age welfare rested solely with the members of one's immediate family, though in some societies (notably classical Athens) this moral obligation was reinforced by law. The medieval Church had some pension schemes for retired clergymen who were feeble, ill, deaf or senile, but poor parish priests received only meagre sums which did not suffice for subsistence. Yet in early modern England, long before the introduction of formalised pensions for public servants, there appears to have existed a very widespread system of public provision for the needy elderly. Smith's detailed study of pauper 'case histories' derived through the linking of families reconstituted from parish registers with Poor Law account books challenges many easy assertions about the importance of family support in old age and the relatively recent creation of the idea of a 'right' to public support.

Smith shows that in many circumstances 40 to 50 per cent of elderly persons might be without either a son or a daughter, and 30 to 40 per cent may have lacked both. Moreover, because of the pattern of nuclear household formation, the parents of married couples would have begun to lose their children's income, and to lose each other in widowhood, at just the point in the life course when their children would have been starting their own families and thus under severe financial pressure. Even when lineally descendent kin were both alive and geographically proximate, therefore, there was no guarantee that resources would flow from children to parents. These demographic conditions, though far from fixed, were present in large parts of north-west Europe, and so raise a general question about how needy elderly people were supported.

In the English case it is clear from Smith's research that the overseers of the poor provided where families were unable or unwilling to do so. He finds, for instance, that in the south Oxfordshire community of Whitchurch in the late seventeenth century, between 40 and 50 per cent of those over the age of 60 were likely to have a Poor Law pension for some period prior to death, a figure not dissimilar to Thomson's estimates of the provision of Poor Law pensions for the aged in the 1840s.[8] The pension records demonstrate that the pension was not a strictly age-related benefit, nor was it provided as an absolute right. It appears frequently to have been given as a supplement to earnings, and the steady increase in its value as the beneficiary ages reflects an increasing incapacity to work. There was a clear gender bias in pensions (more so in the late seventeenth than the mid eighteenth century): women received support at an earlier age than men and, because also of their higher life expectancy, always outnumbered male pensioners. By age 70 a sizeable majority of women in the parishes studied were in receipt of a regular pension, and some had been for many years before this age.

Although these pensions were neither legal entitlements nor directly age related, the very high rates of coverage are, says Smith, indicative of a sentiment that the elderly were entitled to communal support, even if there were close kin available to help them. Such familial help, where it existed, was usually supplementary to, rather than a substitute for, regular parish pensions (indeed, relatives of the elderly sick were frequently paid by the parish to look after them). It seems, then, that there was a generally held social expectation that communities would normally provide financial support to ordinary working people aged over 70, and this at a time, in the late seventeenth century, when the proportion of over sixties in the English population was almost 10 per cent, a level not to be reached again until the 1930s.

How these expectations came to be formed and altered are questions that require further investigation. Smith shows that Poor Law practice was not fixed: pensions tended to be higher in the southern counties than in the north, the real value of pensions rose towards the 1730s and then fell towards the end of the century, the ratio of elderly female to male pensioners also fell between the late seventeenth and late eighteenth centuries, and after 1750 an increasing number of elderly pensioners appear to have been institutionalised in workhouses rather than supported in their own homes. Although there are particular problems in interpreting the late eighteenth-century evidence, Smith finds that it is consistent with the evolution of new Poor Law practices that involved the exclusion of the elderly, especially female pensioners, from contexts in which they managed their own households or were supported in their own homes with the assistance of public funds. This, it should be noted, is at exactly the same moment that Bourdelais and Troyansky see increasing respect for old age in French culture, and the development of pension schemes for public servants. Such divergent national tendencies, though established by very different research methodologies, clearly require further investigation and comparison. If Poor Law support for older people was so widespread and so necessary in seventeenth- and eighteenth-century England, how did older people survive in other, generally poorer, parts of Europe where there existed no legally binding entitlement to relief from destitution? According to recent estimates by Peter Lindert, in late eighteenth- and early nineteenth-century Europe only in England and the Netherlands did public poor relief expenditure exceed 1.5 per cent of national product. Elsewhere, church and private charitable giving 'offered the poor a high ratio of salvation to sustenance', amounting to something less than half of 1 per cent of national product.[9] How this apparent 'funding gap' between the needs and the resources of the mass of older people in past societies was filled remains an open question.

One likely source of support for older people was that most resilient and flexible of social institutions, the family. In Chapter 9 Pat Thane shows how family support – both practical and emotional – has often been overlooked or undervalued by modern social researchers. Wave after wave of social investigators in post-war Britain approached their studies of older people with a strong preconception that intergenerational familial bonds had been weakened or dissolved by processes of modernisation – suburban growth, migration, declining fertility. Yet they consistently found that the family ties of older people were strong – not in economic terms (public pensions had removed the most pressing financial worries of old age), but in terms of social contact and psychological support. If the continuation of close family ties into old age was the norm in the second half of the twentieth century, then, suggests Thane, it is plausible to presume that similar intergenerational ties existed at least as strongly in earlier times, even though these cannot be reconstructed through Poor Law or demographic sources. The problem faced by the historian is that interfamilial exchange which is both non-market and non-monetary leaves few if any direct records; before the advent of the social survey and the tape recorder, such exchange is a shadowy presence (or sometimes absence) in a rather thin, and far from representative, corpus of autobiographical and diary literature.

The hidden strength of family ties identified by Thane must be weighed against the demonstrable failings of many kinship support networks documented in Chapter 8 by David Thomson in his analysis of public welfare provision for older people in the politically and demographically young society of late nineteenth-century New Zealand. An explicit colonial goal of self-sufficiency and minimal public support for the dependent, whatever their age, was put to the test in the 1890s by rapid population ageing and a levelling off, or even decline, in the proportion of owner-occupiers. Some old people did become dependent, self-help and charitable provision was never entirely adequate, families could not always provide for their kin even when coerced by law, and many older people had no kin to whom they could turn. The colonial experiment in self-sufficiency in old age revealed limits to the capacity of the family to provide support for elders; the limits were such that in 1898 New Zealand led the world in introducing a tax-funded, non-contributory old-age pension.

These different readings of the role of the family in promoting the well-being of older people reflect both the importance of specific historical contingency and the diverse perspectives that different types of source material offer the historian. Similar differences in evidence and interpretation infect historical writings on the way in which older people's health needs have been met in past societies. Bourdelais suggests that the early development, in nineteenth-century France, of geriatrics as a distinct medical specialisation, reinforced a negative image of the dysfunctionality of old age. This has continued in the twentieth century; he suggests that the 1958 hospital reforms in France which created university teaching hospitals further emphasised the scientific quest for medical 'cures', and so denigrated and marginalised the medical needs of older people who were typically seen as 'incurable' and deserving of only unsophisticated care. Conrad, however, views these same developments very differently, arguing, largely from German evidence, that the elderly as a group and old age as an issue have moved from the margins to the centre of the health system since the middle of the nineteenth century. From being neglected a century ago, old people's health needs have, since the 1940s and 1950s, formed the very core of the modern welfare state.

Although demographic pressure – the ageing of the population – is part of this process, its role is not automatic. Changes in population structure need first to be recognised and problematised by experts and policy-makers, and increasing numbers in any category can lead as easily to a negative evaluation and a relative reduction in resources as to favouritism and expansion. Conrad accepts that evidence of the place of ageing in medical science does point to some marginalisation of old age in the late nineteenth century. On the other hand, for those demographic groups who were more or less excluded from medical services in the nineteenth century (children, women and the elderly), their inclusion in the insurance coverage of the emerging welfare state from the 1880s was crucial in recognising their need and ultimately in giving them voice.

Conrad's key evidence, however, relates to patterns of medical consumption, particularly of inpatient hospital care, during the last 100 or so years. He examines, for instance, age-specific deaths in hospital as a percentage of all deaths of the same age. In late nineteenth-century Prussia, young and middle-aged adults, especially men, were the people most likely to die in hospital, with children and the elderly both under-represented – the life-cycle pattern was 'n'-shaped. But by the second half of the twentieth century both the young and the old have been fully integrated into the health care system to the extent that they dominate medical institutions, so that hospital utilisation now follows a 'u'-shaped life-cycle curve. Former under-medicali-sation has been replaced by a double dynamic of longer lives and growing numbers on the one hand, and increasing inclusion in and demand towards the welfare state on the other – something which Conrad identifies as a health system transition which parallels the demographic and epidemiolog-ical transitions.

As the elderly have increased their relative weight in the population, so they have also disproportionately increased their claims on health service resources. This, argues Conrad, is simply not consistent with an interpreta-tion of increasing marginalisation, except in so far as medicalisation is itself held to represent social marginalisation. But if old age has been 'medi-calised' in this century, so has everything and everyone, including mothers, infants, athletes, and, in US health maintenance organisations, prime-age, fully fit adults. Again we see the manifest tension between interpretations based on quantitative assessments of policy implementation, and qualitative assessments of policy meanings, and so it is worth turning to consider more explicitly the construction of categories about and by older people.

## Status

Much of the historical investigation of the status of old age in different soci-eties, and about the meaning of old age and ageing for individuals as they interpret their own life course, has been undertaken by cultural historians. Troyanksy suggests that the cultural approach is necessary for an under-standing of old age in early modern society, because analytic categories such as 'participation' and 'well-being' which lie at the core of much economic, demographic and social research by modern historians may best be under-stood in moral rather than economic terms in earlier times. To unpick these moral meanings, the cultural historian has to do more than count people or measure policies, and so must turn to different types of evidence – testimony about individual lives, prescriptive literature on how one ought to age, graphic representations of the ages of man, scientific discourse dealing with the body, religious texts dealing with the soul. Moreover, these sources must be situated in their historical context of authority and power relationships, and must be read for their multiple meanings. In this way cultural historians attempt to recover not just details of the existential conditions of old people in past society, but also the spiritual and intangible meanings of old age and the individual ageing process.

The extent to which historians have a choice about whether to adopt a cultural approach and to focus on issues of status and meaning depends to some extent on the availability of evidence. Parkin points out that there is a basic problem of methodology in attempting a study of old age in antiquity. Literary sources predominate, and although use can be made of legal and other records, on their own they are not enough in dealing with a section of society as silent as the elderly (a silence which itself may speak volumes). Descriptions in classical literature of old age or of elderly individuals were not written primarily to tell us objectively about old age in ancient times, but to use the concept of and images associated with old age for the writer's own purpose. A positive line of defence of old age by Cicero, or a negative jibe at the elderly by Juvenal, must be assessed in the light of the author's (and the audience's) motives and expectations. Without this contextualisation, little can be inferred, because a literary reference may readily be found to 'substantiate' or 'disprove' almost any preconceived idea about any feature of ancient society.

Within the corpus of ancient philosophical and literary writing there are some remarkably familiar sentiments. Cicero calls for a recognition of the positive qualities of old age, particularly wisdom and moderation, and for old men to be shown the sort of respect that was (allegedly) accorded to them in former times – an early expression of the 'golden age' belief. Seneca, however, presents a more realistic image of physical and mental decline in old age, and draws a distinction between old age as a lengthening of (active) life, and old age as a lengthening of death through dependency and exclusion. These positive/negative polarities of stereotyped individuals abound in the literary sources, though Parkin concludes that old age was seen by all but the elderly themselves as a threat to the future, and by the elderly as a time to be endured more than enjoyed. He sets the literary evidence against observations of actions, and notes that there is nothing to indicate a significantly positive role for the elderly in ancient society, whether as decision-maker or as advisers, but likewise little evidence of purely chronological age prejudice.

Similarly ambiguous readings of old age can be drawn from medieval evidence. It is only rarely that the voice of an old man, and almost never that of an old woman, is heard from the medieval sources that have survived, so how far literary, religious and artistic images affected attitudes towards old age, and how far attitudes determined behaviour, must remain a matter of conjecture. What is clear, as Shahar shows, is that the images of old age were ambiguous, except in so far as representations of the elderly always contrasted them with adult males, the wielders of authority and power. Since in almost all medieval discourses about old age the body takes central place, it might be thought that the physical and mental deterioration of the body in old age would generate a consistently negative image. While this is generally true of medical texts and of moralistic and didactic writings, transcendental religious texts saw old age as the symbol of spiritual integrity and wisdom. According to St Augustine, the body could not be both young and old, but the soul could – young through alacrity, old through gravity.

Hence the construction in many saintly life histories of the idea of the boy–old man (*puer–senex*), the child or youth who prematurely had been granted the wisdom of old age.

Even the didactic writers who emphasised the negative character traits of old age did not dismiss the final stage of life as meaningless. It was a time for the expiation of sin, and for possible spiritual elevation as the individual could be brought closer to God by means of his or her weak and ailing body. Even greater consolation was offered by the idea of the ever-youthful soul. Only the material and visible – the body – are destined to age. The soul, formed in the image of God, may grow tired and feeble in bodily existence, but it can renew and purify itself. If in old age a man detaches himself from the world and concentrates on Divine Grace, his soul will be renewed. This articulation of death and salvation not only sanctioned a gradual withdrawal of older people from an active engagement in worldly ambitions, but also provided a metaphysical meaning to the individual life course.

As noted above, there are many examples of medieval prelates and nobles paying little or no attention to the idea of withdrawal from active participation in society, but that appears to be because they did not suffer from any severe decline in functional capacity. And for those older people who did make way for the young, it is impossible, as Shahar emphasises, to determine whether religious and transcendental images of old age induced this behaviour or instead provided spiritual consolation for materialistic inevitability.

The disjuncture between real capacities of older people and the set of social expectations about their role and utility in society is examined in Bourdelais' account of the redefinition of old age as a 'scientific' problem in the nineteenth and twentieth centuries. The social category of 'the aged' evolved in late seventeenth-century France in purely functional terms to signify that part of the (male) population too old to bear arms – typically those over 50 or 60 years of age – but it had no direct impact on the broader social representations or status of older people. This changed, however, in the second half of the nineteenth century, particularly because of the demographic situation in France. Low fertility rates, which had been lauded by political economists early in the century, became a matter of concern from the 1860s as it was perceived that the growth of the French population was lagging behind that of other European countries, particularly Prussia. Initially the national population censuses presented the proportionate increase in older people as a progressive indicator of an increase in longevity, but from the 1880s this was matched by concern about a compensating decline in the youthful population. At the same time, says Bourdelais, increasingly negative images of old age were being generated in France, both in the workplace, where it was argued that industrialisation caused premature physical ageing among the workforce, and in medicine through the development of geriatrics.

The conceptual reassessment of the population age structure was powerfully reinforced in 1928 when Alfred Sauvy produced population projections for France which showed a clear trend towards 'progressive ageing' which, he said, could only be countered by an improbably large increase in fertility or by selective immigration. This idea of population ageing, the growing share of people aged over 60, evolved from a new 'scientific' discourse of demographic measurement and projection, but its basis was an age threshold determined by seventeenth-century conceptions of military utility. Moreover, the dynamic societal process of population ageing became associated with negative images of individual physiological and mental decline in old age. National population ageing, according to pro-natalists, would leave the country desiccated, conservative, unproductive, declining.

Bourdelais contends that the reciprocal relationship over more than two centuries between perceptions and constructions of old age, and the notion of population ageing, reveals the way in which inherited subjective categories can directly prejudice actions and policies. Thane, however, is somewhat sceptical of any grand narrative that portrays a history of declining status and respect for the elderly. She notes that the few attempts to demonstrate the current existence of a dominant negative stereotype of old age have produced little positive evidence. Recent work by oral historians in Britain revealed that working-class old people felt more respected as they grew older, and there was little evidence of them having internalised, or even identified in others, the negative views of old age which are the necessary foil for historical accounts of growing marginalisation.[10]

Historians have identified the declining status of old age in all periods from the medieval world to the modern, and have frequently attributed this degradation of the old to a single dominant cause. Whether the source is medicalisation, the changing attitude of the Church or the cultural impact of capitalism, these are all in essence narratives of modernisation. Part of the problem of interpretation arises from comparisons of incomparable sources – for instance, evidence about rich and powerful old men in the distant past with descriptions of the aged poor in more recent times. But of equal or greater significance is the problem that arises in reading any specific source. Since 'old people' at any particular time will be defined in diverse ways and observed from a variety of perspectives by different observers, it is inappropriate to take any one of these perspectives as emblematic of a view generally held in society. Historical texts provide multiple images of old age, as Chapter 10 demonstrates in the case of retirement, and texts and events can be interpreted in multiple ways. Likewise, 'old people' are not and never have been a single, simple category, but rather an amalgam of individuals divided by generation, gender, class, wealth, power, religion and race, so what may be true for one person or group at any time may be quite unrepresentative for others.

The partiality of specific images and texts that present a personal narrative of old age makes them valuable for comprehending the subjective experience of old age in the past, but also creates a problem for the historian in determining how to weight or select contradictory narratives. Troyansky, however, argues that the neglect of cultural materials by most historians of old age in the nineteenth and twentieth centuries has produced unduly narrow and materialistic social and demographic history which is motivated primarily in support or reaction to the logic of welfare state growth. He suggests that the methodological and inferential gap between cultural and social historians might be bridged through an analysis of the role of early modern institutions that catered to the elderly and which have left sources that permit both social and cultural approaches. As an example, he examines the case of the Justice Ministry in Restoration France. The familiar part of the story is how the state left its mark on society; less familiar is the story of how people used the state. The demands and appeals for pensions submitted to the Ministry by judges reveal a set of self-images and reconstructed life histories which embody different models and meanings of retirement, different reflections on the life course, different concepts of generational progression and generational responsibility. But in looking at how careers are constructed and lives remembered, Troyanksy also sees how demands are made of the evolving bureaucratic state structure, and how demands increasingly are couched in terms of expectation and entitlement. This is not a traditional history of the state, of legislation or policies, but a history of the uses of the state and constructions of the self. That keen sense of self, as defined through the secular life review, is just as important as the development of bureaucratic state structures, argues Troyanksy, for the modern creation of individual old-age entitlements. An exclusive concentration on policy cannot, therefore, comprehend the historical logic of welfare state provision for the elderly. Self-image, social attitudes and policy actions are all elements of the same story and should not be relegated to separate spheres of historical enquiry.

## Sources and interpretations

By suggesting the possibility of transcending disciplinary divisions between social and cultural history through a more integrated reading of source material common to both approaches, Troyansky holds out the prospect of a more 'total' history of old age than has so far been achieved. However, the limited range of source material available to the historian of old age severely curtails the scope for 'total' history. As the chapters by Parkin and Shahar make clear, the breadth of vision of the ancient and medieval historian is enormously constrained by the type of source material available. In predominantly illiterate societies, written texts were constructed by and for an elite, and although these texts can be parsed, filtered, deconstructed and reconstructed into fictive interpretations, there are real limits to the degree of access they can give to the experience of old age and ageing of the majority of people in the past.

This is true even for much more recent times. Paul Thompson has noted

the double jeopardy faced by the mass of older people in leaving any historical trace:

> Like ordinary people in general, old people usually show up vividly in
> the record only when they become a problem. At death, in the moment
> of passing, all secure an entry, and some a lasting monument; but of
> most people's later life little is ever known, or now knowable.[11]

In a search through nineteenth-century British diaries and autobiographies
Thompson found surprisingly little reference to old age, and even less to the
personal experience of ageing: 'Old age rarely seems to be regarded by a
writer as interesting in itself: it is relevant above all as an influence on a
young, new life, and never as the culmination of life.'[12]

This shadowy historical presence (or absence) of old age and ageing sets
real limits to post-modern historical methodology. The tropes of old age
that appear with a certain monotony in texts on health and morals from the
ancient world to the modern are rightly viewed as literary constructions, ripe
for any number of equally valid readings of the way old age was socially and
culturally formed in past times. Language is metaphoric, and 'old age' can
be a metaphor for a vast range of real and imagined values, circumstances
and aspirations. But if there is no language, no discourse, no text, and no
possibility of direct anthropological observation, then there can be no
historical construction. Post-modern history requires not just texts, but rich
texts, nuanced and densely packed with self-reflective comments. When
historical subjects leave no conscious representation of their 'self' – as has
been true of the great majority of aged people in past times – they preclude
the type of deep reading of individual experience which has been one of the
most innovative aspects of post-modern historical scholarship.[13] In this
important respect, therefore, post-modern historical writing can be
extremely elitist, reimposing on the illiterate or inarticulate masses the
'condescension of posterity' from which earlier scholars had attempted to
rescue them.[14]

When the records of old people living in past societies are no more than
the desiccated listings of household structure, pension payments, hospital
admissions or burials, deep reading of the texts offers little return. Instead,
as Smith and Conrad show, much can be achieved by reading widely – by
counting occurrences in different places and at different times, looking for
patterns of continuity and moments of change. Of course the difference
between positivistic and relativistic histories of old age involves much more
than resort to different types of evidence. It involves a different privileging
of questions as much as of sources, a difference that is epistemological
rather than historical. Whether this gap can be bridged, in the history of old
age or in any other area of the subject, is a dominant question in historical
scholarship. Perhaps we should resist the attempt to integrate, to construct a
meta-narrative old age. Yet this should not deflect the attention of historians

of old age from a number of other, smaller, more specific issues which can enhance our understanding of the past and the present – issues about continuities and discontinuities of images, ideas and policies, about national and regional and gender and class differences, about dissimilar trends in similar places. If we can strengthen our understanding of the smaller questions, then we may produce a better history of old age and ageing, even if the epistemological tensions between different approaches remain unresolved.

## Notes

1  Peter Stearns, *Old Age in European Society*, London, 1977, p. 13.
2  For recent surveys of this historical literature, see the essays – particularly the editors' introductory survey – in M. Pelling and R. Smith (eds), *Life, Death and the Elderly: Historical Perspectives*, London, 1991; D. I. Kertzer and P. Laslett (eds), *Aging in the Past: Demography, Society and Old Age*, Berkeley, CA, 1995. For a brief critical comment on some of this literature, see David Troyansky, 'Progress report: the history of old age in the western world', *Ageing and Society*, 1996, vol. 16, pp. 233–43.
3  For a recent survey of tensions within and between positivistic and relativistic strands of historical enquiry, see Richard J. Evans, *In Defence of History*, London, 1997, and the references therein.
4  Martin Kohli, 'The world we forgot: a historical review of the life course', in V. W. Marshall (ed.), *Later Life: The Social Psychology of Aging*, Beverly Hills, CA, 1986, pp. 271–303; Chris Phillipson, *Capitalism and the Construction of Old Age*, London, 1982.
5  Pat Thane, 'The cultural history of old age', *Australian Cultural History*, 1995, vol. 14, pp. 23–9.
6  Klaus Jacobs, Martin Kohli and Martin Rein, 'The evolution of early exit: a comparative analysis of labor force participation patterns', in Martin Kohli *et al.* (eds), *Time for Retirement*, Cambridge, 1991, pp. 36–66.
7  M. Featherstone and M. Hepworth, 'The mask of ageing and the postmodern lifecourse', in M. Featherstone *et al.* (eds), *The Body*, London, 1991.
8  David Thomson, 'Provision for the elderly in England, 1830–1908', Unpublished Ph.D. thesis, University of Cambridge, 1980.
9  Peter Lindert, 'Poor relief before the welfare state: Britain versus the continent, 1780–1880', mimeo, University of California, Davis, October 1997.
10  Paul Thompson, Catherine Itzin and Michele Abenstern, *I Don't Feel Old*, Oxford, 1990.
11  Ibid., p. 19.
12  Ibid., p. 45.
13  A good example is a study by Patrick Joyce of working- and middle-class identities in mid-nineteenth-century England. This work depends crucially on the extensive unpublished and published writings of the two central characters, Edwin Waugh and John Bright. See P. Joyce, *Democratic Subjects*, Cambridge, 1994.
14  The phrase is E. P. Thompson's, from his *The Making of the English Working Class*, London, 1963. A similar sentiment, 'to rescue the landless ex-peasantry from posterity's enormous silence', is proclaimed by Christopher Hill in *Liberty Against the Law*, Harmondsworth, 1997, p. x.

# 2 Ageing in antiquity

## Status and participation

*Tim G. Parkin*

He used to be somebody – but now he's grown old.

(Herondas, third century BC)

I am not the man I once was – the greatest part of me has perished.

(Maximianus, *Elegies on Old Age*, sixth century AD)

## Introduction

While the study of ancient social history has developed over the last century, the role of the private individual *as an individual* in daily life in Ancient Greek and Roman society and the realities of his or her existence (as opposed to legal status) have only more recently come under detailed scrutiny. One aspect of such study has been the consideration of the position of different age groups within ancient societies, though the focus here has been almost exclusively directed towards the young (and their parents). Some study has also been made of *rites de passage*, following the lead of sociological and anthropological literature,[1] but such interests have tended to exclude the study of the elderly of antiquity.

For so long the traditional treatment of 'life and customs' in, for example, Ancient Roman society has tended to present the picture only of an upper class male, from his first years, his education and entry into marriage and public life, culminating in his climb up the political ladder; the next time we meet our Roman subject is generally at his funeral. All too often a Roman disappears from the extant historical record once he has attained the consulship; at best he may warrant a brief mention subsequently as a provincial governor. My point is not so much the broader issue – that such a career would have applied to only the tiniest subfraction of the population of the time (though this is true) – but that on attaining the consulship this Roman's life may only have been half over. What happened to him in his old age? The problem, of course, lies in the silence of the sources, or – more fundamentally – in the interests and concerns of ancient writers and readers. When old people do appear, whether in ancient literature or in modern studies of antiquity, it is usually on the sideline or as a special case. A few notable old people may be mentioned (a Nestor, Sophocles or Augustus), but the subject of old age itself seems scarcely to warrant investigation.

In the same vein the ancient accounts of old age are often little more than lists of characters, mythical and historical, who purportedly lived to a ripe old age. But, in the case of historical characters in particular, posterity did not remember them primarily for their old age, but rather for their achievements: their age is generally irrelevant or, at best, it is remarked or inferred that they performed such feats *even in spite of* their advanced age. There appears, in short, to be a general lack of interest in old people in antiquity. This very fact is itself important and may provide clues as to the treatment of the elderly in Greek and Roman society; the reasons behind it are also important – was it simply because there were comparatively few old people in the society or, rather, few *visible* within the society?

There is a basic problem of methodology in attempting a study of old age in classical antiquity. The central questions to be confronted first are the use of literary sources, a problem of general import to the study of ancient history, and, more basically, the purpose and value of a study such as this. The usefulness of a simple catalogue of literary references to old age is limited, at least in an historical sense.[2] I shall attempt in this chapter only to give a sketch of various literary images of old age as they relate to the themes of this book. My purpose in this regard is to provide a background to historical considerations. Apart from the literary sources, use can be made of the legal corpus, papyri and epigraphy. On their own these are not enough in dealing with a section of society as relatively silent as the elderly. Comparative material must be employed, and judicious use must be made of inference, supposition and models.[3]

The aim here is not to make a single, definitive conclusion about 'the reality of old age in the ancient world', since such reality, even if it may be discerned, will have varied from place to place, from time to time, and indeed from individual to individual. The literary sources on occasion may give subjective views and opinions on old age, statements influenced by individual impressions as well as, perhaps, by ulterior political, social or economic motivations and by adherence to literary or philosophical *topoi*. Such references cannot and should not be held to be generally representative of any time, place or social class, if indeed of any one individual. Does a particular author – and in terms of antiquity we are almost always confined to the male view – portray the situation as it really existed (at least in his eyes), as he wanted it to exist, as he wanted others to believe it existed, or even as a patently absurd distortion of the facts for its own sake? A positive line of defence of old age by Cicero, or a negative jibe at the elderly by Juvenal, must be considered not just in terms of what is said, but also of *why* it is said, in the light of the author's (and the audience's) influences, motives and expectations. Even if accurate in any specific regard, such a reference cannot be automatically assumed to reveal general opinions or practices at any one time, or to point to changes over various generations, as affected by political, social, economic and even religious conditions. Anecdotes need not necessarily reflect a typical situation; more often, they are related for the very reason that they are unusual or remarkable. Descriptions in literature of old age or of elderly individuals were not written primarily to tell us objectively about old age in ancient times, but to use the concept of and images associated with old age for the writer's own purposes. When the literary sources on old age are as few and sparsely spread as they are (though not as few as one might at first suppose), this inevitably makes the interpretation of the evidence on this level doubly difficult. But the literary evidence and its interpretation are still of interest and of real historical value, provided that due caution and critical judgement are used, since they allow us to consider the avowed impression of and reaction to old age and the elderly by various individuals for an intended audience, both young and old, within the various genres of Greek and Latin literature. It is the task of the historian – and the ancient social historian in particular is faced with this exercise – to interpret and make judicious use of whatever genuine testimony is at hand.

As to what the ancients understood by concepts such as 'old age' in terms of a specific number of years, space precludes a detailed treatment.[4] Suffice it to say that in my opinion, and despite the philosophical and literary tradition of the *aetates hominum* (ages of humankind), no specific age limit applied. Literary evidence from antiquity may be adduced to 'show' that old age could be stated as beginning as early as the age of 42 years or as late as 77 years. A word like *senex* (old man) was not strictly defined in terms of number of years, but was related more to appearance and circumstances. In certain contexts an ancient author might call a 44 year old an *adulescens* (e.g. Cicero at the height of his prestige) or a *senex* (such as Hannibal at the time of defeat). One tombstone from Roman Mauretania (modern Algeria) even records a 50-year-old man as dying 'in the flower of his youth'. Physical appearance, mental attitude, circumstances and intention also affect the way a person thinks of him- or herself and is regarded by others.[5] Some people, then as now, may have felt older than their years (some ancient philosophers held that debauchery in one's younger years could lead to a premature old age), and may indeed have looked older than they were – such was a conventional complaint, for example, of poets.[6] A passage from the fourth-century BC Athenian orator Aeschines is quite instructive in this regard, displaying as it does an awareness of the fact that people of the same age may look and feel considerably different. Aeschines' point here is to stress that Misgolas, who took in Timarchus as his lover, is much older than he looks:

> There are some men who by nature differ markedly from the rest of us in respect to their age. For some men who are young seem mature and older than they are; others, who are old in terms of number of years, seem to be mere youngsters. Misgolas is such a man. He happens, indeed, to be of my own age, and was an ephebe with me; we are now in our 45th year. I am quite grey, as you see, but not he.

Comparative historical and medical evidence would suggest that in purely biological terms people in antiquity did not age at a faster rate than they do today, at least not to any significant degree. General standards of health and nutrition may have in some cases speeded up the ageing process, making people both look and feel older.[7] What may have changed to a more significant degree, however, were attitudes towards old age, and it is this aspect which is of particular interest to us here.[8]

## Old age in antiquity: images and attitudes

What attention has been paid to the elderly in ancient societies by classical scholars in the last century has tended to focus on the portrayal of the elderly in literature; the bibliography is becoming vast.[9] It is not my intention here to provide a detailed analysis of the literary image of old age in antiquity, but only to remark on apparently prevalent attitudes, in particular in regard to the themes of status and participation. Old age was a reality for a significant proportion of the population in the ancient world, and it was a reality that presented itself as a potential future for the entire population.[10] So it is of little surprise that old age attracts the attention of writers in almost every genre of literature, from philosophy to comedy, from love poetry to satire. The way that ancient literary testimony can be used to present a positive or negative image of old age (as indeed it has been depicted in many modern studies) is perhaps best exemplified in the collection of references περὶ γήρως ('on old age') from Greek literature preserved in Stobaeus' *Florilegium* or *Anthology*, compiled in the fifth century AD. Stobaeus amassed a total of ninety-five passages from forty-two different authors (plus three anonymous citations), ranging in date from the seventh century BC to the fourth century AD, which he grouped under three headings: praise of old age (thirty-one passages); blame of old age (fifty-five passages); and 'that good sense makes old age unburdensome and worthy of much respect' (nine passages).[11] Of these ninety-five passages, thirty are from Greek tragedy (11 + 16 + 3), twenty-six from comedy and satire (5 + 20 + 1), twenty-five from philosophers (13 + 9 + 3), nine from other poets (2 + 7 + 0), and five from other prose writers (four historians and one orator, 0 + 3 + 2). This distribution alone is quite instructive of the picture of old age one might expect according to the literary genre – in comedy, for example, a negative picture of old age comes as little surprise, while philosophers grappled with the problem of the role of the elderly in society, particularly as they themselves grew older, and presented an image with both positive and negative aspects. In tragedy the picture of the old person might vary between the positive and the negative depending upon the individual concerned – the wise old counsellor or the garrulous old fool.

Quite apart from the interest of the individual passages presented by Stobaeus, his collection serves to highlight the problem of interpreting the position and status of the elderly by reference to isolated literary depictions.

A literary reference may readily be found to 'substantiate' or 'disprove' almost any preconceived idea one might have about any feature of ancient society. In a study of old age in history it is precisely the Stobaean model that one must avoid. It is perhaps inevitable in looking at the literary testimony that a positive/negative dichotomy emerges. What needs to be borne in mind is that the two attitudes are not necessarily exclusive, that both trains of thought are valid depending upon the circumstance of the person(s) described, the intention of the author, and the expectations of his audience.

Old age as a philosophical *topos* in antiquity had a long, if undistinguished, history, and was related both to the observed condition of the elderly of the time and to the stereotypical images derived from popular literature. Philosophical works specifically on old age were written by some; we hear of such tracts by several peripatetic philosophers. Cicero's dialogue *de Senectute* is the only complete work of this kind extant.

The tradition of philosophical writings περὶ γήρως can be traced back, however, to Plato's *Republic*, at the beginning of which Plato has Socrates report on a conversation he had with an elderly manufacturer living at the Piraeus, Cephalus, the father of Lysias.[12] Socrates, himself in his late fifties in the year in which the dialogue is set, 411 BC, questions Cephalus (whose sons are in their forties) about his old age. Cephalus notes that most old people complain about their old age, but he puts their troubles down not to old age but to their characters (τρόποι). In fact old age is in many respects a blessing, he says, since it frees one from physical desires, and leaves the mind free for philosophy – not that Cephalus is a philosopher, but rather a man who enjoys his leisure. Socrates teases Cephalus a little: many would say that he finds old age easy to bear because he has wealth to provide him with comforts. Cephalus admits that there is some truth to this: a poor man who is good will find old age no easier to bear than a bad man who is rich. Cephalus tells Socrates that he uses his wealth wisely, to render to the gods and to other men their due. With that Cephalus rushes off to perform a sacrifice, his son Polemarchus takes over, and the philosophical dialogue proper then begins.

A brief passage, but an effective and important one, both for the contrast it provides with the generally negative literary image of old age that precedes it from the time of Homer onwards, and for the philosophical treatments of old age to follow – Cicero in particular was influenced by this passage of Plato when he came to write his *de Senectute* over 300 years later, and it is this dialogue which in chronological terms provides us with the next, substantial moralising tract defending old age.

Cicero probably wrote his *Cato Maior de Senectute* early in 44 BC, before the Ides of March, when he was 62 and Atticus, to whom the work is dedicated, 65 years old. The dialogue, set in the year 150 BC, takes place between the venerable Cato the Elder (83 years old; he died in the next year) and his two young (in their mid thirties) friends Scipio Aemilianus and Gaius Laelius. In reality, however, the work represents a monologue delivered by

Cato in a role very similar to that of Plato's Cephalus. The preliminary discussion provides striking parallels to Plato's treatment: Scipio and Laelius express their surprise at how well Cato bears his old age when most men find it a burden heavier than Mount Etna. Like Cephalus, Cato replies that those who find old age a burden have only themselves to blame; anyone with any sense will prepare for old age and accept it. The man who complains of old age, he says, is a fool, and any faults in him are due not to old age but to his own character. Like Socrates, Laelius raises the point that perhaps it is Cato's wealth, resources and position that help him to find old age tolerable. Like Cephalus, Cato must admit to the truth of this.

Cicero, through Cato, then proceeds to answer four specific complaints (*vituperationes*) against old age, as follows:[13]

1   Old age takes a person away from activities. The defence is that it is only right for old men to pass from mere physical labours to more fitting, spiritual ones (political, intellectual, agricultural and educational), since old age is marked by its wisdom[14] and the old man can provide a good example of moderation and good sense, together with sound advice: the exemplar of Nestor is something of a cliché, but other active elderly persons, Greek and Roman, are also mentioned. Cato feels that by the end of this section he has made his point (8.26):

> But you see how old age is not only not drooping or feeble, but is even active, always doing and striving for something, the kind of thing, naturally, that was each man's pursuit in his earlier life.

2   Old age weakens the body. It is not denied that in old age physical strength wanes, but Cato states that this is no great hardship. The main reason why most people's physical strength fails in old age is that they have led a 'lustful and intemperate youth' which 'has handed on to old age a weakened body'. Old age must be prepared for by a frugal way of life. Stress is repeatedly placed upon what is said to be the best, perhaps the only true way to prepare for old age – through philosophy. The enjoyment of philosophy, Cicero says, makes up for the loss of physical pleasures, which leads in to the next section.

3   'There follows the third attack on old age, the fact that they say it is lacking in pleasures.'[15] The argument continues along the same lines as the earlier two sections. That physical pleasures, in particular sexual desire (*libido*), are lost is not denied. Cicero/Cato says that this is no hardship, whatever most people might think – rather it is a marvellous boon (*o praeclarum munus!*), and a long list of historical exemplars is again produced.[16] Old age, it is argued, should be praised rather than blamed in this regard, since it gives one freedom to pursue more intellectual activities. Farming is adduced as a worthwhile pursuit and is here discussed at very great length.[17] An even greater pleasure, the *apex*

*senectutis*, is held to be *auctoritas*, the prestige and respect an old man may enjoy if he has led an active public life – a telling argument, to which we shall return.

4    Cicero finally has Cato return to the proper train of the dialogue to answer the fourth *vituperatio*, namely that old age is not far from death. The sense of Cicero's reply is, in true Stoic fashion, 'Death, where is thy sting?' A mind trained in philosophy, he has Cato say, will realise that death is either complete oblivion, where there can be no unhappiness, or else it is eternal life and thus endless happiness. All this is familiar from Greek philosophy (notably Plato's Socrates). Death is inevitable, it is argued, and philosophy helps one to prepare for it and not fear it. The remainder of Cato's address is spent discussing the afterlife, in support of the statements Cato has just made about there being no need to fear death, and on this philosophical note Cicero has Cato close his *consolatio* of old age, with the hope that Scipio and Laelius will both reach old age and with the condition that 'old age is the final scene of life, just as in a play, a final scene whose tiresomeness we ought to flee from, especially when we have had more than enough of it'.

*Consolatio* (consolation), not praise, is the primary aim that Cicero alludes to in dedicating the dialogue to Atticus:

> At this time I thought I would write something for you on old age. For I want both you and myself to be relieved of this burden which I have in common with you, as old age either now presses upon us or at least makes its approach.

Cicero's sincerity in this is not to be doubted, even if he did not himself believe all that he has Cato say in defence of old age. While following a Greek tradition which he admired greatly, he did more than just produce a polished literary exercise. He also sought to provide real *consolatio* for his own old age, upset as he was at the time by personal worries and political uncertainties. His daughter Tullia had died in the previous year, and the extent of his grief is evident from the letters of the period. Politically, he was well aware of the turbulent times he was living in, yet in the months before the Ides of March he was powerless to come to the aid of the *res publica*. *Consolatio* in this regard was more difficult to find.

Philosophy became Cicero's refuge in the mid 40s BC, and also served as a means of expression for his greatest cares. His concern over the political situation was not centred entirely on his own position. In defending old age, he also seeks to promote the status of the elderly, to show that *seniores* still have a role to play in the state.[18] He sets his dialogue in the golden aura of the past when, he asserts, the old man held the prominence, the *auctoritas*, that he deserved and when morals were what they should have been; Cato the Censor serves as a good exemplar. The ancient system in the conservative state of Sparta is cited with approval, by Cicero and by others, Greek and Roman, for the way that precedence was given to the aged. Sparta's *gerousia*, or senate, whose members were at least 60 years of age, is as close as antiquity came to a gerontocracy, but even there the power of the *gerontes* was not absolute. By contrast, in democratic Athens age carried no obvious privilege.

Cicero calls for a recognition of old men's positive qualities and for them to be shown due respect, the sort of respect (allegedly) accorded to them in the old days but sadly lacking, it is felt, in the present. This contrast between an idealised past and the harsh reality of the present is a common one in this context. The idea, itself doubtless propagated by the elderly in the face of some degree of pressure from younger generations, that it is the place of the young (being rash and inexperienced) to obey, of the old (having sound judgement and practical wisdom) to rule, likewise has a long history, whatever the truth underlying it.[19] It was just such a message that Cicero sought to assert.

This underlying line of argument in the *de Senectute* became very explicit and more extreme some 150 years later in Plutarch's pamphlet Εἰ πρεσβυτέρῳ πολιτευτέον ('On whether an old man should engage in public affairs') which he wrote in his own old age. The basic message is made very clear, and repeated at length: the man of state must not retire on account of his age, for there are many useful tasks that he is capable of *and has a duty* to perform. Old age, a time of honour,[20] provides the statesman with qualities such as λόγος (reason), γνώμη (judgement), παρρησία (frankness), σωφροσύνη (soundness of mind), and φρόνησις (practical wisdom), all of which not only entitle but actually require the old man to continue to serve in politics. If nothing else he should at least instruct the young, who should be allowed to perform the menial duties so that in time they may be ready to take over the more prestigious positions which are the realm of the elder statesmen. For an old man to perform burdensome, trivial tasks, on the other hand, is foolish and shameful.

But even worse is for an old man to retreat from public life entirely, argues Plutarch – this is pure laziness, befitting mere women, to slink off to one's farm when one has duties in the city to perform; the contrast here with Cicero's depiction of a fine old age is evident. The pleasures derived from sex, food and drink that are lost in old age, it is asserted, are well compensated for by the pleasure to be derived from politics (as opposed to Cicero's philosophical pleasures). Mental powers – to answer a possible criticism and to further condemn a life of leisure – are maintained by constant practice.

The philosophical, moralising tradition regarding old age after the time of Cicero is also detectable in other works surviving only in fragments. Perhaps the most interesting in this context are the extracts of a work περὶ γήρως by a certain Juncus, preserved in Stobaeus' *Florilegium*. Exactly who Juncus was is uncertain, but his writings are probably to be dated to the second century AD, to the period of the Second Sophistic. Of the four lengthy extracts preserved by Stobaeus, one comprises an attack on the elderly, which raises many varied negative attributes associated with old age: physical disabilities and illnesses, loss of pleasures and senses, fear of death, impotence, the ridicule of younger generations, exclusion from political and military affairs – and, more originally, the spectre of poverty in old age. The other three represent the old man's replies to these attacks, to the effect that what one loses in old age is more than compensated for by the wisdom and self-control that one attains. The fear of death is answered by considering the afterlife and the pleasures (or oblivion) that will follow death. The influence of the earlier philosophical tradition, in particular Plato and Cicero, in this is clear enough. To what extent, in all these moralising works, we are dealing with simple philosophical *topoi* or with real, personal concerns regarding old age is less obvious. At any rate, there does emerge a very real awareness of the potential attributes of old age, both positive and negative, and underlying this depiction one can detect genuine debate as to the status and role of the aged members of the society, albeit at an impersonal and generalised level.

More personal and immediate discussion of old age in a serious context may be sought elsewhere; two particular writers, of the early Roman empire, will suffice here: Seneca the Younger (*c.* 4 BC/AD 1–65) and Pliny the Younger (*c.* AD 61–*c.* 112). Seneca's letters to Lucilius, written shortly before the former's death, provide several pictures of old age within a philosophical framework. They evince an awareness and certain dread of the disadvantages old age can bring even to a very wealthy man; the overall attitude towards old age and the elderly is sympathetic rather than optimistic. *Epistle* 12 is a particularly good example: on visiting his country estate Seneca is appalled at how run down the building and grounds are looking – all due to old age, the overseer insists, which makes Seneca reflect on his own age, since these stones and trees are his contemporaries, if not younger! Meeting an old slave is the final straw, when he learns that this decrepit figure is none other than his childhood 'pet slave' and therefore the same age as himself: nothing is safe from old age, and all around there are things to remind us of how old we are ourselves. There follows philosophical consolation: 'we should embrace old age and cherish it, for it is full of pleasure, if you know how to make the most of it'.

In a later letter Seneca refers back to these observations and reflects that he now feels even older, though it is only his body that is in decline – his mind is strong 'and rejoices that it has but slight connection with the body'.[21] Similarly, he describes the old age of the Epicurean historian Aufidius Bassus, 'an excellent man, shattered in health and wrestling with his age. . . . Old age has begun to hang over him with its mighty, overpowering weight', like a ship that has begun to sink or a building that is collapsing. In such circumstances, Seneca concludes, 'one needs to look around, to find an exit'.[22] Despite Bassus' physical decrepitude, however, 'his mind is sharp', and for this he has philosophy to thank. Yet the negative aspects of old age are not glossed over:

> He whom old age is leading away to death has nothing to hope for; old age alone grants no reprieve. No ending, to be sure, is more painless; but there is none more lingering.

Elsewhere Seneca speaks of his own old age in a similar fashion. He states that a man should not simply await his fate like a coward and put up with the extreme disabilities that old age may bring. Rather than praising old age, Seneca is coldly realistic – old age is only to be endured if it is endurable (one's mental condition being particularly relevant). The passage warrants quotation at length, for it is one of the most explicit and, I would say, carefully considered and heartfelt statements surviving from antiquity by an old man on the realities of old age as he saw them:

> Frugal living can bring one to old age; and to my mind old age is not to be refused any more than it is to be craved. . . . So the question we need to consider is whether one should shrink from extreme old age and not await the end, but bring it on artificially. A man who sluggishly awaits his fate is almost a coward, just as he is excessively devoted to wine who drains the jar dry and sucks up even the dregs. But we shall ask this question also: Is the final stage of life the dregs, or is it the clearest and purest part of all, provided only that the mind is unimpaired, and the senses, still sound, give their support to the spirit, and the body is not worn out and dead before its time? For it makes a great deal of difference whether a man is drawing out his life or his death. But if the body is useless for service, why should one not free the struggling soul? Perhaps you ought to do this a little before the debt is due, lest, when it falls due, you may be unable to perform the act. And since the danger of living badly is greater than the danger of dying soon, he is a fool who refuses to stake a little time and win a hazard of great gain. Few have lasted through extreme old age to death without impairment, and many have lain inert, making no use of themselves. How much more cruel, then, do you suppose it really is to have lost a portion of your life, than to have lost your right to end that life? . . . I shall not abandon old age, if old age preserves me intact for myself, and intact as regards the better part of myself; but if old age begins to shatter my mind, and to pull its various faculties to pieces, if it leaves me, not life, but only the breath of life, I shall leap from a building that is crumbling and tottering. I shall not avoid illness through death, as long as the illness is curable and does not impede my *animus*. . . . He who dies just because he is in pain is a weakling and a coward; but he who lives merely to brave out this pain, is a fool.

These are Seneca's expressed convictions, though in reality his suicide in AD 65 was forced through political circumstances rather than purely philosophical reasoning. Nonetheless his explicit statement quoted here should be regarded not only as a conclusion based on a philosophical tradition but also as a sincere reflection on the realities of old age for one aristocratic Roman male. The goal was a full life (which for Plutarch meant a politically active one, for Seneca an active one at any rate), not necessarily a long one. This is the explicit message of Seneca's earlier dialogue *de Brevitate Vitae* ('On the Shortness of Life'): it is not that we have a short life to live, as many complain, but that we waste much of it – 'life, if you know how to make the most of it, is long. . . . The period in which we truly live is only a small part of life.'

The professed ideal for Seneca, as for Cicero and no doubt for most elderly aristocratic Roman males of the late republic or the empire, was a healthy old age enjoyed pursuing worthwhile and rewarding activities: *otium honestum*, a phrase heavy with meaning – 'an honourable withdrawal to leisure' – conveys some of the force. For Plutarch, a Greek writing in Roman times, this goal implies service to the state, while for Cicero and Seneca philosophy is the ultimate activity in, as well as refuge from, old age. And it is of just such an ideal that Pliny the Younger in his letters provides concrete examples. Like Seneca, Pliny (writing in his forties) displays an awareness of the negative attributes as well as the potential positive qualities that old age can bring, as embodied in the various elderly aristocratic mentors and friends he describes or addresses. Like Seneca, he witnessed the painful old age and suicide of a friend: he describes the last years of Corellius Rufus, who suffered from gout (*pedum dolor*) from the age of 32; as he grew older the pain became increasingly acute, until eventually he killed himself at the age of 67. Pliny requires *consolatio*; he misses his friend, but he can understand his motivation in killing himself.

But the human condition is not always so wretched. Pliny also expresses his respect for old men who lead a full life, whether in politics or in active retirement. Arrius Antoninus earns Pliny's praise for his political career: 'In virtue, prestige, and age, you are our foremost citizen – so fine a record cannot fail to command respect', though Pliny adds that he respects him even more for his *remissiones* or recreations. Verginius Rufus, who died at the age of 83 years in the same year as his third consulship, provides Pliny with a good model, for he spent his old age 'living in close retirement and deeply respected by us all; his health was good, apart from a trembling of the hands, not enough to trouble him'. The approach of death, however, was difficult and drawn out, but he died *plenus annis, plenus honoribus* ('with a full store of both years and offices'), and his funeral oration was delivered by one of the consuls of that year, the historian Tacitus.

Another prominent individual who wins Pliny's esteem is Pomponius Bassus for planning and spending his *otium* in peace, living in a charming spot, getting exercise on the beach, enjoying conversation and reading:

> This is the right way to grow old for a man who has held the highest
> civil offices, commanded armies, and devoted himself entirely to the
> service of the state as long as it was proper for him to do so.

This is the way a politician should lead his life (*pace* Plutarch again): to
devote the 'first and middle stages of his life' to one's *patria* and keep the
final years for oneself. Yet one is reminded that for most *otium* was an
idealised goal rather than an easy reality: Pliny wonders if he will ever get
the chance to enjoy such a life of leisure. It is important to him that people
see his retirement not as *desidia* or indolence (as Plutarch would have seen it)
but as *tranquillitas*. It is the old age of Vestricius Spurinna, however, that is
Pliny's true ideal: 'There is no one whom I would rather take for an example
in my old age, if I am spared to live so long.' His life in retirement, Pliny
states, was well ordered (including conversation, reading, walking and other
exercise, writing and bathing), and he enjoyed a good, simple diet. Then,
and only then, are we told his age: he has passed his 77th year, 'but his
hearing and sight are strong and unimpaired, and he is physically fit and
energetic; old age has brought him nothing but wisdom'. This is the ideal:
after a lifetime of distinguished service to the state, to enjoy good physical
and mental health in old age, amid comfortable surroundings and with
continued potential to develop one's wisdom. It is just such a goal that Pliny
professes to set for himself – later. In the immediate present he has too much
to do, but he instructs the addressee of this letter to remind him of this
intention later in life, when he is old enough to be able to enjoy such *otium*
without being accused of *inertia* or laziness.

If Spurinna provided the ideal, others around Pliny presented the image
of the extreme (at least for aristocratic males) negative aspects of old age,
Domitius Tullus being a prime example. Despite his wealth, he is a hopeless
invalid, fortunate only in that he has a wife and slaves to tend him. His wife,
we are told, was greatly criticised for marrying him in the first place, and
particularly now that he is so decrepit: 'a wealthy old man and a hopeless
invalid, whom even a wife whom he had married when he was young and
healthy might have found repulsive'. The physical and mental decrepitude of
Tullus is described in brief but disgusting detail:

> Deformed and crippled in every limb, he could only enjoy his enormous
> wealth by contemplating it and could not even turn in bed unless he was
> man-handled. He also had to have his teeth cleaned and brushed for
> him – a squalid and pitiful detail. When complaining about the humilia-
> tions of his infirmity, he was often heard to say that every day he licked
> the fingers of his slaves.

It is just such a depressing image of the end of one's life, and not solely the
welcome one of a Spurinna, that Pliny and his contemporaries had also to

face. The negative realities, helplessness and hopelessness, could not be ignored.

And it should by now be apparent that it was not only the evident physical shortcomings of old age that had to be feared, but also the social liabilities that such negative attributes entailed, particularly in the attitudes of society towards its elderly members. It was just such attitudes in a political sphere that Cicero and, more explicitly, Plutarch were seeking to counteract or redefine. Grey hair, to take a trivial instance, might be seen as a symbol or crown of old age and its inherent nobility, but grey hair alone does not make a man wise and could be taken instead as a sign of decrepitude, 'the mildew and mould of old age', to quote one ancient author. It was an ancient proverb, attributed first to Solon, the sixth-century BC Athenian statesman and poet, that in an ideal old age one should go on learning something new every day, and this, in the eyes of Plato, Cicero and company, is in fact seen as a requisite for a wise old age. Yet here too there is a negative tradition undermining the positive trait, the notion that learning in old age is untimely, foolish and shameful. As Plutarch stressed in his pamphlet in regard to politics, one must continue one's lifelong good habits in old age, and not suddenly try to start from scratch when it is too late. The negative attitude expressed in regard to *opsimathia* (late learning) is surprisingly bitter in tone, drawn as it is by those who feel themselves above such petty behaviour.

Such positive/negative polarities, such ambivalent attitudes in regard to age, abound. Concurrent with the positive arguments of a Plato, a Cicero or a Plutarch, together with the two-sided, veristic discussions by Seneca, Pliny and Juncus, for example, we encounter a coldly negative picture even within the 'serious' tradition. While Cicero might mention in passing, only to dismiss, some negative qualities attributed by some to old age, Aristotle in his *Rhetoric* (fourth century BC) dwelt on just such features at great length. The main factor that is stressed is the old man's wary, pessimistic manner – having lived a long life and having made many mistakes, he is overly cautious, unlike the young man who has yet to learn life's knocks and who therefore overdoes everything and lives to excess; this is in direct contrast to the traditional notion that a long life brings with it wisdom, unless one classifies such an attitude as embodying wisdom. The elderly are, we are told by Aristotle, overly pessimistic, distrustful, malicious, suspicious, and small minded 'because they have been humbled by life and so their greatest hopes are raised to nothing more than staying alive'. They lack generosity, are cowardly and always anticipating danger, and yet they also love life to excess, especially on their last day of life. And so it goes on. The Roman writer Horace (first century BC), among others, provides a similar characterisation.

In short, the 'serious' literary and philosophical traditions in the description of old age provide two main attitudes: a 'positive', consolatory depiction, playing down (while still accepting) the negative attributes associated with old age in order to highlight positive qualities in and the potential of old age and the elderly; and a more negative reality, a coldly analytical, though impersonal and largely objective, depiction of the debilities and unpleasant attributes of old age – a reality of the present contrasted with an idealised past and an imagined or desired future. Turning now to more 'popular' forms of literature, in particular comic and satiric writings, the tradition, though diverse and widespread, is more straightforward to classify. It will be useful, as well as inevitable, if our focus should turn first to some hundred lines of Juvenal (in *Satire* 10, written early in the second century AD), in which is preserved one of the most powerful and bitter attacks on *senectus* in the literature of the ancient world, if not of all time.[23]

In dealing with the pointlessness and misguidedness of most people's prayers, Juvenal comes to a common plea: 'Grant us, Jove, a long life and many years!' But it is a prayer which he immediately rejects, for 'How painful are the endless afflictions of which drawn-out old age is full.' We are then given a detailed catalogue of the (mainly physical) disasters old age brings to a man, with some pertinent examples and with considerable rhetorical distaste. The depiction of old age in Juvenal's tenth satire focuses primarily on the physical manifestations – the wrinkled and sagging face, as a result of which all old people look the same, the shaky voices and limbs of the elderly, their bald heads and drivelling noses, and their toothless gums. As a result of such infirmities the old man – and note that the focus is on the male, not the female – is offensive both to his family and to himself. Even the legacy-hunter, whose job it was to fawn over ailing aristocrats, finds the old man disgusting, a clever (though perhaps exaggerated) effect. Loss of pleasures and of senses follows: no longer can one find enjoyment in food and wine, and sex has long since been forgotten (a recurring theme). Other pleasures are also lacking: one can no longer enjoy singing, music or the theatre – for a start, you are deaf.

This leads on to geriatric illnesses – the old man's chilly frame can be warmed only by a fever. The diseases old age brings are countless (old age was held by many to be a disease itself), along with its other physical shortcomings, to shoulders, loins, hips and eyes; like a swallow's chick the old man cannot even feed himself. Finally, as an endnote to add to the misery, mention of mental failings is also introduced – they are held to be the worst feature of all.[24]

From this unrelievedly vicious attack, Juvenal turns next to consider drawbacks suffered by the elderly, negative features of a more emotional and sentimental nature. Even if his mind retains its vigour, yet the aged man must endure the cruel fate of burying a beloved wife or a child, a brother or a sister: 'this is the price of longevity' – a very real and touching side of old age, a side which Juvenal shows real sensitivity (whatever his motives) in portraying.

But on the whole Juvenal's picture of old age is unpleasantly vivid, brilliantly harsh, and unforgivingly cruel. The message is clear enough: what one should pray for is not length of life, but, as we are told at the end of the satire, *mens sana in corpore sano*', which 'counts long life the least of nature's gifts'. This is one possible response to the realities of old age. There is realism in Juvenal's diatribe as well as rhetorical exaggeration; what is lacking, to be sure, is a genuine concern for the plight of the elderly described.

But negative images and attitudes are common enough, even simply as asides or passing references. The satirical/comic tradition is the harshest, directed especially against women. If Juvenal provides the strongest overall picture, then others, particularly Horace and Martial, have left us the most offensive and devastating indictments of the aged female. The stereotyped old woman is toothless, haggard, sex-crazed and disgusting. Highly unpleasant portrayals abound: from Latin literature one thinks in particular of two epodes by Horace, a score of poems by Martial, and several among the Priapic poems. As marginalised members of society, old women were especially set apart. Past the age of menopause and therefore no longer able to perform their duties as reproducers, they could easily become stereotyped as brothel madams, as witches, or as alcoholics.

The bitterly negative, often extremely personal, indictment of old age, particularly in satirical and erotic poetry, has a long history which Roman writers of the early empire adopted willingly and enthusiastically. Invective against old age can be traced back as far as Homer, and extends in painful and dreary detail to the elegies on old age written by Maximianus in the sixth century AD. As early as the seventh century BC Mimnermus in particular dwells on the flight of time, the loss of youthful pleasures, and the hatefulness of old age. In Greek tragedy and comedy alike old people, especially women, often come in for harsh treatment in their depiction. On the Roman stage, particularly in the plays of Plautus, every possible negative quality associated with old age is highlighted, with special emphasis on the old man's sexual, though impotent, proclivities. The negative images pervade almost every 'popular' branch of classical literature. It is the evident physical disabilities on which the popular literature focuses, highlighting the immediate concerns and fears of what old age will bring, more than on the more 'philosophical' *vituperationes* that concern Cicero.

Pliny the Elder (first century AD), like Juvenal, argued that a short life is nature's greatest gift. How can old age even be considered a part of life, he asks, with all the physical disabilities associated with it? And this is perhaps the dominant attitude or image of old age to come out of the literary sources, both 'serious' and 'popular', whether by a Cicero or by a Juvenal. Literary portrayals concentrate almost exclusively on the stereotyped old person him- or herself, generalising mainly on the physical infirmities old age brings. Plutarch apart, there seems very little attention to the social framework. The emphasis is on the way the elderly are to be pitied (a poor *apologia*) or are derided, and on how old age is to be feared or at best endured. Realities of old age are disguised beneath literary *topoi*.

## The marginality of old age

Two extremes in attitude towards the elderly have been seen to recur, explicitly or implicitly, in the ancient evidence: that old people have a definite role to play and contribution to make; and that old people are an unwelcome burden and at best must be tolerated. These are gross generalisations, but the awareness of the fact that such attitudes, at both extremes, may co-exist, rather than be mutually exclusive, is important. Different people at different times under different circumstances may hold one view or the other – if they hold any attitude at all – about different aged individuals. The extent to which old people in ancient society were an integral part of that society or were in some way excluded from full participation depended to a large extent, apart from questions of gender and status, on the degree of capability of the individual; that individual would not be wholly marginalised so long as he or she was still capable of performing some useful function, be it as a statesman or as a childminder. Just as two very distinct attitudes towards the elderly may be discerned, so the differing circumstances – economic and social, personal and public – of each individual old person may have led to very different attitudes by other members of society towards him or her. In short, the prestige enjoyed, the part played, the actual status of an old person in the ancient world depended more on the person him- or herself than on the general fact that he or she was old. Just as Cephalus and Cato stated that the faults found in an old person were due not to old age but to that person's character, so it may be said that society's view of an elderly individual was dictated by the extent to which that individual continued to find a niche in that society. Old people were not automatically accorded a role or privileged position; hence, perhaps, the insistence of some ancient authors that, for example, old men still have an important part to play in public life. Crucial in this context is the physical and mental well-being of the aged, and another distinction in the definition of old age will need to be borne in mind here, between the healthy and the decrepit elderly, that is between those who enjoy a robust old age during which they are capable of continued activity, physical and/or mental, and those who, owing to the natural consequences of senescence, are no longer able to function as society would wish or expect.[25]

In most pre-industrial societies in the past and in many contemporary societies studied by anthropologists it is the active adult male group which sets the norms, and other sectors of society – children, women, old men (to which one might add for antiquity slaves and foreigners) – are seen as in some respects on the margins of this cultural ideal. In terms of ancient societies the norm may be regarded as the adult male warrior,[26] and one's membership of this privileged minority depends on one's physical capabilities as well as one's inherited status. All other individuals are to some degree distanced from this ideal image. It needs to be further noted that members of such a marginalised body may be of different circumstances. The young, for example, will in time grow up, and through rites of transition will enter into the elite group, whereas older men have had their time at the helm (though to some extent they might rebel against their exclusion) and no *rite de passage* is left apart from death. One difficulty in analysing the position of marginal groups within an historical society is that by their very nature such marginal sectors tend to be the focus of very little attention and therefore leave little in the way of historical record. One advantage, however, with studying the elderly in ancient society is that, unlike other groups on the fringe such as women and slaves, they have left us testimony, particularly in the form of literature, in which they do indeed stress their continued role, as has been seen.

A recurring theme in classical literature is that war is for the young, advice for the old – this is a natural consequence of the physical deterioration evident in many old people, but assumes continued mental capabilities, an assumption which was not always correct. To be old is not enough, one must have positive attributes to outweigh the perceived negative ones. To be sure certain positive qualities were well appreciated, and not just by the elderly themselves – the experience gained by years lived, the social contacts, cultural understanding, and traditional *mores* 'stored' in old people. But one factor did forcefully exclude the elderly, as with women and children, from the active citizen body, and that was their lack of any active military role, at least in terms of actual fighting. Writers such as historians and epic poets often made the observation that the young men go out to fight while the women, children and elderly are left behind at home.[27] The point in most literary examples is to highlight the pathos of the situation, the misery and helplessness of those left behind, rather than to imply that the elderly are a burden or cowardly. But the social reality still meant that the elderly were not normally called to arms and were not seen in the same light as the younger, stronger men. As Ovid puts it most bluntly: *turpe senex miles* (an old soldier is disgusting).

If, like Homer's Nestor, the old man accepted that he could play no part in direct military action, the argument could still be made that he had a vital role to play in this sphere as adviser. More broadly, to follow the arguments of Cicero and Plutarch again, the elderly's role in government, as citizens of the state, might be held to make up for their lack of participation in military affairs. Bearing in mind what has already been said, one may consider further the extent to which an old man was regarded as a complete member of the political body, the Greek *polis* or the Roman *civitas*. Aristotle, in defining the nature of citizenship, considers various categories of persons who may not be deemed citizens in the fullest sense; factors he mentions include residence, rights under private law, and age:[28]

> One may dismiss from consideration children who are still too young to be entered on the roll of citizens, or men who are old enough to have been excused from civic duties. There is a sense in which the young and

the old may both be called citizens, but it is not altogether an unqualified sense: we must add the reservation that the young are undeveloped, and the old superannuated citizens (τοὺς δὲ παρηκμακότας: *literally* 'those past their prime'), or we must use some other qualification; the exact term we apply does not matter, for the meaning is clear. What we have to define is the citizen in the strict and unqualified sense, who has no defect that has to be made good before he can bear the name – no defect such as youth or age, or such as those attaching to disfranchised or exiled citizens.

One should note again that while the young will in time overcome the 'defect' of age and thus become citizens in the full sense, the elderly will not. But of course with Aristotle's definition we are dealing with theory, not necessarily practice. Yet the feeling if not the rule seems often to have been that the old man had outlived not only his military but also his political usefulness. The point is made explicitly many centuries after Aristotle by Juncus, whom we have already met and who lists among the many negative attributes of the elderly their exclusion from political and military affairs:

> If the old man has the audacity to enter the public square, he provokes the laughter of those who see him, for he cannot see properly and cannot hear when people shout. Trying to make his way forward he trips and falls. He is accused of getting in the way and of using up the common air of the city. For when he appears in the assembly, he is not included among the ranks of the tribes, nor is he capable of holding office, on account of the aforementioned disabilities: he is bowed and withered, misshapen and feeble, and in spirit, as the saying goes, has become a child again. In war (for this too should be mentioned) he is exempt from service and is left naked and defenceless, since he is not enlisted in the infantry or cavalry, nor indeed as a rower on a ship nor as a marine.

The conclusion is inevitable, that old age is *inutilis*, useless, an epithet that is not irregularly attached to *senectus*. In old age a man is not what he was, much of his usefulness is gone and in some respects, or in some people's eyes, he would be better off dead.

If some old men were disadvantaged by their marginal status, double marginality must have incurred twice the problems. The *puer senex*, the ideal of late paganism and early Christianity in particular whereby the young were precociously invested with (positive) qualities of old age such as wisdom and moderation – the stuff of saints – is one artificial example of such double marginality, with positive implications, at least for the young. The double marginality of the woman, in terms of both sex and age, is not so positive. As has been seen, the literary depiction of the old woman was almost monotonously negative and at times grotesque and cruel. It is a well-known feature of Athenian society (as depicted in extant evidence) that women, especially of the upper classes, enjoyed very little freedom outside the home. In old age, however, after the menopause, a woman was apparently granted the freedom to go outside the family confines. As widows in particular, in both Greek and Roman society, women in old age might in fact enjoy considerable authority, in practice if not also in legal theory, because they controlled the family wealth to some limited extent – always supposing, of course, that the family had wealth in the first place. Any benefits (in our eyes) accruing to a woman through her old age, however, were not due to any privileged or enhanced status, but rather quite the opposite. Because a woman past the menopause could no longer perform her primary function as a producer of legitimate offspring, it became of little concern to the adult male who made and enforced the rules whether or not an old woman followed the conventions of society or not. As a doubly marginalised member of society an old woman became an object of little interest, sexually and otherwise, so far had she strayed from the centre of attention, the world of the adult male citizen. The curse Ovid invokes on the aged whore Dipsas ('Thirsty') sums up well the fate of many an old woman in ancient society, as well as the callous view many a male may have taken: 'May the gods grant you no home and a needy old age and long winters and everlasting thirst.'

To most, however, such marginalised members would have been of little interest. Even in, for example, the extant medical literature from antiquity, there was no separate field of geriatric medicine; at most there exists only limited discussion of old age and its associated ailments. The degenerative ailments of old age were viewed with some helplessness. Medical science in antiquity, and up until the last century, concerned itself, when it turned to the elderly at all, with the possibilities for the prolongation of life through a regimen of diet and exercise, and with the observation of ailments. Since the elderly comprised a not insignificant proportion of the population, we are left again with the conclusion that as a marginal sector of society, the elderly could expect little comfort from the doctor. Death is the only sure cure for the *insanabilis morbus*, the incurable disease of old age.

Similarly, the corpus of law seldom turned its gaze towards the oldest members of the community. Few concessions were granted to age. There was never any institutionalised system of retirement or of pensions in antiquity. Old-age welfare rested solely with the members of one's immediate family, though in some societies, most notably classical Athens, this moral obligation was reinforced by law. With the care this might bring came also a dependence upon the younger generations.[29]

If the participation of the aged person in public affairs was at times debated, his or her role in religious practices was not, and this again is a mark of marginalisation.[30] Prophets and seers in literature were often depicted as marginalised members of society – women and aged men. Plato and Aristotle both remark that in their ideal states religious duties would be reserved for those in old age. In the Roman state the *paterfamilias*, the senior male member of the household, had the duty to observe the customary religious rites, the worship of *Lares*, *Penates* and ancestors. Priests and priestesses at Rome need not be old, though the office normally lasted for life,[31] and, in line with traditional ideas of respect for age, seniority would normally be expected to be given to the oldest member of the college.

The impression remains, however, here as elsewhere, that the continued activity of the elderly depended upon their own proven capability to perform the duties required. As marginal members of society any rights they held were far from automatic, but had to be won and maintained through continued performance and incessant pressure. What may appear at first sight as privileges, such as the greater degree of freedom for women in later life, in many cases should be more closely defined as a diminution of status and a lack of concern by other sectors of society. As the capability or right to execute some functions in the society disappeared, other functions had to be found if old people were not to be dismissed as *inutiles* and therefore regarded as surplus to requirements, as were his aged slaves by Cicero's exemplar of old age, Cato the Elder.

The various aspects discussed in this chapter have pointed to a picture, where old age is seen by all but the elderly themselves as a threat in the future, and where it is seen by the elderly as a time not so much to be enjoyed as to be endured, while ensuring that privileges are accrued rather than that their rights are taken away. While allowing for differences over time and space – subtle differences upon which the available testimony will not allow us to elaborate – I believe it is fair to conclude with a generalisation of this sort, that although criteria of age played an important part in public and private life alike, old age, the inevitable conclusion of a long life and the precursor to death, was not accorded in practice the esteem or authority which people such as Cicero and Plutarch in their own old age felt it merited. Whatever scattered expressions of reverence for old age might suggest, there is nothing to indicate any significantly positive role for the elderly in ancient society, whether as decision-makers or as advisers. Privileges granted to old age generally took the form of *exemptions* from duties (not always freely given at that), rather than positive benefits. The primary factor which finally determined an old person's place in the society was the health, mental and physical, that that person did or did not enjoy.[32] The point Cicero made in 44 BC is a timeless one:

> Ita enim senectus honesta est, si se ipsa defendit, si ius suum retinet, si nemini emancipata est, si usque ad ultimum spiritum dominatur in suos.

> Old age will only be respected if it fights for itself, maintains its own rights, avoids dependence on anyone, and asserts control over its own to the last breath.

There is no reality, therefore, underlying some traditional but usually unsub-
stantiated images of the elderly in the past ('the good old days') still
commonly held, images which usually contrast the allegedly unfavourable
position of old people today with that enjoyed by their ancestors in a mythical golden age. But it might also be added in conclusion that for the
ancients old age was less of a 'problem' than it is regarded all too often by us
today. By this I mean not that old age was a more comfortable state then
than now – what we have seen here precludes such an assessment. Rather it
is the case that old age in antiquity was not seen as a different or distinctive
stage of the life cycle to the same extent that it is in modern western societies. In the absence of wage-labour as the standard way of life and of a
retirement age in general life, people were expected simply to go on doing
whatever they had always done until they dropped. While they had no geriatric skills to speak of, the Greeks and Romans did not in reality seek to
shorten their life span. Old age, with all the negative features it might entail,
was still in reality regarded as part of the course of nature, as part of adulthood. In that regard systematic and deliberate marginalisation of the elderly
did *not* occur.

## Notes

1 The standard work on such rites in a classical society remains J. Gagé, 'Classes
  d'âge, rites et vêtements de passage dans l'ancien Latium', *Cahiers internationaux
  de sociologie*, 1958, vol. 24, pp. 34–64.
2 The only major study to date of ageing in antiquity is B. E. Richardson, *Old Age
  among the Ancient Greeks. The Greek Portrayal of Old Age in Literature, Art, and
  Inscriptions, with a Study of the Duration of Life among the Ancient Greeks on the
  Basis of Inscriptional Evidence*, Baltimore, MD, 1933. Her uncritical and subjective approach enabled her to convey the impression that the elderly in Ancient
  Greece enjoyed something of a golden age. At least one reviewer was convinced:
  'In this age, when it is the tendency to focus attention on the very young, it is
  refreshing to turn to a nation who kept children in their proper place and paid
  due deference to their elders and betters', E. Dobson, review of Richardson, *Old
  Age*, in *Antiquity*, 1934, vol. 8, pp. 365–6. Contrast the review by W. Schmid, in
  *Gnomon*, 1934, vol. 10, pp. 529–32.
3 Finley makes the salutary observation that the central themes of interest in the
  'burgeoning sociological and psychiatric literature' on old age and the elderly in
  modern society are not easily or directly applicable to the study of old age in the
  ancient world, largely because of a lack of awareness of such issues at the time
  and hence a lack of explicit evidence surviving today. To quote Finley here, 'The
  ancient historian is drawn to making bricks without straw. I do not wholly
  despair, but I am necessarily restricted to general statements based as much on
  broad sociological considerations as on ancient documentation.' M. Finley, 'The
  elderly in classical antiquity', *Greece and Rome*, 1981, vol. 28, pp. 156–71;
  reprinted in *Ageing and Society*, 1984, vol. 4, pp. 391–408, and in T. M. Falkner
  and J. de Luce (eds), *Old Age in Greek and Latin Literature*, New York, 1989,
  pp. 1–20.
4 See T. G. Parkin, 'Age and the aged in Roman society: demographic, social, and
  legal aspects', Unpublished D.Phil dissertation, University of Oxford, 1992.

5 One rather touching example of this is provided by the fifth century AD poet Ausonius, where he urges his wife to ignore the arrival of old age and for them to continue calling one another *iuvenis* (young man) and *puella* (girl), as they have since the day they were married: 'let us refuse to know the meaning of ripe old age; it's better to know Time's worth than to count his years'.

6 Grey hair was commonly taken as a sign of premature ageing. Gilbert argues that in the Renaissance people in their forties might be regarded as old – Erasmus wrote his poem 'On the discomforts of old age' when he was only 39/40. But the point is that some people might regard themselves or be regarded as old by their appearance rather than by their exact chronological age. The second century AD Greek writer Phlegon mentions the case of one man who apparently went through the whole life cycle in only seven years! C. Gilbert, 'When did a man in the renaissance grow old?', *Studies in the Renaissance*, 1967, vol. 14, pp. 7–32.

7 The opposite might also have been true: the general lack of fatty and sugar-based foods and the use of walking rather than mechanical transport might have meant that those not carried off by infection or accident looked younger thanks to a comparatively healthy life style.

8 J. S. Siegel, 'On the demography of aging', *Demography*, 1980, vol. 17, pp. 345–64, remarks on the notion, in itself a useful one, that instead of considering someone old after $x$ number of years from birth, we might employ a numerical value for the commencement of old age based on the average number of years *until death*: 'according to this concept, old age covers the period of life beginning with the age after which the particular [population] groups have a specified average number of years to live, say 10 to 15 years'. Using model life tables where $e_0 = 20$–30 years, one can estimate, for example, that Greeks and Romans had on average ten to fifteen more years to live from around the age of 50 to 60 years. Any figure more precise would suffer from spurious accuracy. I am not suggesting, of course, that Greeks and Romans defined old age in this way. For further discussion of this way of defining old age, see the chapter by Bourdelais in this volume.

9 See Emiel Eyben's bibliographical article in Falkner and de Luce, *Old Age in Greek and Latin Literature*, pp. 230–51, and also W. Suder (ed.), *Geras. Old Age in Greco-Roman Antiquity: A Classified Bibliography*, Wroclaw, 1991. The most recent and substantial study of note is T. M. Falkner, *The Poetics of Old Age in Greek Epic, Lyric and Tragedy*, Norman, OK, and London, 1995.

10 See T. G. Parkin, *Demography and Roman Society*, Baltimore, MD, and London, 1992, especially pp. 105–11.

11 That it is not so simple to classify every literary reference under these three headings is highlighted by the fact that a fragment of Sophocles ('no one loves life more than the ageing man') is quoted in both the first and the second sections!

12 *Republic* book 1, 328b–331d. Plato was probably in his fifties when he wrote the *Republic*.

13 Other complaints may spring readily to the reader's mind, but are not rebutted here; Cicero/Cato's primary concern is with the negative aspects of old age as seen by a Roman aristocratic male who enjoys tolerably good health. For an excellent philological commentary on the *de Senectute*, see J. G. F. Powell (ed.), *Cicero, Cato Maior de Senectute*, Cambridge, 1988.

14 An extremely common sentiment in both Greek and Latin literature, from Homer onwards. It is said to be the place of the young to obey and the old to rule; the elderly were often held to be teachers of the young.

15 Though this is later qualified, when Cicero has Cato state that such *voluptates* (pleasures) are not wholly lacking – a noticeable difference from the Platonic model.

16 It is perhaps not fair to note that neither Cato nor Cicero seems in reality to have lived up to this ideal.
17 This digression by Cato, incidentally, provides a marvellous example of the garrulousness of old age; as Cicero has Cato say, 'Old age is by nature rather talkative – just in case I should appear to be absolving it of all faults.'
18 It is worth bearing in mind that Cicero is writing at the beginning of a period when the power of the conservative senate (a body whose very name is linked to the Latin term for old age) will be supplanted by that of an autocrat; the future emperor Augustus first rose to prominence (in 44 BC) at the age of 19 years. The collective influence of the anonymous elderly is in effect replaced by the executive power of the young.
19 In an oral culture, the old might enjoy increased prestige as repositories of traditional wisdom to be passed on to the young, whereas in a literate culture written records could take their place. On the other hand, failing powers of memory and performance skills in old age could mean that the very aged had no role to play, whereas in classical Athens elderly authors (one thinks for a start of men like Aeschylus, Sophocles and Euripides) flourished.
20 Much was made by some Greek authors of the supposed relationship between the Greek terms for honour (γέρας) and for old age (γῆρας).
21 Seneca suffered from a wide variety of ailments in his later years, as he is fond of mentioning.
22 On suicide, see Seneca's well-known 77th letter, and the discussions of ancient attitudes towards suicide and euthanasia in P. Carrick, *Medical Ethics in Antiquity*, Dordrecht, 1985, and B. A. Brody (ed.), *Suicide and Euthanasia*, Dordrecht, 1989. With eighty-seven recorded cases from antiquity of self-killing among the old, A. J. L. van Hooff, *From Autothanasia to Suicide: Self-Killing in Classical Antiquity*, London, 1990, provides a wealth of analytical detail on the elderly's means (starvation being the most common) and motives (most notably to escape pain or public disgrace, and through being weary of living).
23 One remembers Hamlet's reaction:

> Slanders, sir: for the satirical rogue says here that old men have grey beards, that their faces are wrinkled, their eyes purging thick amber and plum-tree gum, and that they have a plentiful lack of wit, together with most weak hams: all of which, sir, though I most powerfully and potently believe, yet I hold it not honesty to have it thus set down.

24 On senile dementia in the Roman world, see T. G. Parkin, 'Out of sight, out of mind: elderly members of the Roman *familia*', in B. Rawson and P. R. C. Weaver (eds), *The Roman Family in Italy: Status, Sentiment, Space*, Oxford, 1997.
25 Such a distinction is made by some Latin authors, between *senectus* and *senium*; a similar dichotomy is occasionally made in the ancient medical texts (e.g. Galen, *Commentaries on Hippocrates' Aphorisms* 3.31 [17B.648 Kühn]). There is rich comparative material in L. W. Simmons, *The Role of the Aged in Primitive Society*, New Haven, CT, 1945; idem, 'Aging in pre-industrial societies', in C. Tibbits (ed.), *Handbook of Social Gerontology: Societal Aspects of Aging*, Chicago, 1960; A. P. Glascock and S. L. Feinman, 'Social asset or social burden: treatment of the aged in non-industrial societies', in C. L. Fry (ed.), *Dimensions: Aging, Culture and Health*, New York, 1981. Note also M. Philibert, 'Le statut de la personne âgée dans les sociétés antiques et préindustrielles', *Sociologie et sociétés*, 1984, vol. 16.2, pp. 15–27, and H. M. Stahmer, 'The aged in two ancient oral cultures: the ancient Hebrews and Homeric Greece', in S. F. Spicker et al. (eds), *Aging and the Elderly: Humanistic Perspectives in Gerontology*, Atlantic Highlands, NJ, 1978.

26 N. Loraux, ''Ηβη et ἀνδρεία: deux versions de la mort du combattant athénien', *Ancient Society*, 1975, vol. 6, pp. 1–31.

27 For example, Homer, *Iliad* 15.660–6, 18.514–15; Thucydides 2.6; Julius Caesar, *Gallic War* 1.29.1; Vergil, *Aeneid* 5.715, 12.131–2. Vergil's depiction (*Aeneid* 2) of the aged Trojan Priam's feeble attempts to go into battle underlines the pathos. Exceptions to the rule are highlighted for the very reason that they are necessitated by highly unusual circumstances. Women, old men, children and the poor are commonly grouped together by ancient authors. The various roles of the age groups are neatly, if somewhat cynically, summed up in a proverb attributed to Hesiod: 'Deeds belong to the young, advice to the middle-aged, prayers to the elderly.'

28 *Politics* 1275a, trans. E. Barker. Compare Seneca, *Controversiae* 10.4 (early first century AD) for some similar logic: the state cannot be harmed by a child, a woman, an old man, or a pauper, since such people are not true members of the state.

29 Parkin, 'Out of sight, out of mind'.

30 T. Wiedemann, *Adults and Children in the Roman Empire*, London, 1989, pp. 176–7.

31 Vestal virgins being one notable exception, whose 'retirement' after the age of 40 years would probably coincide with the menopause.

32 An ancient proverb put it simply: 'It is a fine thing to grow old, but a bad thing to grow too old.' An alternative version is also noteworthy: 'It is a fine thing to grow old, so long as you have someone to look after you.'

# 3 Old age in the high and late Middle Ages

## Image, expectation and status

*Shulamith Shahar*

Contrary to the accepted view that people in the Middle Ages and the Renaissance were considered old from their forties, in fact they were classified as old between the ages of 60 and 70. Though in some of the schemes for the division of the life course into stages old age begins at 40, in others its onset is at 35, 45, 50, 58, 60 or 72. The schemes were developed in different contexts and related to various configurations of nature and time. The authors conveyed the symbolic identity of each stage in human life, and a judgement of its virtues, rather than an evaluation based on a biological or social reality. Several medieval scholars and artists declared at the age of 40 that they were already old; however, there are ample examples of such claims by people in the nineteenth and twentieth centuries. According to medieval legislative texts which are definitely a more reliable source for the question, the onset of old age is between 60 and 70. In all the legislative texts which granted age-linked exemption from military service, trial by battle, service on the town watches, various administrative duties and positions, as well as from payment of taxes and obligatory work, they were granted to those of 60 or 70 years of age. In most of these legislative texts there is no mention of women as they were not liable for most of the duties from which exemption was granted to elderly males. They are mentioned only in the Statute of Labourers promulgated in England in 1349, and in Henry VIII's statute concerning vagabonds and beggars (1503). According to the Statute of Labourers, up to the age of 60 women were required to accept any work offered to them like men. According to the statute of Henry VIII those who were in authority to punish beggars and vagabonds were entitled to diminish the punishment of both men and women over 60 years of age. According to a thirteenth-century compilation of laws from the Crusader Kingdom of Jerusalem, known as the Assises de la Haute Cour, an heiress of a fief, who reached the age of 60, was no longer obliged to marry on order of her feudal lord. In various non-legislative texts as well 60 is the indicator of old age for both men and women.[1]

While there is some distinction in the legislative texts between subgroups in the elderly population (not all the concessions and exemptions apply to the elderly of all strata of society), in all the other various texts they are represented as one group. In the images, attitudes and expectations as to conduct and state of mind that are developed in the various discourses, no distinction is drawn between various social strata. The elderly constitute one marginal group represented along with women, children, invalids, poor folk or foreigners. Sometimes the common denominator attributed to them and to those who are represented alongside them is their physical weakness, sometimes it is their mental weakness, or their social distinctiveness. However, in these representations they are always contrasted with adult males – the wielders of authority and power.[2] Elderly women thus belonged to two marginal groups, that of women and that of the old ones. No defined roles are accorded to the elderly as a group in the normative texts. Even the role they definitely fulfilled as a group in reality, that of witnesses in cases of disputed rights of possession of land, contested demands of service, etc., and of repositories of local custom and tradition, is rarely mentioned in the normative and ascriptive texts.

Attitudes towards the old person were equivocal. Conflicting meanings were also attributed to the old body as regards its moral and spiritual significance and what it contained for man. There was no unanimity of view as to the kind of relationship between body and soul. However, in almost all the discourses about old age, the body takes central place; and in all of them the same unidealised stereotype is attached to it. There were three main conceptions of the relationship between body and soul in old age. According to the first, the person constituted a psychosomatic unity of body and soul. The second conception does not imply a dichotomy between body and soul in old age, but its supporters emphasise the idea of their possible development in two opposite directions. The third conception entailed an explicit separation of body and soul, and the texts that represent it are the only ones that disregard the body.

The conception of the person as a psychosomatic unity of two linked entities, body and soul, was developed in the scientific and medical texts. Old age, it was argued, entailed deterioration of both physical and mental capacities as well as the development of negative traits of character. According to Christian doctrine man forfeited immortality and was condemned to the subsequent process of ageing because of Original Sin. Opinions were divided as to whether, after the Deluge, human life span was curtailed even further and the ageing process was expedited in the wake of divine intervention or natural factors. However, in either case, in medical texts both divine punishment for Original Sin and possible divine intervention after the Deluge are ultimate causes, while focus is on the immediate causes of ageing, and how man ages. The changes in the composition of the humours in the body, that is the increase in external bad humours and the decrease in natural heat and innate radical moisture, were regarded as the immediate cause of all the *accidentia senectutis* which included both physical and mental concomitants. Roger Bacon (1214–92) writes:

All these accidents of old age and senility are white hair, pallor, wrinkling of the skin, excess of mucus, foul phlegm, inflammation of the eyes and general injury of the organs of sense, diminution of blood and spirits, weakness of motion and breathing in the whole body . . . [3]failure of both the animal and natural powers of the soul, sleeplessness, anger and disquietude of mind, and forgetfulness of which the royal Hali says that old age is the home of forgetfulness, and Plato that it is the mother of lethargy.[4]

Aristotle believed that physical and intellectual ability peaked and declined at different ages, the latter occurring later than the former.[5] Thus some medieval writers distinguished between old age and extreme old age, usually denoted *senium*, and attributed the mental decline only to the second stage. At that stage, because of the physiological changes occurring in his body, primarily the decrease in natural heat, man becomes once more like a child.[6] Mary Carruthers demonstrated that in medieval literary culture 'memory' was a literary as well as an ethical concept. It was a sign of the moral strength and humanity of the person.[7] Its weakening was thus a sign of their diminution. Melancholy had an allusion to sin; it signified lack of belief in divine grace. However, the description of the development of these characteristics as well as of negative traits of character is a neutral one with no moral judgement attached. The development of certain negative traits of character is considered part of the inevitable process of ageing, just like the deterioration of the body over which man has no control. Little symbolic significance is attached to the old body in scientific texts. When Vincent of Beauvais (*c.*1190–1264) following Maximianus describes old age as the 'smell of death' and 'death in life', the imagery of death is not of otherworldliness, but rather of a liminal stage between life and death, and of the end of a biological process.[8] There are no expectations of the old person regarding behaviour or state of mind in the medical texts. However, believing that by acting on the soul one can act on the body, some authors offer advice on how to prevent anger and melancholy which reduce the natural heat and thus accelerate the process of ageing. These feelings can be prevented by evoking emotion and joy through aesthetic pleasure, intellectual discourse with friends and, of course, through reading the Holy Scriptures.[9]

The conception that illness and decrepitude are an inevitable component of senescence, combined with the limited medical capacity of the period, determined the attitudes towards the medical needs of the elderly. The purpose of the detailed instructions for the elderly in the health manuals is not therapeutic but preventive; namely, to delay further deterioration, and enhance the person's well-being, not to cure or rehabilitate that person.

The authors of the medical texts as well as those of the schemes of the 'stages of age' do not state explicitly that they refer only to men, but from the contents of the texts it clearly appears that they are concerned exclusively with men. However, some writers did devote a separate discussion to one particular change in the body of the elderly woman: the cessation of menstrual flow. The theory concerning the consequences of this physiological phenomenon is implicit in scientific texts and explicit in works of scientific popularisation. According to both scientific and popular belief menstrual blood was impure, harmful and possessing destructive power.[10] According to this theory, however, after menopause the woman was even more dangerous, because she became incapable of eliminating the superfluous matter from her organism. As stated in *De Secretis Mulierum* attributed to Albert the Great:

> the retention of menses engenders many evil humours. The women being old have almost no natural heat left to consume and control this matter, especially poor women who live on nothing but coarse meat, which greatly contributes to this phenomenon. These women are more venomous than the others.[11]

Being venomous by virtue of her very physiological mechanism, the poor old hag who concocts philtres of love and death is thus merely exercising an activity analogous to the transformation that physiology works on her organism. The conception of the process of ageing of the male was also a deterministic one. The changes in personality attributed to men (including the poor ones), however, were not considered as harbouring social danger and entailing destructive actions.

In religious and didactic writings the old body serves as a metaphor for the transience and vanity of all worldly things. Its unidealised stereotype is aimed at arousing contempt of self and of the world (*contemptus sui, contemptus mundi*). Innocent III (1160–1216), in a text influenced by Horace, and which itself had an impact on various later medieval texts, from sermons to literary works, depicts the vicissitudes, sufferings, sins and vanities of earthly life from conception to death. He devotes a detailed and unsparing description to the old man's body: his heart weakens and his head shakes; his face becomes wrinkled and his back becomes bent; his eyes grow dim and his joints grow shaky; his nose runs and his hair falls out; his hand trembles and he makes awkward movements; his teeth decay and his ears grow deaf. And he adds: 'young men! be not proud in the presence of a decaying old man; he was once that which you are; he is now what you in turn will be'.[12] Innocent III's description of the degradation old age entails is not meant to evoke empathy but to caution against pride and to arouse contempt of the flesh. He does not exhort the young out of respect for the wisdom and morality of the old, but in order to emphasise that old age is part of the human condition which none of those who live long enough can escape. The old body does not merely indicate the approaching biological end as in the medical works, but also symbolises the terrible judgement in the next world which man in his folly and sin chooses to ignore. In Petrarch's

(1309–74) treatise *De Remediis utriusque Fortune* (On the Remedies to the two kinds of Fortune), in a philosophical rather than in a religious context, the metaphoric use of the old body serves the same purpose as in Innocent III's text. In a dialogue between Joy and Reason, the function of pessimistic Reason is to curb Joy, bring home to him the folly of his happiness and convince him that all that now causes him happiness will become a source of evil and pain. The degradation and increasing unloveliness of the body and the loss of bodily pleasures are indicators of the fragility, impermanence and insignificance of this world. Says Reason to Joy: the blond curls will be shed; the single curl which will remain will turn white; wrinkles will plough furrows in the forehead and cheeks; a gloomy cloud will cover the merry rays and the glowing stars in the eyes. Before the teeth fall out they will lose their smoothness and white gleam. The neck and shoulders will lose their nimbleness and become crooked. The hands will dry up, and the feet will bend to such a degree that you will no longer recognise them as yours.[13] The old body suffering from gout, scabies and constant fatigue can no longer jump, play tennis or dance. The young body is like a flower, but a flower whose fading is inherent in its blossoming. Loyal to the concept of the unity of body and soul, after describing the changes in the old body and the diseases which are its lot, he depicts the dimming of understanding, the weakening of memory and the disturbance of speech.[14]

Preachers and authors of moralistic and didactic treatises who depicted in detail the unsightliness of the old male body did not depict the female one. Some of them only mention in general terms the transience of female beauty, and accompany their statement by critical and sarcastic comments on the vain efforts of old women to conceal their loss by lavish clothing, cosmetics and female wiles.[15] It is in the texts that present the binary contrasts of young/old and even more so in those that use the female body as the personification of winter, the enemies of love, evil traits, sin, old age itself and death that there is a detailed and cruel description of the body. One example will suffice. In *Le Pèlerinage de la vie humaine*, written in the fourteenth century by William of Deguileville, the different virtues like Mercy, Charity, Reason, Penitence and Diligence (*occupant*) as well as God's Grace are personified by young women splendidly dressed. While Sloth, Pride, Flattery, Hypocrisy, Envy, Treachery, Anger, Avarice, Gluttony and Lust, as well as Tribulation, Heresy, Disease and Old Age, are represented by ugly old women. Sloth is an ugly, hairy, dirty and stinking old woman. Pride is an old woman of monstrous obesity. Because of this obesity and her swollen legs she cannot walk alone. She rides on Flattery, in her one hand a stick (to spur on Flattery), and in the other a mirror into which she gazes. The image of Hypocrisy is not sharply delineated, but she is covered by a cloak such as is worn by old women to hide their ugliness and infirmities. Envy crawls on her belly like a snake; she is shrivelled and dry without flesh and blood. Disease leans on crutches; and Old Age has legs of lead, while Mercy, leading the pilgrim to the infirmary, is a young woman with an

exposed breast so as to suckle the suffering.[16] The old woman, whose milk
has dried up, can never be the image of the Holy Mother nursing her infant
– the symbol of goodness and unstinting giving. Caroline Bynum demonstrated the association of woman's body with food in medieval culture, and
the use of food as metaphor in describing female mystical experience.[17]
There was no place for that association in relation to the old woman's body.

As already mentioned, the image of the elderly person was an ambiguous
one. Ageing was considered conducive to increased wisdom, 'liberation of
enemies', that is passions and worldly ambitions, as well as to spiritual
growth. These traits of the old person are manifestly elevated in medieval
religious texts presenting the transcendence ideal. The transcendence ideal
(already developed among the Epicureans, the Stoics and early Christians) is
based on the assumption that man as a rational being can overcome the
*cursus aetatis*, the laws of nature and time, and disclose the ideal traits of all
natural ages.[18] As St Augustine wrote: 'in your body you cannot be both
young and old. In your soul, however, you can: young through alacrity, old
through gravity.'[19] But unlike St Augustine who presented as an ideal the
blending of youth and age, the medieval Christian thinkers regarded the
ideal transcendence as the manifestation of the traits of old age in the young
and even in the child. In the *Vitae* of the saints there often recurs the *topos*
of the boy–old man (*puer–senex*). The boy–old man is the image of Daniel
and Jesus in their childhood; he is serious, wise and displays religious piety.[20]
Bernard of Clairvaux denounced the custom of appointing immature young
people to high positions in the Church. At the same time, he adds that some
young people, because of the grace of God, surpass the old in wisdom,
discretion and way of life, and he quotes the verses from the Book of
Wisdom (4, 8–9) which were usually cited in this context: 'For venerable age
is not that of long time, nor counted by the number of years; but the understanding of a man is grey hairs and spotless life.'[21] Like Bernard of
Clairvaux, John of Salisbury, in discussing the question of who were worthy
of serving as counsellors to monarchs, quotes the Book of Wisdom and
adds that where grave, wise men are concerned 'the question of bodily or
physical age is immaterial'.[22] Old age is thus the symbol of spiritual integrity
and wisdom and its sign is white hair. Needless to say that physiology is not
considered determinant. Man is able to transcend his age spiritually
upwards, while old age in itself is no guarantee for wisdom and spiritual
integrity.[23] Moreover, in the same texts the authors often insert the *topos* of
the 'hundred-year-old boy' (*puer centum annorum*). The greatest folly of the
'hundred-year-old boy' is his desire to continue his amorous activities, which
is neither natural, nor fitting for his age.[24]

In the *Vitae*, the *topos* of the boy–old man is paralleled by that of the
girl–old woman. The hagiographer of St Catherine of Siena described her at
the age of 6:

From that hour, the little girl began to grow old. There was a wondrous maturity in her good qualities and her conduct. Her deeds were not those of a child, nor of a young woman, but were entirely in the spirit of old age.[25]

However, in the religious literature, which presented the ideal of spiritual transcendence as something which a young man (and not only the child who was a future saint) could achieve, there is no reference to young women.

All authors of moralistic and didactic treatises denied determinism. However, unlike the elevators of the transcendence ideal they concentrated on the negative image of the old person. They do not distinguish between old age and extreme old age, and also extend the list of the negative characteristics. Aegidius Romanus (*c.* 1247–1316) wrote a manual for the education of kings, which was dedicated to his former pupil and later king of France, Philip the Fair. In this manual following Aristotle he describes the old ones as cowardly, suspicious, shameless (because advantage is more important to them than honour), miserly and lacking in hope. He also states that they tend to show pity and not to pass judgement hurriedly on matters concerning which there is doubt. However, the source of these apparently positive traits is not unequivocal. Unlike the mercifulness of the young which derives from their belief that everybody is as good as themselves who have not yet caused harm to anyone, writes Aegidius, the mercifulness of the aged derives from their weakness. They want everyone to take pity on the weak. They do not hurry to pass judgement because they are no more sure about anything being humiliated by life. Aegidius also concurs with Aristotle's conclusion, which was also adopted by other medieval thinkers, that the most suitable age for power and holding positions is middle age (*in statu*). At this age, the negative traits of youth have disappeared while the negative traits of old age have not yet developed. However, in Aegidius's day, monarchy was hereditary in the Capetian dynasty. Thus, a young man could inherit the throne and, at least theoretically, an old man as well. Aegidius's solution is transcendence upwards as well as downwards: 'Young and old alike can act against the tendency [of their age].'[26] The fourteenth century poet, Eustache Deschamps, in a poem written in the first person, after describing in most cruel terms his old body, adds the negative stereotype of the old man: impatient, miserly, quick to anger, bored and boring, hostile to new customs, laughter and merriment.[27]

Unlike Aegidius Romanus and Eustache Deschamps, Bernardino of Siena distinguishes between 'good' and 'bad' old people. Enumerating the spiritual calamities of old age – impatience, melancholy, ignorance, gloominess, perversity or vice, stupidity and mental blindness – he adds that all these are mainly found in 'bad old men' (*et maxime in senibus malis*).[28] Like most other preachers and authors of moralistic texts Bernardino of Siena rejects determinism and ignores physiology. There are individual differences between people. Vincent of Beauvais, a compiler who recorded various approaches, often without integration, notes the two different conceptions of old age, and in this case, tries to reconcile them. He writes of the good in old age, stemming mainly from the increase in wisdom and decline in passions. He then goes on to list the manifestations of mental decline in old age: absence of energy, forgetfulness, gullibility. Aware of the contradiction, he proposes a solution based on acknowledgement of the individual differences between people based on dissimilarity of personality: just as passions and wantonness are not characteristic of all *adolescentes*, so also senile folly (*stultia que deliratio dicitur senium*) is not evinced in all old people.[29] Unlike Vincent of Beauvais, who wrote an encyclopedia of natural philosophy, and was obliged to refer to the theory of humours, the authors of moralistic and didactic texts were exempt from this duty. They denied determinism and emphasised man's will and choice, together with Divine Grace.

This denial of determinism, emanating from the conception that body and soul can develop in two opposite directions, enabled an elaboration of expectations of the old person as to behaviour and state of mind on the one hand, and on the other hand offered consolation and hope. One can find in the various discourses, expressions of empathy towards the plights of the elderly: their physical sufferings, their poverty and the fact that they are considered a burden and a nuisance. Bartholomaeus the English, author of a popular encyclopedia, describes the old man who coughs and spits, who is a burden to everyone and is judged and despised by all.[30] However, little tolerance was expressed towards diversions of the elderly from the expected state of mind and behaviour. The old person was exhorted to exhibit resignation, refrain from complaining, accept his age and his approaching death and prepare for it, gaze into his own soul and act for his salvation. Old age is presented as a gift the old person was privileged to receive. On the one plane the gift is longevity itself which the old enjoy, while so many others die prematurely, in childhood or in youth. Castigating the elderly for their murmurings and complaints, Bernardino of Siena says (or rather shouts): 'You strove to reach it, you desired to achieve it, you were afraid you'll not reach it, and now, arriving, you lament. Every one wishes to reach old age, but nobody wishes to be old.'[31] On a higher plane the gift consists in the opportunity given to the old person to repent, make penance and come closer to God by means of his weak and ailing body. It is up to him to use the opportunity afforded to him, or not to use it. Nineteenth-century American Evangelical ministers promised their flock, in their sermons, that obedience to the natural laws of health and morality would bring long life, a healthy old age and natural death. Violation of natural law and morality, on the other hand, caused premature wretched old age or early, painful death.[32] Medieval religious thinkers, who regarded the old body as an opportunity and means of expiation of sin and spiritual elevation, in no way linked the right way of conduct and state of mind to the condition of the body. They did not hold out the promise of health in old age as a prize for living a moral life. Moreover, the decline and weakening of the body were perceived as facilitating expiation of sin and spiritual elevation. Unlike young and beautiful ascetics who sought disease or mutilated their bodies in order to expiate their own sins or the sins of others and in order to come close to God, the old person did not have to discipline his body. Old age was perceived as a source of physical suffering and almost as disease. It was also the time of extinction of passions.

The old body is no more the focus of desire, only of pain. The very ageing of the body prevents the commitment of some of the most notorious sins. Having lost his teeth, writes the preacher, the old man will laugh less, gnaw less at the good name of others and talk less. The weakening of sight will relieve him from gluttony, avarice and lust. If his hearing fails, he will be less able to listen to nonsense and instead will read religious books and gaze in silence at the works of God – at heaven and earth and all they contain. The abating of the libido will free him of the sins of the flesh.[33] A lustful old man or woman looking for sexual adventures was considered to be flouting the laws of nature and behaving like a madman or woman. Moral, social, aesthetic and medical arguments combined with views on the 'natural' and 'unnatural' to condemn the amorous old man (*senex amans*) who does not act as befits his advanced years. Philip of Novare (d. 1264) defined the old man's wish for amorous relations as 'desire without need and capacity'; and that of the woman as deriving from her vanity. Her nature no more inclines her to sexual relations, but she wants to prove that she is still desired.[34] In medical texts old men (there is no reference to women) are warned against intercourse, as it might harm their health and accelerate the process of ageing.

In works of fiction the lustful old man is described as pathetic, comic or grotesque. He is, however, usually a man of some standing and property, a rival for the young men who are less prosperous than he. But the old woman, who is expert in the secrets of life and sex, belongs to the lower strata of society (being one of those who feed on coarse meat which increases the proportion of poison in their bodies). She is often presented as more dangerous than grotesque. In moral literature both men and women (but more often men) are condemned for clinging to their sins of youth instead of exploiting the opportunity accorded to them to free themselves of sin and repent.

Notwithstanding the attribution of a long list of negative traits of character to the old person in these religious and didactic texts, and despite the ubiquity of lack of consistency in the arguments and their veering between the two images, they also accorded meaning to the inevitable plights of the last stage of life. Old age was presented as a time not only of expiation of sin but also of possible spiritual elevation. Some of the authors, though referring to both body and soul, ignore the question of the relationship between them. Others presented them as developing in old age in two opposite directions. As John Bromyard, author of an encyclopedia for preachers, asserted: 'To the extent that old age decreases the power of youth, it increases the devotion of the soul; what is suppressed in the one is elevated in the other.'[35] Some writers placed greater emphasis on expiation of sin; others, like Dante, emphasised spiritual elevation. In his *Convivio* he compares the last stage of life to a ship gradually drawing its sails before entering harbour. Tranquilly and tenderly, without bitterness, the ennobled soul proceeds in due order towards its ultimate fruit. Like other thinkers and authors of medical manuals, Dante compares the death of the old person to the ripe apple falling from the tree. In medical works, the emphasis is on the naturalness and lack of pain; in Dante – on the end of the road, acceptance and great peace.[36]

The purest consolation was offered, however, by the idea of the ever-youthful soul, which related to both men and women. The full elaboration of this idea can be found in one of the sermons of Meister Eckhart. This is the sermon on the Epistle to the Romans, 6, 4: 'Therefore we are buried with him by baptism into death; that like as Christ was raised up from the dead by the glory of the father even so we also should walk in newness of life.' God Who created *ex nihilo*, writes Eckhart, Who is always, and Who acts always, is new. Life and newness are his domain. All that is new comes from God and there is no other source of renewal. 'Come close to God', therefore, writes Eckhart; 'draw near, come back, turn round to God'. All those who draw near to God will be renewed (*innovantur*), and purified; they will be good and sanctified, as stated in Psalms 103, 5: 'thy youth is renewed like the eagle'. In a life of grace, man will always renew, and renewal is life. On the other hand, those who move away from God will grow old (*veterascunt*), sin, and be lost. 'For the wages of sin is death' (Epistle to the Romans 6, 23). The soul formed in the image of God is created young. It may have grown tired and feeble in bodily existence, but it can renew itself and purify itself. Only the material and visible are destined to age. Eckhart does not refer to the body, nor does he perceive the old body as an opportunity and means of spiritual purification through suffering, release from passions and expiation of sin. The possibility of the renewal of the soul is a constant factor, and this renewal is not a one-time act but is repeated. If a man delves into his inner resources, detaches himself from the world and concentrates on Divine Grace, he will be renewed. Only the soul of him who draws away from God will grow old, and the further away he moves, the more it will age (*antiquatur*).[37]

The expectations of the old person mentioned so far are that he accept his ageing and the plights it entails without complaint, free himself of worldly ambitions, not to behave like the young and especially avoid the sin of the flesh, achieve a sense of resignation, repent and concentrate on his approaching death and the salvation of his soul. There was, however, one more expectation that had a clearer social significance. The old person was expected to withdraw to the margins and make way for the younger ones. By law an elderly person was entitled to retire from military service and certain offices, and administrative duties; he was not obliged to retire. In the normative texts he is advocated to retire. Philip of Novare stated that a man who reached 60 was exempt from service. From this age on his only obligation was to serve himself, and if he had the means, he should avail himself of the services of others. He also states that pride in an old person is disgraceful. Even if he is rich, being weak in his body he should be meek and modest in all his ways.[38] Jean Gerson, in his essay 'To an Old Man', exhorts him to dedicate the time left to him to reading the Scriptures, prayer and preparation for his death. He is also advocated to cease caring about the affairs of others. When St Antony got old, writes Gerson, an angel appeared to him and said: 'Think about yourself, Antony, and let God direct the lives of others. Mad is the old man who does not conduct himself thus.'[39] Vincent of Beauvais declares that an old man has to disengage himself from all his occupations and from the care of his estates.[40] (Feudal estates in the high Middle Ages entailed administrative rights and many of them also various degrees of ruling power.) Leon Battista Alberti in his *Libri della Famiglia*, written as a guide book for a great Florentine family in the early fifteenth century, introduces two elderly men, Giannozzo and Piero. They are both 64 years old, and both are presented as having already retreated to the margins. Giannozzo helps as much as he can his elderly and needy friends; he recommends them to the Commune's authorities and assists them financially. He also serves as adviser to the young of the extended family. However, he holds no public office, does not conduct business and is already remote from the centre of activities. Piero who in his forties and fifties was involved in political affairs in the service of princes, also no longer holds any public office.[41] As already mentioned, Aegidius Romanus, in the wake of Aristotle, believed that it was the middle-aged males who were the most suitable for exercising authority and for ruling, not the old ones. Writing for a member of hereditary monarchy, however, he could not suggest that aged monarchs should retire. He had to content himself with the idea of a possible transcendence of a man in authority both upwards and downwards. The Florentine Brunetto Latini was apparently the only medieval political thinker who suggested entrusting the highest political offices to the 'old' ones (*vieus*). However, a careful reading of his *Li Livres dou trésor* reveals that in fact his suggestion refers not to the elderly, but to the middle-aged men, and that his main concern was that young men should not be elected to the governing bodies of the republic.[42]

The question to be asked now is what impact did the images, attitudes and expectations developed in the various discourses have on reality, that is on the way old men and women were treated, and on their status? It is known that images influence attitudes, and attitudes can affect reality, that is action. However, it is also known that the causal connection between attitudes and actual conduct is complex and by no means direct, let alone cases where attitudes are ambiguous as they were towards the elderly in medieval culture. It is only rarely that the voice of an old man, and almost never that of an old woman, is heard from the medieval sources that survived, the voice that could tell us how he or she felt in his (her) family and in his (her) community. The little we know about how elderly people were treated comes mainly from indirect evidence. Any attempt to answer this question involves a discussion of the relationship between elderly parents and their offspring, the ways of devolution of property from the older to the younger generation as well as the tensions between the young and the old. These issues are not the subject of this chapter. I will concentrate on the question of the status of elderly people.

The status of the elderly varied according to social strata, economic resources, roles and personalities. There was, however, one common element to all strata of society which was a major factor in determining the status of the elderly. Authority and role were not based on an ascriptive criterion of age. Ideally, mature middle-aged males were expected to wield authority, and a minimal age was fixed by both canon and secular law for appointment or election for various offices. However, many people held office while still young, if only because some senior positions were hereditary. The minimal age at which a person could take hold of his or her inheritance varied according to the type of asset or office involved, but it was always a young age, from 14 to 21.[43] At the other pole, there was no legal age of obligatory retirement. What determined the time of retirement in all strata of society was functioning and not chronological age. Thus if not forced into retirement by family or political circumstances, elderly men who had the functional capacity could continue to fulfil their roles, each in accordance with his social position. The only case of legal disqualification from office due to chronological age I encountered is in the statutes of Lucca. People aged 55 and over could not be elected to public offices.[44] (In other localities exemptions from certain duties and the *right* to retire were accorded only to men of more advanced age.) At the opposite pole, in Venice it was the young who were disqualified from office. According to the laws and statutes of the commune of Venice the minimal age for election to the various public offices did not differ from that fixed in the other Italian communes. For minor offices it was 25, which was also the minimal age for full citizenship; for the higher ones as well as for election to the various councils it was between 32 and 40; and for the highest ones, like that of the Standard Bearer of Justice in Florence, it could be 45. *De facto*, however, definite preference was given in Venice in the election to all the higher offices and ruling bodies to elderly men. Only old men (in their sixties, seventies and sometimes even in their eighties) were elected to the office of doge, and the election was for life. Very rarely was a man under 50 elected to the ruling councils like the Senate, The Council of Ten and the Collegio. The power of the elderly patricians who ruled Venice was based on a combination of the 'ascriptive' criterion of age and an 'achieved' criterion. ('Achievement' in this context included not only economic resources, social connections and suitable personality, but also birth to a patrician family.)[45]

However, both Lucca and Venice were exceptions. In general no preference was given to the elderly on the one hand, nor were they obliged to retire as long as their functional capacity did not fail, on the other hand. Since there was no general retirement policy and no pension schemes (retirement with a pension was, as Rosenthal phrased it, only 'a sporadic practice'),[46] elderly people who had no independent means and their salary was their only means of sustenance postponed their retirement as long as they could. They clung to their minor office until they were forced to retire, or if they were manual labourers who were hired for a limited period, or for a specific task, until no one was ready to hire them. Every retirement entailed a diminution of social status. The 'positive' half of the image of the old person was not enough to ensure respect towards him and maintenance of his status after retirement. For salaried minor office holders or wage labourers retirement entailed not only loss of status but also loss of means of livelihood.

Let us now turn from the elderly as a group and examine very briefly some of the subgroups. The popes were middle aged or old. Some of them were elected when they were in their forties, but most of them were in their fifties or sixties, and some of them were already in their early seventies at their election.[47] They were elected for life, and no pope was required to retire because of his age. (If a pope had to renounce his office it was because of political reasons and the election of an antipope.) At the head of the Church there was thus a middle-aged–old pontiff. As for other prelates – bishops, archbishops, abbots, and heads of religious orders – it appears that they advanced in the ecclesiastical hierarchy at various paces. Many of them, however, reached the peak of their career when they were already in their sixties and even in their seventies. Some of them lived to their eighties, did not retire and served until their last day. Those who did retire did not do so before they reached their sixties, and sometimes much later. A few examples will suffice. Lanfranc (*c.* 1005–89) was appointed Archbishop of Canterbury by William the Conqueror when he was about 65 years old. He died in office when he was 84. Anselm of Canterbury (*c.* 1033–1109) was elected archbishop when he was 60 years old, and served until his death at the age of 75. Arnulf, Bishop of Lisieux, retired to the monastery of St Victor in Paris when he was 81. Hato, Bishop of Troyes in the twelfth century, retired to Cluny when he was 69, while Gilbert of Sempringham finally retired as head of his order when he was (at least) 89. Humbert of Romans retired as Master-General of the Dominican order when he was 65. Another member of the same order, Stephen of Bourbon (1182–1261), an active preacher and Inquisitor, retired only in his late seventies. Hildegard of Bingen (1098–1179) founded her new independent community of nuns at Eibingen when she was 67 years old and remained at its head until her death at the age of 81. Ela, Countess of Salisbury (*c.* 1191–1261), founded after she had been widowed a Cistercian nunnery and became its abbess. She retired at the age of 68 (two years before her death). Parish priests who asked to retire or were forced into retirement (because they were feeble, ill, semi-blind, or deaf or senile) were not allowed to retire or forced to retire before they reached their sixties. The Church had some pension schemes for retired clergymen, but poor parish priests or chantry priests received only meagre sums which did not suffice for subsistence.[48] Monks and nuns were insured in their old age against want as well as against loneliness. As for the standing place accorded to them in the community, it appears that religious communities in the high and late Middle Ages followed the instruction of St Benedict of Nursia (in chapter 63 of his rule): 'under no circumstances should the standing of the brothers be fixed according to age, for Samuel and Daniel, though young boys (*pueri*) judged the old.'[49] The advanced age of the monks or nuns did not guarantee respect towards them or an honourable standing in the community. It was their personality that determined their status.

Unlike the popes, the kings were young. It is not clear whether the election of older men to the highest office in the Church was due to ideology (or at least to conscious preference given to them) or just to contingency. In what concerns kings there was definitely no ideology that made them accede to the throne as young men. It was the dynastic principle that was decisive. Their predecessors died relatively young, and they inherited the throne while still young. Of all the kings of Europe from the eleventh to the beginning of the fifteenth century, only one king, Alfonso VI, King of Castile and Léon (1030–1109), reached the age of 79. Of all his predecessors and successors only two were in their sixties when they died.[50] Only three of the kings of Aragon reached their sixties,[51] and only four of the German emperors.[52] Three of the kings of England died in their sixties,[53] and only one of the kings of France of the Capetian dynasty survived to the age of 60 – Louis VII (1120–80). All the others, in all countries, died younger. In the most dramatic struggles in the Middle Ages between Church and state, young kings confronted elderly popes. At Canossa, in 1077, the Emperor Henry IV was 22 years old; Gregory VII was 57. Frederick II (*Stupor Mundi*, 1194–1250) was 34 years old when he was excommunicated in 1228 by Pope Gregory IX. The latter was 73 years old. When in 1303, Pope Boniface VIII was attacked by the envoys of Philip IV, King of France, the pope was 68 years old; the king was 35.

Among men in the nobility there was a high rate of unnatural death. Noblemen met their death in military training, in wars in Europe, as well as in the crusades, in tournaments or by execution in civil wars (towards the late Middle Ages), often long before they reached old age.[54] Of those who survived and reached old age, some continued to render the military service due for the fief in person as long as they could and to fight in battles. Thus, Raymond IV (*c.* 1041–1105), Count of Toulouse, became one of the leaders of the First Crusade when he was about 60 years old, and fought in battle until his death at the age of 63. William Marshal was appointed regent of England (since Henry III was a minor when he inherited the throne) at the age of 71, and at the age of 72 still took part in battle. And John Howard, Duke of Norfolk, died in battle aged about 75. Others preferred to retire (through commutation of the military service by money payment, or through hiring someone to replace them). They did not lose their fief which was hereditary. They could enjoy its income and control its administration. However, even in the later Middle Ages, when feudal service had long ceased to constitute the main source of military levy, retirement must have entailed diminution of status and must have distanced the person from the centre of activities. Service, like the right of command and honour, constituted a basic element in the ethos of the aristocracy.

There must have been less diminution in the status of the heiresses of fiefs than in that of their male counterparts. Some of them who inherited fiefs that entailed political and legal powers, like Matilda of Tuscany (1046–1115) who died at the age of 69, or Margaret of Flandres (1202–80) who died at the age of 78, ruled their feudal principalities until their death. They did not have to render military service in person at any stage of their lives and though they were heiresses they were debarred from participating in the representative assemblies that developed in the fourteenth century. (Some of the elderly secular peers in the later Middle Ages asked to be exempted from attending the sessions of the House of Lords.)[55] It is known that even when women enter a public realm they are rarely in situations where their ascriptive identity as females is irrelevant. In old age, however, it becomes blurred. It is possible that when they were no longer young, they became more assertive and more free in their contacts and negotiations with both their subordinates and their superiors.

Though there was no legal age of obligatory retirement kings and feudal lords could force into retirement their office holders and servants. Though in theory the appointment of coroners was for life, in fact many of them were forced to retire at a certain stage.[56] And John Russell, who was usher and marshall to Humphrey, Duke of Gloucester, writes in his manual that he was forced to leave the court of the Duke because of his advanced age.[57]

In southern Europe, where the extended family was dominant, elderly peasants did not retire and kept their status as heads of the household. They cultivated their land together with one of their married sons, or with a number of their sons, daughters and sons-in-law, depending on the customary tradition of the region and the demographic condition. All sons and daughters who remained on the family farm also remained under the authority of the elderly head of the household. In Languedoc even his death did not always liberate the younger generation from the control of the old one. The widowed mother replaced the father as head of the household and assumed authority over her married sons and daughters-in-law.[58]

Traditional custom was quite different in northern Europe and some parts of central Europe where the nuclear family was dominant. At a certain stage in his life the peasant handed over his farm to one of his offspring by an agreement (not necessarily a written one) whereby the latter guaranteed to keep him and look after him until the end of his days. If he had no offspring in the village (which was a common case in the second half of the fourteenth century after the Black Death of 1348), because they died or emigrated, the agreement was drawn with a relative or with non-kin. What determined the timing of retirement was not only the decline in functional capacity but also demographic and family circumstances. Some widows handed over their farm before reaching old age because they felt incapable of working on their holding and rendering the lord of the manor the services that their tenement was charged with by themselves. In periods of demographic pressure peasants sometimes retired while still relatively young in order to enable a son to marry and establish a household. In periods of demographic decline when more opportunities were opened to the survivors outside their village (to get work for better wages, or acquire land) many of the young emigrated. In order to ensure that a son (or married daughter) remained in the village to continue cultivation of the land and provide support in old age, older peasants might retire and hand over to the son or daughter. The lord of the manor who wanted his lands to be cultivated properly and manoral services rendered, sometimes exerted pressure on a widow or aged peasant to retire.[59] The retired couple (or widow or widower) moved from the main room to a back room, or to the attic, or to a spare cottage, and the new head of the household settled in the main room – a painful symbol of the change in status of the elderly. In didactic literature there are many detailed stories about the plights of the elderly who handed their property to their children in their lifetime. In the reality there were both 'good' and 'bad' sons and daughters. The warning in the didactic texts as well as sayings that were common in Austria, like 'to sit on the children's bench is hard for the old',[60] express anxiety and fear of ageing and the dependence and the loss of status that it entailed. They also express sadness because of the consciousness of the lack of symmetry in the relations between parents and children, even when the latter are 'good' ones.

Retirement had its disadvantages and doubtless entailed diminution of status. In the idealisation of the attitudes towards the elderly and of their condition in pre-industrial society, the fact that there was no legal age of obligatory retirement was often singled out as one of the advantages the elderly enjoyed in the past. The absence of obligatory retirement, however, also meant absence of pension schemes. It enabled those elderly whose physical and mental capacities did not fail (or those whose status was ensured by the customary tradition of the region) to keep their status and go on living a fuller life than that of the retired ones. However, it also exposed those whose strength did fail and for whom there were no retirement settlements nor assets to be handed down to their offspring, or to non-kin, or to some institution to which one could retire, to dire poverty and humiliation.

The elderly were not counted among those whom the Scriptures defined as deserving assistance as were the widows and orphans. Nevertheless, there was an awareness of the fact that old age was often accompanied by want, and that the elderly could not always be cared for by their offspring. As for the practice, it cannot be said that the elderly were discriminated against by the charity institutions, the village community or the fraternities. They suffered worse because they were unable to take advantage of changes in the land and labour market when these occurred as could younger people, and charity was never sufficient for the needs of any of the groups of the poor.

There is no need to elaborate on the by now acknowledged fact that the 'golden age' for the elderly 'in the past' is a myth. It is also obvious that the social realities of old age in western society have undergone a great change through the centuries separating us from the Middle Ages. However, secularisation and the 'ageing of the population' notwithstanding, the images, the attitudes and expectations of old people have changed less than the social realities underlying them.

## Notes

1 S. Shahar, 'Who were the old in the Middle Ages?', *Social History of Medicine*, 1993, vol. 6, pp. 313–41.
2 Examples: *Annales S. Iustinae Patavini*, in *M.G.H. Script*, vol. 19, Hanover, 1886, p. 179; Matthew Paris, *Chronica majora*, ed. H. R. Luard, Rolls Series 25 (57), London, 1877, p. 134; Thomas Aquinas, *Summa theologiae*, vol. 3a, q. 72, art. 8, trans. The Fathers of Blackfriars, London, 1974, vol. 57, pp. 212–15; M. Lauwers, 'La mort et le corps des saints. La scène de la mort dans les *vitae* du Moyen Age', *Le Moyen Age*, 1988, vol. 94, pp. 37–8, and note 110; *Li livres de jostice et de plet*, ed. L. N. Rapetti, Paris, 1850, vol. L. II, C. XIV, p. 98.
3 Roger Bacon, *Opus majus*, ed. J. H. Bridge, Frankfurt, 1964, vol. 2, p. 206; English trans.: Roger Bacon, *Opus majus*, trans. R. B. Burke, Philadelphia, 1928, vol. 2, p. 619.
4 Roger Bacon, *Opus majus*, vol. 2, p. 206; trans.: vol. 2, p. 619; see also Roger Bacon, *De retardatione accidentium senectutis cum aliis opusculis de rebus medicinalibus*, ed. A. G. Little and E. Withington, Oxford, 1928, pp. 9, 29, 31, 80; there is a long discussion about the question whether human life was shortened after the Deluge because of divine intervention or due to natural causes in Engelbert of Admont's (1250–1331) *Liber de causis longevitatis hominum ante diluvium*, in *Thesaurus anecdotorum novissimus*, ed. J. Pertz, Augsburg, 1721, vol. 1, cols 439–502; the author finally attributes it to natural causes, mainly to the increased foulness of the air. Roger Bacon as well attributed the regression in life expectancy to the foulness of the air, and also to neglect of the right regimen of health and to bad morals: Roger Bacon, *Opus majus*, vol. 2, pp. 205–6; trans. p. 618.
5 According to Aristotle the peak of physical strength is at the age of 30–5, while that of the intellectual one is around the age of 49, Aristotle, *Rhetorica*, bk II, C. 14.
6 Honorius Augustodunensis [Honorius of Autun], *De philosophia mundi libri quattuor*, *PL*, vol. 172, L. 4, C. 36, col. 99; Vincent de Beauvais, *Speculum Naturale*, in *Bibliotheca mundi seu speculum quadruplex,* Douai, 1624, L. 31, C. 87, col. 2360; Arnaldus de Villanova, *De regimine sanitatis*, in *Opera omnia*, Basel, 1585, col. 372; Albertus Magnus [Albert the Great], *De aetate sive de juventute et senectute*, in *Opera omnia*, ed. A. Borgent, Paris, 1890, vol. 9, tractatus 1, C. 6; Gabriele Zerbi, *Gerentocomia*, in *On the Care of the Aged and Maximianus' Elegies on Old Age and Love*, trans. L. R. Lind, Philadelphia, 1988, C. 1.
7 M. Carruthers, *The Book of Memory. A Study of Memory in Medieval Culture*, Cambridge, 1993.

8  Vincent de Beauvais, *Bibliotheca mundi*, L. 31, C. 88, col. 2361.
9  Roger Bacon, *De retardatione*, pp. 9, 71, 178; Arnaldus de Villanova, *De regimine sanitatis*, cols 819, 821; Bernard de Gordon, *De conservatione vitae humanae seu de regimine sanitatis*, Leipzig, 1570, p. 121; see also: M. Ch. Pouchelle, *The Body and Surgery in the Middle Ages*, trans. R. Morris, Oxford, 1990, p. 65.
10  It was not only a woman's menstrual blood that was considered impure and harmful. According to both medical and popular conceptions the foetus in its mother's womb was nourished by her menstrual blood, which was not eliminated from her body during her pregnancy. The blood that served as nourishment for the foetus was thus also considered impure. According to Innocent III the menstrual blood of a woman which does not flow during her pregnancy is so vile and impure that its touch can cause a tree to wither, grass to shrivel, and the loss of fruit. Dogs which licked it would suffer from rabies. And a child conceived as a result of intercourse with a menstruating woman would be born a leper. Innocent III, *Lotharii cardinalis (Innocent III) De miseria humanae conditionis*, ed. M. Maccarrone, Lugano, 1955, L. I, C. 4, pp. 11–12; in the *responsa* of the academic physicians of Salerno it was stated that the infant was incapable of standing, sitting, walking and talking immediately after birth because, unlike the animals, it was nurtured in its mother's womb on menstrual blood from which it was not easily cleansed, while animals were nurtured in the womb on purer food: *The Prose Salernitan Questions*, ed. B. Lawn, Oxford, 1970, Q. 228, p. 155; see also Rufinus, *Summa decretorum de Magister Rufinus*, ed. H. Singer, Aalen, 1963, p. 16.
11  *De Secretis mulierum*, in *Les admirables secrets de magie du Grand et du Petit Albert*, cited in D. Jacquart and C. Thomasset, *Sexuality and Medicine in the Middle Ages*, trans. M. Adamson, Oxford, 1988, p. 75; by the end of the fifteenth century when *fascinatio* (the process by which certain persons harmed others with the power of sight) was brought into the academic medical domain, women were thought to acquire the power to fascinate in their natural process of ageing. The theory was developed by Diego Alvarez Chanca (*Tractatus de fascinatione*, 1494), and by Antonio de Cartagena (*Libellus de fascinatione*, 1529); according to these writers the actions of the old women were not controlled by will, but could be much worse if accompanied by bad intentions. The whole discourse in both treatises is based on the potential or actual venomousness of women's bodies, both while menstruating and after the cease of menses. However, old women whose menses ceased, and thus always carried menstrual blood in their bodies, were considered especially prone to fascinate. Their victims were generally children: F. Salmon and M. Cabré, 'Fascinating Women: The Evil Eye in Medical Scholasticism', paper presented at the Barcelona Conference, Cambridge, September, 1992 (unpublished).
12  Innocent III, *Lotharii cardinalis*, L. I, C. 10, p. 16.
13  Francesco Petrarca, *De remediis utriusque fortune*, Rotterdam, 1649, L. I, pp. 18–19; *idem*, *Phisick against Fortune*, trans. Thomas Twyn, London, 1579, f. 3v.
14  Petrarca, *De remediis*, L. II, pp. 94–5, 353, 564–6; *idem*, *Phisick against Fortune*, f. 162r, 267r–268v.
15  See for example: Giraldus Cambrensis [Gerald of Wales], *Gemma ecclesiastica*, ed. J. Brewer, Rolls Series, vol. 21, London, 1862, p. 182; Philippe de Navarre, *Les quatre âges de l'homme*, ed. M. de Fréville, Paris, 1888, p. 90.
16  Guillaume de Deguileville, *Le pélerinage de la vie humaine*, ed. J. J. Stürzinger, London, 1893, especially pp. 229, 251–2, 255, 374, 407, 414.
17  C. Walker Bynum, *Holy Feast and Holy Fast. The Religious Significance of Food to Medieval Women*, Berkeley, CA, 1987.
18  See on this: J. A. Burrow, *The Ages of Man: A Study in Medieval Writing and Thought*, Oxford, 1986, pp. 95–134.

19 St Augustine, *Retractationes, Libri II*, ed. A. Mutzenbecher, *CCSL*, 1984, vol. 57, Turnhout, I, C. 26, p. 80.
20 S. Shahar, *Childhood in the Middle Ages*, London, 1990, pp. 15–16; Burrow, *Ages of Man*, pp. 137–42.
21 Bernard of Clairvaux, *De moribus et officio episcoporum*, Epist. 42, *PL*, vol. 182, C. 7, cols 826–7.
22 John of Salisbury, *Policraticus*, ed. C. C. J. Webb, Oxford, 1909, vol. I, L. 5, C. 9, p. 321.
23 Thomas Aquinas, *Summa theologiae*, 3a, q. 72, art. 8, vol. 57, pp. 214–15; see also Petrus Berthorius, *Dictionarium*, in *Opera omnia*, Cologne, 1730, pars 3, p. 86.
24 This *topos* was based on Seneca's remark on the *puer elementarius* and on an interpretation of the verse in Isaiah 20, 65, as mistranslated in the Vulgate. An example from a compilation of commentaries on the Bible: Walafrid Strabo,*Glossa ordinaria, PL*, vol. 113, col. 1311; from a popular didactic text: *The Book of Vices and Virtues: A Fourteenth-Century Translation of the 'Somme le roi' of Lorens of Orléans*, ed. W. Francis, London, 1942, p. 287; see also Burrow, *Ages of Man*, pp. 141–62.
25 *Acta Sanctorum*, ed. the Bollandist Fathers, Paris, 1863, p. 870.
26 Aegidius Romanus [Giles of Rome], *De regimine principum*, Rome, 1607, L. I, pars 4, C. 1–4, pp. 188–203; Aristotle on the young and the old: *Rhetorica*, bk II, C. 12–14; *Ethica*, bk IV, C. I, 1121b, bk VIII, C. 3, 1156a, C. 5, 1157b.
27 Eustache Deschamps, *Regrets d'un vieillard*, in *Oeuvres complètes*, ed. le Marquis de Queux de Saint-Hilaire, Paris, 1878–1903, vol. 6, pp. 225–30, vol. 7, MDV, V. 25–8.
28 Bernardino de Sienne, *De calamitatibus et miseriis vitae humanae et maxime senectutis*, in *Opera omnia*, ed. the Fathers of the Collegium S. Bonaventurae, Florence, 1959, vol. 7, sermo 16, pp. 245–6, 258.
29 Vincent of Beauvais, *Bibliotheca mundi*, L. 31, C. 89–90, cols 2361–3.
30 Bartholomaeus Anglicus, *Liber de proprietatibus rerum*, Strasbourg, 1505, L. VI, C. 1, de etate; idem, *On the Properties of Things: John Trevisa's Translation of Bartholomaeus Anglicus' De proprietatibus rerum*, ed. M. C. Seymour, Oxford, 1975, p. 290.
31 Bernardino de Sienne, *De calamitatibus*.
32 T. R. Cole, *The Journey of Life. A Cultural History of Aging in America*, Cambridge, 1992, p. 131.
33 Bernardino de Sienne, *De calamitatibus*, pp. 253, 256–62.
34 Philippe de Navarre, *Les quatre âges*, no. 173, p. 95; no. 184–5, pp. 100–1.
35 John Bromyard, *Summa praedicantium*, Antwerp, 1614, pars 2, C. 5, p. 355.
36 Dante, *Convivio*, in *Le opere di Dante*, ed. M. Barbi, Florence, 1921, C. 4, p. 28.
37 Meister Eckhart, *In novitate ambulamus*, in *Die deutschen und lateinischen Werke*, ed. E. Benz *et al.*, Stuttgart, 1956, IV, sermo 15, pp. 145–54, see especially pp. 149–50.
38 Philipe de Navarre, *Les quatre âges*, no. 194, p. 105, no. 174, pp. 95–6.
39 Jean Gerson, *À un vieillard*, in *Oeuvres complètes*, ed. Mgr. Glorieux, Paris, 1960, vol. 2, XIX, p. 76.
40 Vincent de Beauvais, *Bibliotheca mundi*, L. 31, C. 89, col. 2362.
41 Leon Battista Alberti, *The Family in Renaissance Florence*, trans. R. M. Watkins, Columbia, SC, 1969, bks III–IV, pp. 35–41, 156–7, 167, 170.
42 Brunetto Latini, *Li livres dou trésor*, ed. F. J. Carmody, Berkeley, CA, 1948, L. III, C. 73, 4–6, p. 392, C. 75, 1–2, p. 393.
43 Shahar, *Childhood*, pp. 28–9.
44 A. Pertile, *Storia del diritto italiano della caduca dell'Impero Romano alla codificazione*, Turin, 1892–1902, vol. III, p. 253 and note 48.

62    *Shulamith Shahar*

45 On Genoa: *Regulae communis Iannuae anno 1363*, in *Historiae patriae monu-menta*, vol. 18, ed. C. Desimondi *et al.*, Turin, 1901, pp. 259, 275, 261; on Florence: D. Herlihy, 'Age, property and career in medieval society', in M. M. Sheehan (ed.), *Aging and the Aged in Medieval Europe*, Toronto, 1990, p. 145; on Venice: R. Finlay, 'The Venetian Republic as a gerontocracy', *Journal of Medieval and Renaissance Studies*, 1978, vol. 8, pp. 157–78; on the 85-year-old and semi-blind doge, Dandolo, who was leader of the Venetians in the Fourth Crusade: Geoffroi Villehardouin, *La conquête de Constantinople*, ed. E. Faral, Paris, 1961, vol. 1, pp. 66–70.

46 J. T. Rosenthal, 'Retirement and the life cycle in fifteenth-century England', in M. M. Sheehan (ed.), *Aging and the Aged in Medieval Europe*, Toronto, 1990, pp. 173–88.

47 Innocent III was elected pope when he was 37 years old, which was definitely an exception. Callistus II was elected pope in 1119 when he was about 69; Lucius III in 1181 when he was 71. Both Gregory IX (1227) and John XXII (1310) were elected when they were 72; Honorius IV (1285) was 75 at his election and Celestine V was 85 (his case too was exceptional).

48 See on this: Rosenthal, 'Retirement', pp. 180–3; N. Orme, 'The medieval almshouse for the clergy: Clyst Gabriel Hospital near Exeter', *Journal of Ecclesiastical History*, 1988, vol. 39, pp. 1–15; *idem*, 'Suffering the clergy: illness and old age in Exeter diocese 1300–1540', in M. Pelling and R. M. Smith (eds), *Life, Death and the Elderly: Historical Perspectives*, London, 1991, pp. 62–73.

49 *La Règle de Saint Benoit*, ed. and trans. J. Neufville and A. de Vogüé, Paris, 1972, vol. II, pp. 642–4.

50 Alfonso IX (1166–1230) died at the age of 64, and Alfonso X (1221–84) at the age of 63.

51 James II (1264–1327) was 63 when he died. James I (1208–76) and Pedro IV (1319–87) died at the age of 68.

52 Frederick I Barbarossa (1123–90) drowned in Asia Minor on his way to the Third Crusade at the age of 67; Louis IV, the Bavarian (1287–1347), died at the age of 60; Charles IV of Luxemburg (1316–78) at the age of 62; and Sigismund of Luxemburg (1368–1437) at the age of 69.

53 Henry III (1207–72) and Edward III (1312–77) were 65 at their death, and Edward I (1239–1307) was 68.

54 See: T. H. Hollingsworth, 'A demographic study of the British ducal families', *Population Studies*, 1957, vol. 11, pp. 4–26; J. T. Rosenthal, 'Medieval longevity and the secular peerage 1350–1500', *Population Studies*, 1973, vol. 27, pp. 287–93; G. Duby, 'Dans la France du nord-ouest au XIIe siècle: les jeunes dans la société aristocratique', *Annales ESC*, 1964, vol. 19, pp. 839–43.

55 Rosenthal, 'Retirement', pp. 177–8.

56 Ibid., pp. 175–6.

57 John Russell, *The Boke of Nurture*, ed. F. J. Furnivall, London, 1867, line 1216, p. 81.

58 See *inter alia*: Ch. Klapisch, 'Fiscalité et démographie en Toscane (1427–1430)', *Annales E.S.C.*, 1969, vol. 24, pp. 1313–37; D. Herlihy et Ch. Klapisch, *Les Toscans et leurs familles. Étude du Catasto florentin de 1427*, Paris, 1978, pp. 370–9, 491–7; Ch. Klapisch, '"A uno pane et uno vino": the rural Tuscan family at the beginning of the fifteenth century', in *Women, Family and Ritual in Renaissance Italy*, Chicago, 1985, pp. 36–67; E. Le Roy Ladurie, *Les paysans de Languedoc*, Paris, 1966, pp. 160–8.

59 See: R. M. Smith, 'The manorial court and the elderly tenant in late medieval England', in M. Pelling and R. M. Smith (eds), *Life, Death and the Elderly: Historical Perspectives*, London, 1991, pp. 36–91; E. Clark, 'The quest for security in medieval England', in M. M. Sheehan (ed.), *Aging and the Aged in*

*Medieval Europe*, Toronto, 1990, pp. 189–200; in the Pyrenees the custom of retirement was dominant: E. Le Roy Ladurie, *Montaillou. Village occitan de 1294–1324*, Paris, 1975, pp. 64–6, 288–91, 294–5, 317, 321–3.

60 M. Mitterauer and R. Sieder, *The European Family. Patriarchy to Partnership from the Middle Ages to the Present*, trans. K. Oosterveen and M. Hörzinger, Oxford, 1982, pp. 166–7.

# 4 Ageing and well-being in early modern England

## Pension trends and gender preferences under the English Old Poor Law c. 1650–1800

*Richard M. Smith*

> Generally speaking, it was the community not the family which supported
> the elderly in early modern England, and, despite the letter of the 1601 Act,
> the machinery of poor relief reinforced the pattern.[1]

When Paul Slack, in an important overview of almost all aspects of poverty,
poor relief and social conditions in early modern England, wrote the above
lines he was doing so against the background of research, by no means large
in quantity, that had been undertaken in the 1980s. One strain of thinking
influencing Slack's interpretation concerns the legal framework of welfare
responsibilities. It has been common to quote the legal theory regarding
such responsibilities as embodied in a famous clause in the Elizabethan Poor
Law Act of 1601:

> The father and grandfather, mother and grandmother, and children of
> every poor, old, blind, lame and impotent person, or other poor person
> not able to work, being of sufficient ability, shall at their own charges
> relieve and maintain every such poor person, in that manner and
> according to that rate, as by the justices . . . in their sessions shall be
> assessed.[2]

The latter appears as a clear statement of certain highly specific obligations
that were or would be heaped upon individuals to care for their immediate
relatives. It has been observed that these were obligations buried deep in
legislation enacted to provide a public provision for the needy. Furthermore,
it is important to note the very limited range of familial obligations which
any individual under the law might be asked to meet. For the elderly it was
their children, their direct offspring, who bore a legal duty to care. Brothers,
sisters, nephews, nieces, grandchildren – all were exempted from legal duties.
Children, too, were liable to assist only if the elder was destitute, not poor or
needy, and only if they were 'of sufficient means' to do so. Obligations

extended down the line of descent, so grandparents could be taken to court to enforce payments towards grandchildren, but no reverse duty existed.[3] The law was not structured so as to enable a net flow of resources from young to old, rather the reverse directional bias applied, contrary to much 'orthodox' thinking about such intergenerational flows in pre-industrial societies.[4] In early modern England sons and unmarried daughters in theory could not be compelled to take an impoverished elder into their homes; monetary payment was all that could be imposed. It is now known that magistrates in their interpretation of this law did take a hard line with men who abandoned their wives and children but were reluctant to prosecute children who failed to provision destitute parents.[5]

Another area of the research that inclined Paul Slack, by implication, to demote the family and promote the community in the provision of care for elderly persons arose as a by-product of investigations of co-residential group arrangements based upon a fairly simply conceived premise concerning the relationship between patterns of co-residence and implied mutual assistance. Until the early 1970s two very durable ideas had held sway: one was that co-resident group structures in early modern English and European societies had been large and complex and that all older people lived in families, mostly their own, but if not, the families of their relatives, usually of their married children. In fact, the family as a residential unit was thought to be multigenerational and kin enfolding; the other widely held view was that society hung together, indeed cohered around allegiances to kin which had primacy over other social bonds or relationships. A particularly prevalent notion was that this relationship owed a great deal to patriarchy and deference of the young to the old which ensured a flow of resources, particularly of personal services, from children to parents.[6]

In considering the first of these premises we may refer to evidence assembled from what is still a disturbingly small number of early modern English listings of inhabitants so far discovered for communities in the seventeenth and eighteenth centuries (see Table 4.1). For males over age 65 the most common residential arrangement prior to 1800 was that they would still have had wives alive and co-resident. More than half of the males were so situated. This pattern appears to have been remarkably durable and persisted into the interwar years of the present century, although by 1921 fewer men lived as lone parents with an unmarried child. The living arrangements of elderly females take on a different appearance. Fewer women than men from this age group still had co-resident husbands and a considerably higher proportion of the females lived alone, or with other relatives. The commonest co-residential arrangement involved co-habiting with the spouse, but no more than one in five lived with kin who were not unmarried offspring. There is a real possibility that proportions co-residing with kin had substantially increased by the early twentieth century.[7] However, perhaps the most prominent feature of the early modern data concerns the fact that approximately one in three of elderly females lived either alone or with persons to whom they were not related. This frequency was considerably greater than co-residence of elderly females with ever-married children or other kin.[8]

There are some obvious demographic developments accounting for these trends. In the seventeenth and eighteenth centuries the marriage age of both sexes was relatively high. Over the twentieth century first marriage and/or

*Table 4.1*   Living arrangements of persons aged 65+, England and Wales, sixteenth to twentieth century

| Living arrangements | Rural English populations before 1800[1] | Lichfield 1692 | England and Wales | | | |
|---|---|---|---|---|---|---|
| | | | 1891[2] | 1921[2] | 1971[3] | 1981[3] |
| *Males* | | | | | | |
| Living alone | 2 | 5 | 5 | 6 | 13 | 17 |
| Non-relatives only | 11 | 8 | 13 | 10 | 4 | 3 |
| Spouse (with/without others) | 58 | 68 | 57 | 57 | 73 | 73 |
| Lone parent with never-married child | 16 | 16 | 10 | 12 | 3 | 2 |
| Other relatives only | 14 | 3 | 15 | 15 | 7 | 5 |
| Total[4] | 100 | 100 | 100 | 100 | 100 | 100 |
| *N* | 102 | 38 | 1,699 | 2,620 | 24,836 | 30,175 |
| *Females* | | | | | | |
| Living alone | 15 | 17 | 11 | 11 | 36 | 42 |
| Non-relatives only | 17 | 32 | 14 | 11 | 5 | 3 |
| Spouse (with/without others) | 40 | 23 | 30 | 32 | 36 | 38 |
| Lone parent with never-married child | 6 | 20 | 18 | 20 | 7 | 6 |
| Other relatives only | 23 | 9 | 28 | 26 | 15 | 11 |
| Total[4] | 100 | 100 | 100 | 100 | 100 | 100 |
| *N* | 102 | 66 | 2,121 | 3,295 | 38,361 | 45,123 |

*Source*:  From data presented in Wall, 'Elderly persons and members of their households in England and Wales'.

*Notes*:
[1] Derived from an analysis of the censuses of Ealing (Middlesex) in 1599, Chilvers Coton (Warwickshire) in 1684, Wetherby (Yorkshire) in 1776, Wembworthy (Devon) in 1779, Corfe Castle (Dorset) in 1790 and Ardleigh (Essex) in 1796.
[2] Anonymised data from census returns for parts of the following areas: Abergavenny (Monmouthshire), Axminster (Devon), Banbury (Oxfordshire), Bethnal Green (London), Bolton (Lancashire), Earsdon (Northumberland), Morland (Westmorland), Pinner (Middlesex), Saffron Walden (Essex), Stoke (Staffordshire), Swansea (Glamorgan), Walthamstow (Essex) and the city of York.
[3] Calculated from the national samples of the English and Welsh populations taken by the Office of Population Censuses and Surveys for the purpose of the Longitudinal Study.
[4] Includes a few cases of never-married persons aged 65+ living with a parent.

co-habitation has increasingly taken place earlier rather than later in the twenties or indeed the thirties. At the same time, the average age at which the last child was born has fallen and a closer spacing of surviving children as a consequence of conscious family planning and lower infant mortality rates have led to a shortening of the duration of the nuclear family and a corresponding lengthening of the 'empty-nest phase', as the married couple age together by themselves. These tendencies have been exacerbated amongst contemporary 70 and 80 year olds by the high incidence within those age groups of childless marriages formed in the interwar years. Furthermore increasing sex differentials in mortality have extended life expectancy at higher ages for females so that 80 per cent of those living alone today are widows. There may in the latter half of the twentieth century have been a growth in the housing stock and rising incomes which have enabled the elderly to retain separate residences. These are all interesting and under-researched issues, but cannot be pursued in the present discussion.[9]

In considering the legal evidence and patterns of co-residence in early modern England it is easy to exaggerate both the extent of residential isolation on the one hand and to overemphasise the degree of residential interdependence of the generations, on the other hand. In isolation the evidence on residence is difficult to interpret, although when viewed against the background of certain underlying demographic rates it becomes easier to account for these patterns. We now know much more about the availability of kin to an individual in past populations, thanks to the technique of microsimulation and especially the outcomes created by the CAMSIM computer program or suite of programs. With such techniques we can now reconstruct past populations based upon the use of demographic parameters that have been securely identified in historical demographic research. We can estimate the extent to which secular demographic trends in pre-industrial England implied secular trends in the number of living near-kin which people had over their life course. Such calculations reveal an interesting paradox. If at later ages (i.e. over 55 or 60 years) people showed a wish to live with mature, independent children, or with other relatives, and those children or relatives were willing to provide that facility, both children and other kin are considerably more likely to be available today than they were in the seventeenth century (see Table 4.2).[10]

Such measures of kin availability are quite sensitive to shifts in the underlying demographic rates. The contrast between the late seventeenth and late twentieth centuries is very evident in Table 4.2. The apparent advantage of the present-day elderly and the disadvantage of the late seventeenth-century elderly were both less when the conditions of late Georgian England are considered. Between the 1780s and the Poor Law Report of 1834 marriage ages were early and fertility very high in comparison with preceding and subsequent periods, and almost 80 per cent of the elderly would have had children alive and potentially available to support them.[11]

Notwithstanding the changes in kin availability that occurred through the

Table 4.2    Numbers of kin at later ages, late seventeenth and late twentieth century, England (kin of women)

|  | At age | Late 17th century | Late 20th century |
|---|---|---|---|
| Numbers of children | 55 | 2.1 | 1.7 |
|  | 65 | 1.9 | 1.7 |
|  | 90 | 1.2 | 1.5 |
| Proportion with no children | 55 | 0.31 | 0.21 |
|  | 65 | 0.33 | 0.21 |
|  | 90 | 0.41 | 0.24 |
| Numbers of descending kin | 55 | 6.2 | 5.4 |
|  | 65 | 7.2 | 6.6 |
|  | 90 | 8.5 | 10.7 |
| Numbers of lateral kin | 55 | 4.83 | 4.8 |
|  | 65 | 3.11 | 4.1 |
|  | 90 | 0.60 | 0.8 |

Source: Laslett, A Fresh Map of Life, p. 116.

Old Poor Law era, we should note the flawed capacity of the early modern demographic system to provide kin-based assistance to elderly persons. Given that childlessness in old age was relatively common, if welfare obligations for fathers and mothers were assumed to fall primarily upon offspring, in many circumstances 40 to 50 per cent of elderly persons might be without either a son or a daughter and 30 to 40 per cent may have lacked both. When marriage was late for both sexes (the late twenties or early thirties), neo-local and based upon assumed economic independence for the newly formed household, as it was throughout most of north-west Europe, the parents of married couples would have begun to lose their children's earnings or labour power, and to lose each other in widowhood at the point in the life course when those children in their turn may have been severely pressed by the unfavourable balance of consumers to producers or earners in their own still youthful households.[12] This problem was summed up by one correspondent from Warwickshire reported in Booth's survey of The Aged Poor (1895) who noted 'that the children's own families are costing most just at the time of greatest parental need'.[13] A similar recognition of an incompatibility of intergenerational interests emerges from a letter written in 1810 by an elderly pauper resident in Bethnal Green to the overseer of the parish of St John's in Colchester: 'My children are all married and got familys which these dear times they have as much as they can do to support and therefore are not able to assist me.'[14] These are relatively frequently encountered sentiments that surface in the Essex pauper correspondence of the early nineteenth century.[15] They are also interesting in so far as they imply that availability of lineal kin (an availability that had increased for the elderly generations of the Napoleonic- and Post-

Napoleonic-War eras) was no guarantee of a flow of resources from children to parents.

If families were frequently unable or unwilling to provide this support the overseers of the poor do seem frequently to have provided it in their stead. Dr David Thomson, a pioneer researcher in this field in the 1980s, provides particularly revealing evidence. The bulk of his investigations are concerned with the years immediately following the Poor Law reforms of the 1830s when the values of self-responsibility and familial duty were supposedly held, at least by Poor Law administrators and rate-payers, with particular fervour. On the basis of a scattering of community case studies, Thomson argues that the majority of all elderly persons in England were maintained by the Poor Law, receiving weekly pensions with a relative value in excess of pensions paid by the late twentieth-century welfare state.[16] While we need not accept Thomson's overgenerous assessment of the level of Poor Law provision, we can note that in the early 1840s perhaps two-thirds of women of the age of 70 and one-half of the men of that age, one-half of the women aged 65–9 and a significant minority of women 55–60 and men in their 60s received a weekly pension that bore a very close relationship to the wages received by labourers.[17] In addition extra payments were not infrequently granted for quite extensive periods of need, for special diets, medicine, the employment of nurses or home-helps, the purchase of alcoholic beverages, shoes and clothing.[18]

The Old Poor Law, at least from the late seventeenth century when reasonably complete Poor Law account books begin to survive with increasing frequency through to the Poor Law Report of 1834, has yet to be investigated along the lines adopted by Thomson in his nineteenth century studies. The remainder of this chapter reports on research into the construction of pauper 'case histories' derived through the linking of families reconstituted from parish registers with Poor Law account books. The research is based upon a selection, made in part for time-saving reasons, of six parishes whose registers have already been fully reconstituted in a machine-readable form. A number have been so reconstituted by the Cambridge Group for the History of Population and Social Structure.[19] Of course, it was also necessary that they possessed Poor Law accounts of high quality. The seven communities currently available in this form constitute a mixture of villages, market towns, both inland and coastal, and one large, rapidly growing London parish: Dawlish, a coastal community in Devon, Tavistock in the same county in the Tamar valley abutting the border with Cornwall, Worfield in Shropshire, Terling in central Essex, a village that has been much studied by Tudor and Stuart historians although principally before the Poor Law accounts become available after 1690, Lowestoft, an east-coast fishing port and St James Clerkenwell in London and finally the Oxfordshire community of Whitchurch in the Thames valley near to Reading. In addition a partial family reconstitution of the West Yorkshire mining community of Whitkirk has been undertaken to enable what is rarely possible with evidence from the north of England – linkage between parish registers and Poor Law accounts.[20]

This chapter also assesses a larger body of data on pension payments from fourteen other parishes: three in the East Riding, one in the North Riding and one in the West Riding of Yorkshire, two in Lancashire, two in Lincolnshire, one in Oxfordshire, two in Gwent and two in Devon. In addition a significant body of evidence relating to the elderly poor collected by Dr Mary Barker-Read for five Kentish communities in a region of heavy outmigration and declining industry (Cowden and Wrotham, rural parishes; Cranbrook and Tonbridge, market towns with large rural hinterlands; and Maidstone, the county town) is incorporated into this analysis.[21]

The focus of this chapter is principally, although not exclusively, upon the century *c*.1650–1750 and addresses the issue of elderly persons whose Poor Law benefit histories can be reconstructed. This period of English history is particularly interesting as it constitutes a phase when 9–10 per cent of the population was 60 years and over (see Figure 4.1).[22] Such a 'mature' age structure is primarily a product of the low fertility levels in England during this period which, when combined with high rates of outmigration to North America, the Caribbean and Ireland, largely of young adults, increased the probability that in excess of 33 per cent of persons aged 60 and over would not have had children living nearby.[23] These problems were undoubtedly exacerbated by the high migration rates to London that in combination with high rates of emigration led to quite severe rural depopulation in many areas of southern and eastern England with a resulting ageing and shrinkage of many communities.[24] The way in which this society, with, by pre-industrial standards, its top-heavy age structure and its relative deficiency of kin, coped with the care of the elderly is the central concern of this study. The

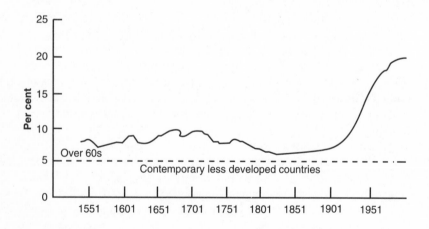

*Figure 4.1* The elderly in the English population, 1541–1981
*Source*: P. Laslett, 'Necessary knowledge', p. 15.

data that have been assembled in the first instance allow us to gain answers to two rather obvious questions: quite simply, how many pensioners were there and how much were they paid?

Identifying pensioners when well-kept Poor Law account books are available is not difficult although it is hard to be sure that we are dealing with individuals when only individuals are listed as recipients. The possibility of other recipients or dependants lurking behind the person named in the Poor Law account book is ever present. In the case, for instance, of young widows there are likely to have been children or younger dependants to whom the 'doles' or 'collections' were also directed. Paul Slack has suggested on the basis of listings of the poor from a scattering of parishes, both rural and urban, that it would be acceptable to double the number of pensioners to establish the overall size of the group dependent upon parish pensions or doles.[25] If this is done in conjunction with the establishment of fairly rudimentary estimates of parish populations it can be seen from Table 4.3 that pensioners and their dependants constituted from 2 to 8 per cent of the total populations of the communities in this sample. A level of about 4–5 per cent might capture the modal proportion.

Such proportions may seem small, but only if we fail to recognise that in observing this group we are considering those most likely to be entirely or very largely dependent on the parish for their livelihood. This type of estimate does not take into account the proportions of overall parish

*Table 4.3*  Pensioners per head of population

| Parish | Cohort | Average births | Estimated population | Average pensioners | Pensioners/ population (%) | Proportion |
|---|---|---|---|---|---|---|
| Lowestoft (Suffolk) | 1657–62 | 44.81 | 1,490 | 28.1 | 1.9 | 3.8 |
| Lowestoft | 1686–91 | 59.7 | 1,990 | 16.6 | 0.8 | 1.7 |
| Whitkirk (WR Yorks) | 1682–4 | 45.2 | 1,500 | 55.3 | 3.7 | 7.4 |
| Whitchurch (Oxon) | 1673–8 | 8.9 | 300 | 10.6 | 3.5 | 7.0 |
| Whitchurch | 1701–20 | 11.9 | 400 | 8.4 | 2.1 | 4.2 |
| Tavistock (Devon) | 1709–10 | 69.9 | 2,160 | 86.3 | 3.7 | 7.8 |
| Terling (Essex) | 1716–25 | 19.4 | 600 | 7.0 | 1.2 | 2.3 |
| Whitchurch | 1731–40 | 18.5 | 620 | 8.2 | 1.3 | 2.5 |
| Tavistock | 1735–6 | 75.4 | 2,510 | 109.0 | 4.2 | 8.7 |
| Terling | 1744–50 | 17.3 | 540 | 11.9 | 2.2 | 4.4 |
| Whitchurch | 1751–70 | 16.3 | 540 | 22.2 | 4.1 | 8.1 |
| Tavistock | 1760–1 | 74.8 | 2,490 | 64.5 | 2.6 | 5.2 |
| Terling | 1770–8 | 21.3 | 660 | 64.0 | 1.0 | 2.0 |

expenditure that was allocated to casual payments. During the period upon which we are principally focused casual payments constituted a smaller proportion of total payments than did expenditure on weekly doles or collections. For example, the Oxfordshire parish of Shipton-under-Wychwood (for which Poor Law accounts of two of its townships survive) displays a far from atypical pattern (Table 4.4).[26]

*Table 4.4(a)*   Poor relief expenditure categories

| Years | Annual expenditure | | | Weekly cash payments | | | Assistance in kind and occasional cash payments | | |
|---|---|---|---|---|---|---|---|---|---|
| | £ | s. | d. | £ | s. | d. | £ | s. | d. |
| *Shipton-under-Wychwood, Oxfordshire, 1740–62* | | | | | | | | | |
| 1740–1 | 31 | 6 | 6 | 12 | 17 | 6 | 18 | 9 | 0 |
| 1741–2 | 46 | 5 | 7 | 27 | 6 | 0 | 18 | 9 | 7 |
| 1742–3 | 33 | 1 | 10 | 27 | 6 | 6 | 15 | 15 | 4 |
| 1743–4* | 52 | 7 | 3 | 39 | 8 | 0 | 12 | 19 | 3 |
| 1744–5 | 49 | 1 | 5 | 36 | 8 | 6 | 12 | 12 | 11 |
| 1745–6 | 38 | 7 | 8 | 30 | 12 | 6 | 7 | 15 | 2 |
| 1746–7* | 55 | 1 | 5 | 31 | 14 | 6 | 23 | 6 | 11 |
| 1747–8 | 31 | 1 | 1 | 24 | 2 | 6 | 6 | 18 | 7 |
| 1748–9 | 35 | 19 | 10 | 23 | 11 | 6 | 12 | 8 | 4 |
| 1749–50 | 38 | 1 | 2 | 31 | 6 | 6 | 6 | 14 | 8 |
| 1750–1 | 34 | 19 | 6 | 29 | 0 | 6 | 5 | 19 | 7 |
| 1751–2 | 34 | 17 | 7 | 29 | 0 | 6 | 5 | 17 | 7 |
| 1752–3* | 52 | 4 | 2 | 37 | 4 | 6 | 14 | 19 | 8 |
| 1753–4* | 55 | 1 | 2 | 33 | 9 | 6 | 21 | 11 | 8 |
| 1754–5 | 43 | 8 | 8 | 31 | 15 | 0 | 11 | 13 | 8 |
| 1755–6* | 45 | 5 | 6 | 36 | 0 | 6 | 9 | 0 | 0 |
| 1756–7* | 56 | 3 | 1 | 33 | 16 | 0 | 22 | 7 | 1 |
| 1757–8* | 53 | 18 | 10 | 46 | 1 | 0 | 7 | 17 | 10 |
| 1758–9* | 61 | 7 | 11 | 41 | 18 | 0 | 19 | 9 | 11 |
| 1759–60* | 45 | 3 | 1 | 41 | 12 | 0 | 3 | 11 | 1 |
| 1760–1 | 35 | 9 | 4 | 34 | 2 | 0 | 1 | 7 | 4 |
| 1761–2 | 43 | 12 | 11 | 34 | 4 | 9 | 9 | 8 | 2 |
| Total | 972 | 5 | 6 | 740 | 17 | 9 | 259 | 5 | 5 |
| *Leafield, Oxfordshire, 1740–62* | | | | | | | | | |
| 1740–1* | 56 | 9 | 11 | 19 | 8 | 3[1] | 37 | 1 | 8 |
| 1741–2* | 91 | 1 | 8 | 41 | 19 | 3 | 49 | 2 | 5 |
| 1742–3 | 58 | 14 | 7 | 31 | 0 | 3 | 27 | 14 | 4[3] |
| 1743–4 | 38 | 5 | 9 | 31 | 12 | 10 | 6 | 12 | 11[4] |
| 1744–5 | 51 | 9 | 7 | 33 | 18 | 5 | 17 | 11 | 2 |
| 1745–6 | 63 | 10 | 10 | 39 | 19 | 6 | 23 | 11 | 4 |
| 1746–7* | 44 | 14 | 0 | 4 | 8 | 0[2] | 40 | 6 | 0 |
| 1747–8 | 35 | 0 | 1 | 20 | 6 | 6 | 14 | 13 | 7 |
| 1748–9 | 50 | 8 | 0 | 23 | 5 | 0 | 27 | 3 | 0 |
| 1749–50 | 69 | 12 | 8 | 39 | 13 | 2 | 29 | 19 | 6 |
| 1750–1 | 51 | 13 | 5 | 39 | 4 | 6 | 12 | 8 | 11 |
| 1751–2* | 57 | 4 | 10 | 47 | 19 | 0 | 9 | 5 | 10 |

*Table 4.4(a)* (cont.)

| Years | Annual expenditure | | | Weekly cash payments | | | Assistance in kind and occasional cash payments | | |
|---|---|---|---|---|---|---|---|---|---|
| | £ | s. | d. | £ | s. | d. | £ | s. | d. |
| 1752–3* | 69 | 11 | 3 | 49 | 5 | 0 | 20 | 6 | 3 |
| 1753–4* | 88 | 6 | 5 | 48 | 11 | 0 | 39 | 15 | 5 |
| 1754–5* | 66 | 18 | 6 | 49 | 3 | 6 | 17 | 15 | 0 |
| 1755–6* | 71 | 16 | 0 | 42 | 0 | 6 | 29 | 15 | 6 |
| 1756–7 | 75 | 2 | 4 | 31 | 10 | 8 | 43 | 11 | 8 |
| 1757–8* | 55 | 3 | 4 | 30 | 17 | 6 | 24 | 5 | 10 |
| 1758–9* | 66 | 15 | 6 | 26 | 10 | 6 | 40 | 4 | 6 |
| 1759–60 | 35 | 14 | 0 | 25 | 15 | 0 | 9 | 19 | 0 |
| 1760–1 | 27 | 15 | 0 | 18 | 18 | 0 | 8 | 17 | 0 |
| 1761–2 | 41 | 12 | 2 | 8 | 11 | 0 | 33 | 1 | 2 |
| Total | 1,266 | 19 | 4 | 694 | 16 | 4 | 563 | 2 | 0 |

\* = smallpox year
[1] Six months
[2] Five weeks only
[3] Eight weeks missing
[4] Seven weeks missing

Just about two-thirds of expenditure in the early to middle eighteenth century was directed to weekly pensions or doles. If we consider a very different type of parish, that of St Martins-in-the-Fields in London, which is being intensively studied by Dr Jeremy Boulton, we will see that poor

*Table 4.4(b)* Costs of benefits in kind

| Item | Shipton | | | Leafield | | |
|---|---|---|---|---|---|---|
| | £ | s. | d. | £ | s. | d. |
| Food | 33 | 7 | 11 | 7 | 19 | 0 |
| House goods/fuel | 5 | 16 | 7 | 3 | 12 | 0 |
| Clothes | 19 | 0 | 0 | 89 | 5 | 2 |
| Medical treatment | 103 | 7 | 6 | 60 | 16 | 4 |
| Rent | – | – | – | 123 | 10 | 9 |
| Boarding out | 1 | 0 | 6 | 51 | 1 | 0 |
| Workhouse | – | – | – | 40 | 0 | 0 |
| Employment | 1 | 16 | 5 | 9 | | 0 |
| Indoor work | | 2 | 6 | | 17 | 2 |
| Funerals | 29 | 12 | 3 | 29 | 2 | 8 |
| Marriage/bastardy | 2 | 1 | 1 | | 7 | 10 |
| Settlement | 21 | 2 | 2 | 24 | 5 | 1 |
| Legal | 5 | 17 | 4 | 9 | 8 | 6 |
| Apprenticeships | 1 | 18 | 2 | 34 | 19 | 6 |
| Miscellaneous | 30 | 3 | 7 | 31 | 8 | 7 |
| Total | 255 | 6 | 0 | 507 | 3 | 1 |

relief expenditure rose from about £200 to in excess of £4,000 annually over the seventeenth century when population grew from about 3,500 to almost 40,000. Such trends suggest that while expenditure on relief grew twenty-fold population grew ten-fold. Nonetheless, while there are signs that casual or extraordinary payments rose in the very last decades of the century, expenditure on orphans and pensioners made up almost three-quarters of the monies disbursed. The extraordinary or casual expenditure generally accounted for less than 25 per cent of the total sums disbursed by the overseers of this London parish.[27]

By linking information concerning individuals derived from family reconstitution of parish registers with the information in the Poor Law accounts it becomes possible to discover much about the pensioners and in particular to distinguish their ages. This technique is not always as forthcoming as one might expect in the case of English communities because of the high rates of interparochial mobility. However, it seems that depending on parish size, migratory characteristics and time period, 60–70 per cent of those appearing as recipients of poor relief in the pensioner category can be linked in one way or another with at least one entry in a parish register. That 30–40 per cent, or more, of pensioners were never recorded as being born, married or buried in the parish in which their welfare was provided is, however, a noteworthy feature. It suggests that for a far from inconsequential minority of poor relief recipients possession of a 'settlement' may not have been critical or a *sine qua non* regarding eligibility, and it also suggests, or is consistent with the view, that being away from or lacking geographically accessible kin may have been key factors that necessitated parochial support for an individual.

What of the age attributes of those pensioners who are identifiable and linkable between sources? We will confine our consideration of this matter by reference to the south Oxfordshire community of Whitchurch. Here we are able to establish those of a certain age who were in receipt of pensions and the proportion of those dying in the parish and of a certain age who had prior to death become parish pensioners. After 1761 ages at death are given in the burial register and when those dying can be linked with their baptismal entries in the parish register those ages fairly consistently appear to be accurate, rarely overestimated or underestimated by more than a year or eighteen months. It appears that between 40 and 50 per cent of those over the age of 60 in this community by the late seventeenth century were likely to have a Poor Law pension for some period prior to their death. Such figures are certainly comparable with the estimates of the incidence of Poor Law pension provision by age from the 1840s that have been reported by Thomson.[28]

It is a rather easier task to establish what proportion of all pensioners were of a specific age, which is, of course, not synonymous with knowing what proportion of a particular age group received pensions. The results of analyses of a somewhat larger set of our sample parishes in which a broad division is made of pension-weeks paid to those pensioners aged 0–50 and those over 61 years are reported below. This approach has the advantage of isolating the elderly and seeing how their representation in the parish pensioner population varied across space and through time.

The results flowing from this approach are reported in Table 4.5, which reveals that pensioners or collectioners aged 0–50 years received about 30–35 per cent of the pension-weeks while those aged 61 years and over received 35–55 per cent of the weekly payments. The important point to note in relation to the data presented in Table 4.5 is that persons aged over 60 rarely constituted more than 10 per cent, and were generally 7–8 per cent, of the total population in this period. Another way of considering these data suggests that those over 60 received a share of the pension payments that varied from five to nine times more than their proportional share of the population. Here we observe a very definite preference for prioritising the elderly as a category of the 'deserving poor'.

We may turn now to consider the distribution of pension payments according to the sex of the recipient. A simple count of adult pensioners by sex from Lowestoft, Dawlish, Worfield, Whitkirk and Whitchurch has been made and is presented in Table 4.6. There are difficulties in undertaking this type of analysis because of the 'hidden beneficiary' problem to which reference was made earlier, since younger females, especially if widowed, were more likely to have dependent offspring in their households than those in the older age groups. Overall, females outnumbered males by about 2.5 to 3 to 1, although the pensioner populations appear to have been even more feminised in the late seventeenth century than they were to be by the mid eighteenth century.

We proceed now to consider the value of the Poor Law pension. This part of the analysis is based upon a large sample. Over 120,000 actual weekly pension payments have been assembled in this sample from twenty-five communities. While the analysis of these data has not yet reached the point

*Table 4.5*  Proportion of pensioners in various age groups, 1663–1742

| Parish | Period | 0–50 years (%) | 61 years or over (%) |
|---|---|---|---|
| Whitkirk | 1663–87 | 6,642/15,930 = 41.7 | 5,048/15,930 = 31.7 |
| Lowestoft | 1670–90 | 6,244/15,660 = 39.9 | 5,630/15,660 = 36.0 |
| Whitchurch | 1672–1700 | 4,228/11,121 = 38.0 | 5,032/11,121 = 45.2 |
| Subtotal | | 17,114/42,711 = 40.1 | 15,710/42,711 = 36.8 |
| Whitchurch | 1700–30 | 3,298/10,055 = 32.8 | 4,936/10,055 = 49.1 |
| Worfield | 1722–30 | 707/3,272 = 21.6 | 2,404/3,272 = 73.5 |
| Dawlish | 1727–42 | 1,080/2,441 = 44.2 | 1,040/2,441 = 42.6 |
| Subtotal | | 5,085/15,768 = 32.2 | 8,380/15,768 = 53.1 |

*Table 4.6*    Age groups of adult pensioners by sex, 1663–1742

| Parish | Period | Males | | | Females | | |
|---|---|---|---|---|---|---|---|
| | | *21–50 (%)* | *61+ (%)* | *N* | *21–50 (%)* | *61+ (%)* | *N* |
| Whitkirk | 1663–87 | 24.1 | 52.4 | 5,604 | 40.2 | 25.1 | 8,416 |
| Lowestoft | 1670–90 | 4.0 | 62.2 | 2,318 | 40.2 | 34.8 | 12,022 |
| Whitchurch | 1672–1700 | 42.1 | 57.9 | 990 | 34.0 | 46.5 | 9,579 |
| Subtotal | | 20.9 | 55.6 | 8,912 | 38.2 | 35.8 | 30,017 |
| Whitchurch | 1700–30 | 32.8 | 49.2 | 2,559 | 24.6 | 55.1 | 6,678 |
| Worfield | 1722–30 | 1.3 | 87.0 | 1,044 | 28.3 | 70.0 | 2,141 |
| Dawlish | 1727–42 | 8.5 | 67.3 | 565 | 31.4 | 53.7 | 1,230 |
| Subtotal | | 21.6 | 61.1 | 4,168 | 26.2 | 58.0 | 10,049 |

where it is possible to isolate the value of pensions being paid to the elderly as opposed to other age groups for all parishes in our sample, it is possible with care to use these data to gain some interesting insights. The initial observation which can be drawn from Tables 4.7 and 4.8 is that the modal value of pensions in the large majority of communities was lower than the mean. Between 1650 and 1750 this was so in twenty-three out of twenty-eight cases – consistent with a situation in which a fairly small basic sum was paid to most pensioners, with a relatively small number of pensioners in greater need or with fewer means of support obtaining more than this; the elderly loom especially large in this latter category. Between 1650 and 1700 it

*Table 4.7*    Pension payments, 1650–1700

| Parish | County | Date | N | Mean | Median | Mode | Average no. of pensioners |
|---|---|---|---|---|---|---|---|
| Whitkirk | WR Yorks | 1663–9 | 3,376 | 0/4 | 0/3 | 0/1/5 | 14.1 |
| | | 1682–4 | 5,312 | 0/5 | 0/4.5 | 0/6 | 55.3 |
| Lockington | ER Yorks | 1653–9 | 1,579 | 0/8 | 0/8 | 0/4 | |
| Routh | ER Yorks | 1679–83 | 1,040 | 0/5 | 0/4 | 0/4 | |
| North Ferriby | ER Yorks | 1658–63 | 1,824 | 0/4 | 0/4 | 0/3 | |
| Woodplumpton | Lancs | 1700 | 1,066 | 0/9 | 0/6 | 0/5 | 41 |
| Whitchurch | Oxon | 1673–8 | 2,737 | 1/4 | 1/2 | 1/0 | |
| Lowestoft | Suffolk | 1657–62 | 6,238 | 1/0 | 0/10 | 0/6 | 28.1 |
| | | 1686–91 | 4,324 | 1/5 | 1/6 | 2/0 | 16.6 |
| Clerkenwell | Middlesex | | | | | | |
| Pensioners | | 1661 | 4,940 | 0/8 | 0/6 | 0/6 | 95 |
| Orphans | | 1661 | 1,872 | 1/6 | 1/6 | 1/6 | 41 |
| Total | | 1661 | 6,812 | 0/11 | 0/9 | 0/6 | 136 |
| Bere Ferrers | Devon | 1648–51 | 826 | 0/11 | 1/0 | 0/6 | |

*Table 4.8* Pension payments, 1700–50

| Parish | County | Date | N | Mean | Median | Mode | Average no. of pensioners |
|---|---|---|---|---|---|---|---|
| Danby in Cleveland | NR Yorks | 1741–50 | 3,900 | 0/9 | 0/6 | 0/6 | |
| Calverley | WR Yorks | 1731–8 | 1,744 | 0/11 | 0/9 | 0/9 | 9.1 |
| Tarleton | Lancs | 1715–23 | 2,189 | 0/10 | 0/8 | 0/6 | n/a |
| Gosberton | Lincs | 1720–4 | 2,320 | 1/2 | 1/0 | 1/0 | |
| Worfield | Shrops | 1722–30 | 7,209 | 1/1 | 1/0 | 1/0 | |
| Panteg | Gwent | 1727–33 | 1,970 | 1/0 | 1/0 | 1/0 | 6.2 |
| Whitchurch | Oxon | 1701–20 | 6,585 | 1/6 | 1/6 | 1/0 | 8.4 |
| | | 1731–40 | 3,426 | 1/10 | 1/6 | 1/6 | 8.2 |
| Terling | Essex | 1716–25 | 3,109 | 1/7 | 1/6 | 1/0 | 7.0 |
| | | 1744–50 | 3,543 | 1/5 | 1/6 | 1/0 | 11.9 |
| Clerkenwell | Middlesex | | | | | | |
| Pensioners | | 1701 | (142) | 0/9 | 0/9 | 0/9 | 142 |
| Orphans | | 1701 | (41) | 1/7 | 1/6 | 1/6 | 42 |
| Total | | 1701 | (183) | 0/11 | 0/9 | 0/9 | 184 |
| Pensioners | | 1723 | 2,679 | 1/11 | 2/0 | 1/6 | 255 |
| Orphans | | 1723 | 641 | 1/7 | 1/8 | 1/8 | 65 |
| Total | | 1723 | 3,320 | 1/10 | 1/8 | 2/0 | 320 |
| Tavistock | Devon | 1709–10 | 4,317 | 1/3 | 1/0 | 1/0 | 86.3 |
| | | 1735–6 | 5,862 | 1/3 | 1/0 | 1/0 | 109 |
| Dawlish | Devon | 1713–19 | 1,225 | 1/4 | 1/3 | 1/0 | |
| | | 1747–50 | 2,806 | 1/1 | 1/0 | 1/0 | 18.0 |

can be clearly seen in Table 4.7 that lower levels of pensions were paid in the north than in the south of England. Average weekly payments in the case studies from Yorkshire were around about 4*d*. or 5*d*. in the 1660s and 1670s. This contrasts with 1*s*. 0*d*. and 1/4*d*. in the southern communities. Whitchurch, Terling and St James Clerkenwell stand out as particularly 'generous' parishes.

A small rural parish such as Whitchurch in south Oxfordshire might have a rather low proportion of its elderly in receipt of pensions, although those who were beneficiaries would have received very substantial allowances, indeed were almost totally dependent on the parish. Such a parish had no charitable funds of the kind that were frequently available in market towns and larger communities.[29] Similarly the nature of the local, undiversified, economy may not have provided the elderly with the range of jobs that would have enabled them to piece together incomes that were partially welfare based and partially dependent on remuneration from part-time and irregular work. For instance, in the market towns, such as Tavistock, a higher proportion of the elderly received relief but the amounts often averaged below 1s. 0d. per week, which would have certainly been inadequate for survival. We know, too, that in market towns rather than in agricultural villages local charities made substantial contributions to the total quantity of welfare provided and that rather lower proportions of beneficiaries from these sources as a whole were to be found in the younger age groups. Whitkirk, in West Yorkshire, was a mining community by the late seventeenth century and wage rates there were most likely higher than in the remainder of our sample. The proportions in receipt of relief in old age were, however, comparable with those found in communities in the south and east of the country, but the weekly amounts pensioners received were much smaller, rarely in excess of 6d. and certainly inadequate as a basis for self-sufficiency. We can only speculate whether this reflects a less efficient system, an inadequate rate-base for welfare funds, or possibly higher incomes, a more viable family economy or greater commitment to kin-based support. Only more research in northern communities will enable the wider significance of these features to be assessed.[30]

From the incidence of pension provision within local communities we know that the pension was by no means a strictly age-related benefit, nor was it provided as a right. There is frequently a sense in which we can observe the pension given as a supplement to earnings and the steady increase in its value as the beneficiary ages reflects an increasing incapacity to work for reasons of deteriorating health and growing decrepitude. As noted previously, women predominate among those collecting pensions and begin to receive support at an earlier age than men, so that by age 70 a sizeable majority of women will have been in receipt of a regular pension, some for many years. This pattern is clearly present by 1700 and in this respect mirrors those characteristics that have been recovered by David Thomson, through his superior, more accurate, census-based research from 1841 onwards. Males, however, were less readily apparent among those receiving assistance over the age of 65 than would appear to be the case in Thomson's earlier nineteenth-century samples. This may, however, reflect the fact that many of Thomson's samples come from areas of low agricultural wages and high rural unemployment in the south and east of England, with the result that his data have been distorted by the presence of a larger number of elderly males receiving income supplements or unemployment benefit through the poor rates rather than retirement or disability pensions. These may well have been characteristics that were beginning to make their presence felt in the later eighteenth century in our sample as we will see later in this discussion.[31]

It is important to stress that the pattern we observe in the late seventeenth and early eighteenth centuries in which elderly pensioners loom large among Poor Law beneficiaries was not one which displayed a constancy throughout the Old Poor Law period. We would confirm suggestions already made by William Newman-Brown in his research on Aldeham, Hertfordshire, Tim

Wales in his investigation of Norfolk poor relief, and by Andrew Wear in his pioneering investigations of the London parish of St Bartholomew, that much more was being spent regularly on orphans and young widows with children earlier in the seventeenth century.[32] The relative decline in the proportional significance of these categories of beneficiary is interesting and may owe much to changes in the broader relationship between population and resources – improving in the late seventeenth century as fertility fell and the population became less youthful.[33] Another development that could have reduced the significance of orphans among the recipients of relief may have been a decline in the severity and frequency of epidemic mortalities that often left parishes with a large number of parentless 'survivors' in need of parochial support.[34]

By the end of the seventeenth century it is clear that weekly doles or pensions had risen on average to almost 1s. 0d. and over. By the 1720s or 1730s their level had reached 1s. 6d. in most places in southern and eastern England. These levels of weekly doles in the early eighteenth century, given the deflationary forces then at work and the relatively low price of bread, were consistent not just with an increased nominal but with a real rise in the value of the pension. To this point in the discussion we have considered the recipients of poor relief in somewhat impersonal terms. We now consider some sample case histories of elderly pensioners whose experiences, it may be suggested, were characteristic of a sizeable majority of those living past the age of 60 in communities in southern and eastern England in the century after 1650.

Richard Sheaf married Katherine Miller in Cranbrook in Kent in 1648, where they settled. A son was born in 1649. Katherine was 25 years of age at marriage and 26 when her son was born. She was widowed in 1678 when she was 55. From that moment in 1678 until 1682 she received occasional relief during fairly frequent periods of 'sickness'. From 1682 when Katherine was almost 60 she was given a pension of 2s. 6d. per month (less than 1s. 0d. per week), but continued to receive supplements during her recurrent periods of 'sickness'. Her rent was paid, although her weekly allowance of 9d. was almost certainly insufficient to maintain her, given her frail condition. What other income might she have received? It is not until 1686 when the Poor Law accounts reveal a payment made for 'cards' for her that we can establish that she derived some earnings from the carding of wool. More cards are supplied by the overseer in 1690 when in her 67th year she is referred to for the first time as 'old widow Sheaf'. In her 68th year her pension was raised to 3s. 0d. per month when she was also provided with winter fuel, indicative of her failing capacity to sustain herself. That year in June she was given a rather large casual payment of 11s. 0d. on account of illness, after which she was removed from her home to be lodged with a young widow who was paid 6d. per week by the overseer for her houseroom. By this time widow Sheaf was receiving a pension of 1s. 6d. per week, a sum adequate to meet all of her basic needs. Indeed the parish, it seems, was supporting her completely in her 68th year at the end of which she died. Throughout this period her son was resident in Cranbrook and we know from later Poor Law accounts that he went on to be one of the first inmates of the Cranbrook workhouse at the age of 73 after it was built in 1722.[35]

The widow Foster (see the displayed text below) does not appear in the reconstitution of the Whitchurch (Oxfordshire) parish register, despite being a pensioner for nearly twenty-four years. She went on the parish within a few years of her husband's death when she was in her mid fifties. Although no family is traceable from the parish registers, it is apparent from a casual payment of 1686–7 that she had at least one child. She starts off with a modest pension of 1*s.*, with occasional help with clothing and house repairs. By the time she had reached her mid seventies she was receiving a weekly pension of 2*s.* 6*d.* Those entering the system at a more advanced age than the widow Foster tended to be given a fairly small and rudimentary pension which only grew as and if they approached extreme old age and their dependency increased. With many in this category either death came suddenly without long illness or incapacity allowing little time for the pension to increase, or the final illness provided the catalyst for an elderly man or woman to go onto the pension list in the first place, usually for a brief period in such instances. There is some sign of widow Foster's deteriorating health suggested by payments of 2*s.* 6*d.* to a surgeon apothecary in 1689–90, of 5*s.* 0*d.* in 1691–2 for medicines and a substantial growth in casual payments up to her death in 1693 as she gradually became less and less able to support herself. In her final years of life she was receiving a pension of 3*s.* 6*d.* per week. Widow Foster's is an unspectacular, but very good, example of the incremental withdrawal from economic productivity and self-support that represents something close to a modal experience for the ageing female.

---

*Poor relief payments to Widow Ann Foster, Whitchurch, Oxon., 1669–93*

*Birth:*     *Not known*
*Marriage:* *?1642-1-16 Thos Foster/Anne Hanks (Witney)*
*Buried:*    *1693-3-22, widow Ann Foester (unattributed)*
         *At least one daughter*

| Year | Description | | Amount |
|---|---|---|---|
| 1668–9 | Paid to the wid F | | 0-3-0 |
| 1669–70 | Paid to the wid F | | 1-0-6 |
| 1670–1 | Paid to the wid F | | 2-14-0 |
| 1672–3 | Paid to the wid F | 48w @ 12*d.* | 2-8-0 |
| 1673–4 | Paid to the wid F | 55w @ 12*d.* | 2-15-0 |
| 1674–5 | Paid to the wid F | 50w @ 12*d.* | 2-10-0 |
| 1675–6 | Paid to the wid F | 51w @ 12*d.* | 2-11-0 |
| 1676–7 | Paid to the wid F | 52w @ 12*d.* | 2-12-0 |
| | Paid to the wid F | | 0-2-6 |
| 1677–8 | Paid to the wid F | 51w @ 1*s.* | 2-11-0 |
| 1679–80 | Paid to the wid F | 51w @ 1*s.* | 2-11-0 |
| | Paid for mending the wid F's house | | 0-2-8 |

---

| 1680–1 | Paid to the wid F | 51w @ 1s. | 2-1-0 |
|---|---|---|---|
| 1681–2 | Paid to the wid F | 54w @ 1s. | 2-14-0 |
| | Paid to the wid F in her lameness | | 0-8-0 |
| 1682–3 | Paid to the wid F | 51w @ 1s. | 2-11-0 |
| | Paid to the wid F in her lameness | | 0-5-0 |
| | Paid for straw and mending her house | | 0-5-0 |
| 1683–4 | Paid to the wid F | 51w @ 1s. | 2-11-0 |
| 1684–5 | Paid to the wid F | 55w @ 1s. | 2-15-0 |
| | Paid to her besides her weekly Collection | | 0-7-0 |
| 1685–6 | Paid to the wid F | 50w @ 1s. 3d. | 3-2-6 |
| | Paid to the wid F besides her weekely Collection | | 0-3-0 |
| 1686–7 | Paid to the wid | 26w @ 1s. 3d. | 1-12-6 |
| | | 25w @ 1s. 6d. | 1-17-6 |
| | Paid to the wid F besides her Collection | | 0-6-0 |
| | Paid to her daughter for tending her | | 0-6-0 |
| 1687–8 | Paid to the wid F | 36w @ 1s. 6d. | 2-14-0 |
| | | 19w @ 1s. 6d. | 2-7-6 |
| | Paid to her besides her weekely Collection | | 1-17-10 |
| 1688–9 | Paid to the wid F | 50w @ 2s. 6d. | 6-5-0 |
| | Paid for linnen cloathes & a pair of stockings for wid F | | 0-4-0 |
| | Paid for a paire of shooes for wid F | | 0-2-8 |
| | Paid for a night wastcoate for the wid F. | | 0-2-6 |
| 1689–90 | Paid to the wid F | 55w @ 2s. 6d. | 6-17-6 |
| | Paid to Mr Hinderson for Comeing to the wid F | | 0-2-6 |
| | Paid for a paire of boddice for wid F | | 0-3-6 |
| 1690–1 | Paid to the wid F | 51w @ 2s. 6d. | 6-7-6 |
| | Paid for a paire of stockings for the wid F | | 0-1-2 |
| | Paid for a new pair of sleeves and mending the wid F's wastcoat | | 0-1-4 |
| | Paid for makeing small linnen for thi wid F | | 0-1-6 |
| | Paid for a Coate for the wid F | | 0-6-7 |
| 1691–2 | Paid to the wid F | 50w @ 2s. 6d. | 6-5-0 |
| | Paid for an Aporne for the wid F | | 0-1-3 |
| | Paid for 2 Coifes for the wid F | | 0-1-0 |
| | Paid for Laces for the wid F | | 0-0-2 |
| | Paid for a Aporn for the wid F | | 0-1-3 |
| | Paid for medicine for the wid F for 3 yeares past & dressing her Legg | | 0-5-0 |
| | Paid for bindings for her Coates | | 0-0-2 |
| 1692–3 | Paid to the wid F | 52w @ 3s. 6d. | 9-2-6 |
| | Paid for Linsey woosey & an under coate for the wid F | | 0-3-0 |
| | Paid for a sheet for the wid F | | 0-3-9 |
| | Paid for a wastcoate for the wid F | | 0-5-6 |
| | Paid for mending and making Linen cloathes for her | | 0-1-0 |
| | Paid for a shroud for the wid F | | 0-5-0 |
| | Paid for Layer her forth | | 0-1-0 |
| | Paid for a Coffin for her | | 0-6-0 |
| | Paid for bread and beere when she was buried | | 0-5-0 |
| | Paid for Ringing the bell and digging the Grave for her | | 0-3-0 |
| | Paid for the Affidavitt and fetching him [sic] | | 0-1-0 |

While we encounter a surprisingly large quantity of information concerning payments of the surgeon's bills the detail recorded of treatments given is somewhat sparse. We do see a pattern of treatments in which surgeons and local healers interact in ways that suggest how unrealistic it would be to regard the amateur and professional healers as non-communicating sectors. Nevertheless, as might be expected, 'medical provision' for the ageing pensioner is principally funded through Poor Law payments for nursing, lodging and dietary supplements as well as subsidies for rents and fuel. In an accounting sense it is difficult to separate these categories. If we were to focus on payments for practitioners' bills and specific medicines the outlays, as we have shown above, would rarely exceed a few per cent of total rate-based expenditure, but if the other categories that entailed a more comprehensive definition of 'care' are considered, in excess of 20 per cent of Poor Law casual expenditure could be regarded as directed to servicing the health needs of the parish population. The elderly are a very prominent group of recipients of such casual payments.[36]

It is very clear that the nursing of the aged sick cannot be divorced from their medical treatment, for in many cases they were performed by the same person. For example, Anne Tully of Cowden in Kent in 1687 received 6*d*. per week for 'lodging and attendance' with a number of widows, a further £2. 10*s*. 0*d*. paid to her as 'casual sums' for her medicine when treating 'old widow Woodman'. It was common practice to pay the poor to look after the poor, particularly the aged poor. A provisional finding from our parish sample suggests that nursing was in the hands of several groups of people: those who worked for the parish on a full-time basis, being very experienced, who would and did assume responsible positions in the many disease outbreaks. In this respect it is worth noting the role played by the elderly themselves who seem at least in the eighteenth century in the case of smallpox to have assumed a prominent function as 'carers'. From the late seventeenth century onwards, there appeared among the older members of the communities numbers of men and women who had survived smallpox and who could approach other victims in relative safety. Widow Sturt of Tonbridge in Kent, who survived an epidemic of 1681, while her husband succumbed, took charge of the nursing in the pest house when members of fifteen different families were moved there in an outbreak of the disease in 1698. A second group of 'carers' attended their neighbours or were paid to attend their parents for short periods, while a third group acted as irregularly employed ancillaries, as watchers of the dying, or assistants of full-time nurses.[37]

Our evidence suggests that by the end of the seventeenth century there had emerged a detectable sentiment that the elderly were entitled to communal support, even if there were close kin available and able to help. This is not to say that no help of any kind passed between the elderly and their children resident in the parish, but that such help, where it existed, was usually supplementary and no substitute for regular parish pensions. It has been noted many times, a good example being Andrew Wear's work on seventeenth-century London, already mentioned, that relatives of the elderly sick were paid by the parish to look after them.[38] In Whitchurch we read in the account for 4 October 1755 'paid John Allom's wife to nurse her father 8s'. To take a further example from Whitchurch, the widow Sadgrove was probably around the age of 70 when she became a pensioner in the late 1690s, almost a quarter century after her husband's death. She is an example of the commonest sort of widow in receipt of parish support: those without children living at home. Although at first the pension was small, it quickly escalated to proportions which probably provided her full support without the necessity of further supplement. One daughter was baptised in the parish, but an Edward Sadgrove makes appearances in the accounts from time to time and it seems from the records of casual payments in 1699–1700 that widow Sadgrave had a son living across the county border at Moulsford in Berkshire who was given money to buy her clothes, but seems not to have been responsible for providing her with support from his own purse. Indeed her funeral expenses were met entirely by the parish when she was buried in 1705. The case of widow Sadgrove and her son Edward should in no sense be regarded as atypical. Some historians have regarded such instances involving the payment of daughters or daughters-in-law to provide nursing care for a parent as indicative of the transformation of care from an obligation into a commodity.[39] Such actions, some would argue, served to undermine mutuality of familial support.[40] Others, I believe correctly, prefer to see such actions on the part of Poor Law authorities as a means of inducing children to maximise the care and attention they were willing *in toto* to give, thereby buttressing or enhancing the level of familial support.[41] Such an interpretation would seem consistent with a view of welfare that served to promote self-sufficiency by simultaneously promoting familial self-sufficiency.[42]

## The late eighteenth century

Our findings would seem to reveal that the century between 1650 and 1750 was one in which the share that the elderly were receiving of the rate-based funds had grown. Furthermore the value of the allocations to individual pensioners may have also increased so that weekly doles bore an increasingly favourable relationship to prices and wages. Rate-based expenditure in most of the parishes in this sample had increased significantly in the last third of the seventeenth century.[43] We proceed to make some provisional observations on certain features of our data relating to the second half of the eighteenth century considering in turn the evidence bearing upon the value of pensions, the age patterns of the pensioners and their sexual composition.

Table 4.9, based on almost 45,000 pension payments between 1750 and 1800 in fourteen sets of statistics taken from parishes drawn from the north, east, west and south of England, displays features indicative of changes that may have become even more marked by the turn of the century. Of the fourteen sets of statistics for the parishes in Table 4.9 only seven show a modal weekly pension amount as high as or higher than the mean. Where the mode was higher, it would have required a larger number of very small and clearly supplementary pensions to have been paid to balance the equation. Such a finding is consistent with an increasing presence of married couples and their overburdening children in the population of Poor Law beneficiaries and represents a striking development after 1770. Furthermore, the evident stabilisation of mean and median values of weekly pensions suggests a decline in their real value given what is known of price movements during this phase. This was also a period when overall Poor Law expenditure after a period of relative stability in the middle of the century increased noticeably.[44] It is clear that the rise of overall expenditure was not the result of a growth in the size of the pensions paid to individuals. As the absolute number of pensioners rose over the course of the late eighteenth century, given demographic growth, it may have been that the capacity as well as the will of the rate-payers to keep up the level of pension payments was seriously stretched. It is also necessary to take into account the possible structural changes in the composition of the pensioner body over the period. It is often supposed that as the eighteenth century wore on many more labourers with large families may have needed relief than previously, but this was increasingly supplementary in nature and therefore involved smaller sums of money.[45] Such a compositional shift in the character of pension recipients would have had the effect of holding average amounts down.

Another development that may have served to distort the measurement of pension and pensioner statistics concerns a growth in the number of work-

*Table 4.9*   Pension payments, 1750–1800

| Parish | County | Date | N | Mean | Median | Mode | Average no. of pensioners |
|---|---|---|---|---|---|---|---|
| Calverley | WR Yorks | 1766–71 | 2,328 | 0/10 | 0/9 | 0/6 | 16.2 |
|  |  | 1791–6 | 2,980 | 0/10 | 0/9 | 1/0 | 15.5 |
| Wawne | ER Yorks | 1772–9 | 1,718 | 1/6 | 1/6 | 1/6 |  |
| Easington | Lancs | 1760–4 | 2,544 | 1/0 | 1/0 | 1/0 | 12.2 |
| Woodplumpton | Lancs | 1775–9 | 5,044 | 1/10 | 2/0 | 2/0 | 24.3 |
| Skendleby | Lincs | 1769–78 | 2,079 | 1/2 | 1/0 | 1/0 | 5.6 |
| Potterhanworth | Lincs | 1774–91 | 2,132 | 1/3 | 1/0 | 1/0 | 6.8 |
| Trevethin | Gwent | 1768–72 | 4,021 | 1/4 | 1/3 | 1/0 | 19.3 |
| Whitchurch | Oxon | 1759–62 | 3,289 | 1/8 | 1/6 | 1/6 |  |
| Dorchester | Oxon | 1772–80 | 5,285 | 1/8 | 1/6 | 1/6 | n/a |
| Terling | Essex | 1770–8 | 2,531 | 1/5 | 1/6 | 1/0 | 6.4 |
| Tavistock | Devon | 1760–1 | 3,226 | 1/0 | 1/0 | 1/0 | 64.5 |
| Bere Ferrers | Devon | 1778–80 | 4,373 | 1/3 | 1/3 | 1/3 |  |
| Stoke Fleming | Devon | 1783–8 | 5,925 | 1/8 | 1/6 | 2/0 |  |

houses and workhouse populations. If those siphoned off into workhouses were not representative of those left on outdoor relief and hence visible in Poor Law account books, then the patterns of pension development that we have considered above may have been, at least partially, explicable in these terms. We will return to discuss this possibility below.

In Table 4.10, which represents a small sample with all the inherent dangers of unrepresentativeness, we see some suggestive developments. Terling, in particular, reveals a decline in the relative importance of females, especially elderly females within its pensioner population. Indeed there is a great deal of evidence to suggest that there was a significant shift in the gender composition of the pensioner population in these sample parishes. A comparison of Tables 4.6 and 4.10 reveals a tendency for the male pensioner population to age. The proportion of male pensioner weeks paid to the elderly rose from 55–60 per cent to 73 per cent in the period after 1745. While, for example, absolute levels differed in Whitchurch and Terling the drift in both parishes was in the same direction. Female pensioner weeks paid to those persons 61 years and over dropped from 55 to 42 per cent of the total in Whitchurch and from 65 to 39 per cent in Terling.

In Tables 4.6 and 4.11 we are able to observe changes in the absolute numbers of male and female pensioners over more than a century. In Table 4.12 we see in summary form the ratios of all male to all female pensioners and elderly male to elderly female pensioners for all the parishes that have been the subject of investigation in this study and separately for the parish of Whitchurch. A steady drop in the ratio of female to male pensioners is apparent over the eighteenth century. There is also a

*Table 4.10(a)* Proportion of pensioners in various age groups, 1745–1800

| Parish | Period | 0–50 years (%) | 61 years or over (%) |
| --- | --- | --- | --- |
| Terling | 1745–65 | 2,675/7,158 = 37.4 | 3,619/7,158 = 50.6 |
| Whitchurch | 1750–65 | 3,985/8,871 = 44.9 | 4,806/8,871 = 54.2 |
| Terling | 1783–1800 | 2,875/7,812 = 36.8 | 3,655/7,812 = 46.8 |
| Subtotal | | 9,535/23,841 = 40.0 | 12,080/23,841 = 50.7 |

*Table 4.10(b)* Age group of adult pensioners by sex, 1745–1800

| Parish | Period | Males | | | Females | | |
| --- | --- | --- | --- | --- | --- | --- | --- |
| | | 21–50 (%) | 61+ (%) | N | 21–50 (%) | 61+ (%) | N |
| Terling | 1745–65 | 35.8 | 51.2 | 3,858 | 21.3 | 64.5 | 2,549 |
| Whitchurch | 1750–65 | 0.0 | 99.2 | 2,716 | 57.1 | 41.7 | 5,064 |
| Terling | 1783–1800 | 14.2 | 77.1 | 2,260 | 38.2 | 39.4 | 4,854 |
| Subtotal | | 19.3 | 72.6 | 8,834 | 42.4 | 45.5 | 12,467 |

*Table 4.11* Age groups of pensioners: sex

| Parish | Period | Males | | | Females | | |
|---|---|---|---|---|---|---|---|
| | | *21–50 (%)* | *61+ (%)* | *N* | *21–50 (%)* | *61+ (%)* | *N* |
| Terling | 1745–65 | 46.6 | 34.9 | 2,909 | 16.2 | 74.4 | 3,498 |
| Whitchurch | 1750–65 | 31.7 | 67.8 | 2,762 | 40.2 | 58.5 | 5,018 |
| Terling | 1783–1800 | 24.5 | 62.5 | 4,316 | 39.9 | 34.3 | 2,798 |
| Subtotal | | 32.9 | 55.9 | 9,987 | 32.7 | 57.4 | 11,314 |

particularly sharp drop in the ratio of elderly female to elderly male pensioners between the early and late eighteenth century.

A drop in both the nominal and real value of pensions and a significant decline in the presence of females in the population of those pensioners in receipt of outdoor relief would seem to have been developments that these investigations have detected. We will need to proceed cautiously in drawing such conclusions since complications may have been introduced into our 'statistics' caused by the growth in workhouses after 1722. How might the establishment and populating of workhouses have influenced the data relating to recipients of outdoor relief that have formed the focus of this chapter? At this stage in investigations into this subject we are obliged to restrict our consideration of this issue to the parish of Terling. For this parish we are blessed with a set of concurrent lists of parish pensioners and workhouse inmates in the second half of the eighteenth century. Between 29 May 1775 and 29 September 1783 there are monthly lists of workhouse inmates for Terling. Between these dates sixty-six persons were maintained in the workhouse for some period of time. Of those inmates, twenty-one were male and forty-five female. Over the comparable period the parish was supporting thirty-six individual pensioners on outrelief, ten of whom were male and twenty-six female. Fourteen persons appeared for varying periods of time on both lists between 1775 and 1783. The considerable degree of overlap neatly demonstrates the intertwined nature of Poor Law provision. There was a clear sense in which the elderly moved into workhouses in the

*Table 4.12* Sex ratios of pensioners

| Period | Sex ratio of female/male pensioners | Sex ratio of elderly pensioners (61+) |
|---|---|---|
| Late 17th century | 30,017:8,912 = 3.4:1 | 10,759:4,951 = 2.2:1 |
| Whitchurch 1672–1700 | 9,579:990 = 9.7:1 | 4,459:573 = 7.8:1 |
| Early 18th century | 10,049:4,168 = 2.4:1 | 5,833:2,547 = 2.3:1 |
| Whitchurch 1700–30 | 6,678:2,559 = 2.6:1 | 3,677:1,259 = 2.9:1 |
| Late 18th century | 12,467:8,834 = 1.4:1 | 5,670:6,412 = 0.9:1 |
| Whitchurch 1750–65 | 5,064:2,716 = 1.9:1 | 2,112:2,694 = 0.8:1 |

latter stages of their lives shortly before their death, which as we have seen from some of the individual case studies was the phase when weekly parish expenditure on them reached particularly high levels. If sizeable numbers were being removed from the pension lists through their placement in the workhouse this could have been a practice which would have had the effect of reducing the observed size of the pensions paid as forms of outdoor relief and recorded in the Poor Law accounts. A cursory examination of that set of detailed listings of workhouse inmates from a selection of English parishes collected by Sir Frederic Morton Eden suggests that such practices were occurring. The example of Epsom (displayed below) in 1796 reveals an inmate population made up of a large number of elderly persons, especially females, with quite severe ailments, and a smaller number of rather younger persons, with few of intermediate ages.[46]

*The adult workhouse inmates of Epsom in January 1796*

| **Men** | **Women** |
|---|---|
| 1 J.H. aged 43. The little work he ever did, or could do, was as a labourer; but, having always been somewhat of an idiot, he is now become quite a driveller. | 1 S.C. aged 56; a lunatic. |
| | 2 M.W. aged 51; paralytic, and impotent. |
| | 3 C.D. aged 60; has sore legs, from bad diseases. |
| 2 R.M. aged 77; worn out, and paralytic: he was a bricklayer. | 4 E.E. aged 62; of a sluggish, stupid character; and never able to earn more than an immediate subsistence. |
| 3 J.C. aged 76; heretofore a labourer: he has been, 8 years, incurably asthmatic. | 5 M.D. aged 59; the widow of a labourer; very feeble, and valetudinary. |
| 4 J.P. aged 69; a labourer; impotent and a cripple. | 6 M.B. aged 60; a native of Ireland; with no regular habits of industry, yet can be made to do work enough to maintain herself. |
| 5 W.F. aged 65, he was a carpenter: but always a slow, stupid and improvident man. | 7 M.A. aged 41; a lunatic. |
| 6 T.H. aged 65; deformed, and heretofore employed as a shepherd, on very low wages. | 8 E.P. aged 76; worn out. |
| 7 D.F. aged 54; he was a postillion, and employed about stables; addicted to drinking, and an idle, worthless man. | 9 M.J. aged 75; impotent: has been a servant the greater part of her life. |
| | 10 A.M. aged 75; the wife of J.M. (see Men No. 9) [*sic*] |
| | 11 M.C. aged 65; of a feeble make, and always sickly. |
| 8 J.T. aged 62; was a whitesmith, but has now a sore leg, probably occasioned by intemperance. | 12 A.M. aged 26; afflicted with a leprosy. |
| | 13 E.K. aged 19; of idle and profligate habits, and often wretchedly diseased. |

| Men | Women |
|---|---|
| 9 T.M. aged 77; he was a barber, but an unsteady unsettled fellow, and of course he never earned much. | 14 E.K. aged 41; somewhat of an idiot: her husband is at present in Newgate. |
| 10 J.B. aged 28; has been a soldier: he is shockingly afflicted with bad disorders. | 15 C.W. aged 18; a native of Switzerland; and now with child, it is supposewd, by a gentleman's butler. |
| 11 J.R. aged 17, His parents having neglectd putting him to a trade, or bringing him up to a regular course of industry, he has contracted many loose and disorderly habits. Twice he has been put out to service, but was always turned off for ill behaviour. Decent people will not employ him; and he can neither be persuaded nor forced, either to go to sea, or to enlist for a soldier. | 16 A.B. aged 27; an idiot. |

*Source*: Eden, *The State of the Poor*, vol. 3, pp. 693–7.

## Conclusions

Our evidence, still in the early stages of assembly and interpretation, reveals a significant minority, and, in some communities, a noteworthy majority, of elderly persons in receipt of parish support in the phase between 1670 and 1740 when such individuals accounted for a share of the total population that they all were not to reach again at a national level until the 1930s. We note too that the level of the pensions or doles provided also increased significantly during this phase when the number of youthful dependants in the population was to reach a minimum level for the whole of the period of the Old Poor Law. Similarly, the sexual balance of the recipient population was markedly skewed in favour of females. These are a set of conditions that it must be emphasised loomed largest in southern rural parishes. Market towns had rather higher proportions of their elderly persons in receipt of relief, although the value of the weekly pensions they received was lower, suggesting a larger proportion of individuals whose assets or earnings were insufficient to sustain them without recourse to welfare. However, there may have been more part-time or irregular employment opportunities available to them than would have been at their disposal in the rural, less differentiated, economies so their dependence was far from complete. It is also probable that such urban settlements were better endowed with charitable resources that served to limit the charges placed upon the rate-payers. In the northern parishes our still scanty evidence shows a similar incidence of pensioners per head of the population, although the doles they received were especially low, often half or less of the weekly amount paid to pensioners in southern parishes.

Later eighteenth-century developments cannot yet be identified with the assurance that characterises our comments on the period before 1750. We have asked whether the decline or stagnation of pension payments in the course of the mid- to late eighteenth century was real rather than an artefact of institutional or compositional changes in the population of welfare recipients. There are many signs that in some parishes the depression of pension values was very real and purchasing power declined. The rural parishes of the south of England, exemplified by Whitchurch, are unambiguously of this type. Mary Barker-Read in her regional study of Poor Law provision for the elderly in Kent has noted a similar stagnation of pensions given to the elderly at 1s. 6d. per week through the whole of the late eighteenth century as well as a later age of commencement of pension payments to both sexes.[47]

However, our consideration of the Terling case should alert our attention to the obvious possibility that workhouses may have drawn in a number of individuals who might, had they not become inmates, have been recipients of large quantities of outdoor relief in the last year or months immediately prior to their death, when nursing expenses, fuel allowances and dietary supplements may have been especially costly. A detailed analysis of 'patient histories' indicates how often outrelief allocations to elderly pensioners frequently rose by 50 to 100 per cent in the final stages of their lives. Widow Foster of Whitchurch is a very good example of this phenomenon (see the displayed text above). In Table 4.8 it is clear that in Terling between 1716 and 1725 the ten years reveal 3,109 pension payments amounting on average to 1s. 7d. to an annual average of seven pensioners. During the seven years from 1744 to 1750, 3,543 pension payments were made to an annual average of twelve pensioners. From 1770 to 1778 (see Table 4.9), after the workhouse had been established only 2,531 pension payments were made to an annual average of only six pensioners who received a weekly dole of 1s. 5d. These changes are reflected in a shift from 2 to 4 and back to 2 per cent of the local population in receipt of pensions over the period as a whole. In Tavistock a workhouse was opened in 1747. Dr Tim Hitchcock has recently observed that in the years immediately prior to the opening of the workhouse thirty-one pensioners were listed in the parish books. When the workhouse opened Hitchcock noted that fourteen persons entered and the remainder of the former pensioners ceased to receive parish doles.[48] Our research does not confirm Hitchcock's finding that outrelief disappeared entirely, but we do confirm a sharp decline in the number of persons receiving weekly pensions and their average value. In Tavistock the Poor Law accounts show that between 1708 and 1710 eighty-six pensioners received 4,317 payments averaging 1s. 3d. per week; from 1735 to 1736, 109 pensioners received 5,862 payments averaging 1s. 3d. per week (see Table 4.8). From 1760 to 1761 we note that thirteen years after the opening of the workhouse sixty-four pensioners received 3,226 payments of 1*s*. 0*d*. per week (see Table 4.9).

The more clearly detectable fall in the presence of female pensioners in the pauper population may help us to understand some other features that have been encountered by one researcher who has studied the residential position of the elderly at the close of the eighteenth century. Dr Tom Sokoll has recently waged a campaign against the 'orthodox' notion that pauper households in early modern England were small and frequently composed of the solitary aged. His position stems from an analysis he has made of the extremely fine listing of Ardleigh's inhabitants in 1796. The combination of an excellent listing of inhabitants for this Essex village and fine Poor Law accounts enables him to establish that there was an almost complete absence of female solitaries. Only one pauper household in eighty-two was so consti-tuted. Furthermore, one-half of all poor women aged 50 and over lived in lineally extended households with their married daughters. The severe economic difficulties brought on by the high prices, harvest failures and severe winter weather conditions clearly placed extreme pressures on parish rates in the late 1790s.[49] Here we must seriously entertain the possibility that we are observing the consequences of practices that involved the exclusion of the elderly, especially female pensioners, from contexts in which they managed their own households or were supported in their own homes with the assistance of parish funds.[50]

There are indications that Malthus may have been troubled by these developments that reduced the residential 'freedoms' of the elderly, espe-cially if they were widows. A commitment to protect the elderly from institutions of a more impersonal kind is very detectable in his sentiments. Malthus, who is sometimes misunderstood in certain aspects of his attitude towards the poor, defended the Old Poor practice or preference of relieving the aged poor in their own homes rather than sending them to workhouses. In 1796 he wrote:

> it is the duty of society to maintain such of its members as are abso-lutely unable to maintain themselves, it is certainly desirable that the assistance in this case should be given in the way that is most agreeable to the persons who are to receive it . . . it seems peculiarly hard upon old people, who perhaps have been useful and respectable members of society, and in their day, 'have done the state some service', that as soon as they are past their work, they should be obliged to quit the village where they have always lived, the cottage to which time has attached them, the circle of their friends, their children and their grand-children, and be forced to spend the evening of their days in noise and unquiet-

ness among strangers, and wait their last moments forlorn and separated from all they hold dear.[51]

If the later eighteenth and early nineteenth centuries did witness a rise in the institutionalisation of the elderly, especially elderly females, and if it proves possible to establish further evidence of a growing tendency for the elderly, especially widows, to co-reside with married daughters, which the listings of the late seventeenth century suggest was a fairly infrequent practice, we can only speculate on what these changes may have implied for the quality of the care the elderly received.[52] Evidence is certainly accumulating to suggest that the late eighteenth and early nineteenth centuries saw a substantial decline, at least in the southern agrarian economies, in the well-being of the elderly female. In Amartya Sen's terms their 'capabilities' were severely trimmed.[53]

## Notes

1  P. Slack, *Poverty and Social Policy in Tudor and Stuart England*, London, 1988, pp. 84–5.
2  E. M. Leonard, *The Early History of English Poor Relief*, Cambridge, 1900, pp. 133–4.
3  D. M. Thomson, ' "I am not my father's keeper": families and the elderly in nineteenth-century England', *Law and History Review*, 1984, vol. 2, pp. 265–86.
4  The most emphatic advocate of such a view is J. C. Caldwell, *A Theory of Fertility Decline*, London, 1982.
5  Thomson, ' "I am not my father's keeper" ', pp. 268–9. As Professor Thane has argued, the absence of case law revealing implementation of this clause should not be interpreted to mean that Poor Law officials made no efforts to secure intra-familial support for actual or potential recipients of poor relief. However, the relative infrequency of such efforts may reflect the costly nature of the enforcement procedures in relation to the small savings provided to the ratepayers or, and more likely, reveals a sympathetic understanding on the part of the local officers, highly knowledgeable of their local communities and fully aware that the care being provided by individuals whose own resources were insufficient to assist, let alone maintain, their close kin, could not be increased still further. See P. Thane, 'Old people and their families in the English past', in M. Daunton (ed.), *Charity. Self-interest and Welfare in the English Past*, London, 1996, pp.116–23.
6  For reflections on these misbeliefs see P. Laslett, *A Fresh Map of Life: The Emergence of the Third Age*, London, 1989, pp.107–21.
7  R. Wall, 'Elderly persons and members of their households in England and Wales from preindustrial times to the present', in D. I. Kertzer and P. Laslett (eds), *Aging in the Past: Demography, Society and Old Age*, London, 1995, pp. 81–106.
8  Ibid., p. 88; R. M. Smith, 'The structured dependency of the elderly as a recent development: some sceptical historical thoughts', *Ageing and Society*, 1984, vol. 4, pp. 417–19. A more nuanced analysis of this question by Susannah Ottaway employing the largest set of listing so far available for the period *c.*1687–1831 reveals that, depending on time and place, between 71 and 67 per cent of males over 60 headed their own households with co-resident wife and/or children, whereas between 52 and 59 per cent of women of similar ages did so. Women were somewhat less likely to reside in households headed by children or

kin (12 to 23 per cent) than to live alone or with persons to whom they were not related (21 to 27 per cent), S. Ottaway, ' "The decline of life": aspects of aging in eighteenth-century England', Unpublished Ph.D. thesis, Brown University, 1997, p. 125.

9  P. Johnson and J. Falkingham, *Ageing and Economic Welfare*, London, 1992, pp. 34–6; Wall, 'Elderly persons and members of their households', pp. 99–104.

10  Laslett, *A Fresh Map of Life*, pp.115–17; J. Smith, 'The computer simulation of kin sets and kin counts', in J. Bongaarts *et al.* (eds), *Family Demography: Methods and Their Applications*, Oxford, 1987, pp. 261–5.

11  Laslett, *A Fresh Map of Life*, p. 117. Susannah Ottaway presents estimates for samples of rural communities which suggest that 62 per cent of elderly females resided with children in the early nineteenth century compared with 46 per cent in the late seventeenth century. She also shows in a highly innovative analysis in which she constructs an 'index of residential security' that females were considerably more likely in the early nineteenth century to reside with spouse and/or children. Making the assumption that security was maximised by residence with spouse and/or children, she concludes that elderly females were, from a residential perspective, far more secure in the early nineteenth century than in the late seventeenth or even late eighteenth centuries, Ottaway, ' "The decline of life" ', pp.135–7 and 141–53.

12  Smith, 'The structured dependency of the elderly', pp. 42–5; see also P. Laslett, 'Family, kinship and collectivity as systems of support in preindustrial Europe: a consideration of the "nuclear hardship" hypothesis', *Continuity and Change*, 1988, vol. 3, pp. 153–75.

13  Reported in M. Anderson, 'The impact on the family relationships of the elderly of changes since Victorian times in government income maintenance provisions', in E. Shanas and M. B. Sussman (eds), *Family, Bureaucracy and the Elderly*, Durham, NC, 1977, p. 56.

14  T. Sokoll, 'Old age in poverty: the record of Essex pauper letters, 1780–1834', in T. Hitchcock *et al.* (eds), *Chronicling Poverty: The Voices and Strategies of the English Poor, 1640–1840*, London, 1997, p.138.

15  Dr Sokoll is preparing a full edition of the Essex pauper correspondence to appear in the British Academy's *Records in Economic and Social History* series.

16  For an article which conveniently summarises his key findings and arguments see D. Thomson, 'The welfare of the elderly in the past: a family or community responsibility?', in M. Pelling and R. M. Smith (eds), *Life, Death and the Elderly: Historical Perspectives*, London, 1991, pp. 194–221.

17  For criticisms of Thomson's views see E. H. Hunt, 'Paupers and pensioners, past and present', *Ageing and Society*, 1989, vol. 9, pp. 407–30.

18  For a similar view of the Old Poor Law's noteworthy generosity, see K. D. M. Snell, *Annals of the Labouring Poor: Social Change and Agrarian England 1600–1900*, Cambridge, 1985, pp. 104–9. See also W. Newman-Brown, 'The receipt of poor relief and family situation, Aldenham, Hertfordshire, 1630–90', in R. M. Smith (ed.), *Land, Kinship and Life-Cycle*, Cambridge, 1984, pp. 123–43.

19  E. A. Wrigley, R. S. Davies, J. E. Oeppen and R. S. Schofield, *English Population History from Family Reconstitutions 1580–1837*, Cambridge, 1997.

20  The recent research of Dr S. A. King of Oxford Brookes University on the Poor Law records of Lancashire and West Yorkshire is beginning to rectify this imbalance.

21  M. Barker-Read, 'The treatment of the aged poor in five selected west Kent parishes from settlement to Speenhamland (1662–1797)', Unpublished Ph.D. thesis, Open University, 1988.

22 The relevant evidence is to be found in E. A. Wrigley and R. S. Schofield, *The Population History of England 1541–1871: A Reconstruction*, London, 1981, pp. 215–19.
23 Ibid., pp. 219–28.
24 R. M. Smith, 'Les influences exogènes sur le "frein préventif" en Angleterre 1600–1750', in A. Blum *et al.* (eds), *Modèles de Démographie Historique*, Paris, 1992, pp. 173–91.
25 Slack, *Poverty and Policy in Tudor and Stuart England*, p. 174.
26 Oxfordshire County Record Office, Shipton-under-Wychwood Poor Accounts, 1740–61
27 J. Boulton, 'Going on the parish: the parish pension and its meaning in the London suburbs, 1640–1724', in Hitchcock *et al.*, *The Voices and Strategies of the English Poor*, pp. 22–4.
28 D. Thomson, 'The decline of social welfare: falling state support for the elderly since early Victorian times', *Ageing and Society*, 1984, vol. 4, p. 468.
29 For evidence revealing a larger role for charities relative to rate-based poor relief in urban centres and even relatively small market towns see the following: Barker-Read, 'The treatment of the aged poor', p. 287; P. Sharpe, 'Gender-specific demographic adjustment to changing economic circumstances: Colyton 1538–1837', Unpublished Ph.D. thesis, University of Cambridge, 1988, pp. 103–17; J. Innes, 'The "mixed economy of welfare" in early modern England: assessments of the options from Hale to Malthus', in Daunton (ed.), *Charity, Self-interest and Welfare in the English Past*, pp. 139–80; A. Tomkins, 'The experience of urban poverty: a comparison of Oxford and Shrewsbury 1740–70', Unpublished D.Phil. thesis, University of Oxford, 1994; G. B. Hindle, *Provision for the Relief of the Poor in Manchester 1754–1826*, Cheetham Society, Manchester, 1975, pp. 141–69.
30 This is an issue which has recently attracted a good deal of debate in relation to discussions about the character of English poor relief, in particular the question of how far it might be supposed that a national 'system' existed in the eighteenth century. For advocacy of a coherent and remarkably well-integrated set of practices in contrast to provisions in much of continental Europe see the case made by P. Solar, 'Poor relief and English economic development before the industrial revolution', *Economic History Review*, 1995, vol. 48, pp. 1–22. Steven King has argued forcefully that practices in northern parishes were fundamentally unlike those further south with not only smaller pensions, smaller proportions of local populations as beneficiaries but a harsher treatment of recipients as a whole. See S. A. King, 'Poor relief and English economic development reappraised', *Economic History Review*, 1997, vol. 50, pp. 360–8, and especially, S. A. King, 'Reconstructing lives: the poor, the Poor Law, and welfare in Calverley, 1650–1820', *Social History*, 1997, vol. 22, pp. 318–38. Lower pension sums in northern parishes are certainly a feature of the evidence presented in Tables 4.7 and 4.8 above. A similar feature appears readily detectable in the evidence assembled by Sir Frederick Morton Eden, *The State of the Poor*, 3 vols, London, 1797, where information on pensions paid to 1,249 persons from thirty-two geographically widely scattered parishes is reported. Proportions of elderly pensions of all pensioners are remarkably similar across the 'sample', although somewhat lower in industrial communities, which is not surprising given that they were likely to have possessed especially youthful age structures. However, pensions paid to elderly persons in 1795 were often 1s. 0d. per week less in northern than in southern and eastern parishes. King has argued that in the rural industrial township of Calverley in West Yorkshire no more than 15 per cent of elderly persons can be traced receiving Poor Law pensions in the late eighteenth century and that there was no consistency in the patterns displayed by their pension benefits.

Elderly persons on receiving a pension in this community were not likely to proceed to remain as recipients of parish-rate funded relief with steadily rising allowances for the remainder of their lives. A recent study of Ovenden, close by Halifax in West Yorkshire, confirms the smaller size of pensions in that locality and also establishes that no more than 20 per cent of the community's elderly received Poor Law pensions. However, this study shows that upon entering the pension list elderly persons did remain there almost continuously thereafter as well as receiving a pension that grew in size as the recipient aged, contrary to King's findings in nearby Calverley. See Ottaway, ' "The decline of life" ', ch. 5. It is clear that this matter is in need of further research, although it would seem too early to conclude that the north of England was not part of a larger 'system' since the sums expended and the social incidence of provision from rate-based funds were significantly larger in most of the northern communities so far investigated and the predictability of relief greater than that discovered in most continental European situations described in the secondary literature on this subject. See P. Solar, 'Poor relief and English economic development: a renewed plea for comparative history', *Economic History Review*, 1997, vol. 50, pp. 369–74.

31  Hunt, 'Paupers and pensioners', pp. 421–3. See note 53 below.
32  Newman-Brown, 'The receipt of poor relief and family situation'; T. Wales, 'Poverty, poor relief and the life-cycle: some evidence from seventeenth-century Norfolk', in Smith (ed.), *Land, Kinship and Life-Cycle*, pp. 351–404; A. Wear, 'Caring for the sick poor in St. Bartholomew's Exchange, 1580–1676', *Medical History*, 1991, suppl. no. 11, pp. 41–60.
33  R. M. Smith, 'Welfare and the management of demographic uncertainty', in M. Keynes *et al.* (eds), *The Political Economy of Health and Welfare*, London, 1988, p. 130.
34  Wrigley and Schofield, *The Population History of England*, pp. 332–6.
35  Barker-Read, 'The treatment of the aged poor', pp. 66–7.
36  See the pioneering work of Samantha Williams, 'Medical care and demographic context in East Bedfordshire in the late eighteenth century', Unpublished M.Sc. thesis, University of Oxford, 1994, now further developed as chapter 5 of her forthcoming University of Cambridge Ph.D. thesis, 'Poor relief and medical provision in Bedfordshire: the social, economic and demographic contexts, c. 1750–1850'.
37  Barker-Read, 'The treatment of the aged poor', pp. 99–104.
38  Wear, 'Caring for the sick poor in St. Bartholomew's Exchange', p. 48.
39  Ibid., pp. 48–9.
40  For an exemplary statement of such a position see L. Stone, *The Family, Sex and Marriage in England 1500–1800*, London, 1977, pp. 148–9.
41  The most sophisticated set of reflections on this issue can be found in J. Finch, *Family Obligations and Social Change*, Cambridge, 1989, pp. 57–85. See also R. M. Smith, 'Charity, self-interest and welfare: reflections from demographic and family history', in Daunton (ed.), *Charity, Self-interest and Welfare*, pp. 43–5.
42  Such a view is also fully compatible with a more positive view of the Old Poor Law's role in promoting economic growth and social development in seventeenth- and eighteenth-century England which is represented in its most provocative and stimulating form in Solar, 'Poor relief and English economic development'.
43  These are developments which have been detected in a number of case studies. See Newman-Brown, 'The receipt of poor relief and family situation', pp. 409–11; Wales, 'Poverty, poor relief and the life-cycle', pp. 353–8; Slack, *Poverty and Policy in Tudor and Stuart England*, pp. 173–82.
44  P. Slack, *The English Poor Law 1531–1782*, London, 1990, pp. 29–34.

45  Ibid., pp. 53–6.
46  Sir F. M. Eden, *The State of the Poor*, vol. 3 , London, 1797, pp. 693–6.
47  Barker-Read, 'The treatment of the aged poor', pp. 160–94. See also the detailed analysis of pension payments in relation to wheat prices in the parishes of Terling (Essex) and Puddletown (Dorset) in the second half of the eighteenth century. In both parishes there was a significant decline in the 'value' of pensions given the severe price inflation that was being experienced, Ottaway, ' "The decline of life" ', pp. 250–7.
48  T. Hitchcock, 'Paupers and preachers: the SPCK and the parochial workhouse movement', in L. Davison *et al.* (eds), *Still the Grumbling Hive: The Response to Social and Economic Problems in England 1689–1750*, Stroud, 1992, p. 163.
49  T. Sokoll, 'The household position of elderly widows in poverty. Evidence from two Essex communities in the late eighteenth century', in J. Henderson and R. Wall (eds), *Poor Women and Children in the European Past*, London, 1994, pp. 207–24; T. Sokoll, 'The pauper household: small and simple? The evidence from listings of inhabitants and pauper lists in early modern England reassessed', *Ethnologia Europaea*, 1987, vol. 17, pp. 21–33; T. Sokoll, *Household and Family Among the Poor: The Case of Two Essex Communities in the Late Eighteenth and Early Nineteenth Centuries*, Bochum, 1992, ch. 2.
50  Ottaway's research on Terling and Puddletown points in the same direction. In Puddletown the number of old men on assistance rose just as the number of old female paupers declined in the final decade of the eighteenth century. Her chronologically more extensive analysis of Terling's Poor Law accounts and vestry minutes than is attempted in this chapter shows that although the number of women receiving relief relative to men held up in the late eighteenth century, the proportion of relief by value going to males rose significantly. Furthermore, whereas female pensions in both communities stagnated, the weekly payments to males increased. See Ottaway, ' "The decline of life" ', ch. 4.
51  William Otter, 'Memoir of Robert Malthus', published with posthumous 2nd edn of Malthus' *Principles of Political Economy*, London, 1816, pp. xxi–xxii.
52  As suggested in the exhaustive analysis by Ottaway, ' "The decline of life" ', ch. 2.
53  A. Sen, *Inequality Reexamined*, Oxford, 1992, pp. 39–53. In her current research (forthcoming University of Cambridge Ph.D. thesis, 'Poor relief and medical provision'), Samantha Williams has found that in the Bedfordshire village of Campton female beneficiaries increased absolutely in number from 1780 to 1813, although their proportional significance was declining steadily. From 1814 the elderly displayed a noteworthy increase in their relative importance in the pensioner list. This growing prominence was particularly characteristic of elderly male pensioners. Williams concludes that this development most likely reflects an increasing discrimination against elderly male farm labourers in an overstocked agrarian labour market, and sensibly suggests that it would be appropriate to regard these benefits as unemployment or disability payments rather than retirement pensions *per se*. In reaching such a conclusion she is clearly offering support to the position of Hunt in his criticism of Thomson's treatment of the pension in the decades immediately after 1834 (see note 17 above).

# 5 Balancing social and cultural approaches to the history of old age and ageing in Europe

## A review and an example from post-Revolutionary France

*David G. Troyansky*

The history of old age has sometimes been offered as yet another example of the fragmentation of historical research into an increasing number of subspecialities. However, historians working on old age and ageing have found that these topics demand multidisciplinary treatment. Far from producing a subspeciality that has little to do with other historical endeavours, the history of old age has encouraged an attempt to balance social and cultural history at a time when those fields appear to be at odds with each other.

Even in the history of old age, however, the balance may go awry, as Peter Stearns contends has happened in recent work favouring cultural history at the expense of social history. The occasion for that complaint was a long review of the survey of the history of old age from the ancient world to the sixteenth century by Georges Minois.[1] That book was emblematic of early attempts at surveying the landscape in any number of subdisciplines, for it tended to slide back and forth between cultural and social approaches and to try on and abandon formulae for putting those approaches together. Thus, Minois played with ideas of the relative security of the aged based upon their percentage of the total population and with representations of elders in different social, cultural and political contexts. He offered little, however, on household structure, family types or control of property. Part of the problem was that the survey was premature – perhaps this is how we operate as historians, beginning with premature surveys, attacking them when we discover their inadequacy, and finding few satisfactory ways of generalising once we actually know something – but part of the problem lay in its inconsistency and lack of a thesis. In Stearns' words, 'there is no ultimate handle' (p. 269).

Paul Johnson's introduction to this volume may be more to Stearns' liking, as it has a handle, and it is very much a social one. Although 'status', in Johnson's text, involves a great deal of cultural construction, the themes of participation, well-being and status are all classic social historical categories that transcend the history of old age and ageing. They are heavily weighted towards issues, such as employment, property ownership and the transmission of household authority, that have been crucial in the development of a history of old age in England.[2] Indeed, except for some medieval work on the ages of man, the English literature has had little in common with the concerns of Minois and others working on the European continent.[3]

This chapter examines the degree to which research on early modern old age and ageing has been characterised by one or another imbalance and the possibility of transcending disciplinary divisions between social and cultural history. Eventually it proposes a way of uniting those approaches and presents as one example my current work on retirement in the early nineteenth century. Along the way, it also addresses the usefulness of Johnson's categories for early modern society. They are clearly appropriate for studying the nineteenth and twentieth centuries. The first two are crucial, as the roles of work and health have become so important in the modern world of ageing. But in early modern society, participation and well-being may best be understood in moral rather than economic terms. At least that is how early modern representations of old age would treat such categories. Of course we can and must still ask what percentage of artisans or peasants over a particular age continued to be active, and social historical investigations have revealed different patterns of 'stepping down', the emergence of institutions dedicated to the care of the elderly, and the impact on older Europeans of particular regimes of marriage, remarriage and inheritance.[4] But the category of old age was constructed in moral ways to laud and censure forms of behaviour deemed appropriate and inappropriate.

Historians working in the vein of Minois – actually they are continuing in the tradition of Philippe Ariès, with all his brilliance and all his naïvety, whether in his work on childhood or on death[5] – have been tempted by the variety of topics to be treated under the rubric of old age: demography, family, religion, art, death, medicine, retirement, the state, etc. Casting our nets widely has been a good way of avoiding anachronism. We have sought how the very idea of old age was constituted in the past rather than applying twentieth-century definitions. By looking at a range of materials, moreover, we may discover that old chronologies do not work. Any break between early modern and modern worlds may or may not correspond to traditional political or cultural turning points, and a totalising chronology will probably prove illusory. Nevertheless, some political events, whether creating new opportunities or catastrophe, clearly have changed the situation for the aged. One thinks naturally of world wars and great depressions as well as of welfare state legislation, but shortly I will refer to an earlier experience of revolution and restoration.

Stearns is right about the problems in Minois. But many of us have gone down that path, particularly scholars working on the European continent, and for good reason. We have seen material on old age, testimony about individual lives, prescriptive literature on how one ought to age, graphic representations of classic tropes of youth and age. The art historical materials go well beyond mere repetition of *Die Lebenstreppe* as is revealed in the catalogue of a Dutch exhibition on old age, which includes images juxtaposing youth and age and enforcing social and sexual norms whose transgression might be studied through demographic data, thus permitting a link between the social and the cultural.[6] We have recognised the existence of institutions that catered to, among others, the older people of early modern times. We have seen a range in treatment of elderly characters in literature and a fascination with longevity in science. All of these approaches to the history of old age are worth making. The problem lies in putting them together. And Minois, perhaps in spite of himself, demonstrates just how difficult that is. Pat Thane makes the point more consciously.[7]

Paralleling the work of Minois in France is Peter Borscheid's work on early modern Germany.[8] He too uses the widest range of sources and tries to gather from other kinds of research what life was like for the aged. While he provides more than Minois on family and household structure, his categories are very much the literary/moral ones. Indeed, he briefly compares Catholic and Protestant views, with a Reformed German culture encouraging the emergence of a kind of patriarchy in which the father is a stand-in for God (p. 32). How that symbolism plays out psychohistorically has not been addressed by historians of old age, but the creation of the ideal patriarch is his central early modern theme.[9] In Borscheid's account, patriarchy is encouraged even more in the rebuilding of central European society after the Thirty Years War. But this time the key institution cuts across confessional differences, as his story of the civilisation process, relying upon Norbert Elias and Jean-Louis Flandrin, is one of an increasingly absolutist state. Parental authority parallels political authority. Religion plays a role again in the eighteenth-century Pietist desire to reform the world, which complements an Enlightenment urge. But as he gets closer to the nineteenth century, Borscheid attempts to use demographic and economic categories. The cluster of works on France in the eighteenth century displays the same intention and the same problems.[10] Attention shifts from cultural representations, including that of old age as social problem, to social policy. For Simone de Beauvoir, the history of representations was a history of lies, for Minois a history of distorting lenses. The key is to figure out what the leading distortions were and how they functioned.

Work on the eighteenth century describes a shift from ridicule to respect. It does not mean behaviour changed in any particular way, but it does mark a shift in image on both sides of the Rhine in a period of greater longevity and secularisation. This chronology fits conveniently with the history of childhood and the family. It confirms the idea of a 'creation' of man and society, of modern politics, and of a modern politics of the family.[11] Without falling into the trap of anachronism, one may see in the French Revolutionary period a new social and political view of the life course and anticipations of the welfare state. The discovery or construction of social problems, however, seems to allow social historians to ignore culture.

Consider the difference between Borscheid's book and Josef Ehmer's social history, which dispenses completely with cultural materials.[12] Ehmer's work is all about social policy, demands by organised labour, working-class households, now more thoroughly studied by Christoph Conrad,[13] and the welfare state. Jean-Pierre Bois and Jean-Pierre Gutton kept high cultural materials in their sections on the early modern period, but set them aside in their treatments of the nineteenth century. The only work that uses them in any sustained way is an unpublished *mémoire de maîtrise* which remains in the world of literature.[14] The *thèses* of Gilles Pollet and Bruno Dumons essentially concern the emergence of modern retirement.[15] Dumons has traced the retirement experiences of civil servants in the Lyons area, examining where they went, how long they lived, and what material resources they possessed. Until we have comparative data, the work will remain a rich regional description. Pollet's thesis begins to suggest that the idea of retirement emerging from the Enlightenment and the development of the public sector provided a new model for the life course, but then he focuses on social policy, losing track of early modern models. This is understandable. After all, demographic ageing – politically defined as Patrice Bourdelais shows us[16] – and the *spread* of retirement are modern 'social problems'. So the modern treatments of a culture of ageing are few and far between. Bourdelais begins to explore the medicalisation of cultural representations, but there is little cultural history in his book. The modern literature has been influenced by sociologists like Martin Kohli and Anne-Marie Guillemard, who have described retirement as a way of managing old age in a world of work.[17] But recent evidence of a greater separation between retirement and old age has thrown this literature into some disarray.[18]

Several contributions to the Pelling and Smith book and various chapters in this volume demonstrate the folly of restricting the history of old age to the last hundred years and to the logic of the welfare state. Studies of retirement since the Middle Ages suggest that questions about career, retirement and public institutions need to be placed in a long-term historical context.[19] But one gets the sense in reading Peter Laslett, Thane or Conrad that the history that counts really begins in the contemporary period.[20] For Laslett, it is a matter of marking a fundamental demographic change; for others, the cultural approach seems to be worth taking mainly to remedy the absence of other kinds of evidence. I would suggest taking seriously the more modern cultural representations and, on the question of retirement, pushing back the chronology by looking at the role of early modern institutions that catered to the elderly and have left sources that permit both social and cultural approaches. Among them were religious institutions, whose records also yield important information on gender and ageing,[21] but here I will focus on the state. Ehmer describes the development of pensions in the Austrian state, Bois demonstrates the importance of the French state, and even the Spanish empire in Mexico has been studied for its contribution to bureaucracy and social welfare.[22] The familiar part of the story is that of how the state left its mark on society; less familiar is the story of how people used the state.

The danger in privileging the state is that one allows the public sphere to determine what one learns about private life. Setters of bureaucratic rules determined to a large extent how people approached the state with their life histories and demands for pensions. But the state was not so completely in control of how people making demands reconstructed their lives. It created an opportunity for relatively privileged individuals to create a sense of their own lives as coherent and meaningful. By using testimony addressed to the state, we are getting at the questions of meaning that Thomas Cole has raised in the American case.[23] He has employed religious and medical texts to tell a story of secularisation. Here I am suggesting the importance of state institutions and ideas of career in the secularisation of the life review and life history.

The French state is a particularly promising area for such investigation. Guy Thuillier has been exploring the bureaucratic angle on French pensions in the nineteenth century and has distinguished between recompense and right, but has still written policy history while hinting at something more.[24] Elise Feller has begun to mine bureaucratic sources from the early twentieth century in the Parisian public transport industry for clues about life experiences.[25] My own current work examines the case of the Justice Ministry in post-Revolutionary France. The system of retirement pensions and widows' and orphans' assistance provides material on people's notions of ageing. The self-portraits of postulants demanding pensions use the stock of representations described in cultural historical studies, but they involve appropriations for individual purposes, especially the desire to convince the ministry to part with money.

When I wrote on changing representations of old age in the eighteenth century, I described a shift from Augustinian to Ciceronian ideas. It should come as no surprise that judges describing their ageing had recourse to Cicero's apology. Magistrates and others pursuing public service were precisely the kinds of individuals who fit Cicero's Roman model of ageing and civic virtue. For example, Gilles Joseph Deligné, an octogenarian judge in Rennes who found himself without a post after a reorganisation of the courts, headed his first demand for a new post on 5 September 1810 with a Latin quotation from *De Senectute* with French translation in a footnote. 'Good sense, reason, and prudence reside in old men. Without them there would be neither cities nor societies'.[26] He used Cicero to argue that despite his age he still had 'all the zeal and all the intellectual and moral means of continuing the functions of judge', and identified his handwriting as proof that he had not fallen into decrepitude. After observing that 'one doesn't die because one is old, but because one is a man', he returned to Cicero for an observation on the importance of continued activity and adding to Cicero's examples of active old men his own cohort of magistrates who had begun their judicial careers in the Parlement de Bretagne under the Old Regime. He then asked a rhetorical question:

> Why should old age, healthy in body and mind, which in all centuries, even among savages, has always obtained marks of veneration, become among the most humane and enlightened people in the universe (the French) an object of rejection and inconsiderateness? Isn't old age, on the contrary, the surest guarantor of maturity of judgement, of a long experience, and the most solid morality[?] I add that if there exists a passion in an honest and upright old man, it is that of dying at the post he has occupied for many years, and in which his hair has whitened. I avow that such is and will always be the dearest wish of my heart.

While Deligné's first wish was for a new post, he expressed a secondary desire to receive a retirement pension. An honourable retirement would save him from the shame and humiliation of being thought to have been fired and from the recrimination of families against whom he had rendered judgement. He fell back on a second line of argument that admitted some physical decline and the increasing difficulty of attending court for long hours and engaging in tiring legal argument that required 'young and vigorous lungs'. Two days later Deligné wrote again, describing a bad debt he had not been able to recover and apologising that his busy schedule did not leave him time to write more briefly, in a less diffuse fashion, or in a hand that, while not noticeably different to my eyes from that of the previous demand (where it was proof of competence), he characterised as clumsy and resembling that of a schoolboy. If, he concluded, he received neither a new post nor an honourable retirement, and were isolated and abandoned by the government, he would quickly die.

Three months later, having received neither a new post nor a retirement pension, Deligné tried another strategy, emphasising an infirmity that dated back twenty-one years. Recognising that physical disability might result in an entitlement, he told a story of an icy New Year's Day 1789 in Rennes, when he fell and broke his right leg, the setting of which resulted in the loss of two and a half inches of bone and a need for crutches. But this was not just any break. It was occasioned by patriotic activity. For while he had left his house in the morning to attend mass, mention of which probably neither helped nor hurt, he braved the weather at 6:00 p.m. to observe a secret 'antipatriotic' meeting of deputies of the Third Estate. 'It is evidently to my patriotic zeal for the success of our revolution that . . . I owe the unfortunate fracture of my leg.' Refusal of a pension would constitute another misfortune. He ended the letter with an accounting of his income, his dependence upon his wife, and the fact that his son-in-law had received a military pension.

The document merits more detailed analysis, for it engages in considerable anachronism, using language concerning patriotism and revolution that reveals the confusion of the era and moving between arguments for continued service and repose. When a new list of judicial appointments drawn up on 14 April 1811 did not include Deligné's name, he wrote again on the 23rd, invoking personal connections in the magistracy and seeking sympathy for his great age and poverty. When speaking of his diet as being reduced to bread and water, he added in parentheses that this was the truth. Perhaps he understood that readers of such demands were bombarded with claims, or maybe he recognised that since his last post had been a temporary one, he did not have the absolute right that some of his colleagues did. Moreover, he was writing in the Napoleonic period, when the system was still uncertain, and funding was often in short supply.

Judges demanding help revealed expectations that derived as much from memories of the Old Regime as from awareness of recent legislation and practice. They described work undertaken in every regime and presented the qualities of a good magistrate, exactitude, zeal and impartiality, as transcending political and constitutional changes. The Ministry had to determine what functions in the Old Regime constituted national service, not a simple matter. Magistrates and *fonctionnaires* had sworn oaths to various regimes. They had purchased Old Regime offices and been appointed or elected since. Loyalties multiplied as they aged. Continuity in their reconstructed careers came from identification with the magistrature itself, with an evolving idea of the state, and with single- or multigenerational narratives. Many postulants presented as a condition of their retirement that they be succeeded by their sons. Otherwise, their demands ought to be ignored. Such conditions blurred the boundary between private property and public office. People who had purchased offices in the Old Regime argued that they had never been properly reimbursed during the Revolution, and habits of thinking of the magistracy as inherited property died hard. The private/public issue has been an essential one for modern historians interested in questions of rights and citizenship, particularly eighteenth-century specialists seeking the proper context for understanding French Revolutionary notions of right, but also historians of the welfare state trying to discern the social contract underlying social legislation.[27] At what point do rights cease being privileges and become entitlements? Do people view entitlements as fulfilling a social contract or as completing a full life? Or both simultaneously?

By reading demands of officials we can gain a sense of how they viewed their careers and their ideas of proper ageing and retirement. Obviously I am not calling simply for a history of external representations but also self-images (recognising the considerable interaction between them). We must find sources that permit a look at subjective experience of ageing and/or retirement in the past. What did people want, expect and achieve in later life? What meaning did they find in retreat or retirement?

Letters to bureaucrats can be explored as a kind of autobiographical writing. Literary scholars have demonstrated that first-person writing is never pure, as it must always draw upon models of personal expression, and they have even begun to look closely at the impact of bureaucratic thinking.[28] If we learn something from them and explore the functioning of bureaucracies, we may discover how ageing individuals appropriated dominant cultural discourses in order to represent their life experiences. If modern youth was invented in the Romantic culture of the early nineteenth century, then perhaps modern age was invented in the bureaucratic culture of the same period. Some individuals may aspire in youth to a Romantic heroism of everyday life; perhaps we are all condemned (or aspire) to the ageing of the bureaucratic self. In the early nineteenth century, these histories are related. The dramatic stories recounted by ageing judges both ran to type and drew attention to themselves as exceptional. This is not a traditional history of the state, of legislation, or policies, but a history of uses of the state and constructions of the self, admittedly one skewed towards public, male experience, but with clues concerning other areas of historical experience.

The career dossiers of judges permit a study of retrospective constructions of lives and anticipations of retirement among public officials over the long term. Retiring judges wrote letters but also constructed charts, outlining their public service before, during and after the Revolution. It took several years of puzzling over home-made charts for the bureaucrats to come up with printed forms for organising the information. One of the models for such a form came from judges' demands in French-occupied Holland.[29] Another came from authorities in Tuscany.[30] Magistrates who had served in areas conquered by the French and were themselves often not of French origin served the French state until they were displaced by international treaties and administrative reorganisation. Upon retiring, they informed the Ministry in Paris of how their systems had functioned in the Old Regimes of Europe. But even as demands became more formulaic, as rules became clearer and careers themselves were more consistently represented, postulants offered elaborate justifications.

Many of the justifications included personal recommendations. Thus, who one was or who might intervene complemented what one did, but it was the service itself that was most important. Service in the Old Regime would be incorporated into a long-term career whose interruptions were often remarkably brief considering the turbulence of the period. Representation of that service, of course, depended upon the time of writing. Demands during the Napoleonic era often expressed moderate support for the Revolution. Demands during the Restoration made more of Old Regime service and loyalty to the Bourbon family. Revolutionary excesses were criticised in both periods, but they were viewed as particularly cruel in the Restoration. Nonetheless, a consistent ideal of moderation and of courageous defence of innocent people became the norm.

Pension legislation was perceived as cumulative, and circumstances encouraged the development of new norms drawing upon diverse precedents. The uncertainties of the Napoleonic period left postulants and administrators relatively free to interpret the meaning of 'right'. Napoleonic decrees of 1806 and 1807 worked out some of the bureaucratic mechanisms for retirement. The decree of 2 October 1807 provided for retirement pensions in individual cases of disability. Postulants appealed through the Ministry or directly to Napoleon. Thus, the demands were personalised and blended the languages of favour and right. They spawned debate within the magistracy. Individuals described how they thought the decrees applied to them as belonging to classes of public servants. Restoration ordinances of 1814 and 1815 created a more bureaucratic system that both responded to perceived needs and provided a model to which ageing judges might conform. Bureaucrats considered time of service, as the law specified – thirty years, or ten with infirmity – but also political, professional and personal behaviour. One man, Romer, headed the accounting department from the Napoleonic era into the 1830s. He issued reports summarising careers and determining financial need. Magistrates might earn his sympathy even as he was overseeing the evolution of a relatively objective operation. Needy magistrates cried for help using language of both traditional charity and Revolutionary welfare, but virtually all described honour and respect as essential to a good retirement. Status, participation and well-being remained moral categories.

Writers of demands bent the rules and reminisced about their years on the public stage of history. Gerontologists who have debated the role of reminiscence but agree that it would not live up to the standards of historical research fail to appreciate historians' recent attraction to subjectivity.[31] Historical actors represented their own life histories against the evolving background of public history. Some began their accounts generations back; others began with their own educations. Some presented the Old Regime as a paradise lost; others recognised how their destinies were linked to the Revolution.

Scholars have described how historians and jurists writing in the early nineteenth century made sense of the Revolutionary past.[32] Some of that historical and legal thinking made its way into autobiographical writing and the arguments of retiring magistrates. Influences ran both ways, between individual experiences and public events. Arguments about justice, paternal kindness, right, equity, welfare, humanity and need depended upon a subjective understanding of the historical moment, but much depended also upon the circumstances of retirement. Was it forced? Was it the result of warfare, institutional in-fighting, political conflict, purge, personal enmities or cutbacks in the Ministry? Was it the result of physical or mental decline? Was it desired or resisted? In some cases, judges presented the decision to retire as part of a plan for the rest of their lives. Some described decisions resulting from months or even years of planning. Others described emergencies. If the initiative did not come from the individual, unless the retirement was the result of complete disability, the judge tended to feign disbelief and describe his remarkably good health and strong desire to continue serving. Sometimes it took months or years, sometimes only a paragraph, for resistance to turn to resignation and proud acceptance. But retirement did not automatically guarantee a pension, and arguments were employed to receive the pension at an appropriate level.

At the very least, many postulants asked to be named honorary judges in their former jurisdictions. Thus, they maintained a certain status, expressed both in a formal role in civic functions and in still being listed in the Imperial or Royal Almanac. While some judges wrote generally of a time of repose, others described a classical return to the country and a humanist retirement to the study. But intellectual labours required the material means that post-Revolutionary magistrates often claimed not to have. Lists of publications and samples of legal, historical and literary work accompanied some demands. Maintenance of a Ciceronian model of retirement would require state support.[33]

The model retirement for a magistrate might have been peaceful, but it followed an active life described in terms of adventure and pathos. Ageing magistrates employed tales of heroic acts and family woes to sway bureaucrats. The heroism involved standing up to terrorists and fighting brigands and draft resisters. The family woes included illness, bankruptcy and the premature deaths of sons in military service. Letters blended statements of loyalty to the regime, an accounting of lives used up or sacrificed, and estimates of the cost of leading a suitable life in retirement.

These men knew how to tell a story, how to shape their reminiscences, and, most impressively, how to complain. They made themselves the heroes of their time. But they also sought sympathy, describing disabilities, misfortunes and poverty. They claimed that poverty itself brought no shame – losing wealth while serving the public suggested virtuous behaviour – but described a shame that might redound to the magistracy and public service if their misery were widely known. We need not accept their stories as unvarnished truth in order to consider them examples of how some ageing men in the early nineteenth century represented their lives. Their subjective understanding of their lives and times infiltrated their objective arguments about recompense and entitlement. Letters from widows and occasionally daughters indicate a gendered distinction between public and private life and a difference in the degree of complaint.[34] The men spoke of politics, loss of property, honour, and even expenses incurred in moving from post to post. The women sought the paternal support of emperor or king and talked about the education of children, something that lasted a long time in the old demographic regime. Their relative unwillingness or inability to complain was in part a function of a weaker right, in part a function of inexperience with rhetorical tools. Some right was implied by ordinance, but it was not absolutely assured. Some women referred to contributions made by their own families. Many more described the need to educate and establish children and grandchildren.

What of the credibility of postulants' accounts? The Ministry faced the same problem that confronts the historian. Documentary evidence was required for time of service, and confidential reports were sometimes requested of colleagues or local administrators. Medical certification also became part of the process. While some postulants claimed that age itself should be proof of deterioration, a medical discourse about the particular hazards of the magistracy and of the ageing of the magistrate evolved. Falling off a horse or cart while on judicial business had immediate consequences, but the more sedentary labours of judges also could be life threatening. Doctors and surgeons described the strokes and heart attacks, gout and asthma, blindness, deafness and paralysis, the difficulty urinating that caused pain, or the incontinence that kept a judge at home. But they went beyond describing illness or disability, and argued that the job itself caused the disability. Long hours of work in unhealthy environments, the emotional strain of the court, and the need to learn new law codes took their toll. Medical arguments passed from doctor and surgeon to judge, colleagues and bureaucrats. Occasionally contradictory testimony made its way into the dossier, and sometimes a medical practitioner seemed to write just what the judge ordered, as in cases where he desired either to be succeeded by a son or to continue working – the certificate indicates that retirement, though desirable, was not yet medically necessary. Whatever the evidentiary status of the medical certificate, and whatever the peculiarity of the magistrature, the physical and 'psychological' descriptions of the ageing of magistrates combined representations of a particular group of individuals and of physiological processes that applied to everyone. Their summing up anticipated that of broader populations in the later nineteenth and twentieth centuries.

In reconstructing careers, remembering and describing lives, and making demands, civil servants blazed a trail for other citizens. They reviewed their lives in a decidedly secular fashion and addressed the state, which was in a position to reward them for their contribution. In another anticipation of the welfare state, French ministries began to withhold a percentage from salaries in order to amass a pension fund. *Fonctionnaires'* contributions were, thus, both monetary and professional. Public discussion of pension funds and entitlement had already begun; civil servants, including magistrates, pioneered a territory that more and more citizens would occupy.

The idea of entitlement, based both on social policy and on individual life experiences as constructed for state authorities, is one that has a long history that remains to be written. When written, it might work at two levels. First, as has been explored in this chapter, is the level of elites and servants of the state, borrowing from various past models, hijacking Enlightenment and Revolutionary notions of human rights, and constructing coherent careers. Second is that of the less privileged, those for whom old age is often presented simply as one of the times of life associated with poverty. How at that second level was old age experienced and culturally constructed by Europe's working classes? The temptation is to fall back on the social scientific model. In his review article, Stearns even has Minois doing that: 'Minois clearly intends his history to help improve attitudes toward the elderly today, though he suggests that modern society already does better than its antecedents by using social science – *real data* – *rather than just literary images*' (p. 264 [my emphasis]). How curious that Stearns manages to enlist even Minois in the call for a social scientific approach to old age! Perhaps we might go beyond the distinction between 'real data' and 'just literary images'. What images described by Minois or Borscheid are employed by social actors in the nineteenth and twentieth centuries? Is there any logic to them? Our discussions of social and cultural categories transcend the subfield of the history of old age and ageing, and concern the most basic historiographical questions of the 1990s.

## Notes

1 Peter N. Stearns, 'Review article', in *History and Theory*, 1991, vol. 30, pp. 261–70; Georges Minois, *Histoire de la vieillesse*, Paris, 1987, trans. as *History of Old Age*, Chicago, 1989. This paragraph and some other brief passages are drawn from my 'Progress report: the history of old age in the western world', in *Ageing and Society*, 1996, vol. 16, pp. 233–43, reprinted with permission of Cambridge University Press.

2 Margaret Pelling and Richard M. Smith (eds), *Life, Death and the Elderly: Historical Perspectives*, London, 1991.

3 John A. Burrow, *The Ages of Man: A Study in Medieval Writing and Thought*, Oxford, 1986; see also Elizabeth Sears, *The Ages of Man: Medieval Interpretations of the Life Cycle*, Princeton, NJ, 1986.

4 Other chapters address these issues, but see also the articles in David I. Kertzer and Warner K. Schaie (eds), *Age Structuring in Comparative Perspective*, Hillsdale, NJ, 1989; Jacques Dupâquier (ed.), *Marriage and Remarriage in Populations of the Past*, London, 1981; *Annales de démographie historique, 1985: Vieillir autrefois*; *Annales de démographie historique, 1991: Grands-Parents, Aïeux*.

5 Philippe Ariès, *Centuries of Childhood*, New York, 1962; idem, *The Hour of Our Death*, New York, 1981.

6 Annemarie de Wildt and Willem van der Ham, *Tijd van Leven: Ouder worden in Nederland vroeger en nu*, Amsterdam, 1993.

7 Pat Thane, 'Old age in English history', in Christoph Conrad and Hans-Joachim von Kondratowitz (eds), *Zur Kulturgeschichte des Alterns/Toward a Cultural History of Aging*, Berlin, 1993, pp. 17–37.

8 Peter Borscheid, *Geschichte des Alters 16.–18. Jahrhundert*, Münster, 1987.

9 See particularly chapter 5: 'Alter als Autorität'.

10 David G. Troyansky, *Old Age in the Old Regime: Image and Experience in Eighteenth-Century France*, Ithaca, NY, 1989; Jean-Pierre Bois, *Les vieux: de Montaigne aux premières retraites*, Paris, 1989; Jean-Pierre Gutton, *Naissance du vieillard: Essai sur l'histoire des rapports entre les vieillards et la société en France*, Paris, 1988.

11 Margaret Darrow, in a review of my book in the *Journal of Social History*, suggested that politics was the way of tying together cultural and social changes

in the history of old age; her own exploration of the impact of the French Revolution on the family in one major town, *Revolution in the House* (Princeton, NJ, 1989), neatly identified long-term and short-term changes in relations between spouses, between siblings and between parents and children, thus permitting a domestic view of liberty, equality and fraternity.

12  Josef Ehmer, *Sozialgeschichte des Alters*, Frankfurt, 1990.

13  Christoph Conrad, *Vom Greis zum Rentner: Der Strukturwandel des Alters in Deutschland zwischen 1830 und 1930*, Göttingen, 1994.

14  Natalie Steiwer, 'Le personnage du vieillard dans le discours littéraire au XIXème siècle', Maîtrise d'histoire, 1990, sous la direction de Michelle Perrot, Université de Paris 7.

15  Gilles Pollet, 'Les retraites en France, 1880–1914: la naissance d'une politique sociale', Université de Lyon 2, 1990; Bruno Dumons, 'Les retraites sous la troisième république: Lyon et sa région (1880–1914). Population, modes de vie et comportements', Université de Lyon 2, 1990.

16  Patrice Bourdelais, *Le nouvel âge de la vieillesse: histoire du vieillissement de la population*, Paris, 1993.

17  Martin Kohli, 'Ageing as a challenge for sociological theory', *Ageing and Society*, 1988, vol. 8, pp. 367–94; *idem*, 'The world we forgot: a historical review of the life course', in V. W. Marshall (ed.), *Later Life: The Social Psychology of Aging*, Beverly Hills, CA, 1986, pp. 271–303; Anne-Marie Guillemard, *La retraite: une mort sociale*, Paris, 1973; *idem*, *Le déclin du social: formation et crise des politiques de la vieillesse*, Paris, 1986.

18  Anne-Marie Guillemard *et al.* (eds), *Entre travail, retraite et vieillesse: Le grand écart*, Paris, 1995.

19  See Andrejs Plakans, 'Stepping down in former times: a comparative assessment of "retirement" in traditional Europe', Aage Sorensen, 'Old age, retirement, and inheritance', and Maris A. Vinovskis, 'Stepping down in former times: the view from colonial and 19th-century America', in Kertzer and Schaie, *Age Structuring*, pp. 175–225.

20  Peter Laslett, *A Fresh Map of Life: The Emergence of the Third Age*, London, 1989.

21  I thank Sherri Klassen for sending me chapters of her work in progress, 'Aging gracefully in the eighteenth century: a study of elderly women in Old Regime Toulouse', Unpublished Ph.D. thesis, Syracuse University.

22  D. S. Chandler, *Social Assistance and Bureaucratic Politics: The Montepíos of Colonial Mexico, 1767–1821*, Albuquerque, NM, 1991.

23  Thomas R. Cole, *The Journey of Life: A Cultural History of Aging in America*, Cambridge, 1992.

24  Most recently, see Guy Thuillier, *Les pensions de retraite des fonctionnaires au XIXème siècle*, Paris, 1994.

25  Elise Feller, 'Agents et retraités des transports parisiens: trajectoires individuelles et changement social dans l'entre-deux-guerres', *Mémoires et Documents*, Vincennes: Mission Archives de la RATP, 1994.

26  Deligné's dossier is found in Archives Nationales, BB25 5. Most of the dossiers used in the study are catalogued in series BB25, but some Napoleonic-era correspondence is found in BB2 10.

27  For eighteenth-century ideas of right that cut across Old Regime and Revolution, see the articles of David Bien and Thomas Kaiser in Dale Van Kley (ed.), *The French Idea of Freedom: The Old Regime and the Declaration of Rights of 1789*, Stanford, CA, 1994; on the evolving civic order, see Isser Woloch, *The New Regime: Transformations of the French Civic Order, 1789–1820s*, New York, 1994. On the welfare state, see Peter Baldwin, *The Politics of Social Solidarity: Class Bases of the European Welfare State 1875–1975*, Cambridge, 1990; Susan

Pedersen, *Family Dependence, and the Origins of the Welfare State: Britain and France, 1914–1945*, Cambridge, 1993; Seth Koven and Sonya Michel (eds), *Mothers of a New World: Maternalist Politics and the Origins of Welfare States*, New York, 1993.

28 See the articles devoted to 'Bureaux and bureaucrats: literature and social theory', in *L'Esprit Créateur*, Spring 1994, vol. 34.

29 The first cartons of series BB25 include many such dossiers. It is worth noting that Bourdelais' discussion of divisions of populations into age groups finds the earliest examples in French Canada before they were taken up in France.

30 See, for example, Barli, BB2 10.

31 See Marc Kaminsky, 'The uses of reminiscence: a discussion of the formative literature', in Marc Kaminsky (ed.), *The Uses of Reminiscence: New Ways of Working with Older Adults*, New York, 1984, p. 156.

32 See, for example, Donald R. Kelley, *Historians and the Law in Postrevolutionary France*, Princeton, NJ, 1984.

33 For particular examples, see David G. Troyansky, 'Old age, retirement, and the social contract in 18th- and 19th-century France', in Conrad and von Kondratowitz (eds), *Zur Kulturgeschichte des Alterns*, pp. 77–95, and 'Retraite, vieillesse, et contrat social: l'exemple des juges de la Haute-Vienne sous la Restauration', in Guillemard *et al.* (eds), *Entre travail, retraite et vieillesse*, pp. 85–101.

34 See David G. Troyansky, '"I was Wife and Mother". French widows present themselves to the Ministry of Justice in the early nineteenth century', published in Dutch in Monique Stavenuiter *et al.* (eds), *Lange levens, stille getuigen: Oudere vrouwen in het verleden*, Zuthpen, 1995, pp. 118–32.

# 6 The ageing of the population
## Relevant question or obsolete notion?[1]

*Patrice Bourdelais*

Just as temperature is measured in degrees and distance in metres, it has been accepted that a population's evolution can be assessed by its ageing. Each month for the past twenty years or so, the press has produced a batch of articles on how France's future is being jeopardised by its ageing citizens: its pension funds will soon be empty, its economic competitiveness and general dynamism weakened, and costs for health and social services will soar. No one would contest, however, that the contemporary sexagenarian has little resemblance to counterparts living between the wars and still less to ancestors from the early nineteenth century. The sexagenarian's expectations of enjoying good health in the years ahead have risen considerably, and his or her place in successive generations has become central. Is there not a glaring contradiction between these changes in age's reality and the notion of an 'ageing' population? It is the notion's scientific pertinence, which for half a century has been built on unchanging statistical categories, that I should like to examine here, as well as the principal consequences of its utilisation.

The history of the French population's ageing is usually summed up in a few figures: in 1750–70, men having reached their 60th birthdays represented only 7 to 8 per cent of the population; in 1860, their proportion rose to 10 per cent; in the first years of the twentieth century, to 12 per cent; then to 14 per cent in 1946; and to more than 15 per cent from 1968 to 1975. The figure shown by the 1982 census fell slightly and temporarily only because of the arrival of the small cohorts born during the First World War. The growing proportion of women living beyond 60 has been even more striking. Until the Second Empire, it was close to that of men. But by the outbreak of the First World War, it was already at 13.5 per cent and reached 16 per cent in 1946. Between 1960 and 1970, it surpassed 21 per cent. One certitude has generally accompanied this observation: the precocity and extent of voluntary birth control have hastened the evolution towards a prematurely ageing population, a condition synonymous with decline. There would be no need, then, to seek other explanations for France's poor performance during the late nineteenth-century crisis, or for the society's waning dynamism. The past and the present weigh on the future. Described as an inexorable 'growing danger', the ageing population's further expansion, we are being warned, is inevitable in the first half of the twenty-first century and will result in numerous economic and social difficulties. Hence, France's misfortunes might be attributed to the egoistic couples who limit their descendants and, consequently, cause the population to age at the expense of their country's economic strength and international position.

To refuse to criticise the notion of an ageing population, to accept this kind of calculation and the fixedness of age categories, is simply an admission that the threshold for old age has not evolved for more than 200 years and will not change for the next fifty, that the starting point of 60 years is immutable. It implies that the significance of age does not evolve historically, that it does not constitute an historical variable. The different ages in life – childhood, adolescence and old age – have inspired many works, but the thresholds defining them appear to have escaped historical development.

## The old age of individuals, ageing of the population

Although old age has always been clearly identified as a stage in life, it became a statistical category only at the end of the seventeenth century, with the reinforcement of the royal state. Colbert introduced it into the colonial administration so as to divide the population according to a dominant criterion: the capacity to bear arms. Gregory King shared his concern and chose the age of 60 as the upper limit for 'fighting men'. The result was a somewhat negative definition of the old as those who could no longer bear arms, which conformed to the conception of a 60 year old in the seventeenth century. The Enlightenment gradually confirmed this threshold: Cicero, who was then fashionable with the French elite, had also thought that old age began at 60. But elderly people were restored to favour by the same elite, and acquired a positive image, which was a decisive break with western tradition. The cultural rupture was concomitant with a demographic upheaval. In the eighteenth century, the more affluent were two to three times more likely to reach their 60th birthday. And the difference in life expectancy persisted beyond that age. This major change in humanity's history was accompanied by a mutation in sensitivities, in perceptions of life and its different ages that transformed the conception of the older generation's role and position in society. Having become venerable, the older generation was charged with educating the younger generations whom it made aware of historical changes and to whom it transmitted the memory of the past.

Reintegrated into society and family, given meaningful functions because old age was no longer synonymous with decrepitude, old people began to be actively esteemed. There arose the first attempts to establish pension schemes, not simply as forms of relief, but as manifestations of the state's, and then the nation's, indebtedness to old people for their past labours. Such a reintegration, which resulted in social conflicts and concern about the financial costs for the rest of society, was bound to highlight the issue of old age in new terms.

Throughout the nineteenth century, the French statistical services never questioned whether the age of 60 did indeed announce the onset of old age. The ongoing concern for estimating human potential was again illustrated just after the Franco-Prussian War when each age group's evolution began to be scrupulously observed at every census. An overall diagnosis of the French population's health was based on the analysis of relative variations within the three broad categories: youth (0–14), adults (15–59) and elderly (over 60). The notion of population ageing, first used by Alfred Sauvy only in 1928, cannot be understood without referring to those final decades in the nineteenth century when the French elite became profoundly worried about the population's future, about its capacity to compete with its neighbours. The optimism of the eighteenth century became a thing of the past. Geriatric studies, sociological surveys, realistic novels, workers' demands and the establishment of pension funds helped to reverse the perception of old age, which once again came to be associated with ebbing strength, decrepitude and decline. In this context, the increasing population of old people was at first interpreted positively, as an indication of French civilisation's excellence. But after 1880, the issue became more questionable, indeed worrisome, because the falling birth rate's effect was underscored, and the economic responsibility of caring for the older generations was viewed with foreboding.

Jacques Bertillon, one of the founders of the Alliance pour l'accroissement de la Population Française (Alliance for the Growth of the French Population) in 1896, spent the last years of the nineteenth century turning out publications destined to alert public opinion to the disastrous consequences of a reduced fertility. A few months after the Alliance's creation, he protested against what he considered an overoptimistic report by Leroy-Beaulieu, who had pointed out that the birth rate was falling in all civilised countries.[2] He also contested the thesis held by many French hygienists and doctors who argued that a determined struggle against mortality, then possible thanks to scientific progress, would partly compensate for the reduced birth rate's effects. Bertillon emphasised the limited nature of the foreseeable gains given the birth deficit's extent. Even if the hygienists were to succeed in reducing mortality, he asked, 'will they have contributed to population growth?' Bertillon's answer left no hope that they would: 'Demography teaches us that this drop in mortality would be followed, everything else being equal, by a fall in the birth rate. Therefore, the population would be older and feebler, but not more numerous.'

Rather than the pertinence of demographic arguments, it is the logical linking that matters here. When Jacques Bertillon concluded that there would be 'an older population', comparing it with a living being, he was breaking new ground and opening the way for the idea that 'a population ages'. When he juxtaposed 'older' and 'feebler', he was abandoning the eighteenth century's optimistic perception by establishing a causal link between the rise in the population's average age and its greater physical fragility. Then in a parable based on botany, Bertillon disclosed the inspiration for his argument:

> A human society might even be compared to a forest of a given surface. After the lumberman has made clearings, seedlings spontaneously burgeon anew and the forest is restored without there having been any need to replant it. If it were otherwise, it would imply the presence of some defect, some harmful germ that was impeding nature's salutary effect. In that case, the forester would have to find the sterility's cause and destroy it. He would have to get rid of the ruinous goats' teeth and other damaging animals who destroy the forest's young plants. But what can be said of someone whose only recourse against such misfortune would be to exclude the lumberman's axe and preserve the trees indefinitely? He would succeed only in uselessly *ageing* his plantation and, in the end, would be defeated in his struggle against death, because the law of living societies, forests as well as nations, is the perpetual replenishment of beings. The impossible task attempted by this ignorant forester is none other than what over-confident doctors are now advising.[3]

Such a mode of thinking can amaze us. To compare a human society to a forest is to ignore completely the differences in the way they function. It overlooks the roles played by the economic and social organisation of human societies, and the individual's psychological and cultural life, his or her ambitions. What place has been left for history, for the evolution of society, for changing life styles and values? And since when have forests been aware of their historical and cultural identity? The demographer, reflecting a tendency characteristic of the second half of the nineteenth century, was joining the economists and looking at human societies as if they were uniquely biological beings. This pedagogical approach oversimplified and misled because it ignored the essential of a human society's dynamics. After having spoken of the 'older population', Bertillon pursued his metaphor by describing its evolution: 'ageing his plantations'. The multidimensional notion of ageing had not yet been coined, but the way had been opened.

These remarks provoked two types of reactions. Lucien March, in charge of the French population census since 1901 and later to become president of the Paris Statistical Society (1907) and director of the *Statistique générale de France* (1910), questioned in particular whether 'the disappearance of a certain number of beings should be an incentive to replace them by others', and felt that Bertillon was neglecting another hypothesis, 'namely, that the respective drops in mortality and fertility for many years are the effect of the same influences acting separately on fertility and mortality.' It was, he argued, one of the results of 'civilisation's' evolution.[4] March thought that 'M. Bertillon's conclusion was not based on the rigorous analysis of statistical data he had consulted', and that the existence of a necessary relationship, of an inescapable 'law', could not be deduced from the evidence he presented. His criticism focused on a crucial point of the debate.

The hygienists, represented by Dr Lowenthal, went over Bertillon's objections to their viewpoints, and reached the one predicting 'a feebler and older population'. They argued that therapeutic progress had not only lowered clinical mortality, but had even eradicated certain illnesses (smallpox, for example). Why then should the population become feebler, since to attain lower levels of mortality, morbidity itself had to be reduced and, hence, the population would be growing healthier?[5] Bertillon's innovation, therefore, did not go unnoticed. It represented a very important stage in the development of the notion of an ageing population.

If one followed Bertillon's logic in his parable of the forest, this 'useless' reduction of the death rate became clearly harmful. Reacting vehemently, Lowenthal quoted this passage in full, continuing with the metaphor, but presenting an opposing argument:

> But after all, if by combating the avoidable illnesses and premature deaths of children, adolescents and adults, we are behaving like ignorant foresters who take away the lumberman's axe so as to preserve their trees 'indefinitely', what epithet can we apply to the shepherd who, seeing his flock decimated by a serious disease, rubs his hands complacently, while envisaging the prodigious quantity of sheep who are destined to be born after a great number of the animals before him . . . will have bitten the dust. And how can we describe this forester who, in the hope of seeing his seedlings flourish, looks on indifferently as the lumberman incessantly fells the youngest, most beautiful and vigorous of his trees?

Lowenthal maintained that men's lives could be saved without violating the laws regarding the replacement of beings.

It was during this debate, therefore, that the two expressions 'an older population' and 'letting his plantation age uselessly' were first employed in the sense that interests us. The latter, closer to the notion of ageing proposed by Alfred Sauvy, was used when comparing the human population and a forest. In spite of objections from March and the hygienists, this metaphor, justifiable perhaps on the botanical level but irrelevant for human societies, was eventually introduced into human demography, and France's population began to age like the trees Bertillon had described. Moreover, this passage from the world of plants to that of men probably contributed to substantiating the idea of certain definitions' immutability. In particular, the threshold chosen to define the onset of old age was settled once and for all, and the idea that it might evolve according to a specific society's characteristics was disregarded.

Bertillon was the first to link explicitly the population's average age and its more or less 'feeble' character. The matrix for the notion of demographic ageing and its negative connotation were thus firmly in place on the eve of the First World War. In his article, written in 1928, on the probable evolution of births and deaths from 1927 to 1956, Alfred Sauvy first used the expression 'ageing of the population' in commenting on the results of his calculations. The surplus of births over deaths, he predicted, would disappear in 1935, making way for a deficit that would reach its nadir in 1945. Sauvy then specified:

> According to the hypotheses concerning the constancy of birth and death rates, it is important to note that these results simply register the consequences of the population's progressive ageing, the effect of which is to raise the death rate in general and lower fertility.[6]

The 'progressive ageing' indicated here that from 1932 to 1938, the number of women in the 15 to 19 age group would be lower than the number in the 45 to 49 age group (a consequence of the *classes creuses*, or lower birth rate from 1914 to 1918). This phenomenon would repeat itself after 1951. The evolution of expected births underlined also that annual newcomers to the base of the pyramid-shaped diagram of age groups used by demographers would be steadily reduced (740,000 in 1927 and fewer than 700,000 after 1937). Therefore, it was the bulge at the pyramid's summit, in contrast with its foundation, that Alfred Sauvy designated simply by the expression 'progressive ageing'. He offered a graphic and efficient instrument to observers of the population's evolution, because with one word, *ageing*, he characterised the entire tendency. During the debate that followed the publication of Sauvy's article, some participants immediately accepted the notion of 'ageing', while others began to contrast it with 'rejuvenation'. Consequently, it had immediate success among statisticians and social commentators.

In the context of the two previous decades of reduced fertility in France and the expansionist policies of the Germans and Italians, the Alliance rapidly adopted this new term since it highlighted the gravity of the decline in progress, and Fernand Boverat devoted an entire book to the subject, *Le vieillissement de la population* (The Ageing of the Population). In the Alliance's propaganda, ageing replaced *dénatalité*, or a falling birth rate, a theme that had had little effect in modifying French behaviour. In its apprehension-based pedagogy, ageing rather than lowered fertility became the scare tactic. For the militant advocating more births, it had the decisive advantage of touching each individual, planting the seed of doubt about the conditions the individual would face in old age : 'What resources will I have when I am elderly?'[7] The very pessimistic answers to that question were motivated by elderly people's high proportion, a result of a low birth rate which, it was said, had been initially favourable to families, but had rebounded on every member of society. The arguments were illustrated with curves and the pyramid-shaped diagrams that had replaced statistical charts. The now customary quantitative approach to ageing was unfurled and for several decades determined the unique way for demographic analysis.

## Sexagenarians at the end of the twentieth century

In two centuries, the French population has moved from a traditional to an entirely new demographic system characterised by voluntary birth control and a significant drop in mortality. The probability of celebrating a 60th birthday has increased dramatically and the sexagenarian's health as well as position in the successive generations have undergone a veritable revolution. The considerably reduced mortality combined with the lowered birth rate and certain changes in marriage patterns have brought about a familial configuration strikingly different from the one that reigned in the eighteenth and nineteenth centuries. In spite of its inadequacies, we can begin with a broad sketch of the average situation. In the eighteenth century, the co-exis-tence of three generations within a family was brief and quite rare. Thus the respect bestowed on the very old was said to be explained by their relatively small numbers: they had 'escaped the common fate'. However, such a causality, slightly simplistic and mechanical, is denied by the history of atti-tudes towards old people in societies with a high death rate. It is precisely at the time when more people began to live beyond 60 years that the perception of old age became positive. Impressive changes have occurred in old people's family situations since the eighteenth century. With a calculation based on death rate tables from that period, we can estimate that the average age at which a person became both fatherless and motherless was 29.5 as compared with 55 during the 1970s. Inasmuch as male life expectancy is now close to 70 years and that of women 80, the number of generations within a family living at the same time has often increased to four and sometimes five. To know one's great-grandchild today, it suffices to become a grand-father at 52 or 53, and to celebrate one's 75th or 77th birthday. Because women tend to marry younger, the timetable is reduced by a few years for them. This fact, plus their lower mortality, leads to a growing frequency of families with four female generations.

A retired woman, aged 55 to 60, thus finds herself surrounded by her mother, aged 82 to 86, and her daughter, aged 28 to 33, who is giving birth to her first child. The falling birth rate reduces somewhat the probability of becoming a grandfather, but on the other hand, the drop in childhood mortality promises a duration of grandparentage that is generally inter-rupted only by the grandparent's death and no longer by that of the grandchild. Sexagenarians are therefore an intermediate generation to which the preceding one turns for care and attention and from which the following one benefits in various ways, having its children tended, for example. However, 60 year olds, once depicted as an aged and worn-out group, rather withdrawn as they approached the end of their lives, quite simply no longer fit that profile. On the contrary, they are likely to be overloaded with sundry demands from their families! All the more so since the successive generations in the family are less dispersed by migrations than one might have believed in the recent past. In the mid 1970s, almost a third of parents aged 50 to 80 lived in the same general areas as their children, and half of them fewer than 20 kilometres apart.[8] A quarter of the children under 3 were looked after daily by their grandmothers, and almost half of the grandchildren spent vacations with their grandparents. In non-agricultural rural areas, the proportions were close to those found in the population as a whole: a third of parents aged 65 or more were living near their children, without necessarily sharing the same roof.[9] Contrary to a firmly fixed idea, it is not farmers' children who are likely to be looked after by their grandmothers, quite simply because almost 80 per cent of them have mothers who do not work outside the home. On the other hand, in the working-class milieu, 41.5 per cent of children under the age of 1 are cared for by a family member; the proportion falls to 38 per cent among employees and 32 per cent among middle management; and 68 per cent of the more affluent mothers employ baby sitters from outside the family, who, in half the cases, come to their homes. In general, the exchange of services concerns almost a third of all families, which does not exclude regular relationships among the other two-thirds, as shown by the frequency of reunions between grandparents and grandchildren during school vacations. The rupture within the family is therefore not as widespread as had been asserted when comparing this situation with that existing in the eighteenth century. Contrary to what is sometimes assumed, changes in family patterns have not nullified the gains from increased longevity. Today, the sexagenarian's position is often central in carrying out the daily jobs for which different members of the successive generations are responsible. Also, one must not underestimate the 60 year olds' role in regard to their own parents, which has transformed them into a veritable pivotal generation of family life. This reminder of the modal situation enables us to sketch roughly a kind of boundary that is clearly detached from the past, but the diversity of behaviours, the dimensions of family relationships as a whole, have also changed enormously.

The study of the relationships which link individuals, a measure of their respective positions within families, as well as the distribution of the different combinations of kinship, has been based on simulations which enable us to compare extreme points of the evolution.[10] What were the main criteria during the 1970s? At 20, only 1 per cent of individuals had lost both father and mother. At 55, the proportion had risen to 50 per cent. Until the age of 17, more than one out of two children knew at least one set of grandparents. The older generation could participate in bringing up that young person, who in turn could witness his or her parents' relationship with their own. Family units no longer follow one another chronologically, but live for several years concomitantly. They overlap, which facilitates a reinforcement of vertical ties, those of lineage, all the more so since those of marriage have become weaker.

Elderly persons who write their wills generally have children who are already at least in their forties, often well established in life. Directly or indirectly, it is the young adults from 15 to 25, the grandchildren of the deceased, who profit from these inheritances, which often help them to 'get settled'.

At the other extreme, in eighteenth- and early nineteenth-century France, 13 per cent of 21 year olds had already lost both parents, and three-quarters of these had no antecedents at all. The privileged relationships between grandparents and grandchildren, which were so well developed according to literature, were probably only exceptional, limited to the well-off classes, principal beneficiaries of the mortality drop at that time. But this did not rule out a new intensity and quality in those exchanges. If 42 per cent of children had at least one complete couple of grandparents witness their birth, death was likely to separate them during childhood: 73 per cent no longer had any forefathers by the time they reached 21. In earlier times, the generations succeeded each other without the overlapping seen today. The present death rate means that the average age for becoming both fatherless and motherless is 48, with the result that there is hardly a difference with the average age of legatees. On the other hand the family unit has proven its resistance, and does not disappear before the children have become adults: 90 per cent of individuals still have a parent or grandparent when they celebrate their 21st birthdays. It is almost never necessary to call on collaterals to bring them up.

From all standpoints discussed above, the elderly population's situation today is entirely different from that in the eighteenth century. But the differences are less striking if one looks at other aspects of family life. Take the example of 60 year olds' integration with their siblings. In the 'Old France', a 65 year old had on average 1.37 surviving brothers or sisters. That figure is not much higher today because of the lower fertility rate: 1.55, with a slightly lower variability than in the eighteenth century. But the age difference among siblings is less than before. Today, 45 per cent of 65 year olds' siblings are older, 55 per cent are younger. This situation contrasts greatly with the one during the Ancien Régime when only 27 per cent were older. Past this age, the survivor was often the eldest of the siblings. Behaviour and perception of age from one period to another are thus markedly different.

As for uncles and aunts, they disappeared just as rapidly as parents in earlier times, whereas they now survive long after their nephews and nieces have reached maturity. Also, because of the narrower age differences among siblings, the generations of uncles and nephews now succeed each other without overlapping. Contemporary direct kinship groups are close in size to those in the eighteenth century, but the age differences were formerly much more important. Today, as then, a 65 year old can count about twenty persons to whom he or she is directly related. But in the past, the group was made up mainly of collaterals, whereas during recent decades, the direct line has occupied a greater place. Finally, the kindred of someone aged 65 once included almost all age groups, whereas today one finds concentrations, corresponding to successive generations, that is those around 35–40, and then those around 10–15.

Taken as a whole, these changes have profoundly modified feelings about age: to be 60 today is to be surrounded by the generations of one's own parents and a kindred made up of collaterals, who are also 60 or slightly more, who are followed by one's children and grandchildren. The situation bears no resemblance to that experienced by older people during the Ancien Régime with no surviving parents and only a few collaterals of the same age or often slightly younger, and with the kinship network spread more uniformly among all ages, in particular up to the age of 40.

The reality of being 60 years old has also changed in terms of demographic expectancy. Between 1750 and 1985, the proportion of young adults having reached 60 years rose from 42 to 82 per cent for men and from 45 to 92 per cent for women. In the mid eighteenth century, a young adult had only four chances in ten of reaching this threshold. By the beginning of the present century, there were six, and for the past few years more than eight (nine, if the young adult is an adolescent). Almost an entire generation will henceforth turn 60, with the result that the age is bound to seem much less extraordinary than it did only half a century ago. How can it still be considered the threshold of old age, especially when the horizon of life expectancy has also evolved enormously? In the mid eighteenth century, the age after which there remained ten years to live was 64; in 1900, it was 65.7 for men and 67.2 for women; today it is 72.3 and 77.6 for the two groups respectively. If one of the criteria for defining the onset of old age is that of being 'well advanced along life's path', then the 60th birthday certainly no longer represents that milestone.

## What does 'being old' mean?

The comparison of the proportion of persons aged 60 and over at the end of the eighteenth century, the beginning of the twentieth and today hardly makes sense because 'elderly' persons are currently so different in their destiny, life expectancy, position in the successive generations and state of health. Who would argue that the human reality designated by the category 'old people of 60 and above' evolved very little between 1850 and 1930, and did not change radically in the past half century? Who would claim that studying the proportion of persons aged 60 and over since the eighteenth century could make the population's multicentury evolution intelligible? What demographic reality would be restored by such a study? The various indicators include the number of persons over 60 or 65. But what do they tell us? Forty years ago, Lucien Febvre pointed out that the historical fact is not a *datum*, it has to be constructed and implemented.[11] And in 1964, Raymond Aron was arguing in favour of an historical knowledge 'whose objective would not be an arbitrarily composed collection of facts standing alone, but an articulated, intelligible whole'.[12]

Is it possible to construct an elucidated and comprehensible series of data on the ageing of the population? The question of the pertinent measure for the ageing phenomenon is posed all the more acutely since we have observed a long period marked by profound changes. The difficulty is to find a new indicator that would account for these changes from the perspective of the new reality attached to being 60 today. We need an indicator that would determine an age equivalent, different from the civil age and applicable to distinct periods in an individual's life. For more than a century, the evaluation of the most important element of change, the state of health, has been possible solely on a quantitative level, by using mortality data, while ignoring numerous qualitative aspects. Can we not venture an initial hypothesis by stating that the greater the probability a 65 year old has of celebrating his or her birthday, the better his or her health? The converse of this statement seems certain: it suffices to examine, for example, the health of sexagenarians in less developed countries. In France, parallel with studies stressing the drop in mortality as one moves up the socio-economic scale, there are those that obtain, for identical civil ages, younger 'biological ages' in the same better-off groups. That the extent of the state of health and the extent of mortality at a given age are interconnected is obvious, but it is impossible to demonstrate the strict proportionality of this relationship.

Undoubtedly it can be objected that recent medical practices can prolong the life of persons who should not be counted among the active population. But on the other hand, and in much greater proportions, medical progress has resulted in the disappearance of many ailments and injuries that were often transformed into disabling handicaps for life. Although the mortality statistics have not recorded it explicitly, progressively fewer sexagenarians are immobile, suffer from poor hearing or uncorrected impaired vision, are recovering from 'bad wounds', or are afflicted with chronic bronchitis, 'gout' or serious circulatory problems. Can it not be argued that the indicators show that the actual qualitative advances compensate in large measure for the years gained at the cost of medical or intensive hospital assistance, which most often occur only in extreme old age?

Unfortunately, it is impossible to go much beyond these few observed data and common-sense observations: morbidity rate statistics according to age group are in general either non-existent or unreliable. From the detailed analysis of the causes of death in various age groups from 1925 to 1978, no conclusions can be drawn as to elderly persons' improved health during the past half century.[13] The smaller proportion of deaths from a specific cause among persons aged 60–74, for example, says nothing about their health or ability to occupy fully a place in society.

And then if we are to consider the change in life's perspective, should we not also look at the age when life expectancy is still ten years? The appropriate indicator is composite: it expresses for two-thirds of its final value the probability of surviving five years when one is between 60 and 75, and for a third, the age at which one still has ten years to live. It would be naïve to think that the result gives the precise age at which the state of health is equivalent, from the beginning of the nineteenth century up to our time. It is an overall estimation whose virtue is above all pedagogical – the data are reported in Table 6.1 and Figure 6.1. It allows us to modify the phenomenon's traditional presentation. Taking an age that currently appears well below that of reduced autonomy, 74 for women, we are able to follow the evolution of its age equivalent as far as the general state of health is concerned.

This age equivalent which evolves according to the changes in conditions of life and diet, progress in public health, personal hygiene and medicine remains stable for men throughout the nineteenth century and up to the period between the wars, whereas the start of an improvement for women emerges as early as the 1880s. In the twentieth century, the female age equivalent rises very rapidly, whereas male progress begins to develop only after the Second World War, in particular, after 1970. Finally, with a retrospective reconstruction using general indicators whose initial value has been adapted to the recent situation, it is rather surprising to end up with a nineteenth-

*Table 6.1* A synthetic indicator for the age of old age

|       | 1825 | 1860 | 1900 | 1910 | 1927 | 1937 | 1947 | 1957 | 1966 | 1975 | 1985 |
|-------|------|------|------|------|------|------|------|------|------|------|------|
| Men   | 59.6 | 60.2 | 59.2 | 59.3 | 60.6 | 60.6 | 63.7 | 63.5 | 64.0 | 65.1 | 67.4 |
| Women | 60.4 | 61.0 | 62.4 | 62.6 | 64.4 | 65.5 | 68.0 | 68.2 | 70.4 | 71.9 | 73.9 |

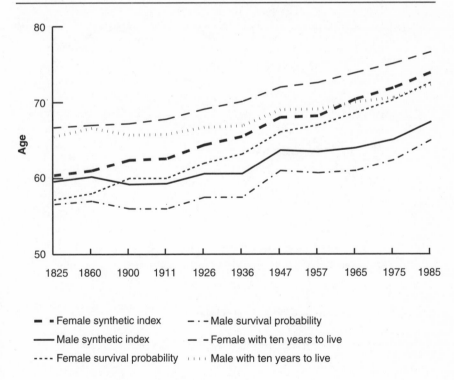

*Figure 6.1* The age of old age

century plateau approaching 60 years for both sexes; that is, precisely with the threshold used by nineteenth century statisticians. Could it be a matter of empirically verifying the proposed method, or else a sort of *a posteriori* justification of the age adopted in the nineteenth century? Let us note simply that there is a convergence of the years representing the onset of old age, the past practice of official statistics and the contemporary theoretical reconstruction. Such a convergence encourages us to continue the investigation.

If the simulation is carried to its conclusion and the fluctuating age thus determined is considered the threshold old age, the proportion of elderly persons is necessarily reduced. Calculation proves that it is even totally cancelled out for women and that a very slight increase is maintained on the male curve only between 1890 and 1940 (Figure 6.2). After all, the portion of the 'really old' has been around 10 per cent for more than a century and a half. Everything depends on how it is presented. The difference between the traditional approach and the one proposed here proves to be particularly sharp in the twentieth century, from the first years for women and from the Second World War for men.

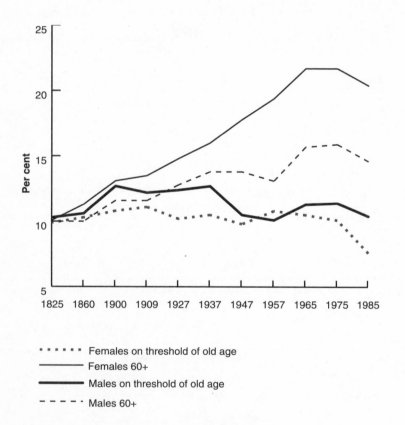

*Figure 6.2* Proportion of elderly people: two measures

## Statistical categories and demographic realities

A supplementary indication of the cultural embeddedness of the statistical classification 'over 60 = old age', used continuously from the eighteenth century to the Second World War, is that it has defined a category and led to a belief that the old-age threshold is immutable. This belief has had a profound impact on policies for the elderly and on more general social analysis. When the Commission for the Study of Problems of Ageing was set up in April 1960, its clearly announced *raison d'être* was to devise a rational approach to old age, which, with increased life expectancy, had taken on a new dimension.[14] Following research presented by INSEE (Institut Nationale de la Statistique et des Études Économiques) and INED (Institut Nationale d'Étude Démographique), the old-age threshold became 60 or 65 years. But this slight modification did not stem from an analysis of the sexagenarian's state of health, it simply reflected the official establishment of a retirement age. However useful on the administrative and accounting levels, this new specification for the onset of old age ignored social realities. Moreover, in the retrospective commentary on the age and sex structure of the French population from 1851 to 1962, published by INSEE in 1968, the grouping together in broad age brackets took 60 and 65 as the dividing line between adults and the elderly, so that a comparison with the past could be made.[15] Thus statistical coherence took precedence over historical argument. It was a question of reconciling the pre-war accounting practice with that of INSEE since 1946. Gradually, the threshold of 65 years emerged as the new norm, so that the 'Sullerot Report' referred to it exclusively. After 65, that is after retirement age, one entered old age.[16]

Since the idea of retirement first appeared around the mid eighteenth century, it has been closely linked to the impossibility of continuing to earn one's living by working, a result of diminished strength and disabilities connected with advancing years. Workers at greater risk – miners or train crews – obtained the right to retire at 50, with a full pension. In spite of changes in the reality of age, the disappearance of many occupational hardships and recent pre-retirement measures destined to ease and control the difficulties inherent in certain jobs, the retirement age remains generally synonymous with entry into old age, whereas twenty years or so separate these two points in the life cycle.

Traditional statistical categories focus also on the analyses of the elderly population's consumption of health care or their dependency. Some present their results by decade, beginning at 60, isolating a five-year bracket made up of persons aged 80 to 84, and then grouping together all those over 85.[17] A summing up then compares those who have reached their 60th birthdays with those who have crossed over this probably decisive hurdle. Such a choice hardly facilitates the observation either of the barrier's pertinence or the precise evolution by age. Such examples are numerous. In a survey on the age of dependency, the figures concern persons from 65 to 74, 75 to 84 and over 85.[18]

The age threshold chosen was once again 65. As a final example, public health studies have shown that 60 was very often automatically adopted as a turning point until quite recently. An enquiry into elderly persons' hospitalisation in Aquitaine presented the results by five-year groups, from 60 to 85 or 90.[19]

Because population data are generally presented in five-year brackets, because a certain administrative consistency leads to it, and because the inertia of the figures' presentation is even stronger than that of the phenomena studied, the old-age threshold remains what it was when it emerged at the end of the eighteenth century! In an editorial contained in a special issue of the journal *Prévenir* devoted to 'ageing', Michel Frossard also chose those 'over 60' as the vital thread for his reflection on demographic ageing.[20] And the recent *Atlas du vieillissement* does the same thing.[21] Its authors, prisoners perhaps of available statistics, did not question whether the onset of old age might have evolved, but organised their observations to correspond to the habitual age groups. They showed that older persons' health has improved, but the threshold for old age remained unchanged. The statistical category has gradually come to define the human category it was supposed to describe.

The opening lines of the report made by the Commission for the Study of the Problems of Ageing witness both the durability of the age threshold inherited from statisticians, and the traditional perception of old age and ageing bequeathed by demographers. The arguments disseminated by the journal of the Alliance are quite simply repeated. For example: 'Politically and psychologically, ageing is expressed by conservatism, attachment to habits, lack of mobility and failure to adapt to the present world.'[22] And elsewhere, one can read that as far as equipment and working methods are concerned, there is no doubt that in sectors where ageing or elderly workers are employed in important proportions, the consequences are disastrous.

In fact this Commission described the consequences of the population's ageing in terms identical to those that had been used ever since the interwar period. It sought to assess the costs that inactive elderly people would create for the active population, costs that would 'burden the French Community's existence'. The ageing condition would henceforth concern politicians because they had been made aware that old age could act as a brake on economic development, provoke social tensions and endanger national solidarity between generations. In an attempt to stabilise institutional housing costs, an integration policy for the elderly population was set up. It acted in particular on incomes, so as to reinsert older people into the consumer circuit and prolong their independence as much as possible. There ensued a determined effort to alter the perception of old age; it sought to replace the image of deterioration by one of preservation.[23]

But the analyses of 'the old age policy's production process' stressed the intersecting of social struggles and state controls, and in the end, hardly mentioned old people's rapidly growing numbers.[24] As for the extraordinary improvement in sexagenarians' health since the last war, it simply went unnoticed. Hence, the exposition on the transformation of old age's cultural model was not entirely convincing. Certainly, the policy for an ageing population was a reflection on the future, because every citizen was likely to reach that future. But it should have added that these contemporary older generations, for whom widespread pensions provide regular and assured incomes, can all the better integrate themselves into a developing society since their health and ability to travel, consume, participate in social life, offer substantial help to their children – in short, their ability to occupy fully their place in society – have improved in undreamed-of ways. A policy that attempted to influence old people's integration by diagnosing their lack of adaptability, adopting the pessimism customarily associated with growing old, fell strangely behind the evolution of ageing's human reality, whereas it was supposed to be preventive!

Nevertheless, the statistical category of the elderly disappeared from administrative and political language. Henceforth, one was more likely to refer to the 'troisième age' (third age). Sociologists stressed that this vocabulary change reflected a determination to break the 'traditional associative chain' of old age–old people's home–decline, to 'liberate the senior citizens from the shackles of old age', and insist that 'a new life style after 60 can and must assert itself'.[25] For the historian, the novelty was not so striking. Did not old age still correspond to the third stage of the broad categories used at the end of the seventeenth century by Colbert and Gregory King, and subsequently by population statisticians from the mid nineteenth century to the Second World War? For administrative and statistical services in general, the continuity was probably going to prevail over the break. The 'third age' had been considered life's third stage for quite a long time. The change came from dropping the 'elderly' category, no doubt because the perception of old age inherited from the nineteenth century and the beginning of the twentieth had at last begun to appear too negative and out of step with the reality of age as revealed by sexagenarians in the 1960s.

Would the expression 'fourth age' be more innovative? The historian would tend to answer no. Might it not be mistaken for the 'decrepit' old age to which seventeenth-century authors referred, because there does gradually emerge a 'fourth age', one characterised by handicaps and dependencies, which accentuate the 'third' one's autonomy and vitality? But does this contrast not push back the traditional perception of the old-age threshold to the former fourth age's edge, that is to 75 or 80?

In this case, the 'Old Age Policy' would have to be reconsidered. If demographers and sociologists have not taken account of the evolution of sexagenarians' capacities during the past thirty years, medical circles and social workers, on the contrary, appear to have noticed vaguely that the new policy has been directed to persons who, in general, could not be described as elderly before 75. This observation has encouraged programmes to help them continue living in their own homes.

The commentaries on the housing needed in specialised establishments or on the growing numbers of isolated old people would also have to be reconsidered. The sustained improvement in sexagenarians' – and then septuagenarians' – health has partially compensated for the older population's greater magnitude. Certainly it makes it possible to understand the success in limiting costs for housing and providing domestic assistance. The latter policy has benefited from a strong demand from families and increasingly numerous older individuals whose improved health lets them remain in their own homes thanks to minimal assistance.

A similar argument leads to a certain relativising of the pessimistic commentaries accompanying statistics emphasising the growing portion of isolated old people. Between 1975 and 1982, for example, the proportion of women over 75 who lived alone rose from 40.6 to 44.9 per cent.[26] Is this merely the sad result of demographic structures' evolution, inexorably destined to worsen? Certainly this category includes numerous difficult cases needing assistance. But there are also more men and women who live alone because they have no need of constant help. Moreover, the age curve of persons living alone supports this hypothesis, because it culminates at 80 to 84 years for women and almost 90 for men, dependence becoming more frequent only beyond these ages.[27] The increase in persons living alone could thus be interpreted as still another indication of the general improvement in elderly people's health, and not as an inevitable 'growing threat'.

In spite of some developments (third and fourth ages), the permanence of the traditional age bracket for the elderly and the values attached to it continue to influence most of the thinking and commentaries on the subject, not only among politicians and decision-makers, but social scientists as well. The fixedness of categories and the arguments applied to them can border on caricatures when calculations of demographic perspectives are presented. Demographic projections, incorporating a variety of fertility and mortality assumptions, make it possible to define the probable future's contours – in the absence, however, of all epidemic, migratory or military upheavals! On the other hand, grouping together the results of simulations by age brackets preserves the limits of 60, 65 or 75 years, until the year 2040. Thus, if the fertility rate is at 1.8 per female, the percentage of sexagenarians goes from 18.1 in 1985 to 20.6 in 2005, and then rises to 29.9 in 2040. Such a presentation inevitably leads to underscoring the difficulties that will ensue from an ever-growing number of persons over 60, 65 or 75.[28] Implicitly, it is assumed that 70 year olds in 2040 will be comparable with those in 1980, whether in their ability to act, their contribution to the economy, their social role, state of health or mental alacrity. Historical evolution not being linear, it cannot be assumed that the changes that will occur between now and 2040 will be as massive as those between 1920 and 1980. Numerous arguments could be advanced on the future's unknowns, such as the emergence of new diseases, but also progress in medical science, genetics, perfected treatments, preventive medicine – all in vain.

## Putting an end to the 'ageing' of the population

The exceedingly negative consequences of using such demographic perspectives reside in their non-evolutionary character. The future looks hopeless because the demographic structures' inertia does not allow a significant modification of the proportion of people: if one accepts the optimistic hypothesis of a fertility rate of 2.1 children per female, the proportion of sexagenarians falls only to 20.0 per cent (instead of 20.6) in 2005 and to 26.1 (instead of 29.9) in 2040. In such a situation, the financial costs of maintaining the elderly would be increasingly heavy. Hence, resignation and pessimism are unavoidable.

We should like to propose another utilisation of these same perspectives, a logical extension of the conclusions reached in the comprehensive historical analysis presented above. With it, the only interesting question would be to determine what progress, what increase in the chronological years at which people enter old age, would be necessary for the population not to become 'truly old', and for the proportion beyond that age to grow only slightly or not at all. The calculations were based on the projected French population, retaining the hypothesis of 1.8 children per female and the low mortality, which increases principally the number of elderly survivors and their probable proportion in the future population (Table 6.2).[29]

The proportion remains stable between the first two dates if the sexagenarians' health improves by three years in two decades. This gain should reach two years if one considers the septuagenarians. The present evolution of life styles, effective preventive medicine and new therapeutics make optimism possible for the first objective. On the other hand, during the subsequent thirty-five years, which will experience great growth at the summit of the age-group pyramid, the gain necessary for stabilising the proportions should be more pronounced: 8.5 years between 63 and 71.5, and 5.0 years between 77 and 82. It is not inconceivable that in half a century the health of a person aged 71.5 will be comparable with that of a sexagenarian in 1985, but there is no certitude that such an evolution will occur. One cannot go from unfounded pessimism to complacent optimism!

This kind of argument presents two advantages, however. First, it underlines the conventionality of most commentaries accompanying population projections. By reversing the approach, and by considering the possibility of (social, medical) evolutions independent of demography, it transforms an

*Table 6.2* The chronological ages at which one becomes old that stabilise the proportion of the elderly

| 1985 | | 2005 | | 2040 | |
|---|---|---|---|---|---|
| 60+ | 18.1% | 63+ | 18.4% | 71.5+ | 18.4% |
| 75+ | 6.3% | 77+ | 6.5% | 82+ | 6.8% |

inescapable future-doom into a future-potentiality, encouraging dynamism rather than resignation. The reality of the number of years a person lives before he or she becomes old will probably follow the evolution started at the turn of the century and accelerating since the Second World War, but its rhythm is impossible to predict.[30] All prognostications in this domain have been refuted by facts. Even if the progress made does not entirely compensate for the growing numbers at the age-group pyramid's summit, the actual ageing will not be that predicted by the statisticians. Thus, a medical and social priority should be to gain some years on age's physical reality. Is it not the only way to combat the ageing of the population? The consequences of such a development would be manifold because, following our contemporary criteria, people enjoying the health of present adults would have little reason to retire from social, political and economic life before reaching very advanced years.

## Conclusion

Finally, the scientific pertinence of the notion that a population 'ages' can be questioned. Undoubtedly, given the very weak evolution shown in the nineteenth century, this kind of measurement was appropriate when Alfred Sauvy introduced it. But the historian has a duty to demonstrate that during the misleading continuity of categories, often unconsciously accepted, realities have changed. Neither the thresholds nor the connotations have budged, and yet everything else has evolved: the sexagenarians' health, their place in the generational chain, their economic resources and life styles. The example of commentaries meant to clarify population projections has shown that the fixedness of categories on which the notion of old age is based and that, in turn, reinforce it, leads to a very narrow conception of the future. The underlying hypothesis is that the health and economic and social roles of the various age groups remain constant. Can it be admitted that such an idea has harmful effects? And is the same not true for the old-age studies and statistics which today, as two centuries ago, use 60 as the threshold? They all contribute to perpetuating the association between retirement age, beginning at 60, and old age, a link that is increasingly refuted by biological and social facts.

Even so, it is not for the historian to argue in favour of raising the retirement age, but rather, at the very most, to point out that certain thinking simply does not correspond to contemporary realities. For most professions, it is no longer justified to cite the work's 'wear and tear' as a reason for early retirement. Striking disparities surely exist among them, but it would be possible to estimate their respective members' life expectancy at retirement and automatically determine different ages for stopping work, based on that life expectancy. Many other scenarios can be envisaged, because the principal constraint is no longer strictly demographic. Setting the retirement age is a political choice that integrates employment policies and a vision of our society. Are we capable of offering our citizens a final third of life devoted to leisure?

The extent to which historical analyses have been imprisoned by the notion of ageing has already been pointed out. On the level of economic analyses, the generally negative interpretation from the end of the nineteenth century and the beginning of the twentieth ensues from the exceptionally precocious character of the demographic ageing of the French population. Sector-based research proving that dynamism and the enterprising spirit had not deserted France in the second half of the nineteenth century changed nothing. Failure to abandon the notion, and even the expression of ageing, can hamper all argument. Michel Loriaux's approach provides a good example of this.[31] After having shown that perceptible increases in numbers of people surviving beyond a hundred years would directly modify all phases of the life cycle and consequently push back old age to beyond 80 or 90, the demographer nevertheless continues to use the term ageing in its traditional sense. Certainly, instead of considering only the quantitative aspect, he proposes giving greater weight to the 'qualitative level', because the elderly are 'in better physical and psychological form', and are endowed with more important economic and social assets. But the reference to the notion of ageing forces him to remain, at least partially, within the framework of traditional perception. What, for example, can he mean by the statement that 'old age has entered our cities' walls and will not be leaving', after his judicious development of a new image of old age for the modern world?

In recent years, the notion of demographic ageing has proved to be devastating for scientific analyses and the presentation of social data. It has even contributed to freezing the threshold for old age whereas its reality has undergone the most important changes ever imagined. Finally, because it is expressed by population projections that do not integrate any probable modifications in the onset of old age, it ends up by predicting the inevitability of increased costs induced by the growing proportion of people over 60. The forecast for the future seems hopeless, and can lead only to resignation and pessimism. Reversing the traditional approach restores the possibility that humans can influence their history. It gives them a power denied by mechanistic thinking on ageing.

The notion of ageing has definitely had its day. Its scientific relevance became blurred shortly after its emergence and it never proved its heuristic worth. Real ageing, more limited than has been imagined, probably never had the effects attributed to it. On the other hand, the notion of ageing has played a major role in French demography's intellectual history, and in the mobilising propaganda of the advocates of a higher birth rate. Because of it, society has only slowly become aware of recent changes in the reality of the age at which a person becomes old.

# Notes

1 This chapter originally appeared in French in *Le Débat*, no. 89, November–December, 1994, and was reissued in *État-providence*. *Arguments pour une réforme*, Gallimard, Paris, 1996. The text was translated by Rebecca Balinska.

2 Jacques Bertillon, 'De la dépopulation de la France', *Journal de la Société de Statistique de Paris*, 1895, no. 12, December, pp. 410–38.

3 Ibid., p. 433; and 'Parallélisme des mouvements de population dans les différents pays d'Europe', *Journal de la Société de Statistique de Paris*, 1904, no. 10, October, pp. 345–8. Emphasis added.

4 Minutes from meetings held on 6 July and 19 October 1904, *Journal de la Société de Statistique de Paris*, 1904, no. 8, August, pp. 268–70, and no. 11, November, pp. 364–6.

5 Dr Lowenthal, *Journal de la Société de Statistique de Paris*, 1905, no. 3, March, p. 100.

6 Alfred Sauvy, 'La population française jusqu'en 1956, essai de prévision démographique', *Journal de la Société de Statistique de Paris*, 1928, no. 12, December, and 1929, no. 1, January.

7 It was the opening sentence of the foreword to Fernand Boverat, *Le vieillissement de la population*, Paris, 1946.

8 Agnès Pitrou, 'A l'ombre des grands-parents', *Autrement*, 1975, no. 3, pp. 104–22; Louis Roussel, *La famille après le mariage des enfants. Etude des relations entre générations*, Travaux et documents (INED), no. 78, Paris, 1976.

9 Jacqueline Maslowski and Paul Paillat, *III, Les ruraux âgés non agricoles*, Travaux et documents (INED), no. 68, Paris, 1976.

10 Hervé Le Bras, 'Parents, grands-parents, bisaieux', *Population*, 1973, no. 1, pp. 9–38; idem, 'Evolution des liens de famille au cours de l'existence, une comparaison entre la France actuelle et la France du XVIIIe siècle', *Les âges de la vie*, vol. 1, Travaux et documents (INED), no. 96, Paris, 1982, pp. 27–45.

11 Lucien Febvre, 'Vers une autre histoire', *Revue de métaphysique et de morale*, 1949, pp. 237–40.

12 Raymond Aron, *Dimensions de la conscience historique*, Paris, 1964, pp. 100–1.

13 Jacques Vallin and France Meslé, *Les causes de décès en France de 1925 à 1978*, Travaux et documents (INED), no. 115, Paris, 1988, pp. 343–466.

14 Laroque Report,*Commission d'étude des problèmes de la vieillesse*, Paris, 1962.

15 *Population par sexe, âge et état matrimonial de 1851 à 1962*, INSEE, Paris, 1968, no. 10.

16 'La situation démographique de la France et ses implications économiques et sociales: bilan et perspectives', known as the Sullerot Report, *Journal Officiel*, 1978, no. 15, pp. 803–38.

17 Michel Gaillard et al., 'La consommation en soins de santé des personnes de plus de 60 ans en 1982', *Carnets statistiques*, 1983, no. 6, December, pp. 80–2.

18 Jean-Marie Robine, 'Bilan de santé des populations âgées: mortalité; dépendance et espérance de vie en bonne santé', in *Les institutions sanitaires et sociales face au vieillissement*, Ecole nationale de santé publique, Rennes, September 1988.

19 Alain Moreau, 'Les personnes âgées à travers le système statistique', *Solidarité santé. Etudes statistiques*, 1987, no. 6, pp. 59–72.

20 'Vieillissements', *Prévenir. Cahiers d'étude et de réflexion édités par la coopérative d'édition de la vie mutualiste*, 1987, no. 15, pp. 3–6.

21 Robert and Laurence Hugonot, *Atlas du vieillissement*, Toulouse, 1988, for example p. 394.

22 Laroque Report, p. 259.

23 The expression comes from Philippe Ariès, *L'Enfant et la vie familiale sous l'Ancien Régime*, Paris, 1960, p. 21.

24 Anne-Marie Guillemard, *La vieillesse et l'Etat*, Paris, 1980.

25 Ibid., p. 81.

26 Joëlle Gaymu, 'Les populations âgées au recensement de 1982', *Population*, 1985, no. 4–5, p. 702.

27 Pierre-Alain Audirac, 'Les personnes âgées, de la vie de famille à l'isolement', *Economie et statistiques*, 1985, no. 175, March, pp. 46–8.

28 For example, Michel Frossard's 'Editorial', *Prévenir*, 'Vieillissements', pp. 3–6.

29 Dinh Quang-Chi and Jean-Claude Labat, *Projection de population totale pour la France, 1985–2040*, Les Collections de l'INSEE, Series D, no. 113, Paris, 1987, Chart A6.

30 A simulation of 'the greatest longevity conceivable' has nevertheless been attempted by Josiane Duchêne and Guillaume Wunsch in 'Les tables de mortalité limite: quand la biologie vient au secours du démographe', *Populations âgées et révolution grise*, ed. M. Loriaux *et al.*, Brussels, 1990, pp. 321–32.

31 Michel Loriaux, 'Il sera une fois ... La révolution grise, jeux et enjeux autour d'une profonde mutation sociétale', in *Populations âgées et révolution grise*, op. cit., p. 21.

# 7  Old age and the health care system in the nineteenth and twentieth centuries

*Christoph Conrad*

This chapter argues that the elderly as a group, and old age as an issue, have moved from the margins to the centre of the health care system in industrialised countries in the last 150 years. In the second half of the nineteenth and early in the twentieth century the health needs of the elderly were marginalised, even neglected, gaining recognition and inclusion only slowly to form the very core of today's welfare state. This is a bold statement about structural shifts in the relative position of old age within a period in which a number of other fundamental changes affecting this stage of the life course have taken place. During the period under consideration, the population aged, the social composition of the elderly population changed, and retirement, as we know it today, emerged.

My main question is: what role did old age play in the health care system? To begin to answer this question one must come to terms with issues concerning the clients, the scientific and socio-political discourse, and the cost and funding of modern medicine. Equally profound changes have affected the medical system itself, including its cognitive basis, its structure as a profession, its institutions and provisions for care in the last hundred years. Charting shifts in the importance of old age for the health care system therefore means examining a dynamic subject in an equally dynamic environment.

The focus I choose here differs from that taken by most studies of ageing in recent historical scholarship. My findings will be related primarily to current debates on issues of population ageing, health costs and social expenditures, while throughout I will compare old with young age groups, especially with women and infants. The attention paid to gender and the life course will help to integrate 'age' into a broader discussion of social change. For the sake of clarity and economy I shall not treat the opposite relationship, that is the impact of modern medicine on the perceptions and realities of ageing,[1] though obviously this distinction has more analytical than descriptive value since these aspects can surely be described as two sides of a single coin.

But could one not argue that there exists a short, causal explanation for the changing relative importance of old age within the health care system, namely the demographic development? Such an argument might go like this: as long as there were relatively few old people, doctors paid little attention to their concerns. As soon as the proportion of the elderly to the overall population markedly increased, the medical world was forced to adapt. Though it is certainly true that the demographic ageing of the population represents an underlying and fundamental aspect of our century that cannot be ignored, its impact on society is neither automatic nor linear. On the one hand, changes in population structure must first be identified and problematised by experts and policy-makers before shifts in policy can be enacted. On the other, the impact of numbers on society works through existing institutions, be they labour markets or social security systems, and cannot therefore be termed direct.

The question 'Who is considered old?', that is 'When does old age begin?', is also crucial in defining the impact of demographic change. In contrast with the argument of Patrice Bourdelais that old age be defined in terms of health and life expectancy,[2] I contend that such a purely functionalist approach should not govern one's definition of old age. Although I agree with Bourdelais that it is important to historicise the concepts of individual and population ageing, it must be acknowledged that the historical trend in delimiting this stage of life, in the twentieth century at least, is characterised both by an earlier exit from the labour force (i.e. a younger numerical age for beginning retirement) as well as by higher inclusiveness (a proportional increase in the pensioner population) rather than exclusively by improvements in health and fitness. In this chapter I pursue a different approach. Instead of choosing a fixed threshold for defining 'old age', all the quantitative data will be analysed in their distribution over the whole range of age groups from birth to death. When using qualitative data I will follow the specific definitions of old age put forward by medical authors, social administrators or law-makers at the time. Mostly, they agreed on age 60 as the lower threshold of old age.

My thesis that old age became a central issue within the health care system will be examined against empirical findings in three different areas. In the following sections evidence will point up that: (1) the attention paid to geriatric themes and subjects in the medical sciences varied over the timespan considered; (2) the inclusion of pensioners and the elderly poor in health insurance and social service systems was gradual; and (3) the profile of people using health services, in terms of age and gender, changed significantly over the course of the twentieth century. In conclusion, the final section presents a tentative model of transition which delineates a fundamental change in the allocation of medical services to different age and sex groups (4). The data come mostly from Germany,[3] but the argument aims to describe a more general model of transition applicable also to other industrialised countries.

## Medical attention to old age

During the course of the nineteenth and twentieth centuries, advances in the biological and medical sciences not only led to an increased reliance on medical professionals for matters concerning ageing and prolongation of life, but also served to minimalise traditional (e.g. religious) constructs about the life–death course. The scientific orientation towards ageing that emerged no doubt assisted in laying the foundations for changes in the relationship between old age and health care systems generally, yet during the nineteenth century old age remained a category of medical study that drew little medical interest overall. Although it is certainly possible to list the names of medical professionals who exclusively addressed issues surrounding old age – such as Carl Canstatt, Lorenz Geist or Carl Mettenheimer in Germany, or C. L. M. Durand-Fardel in France – a comparison of the frequency of interest in old age to the ever-growing interest in paediatrics relegates the former to a negligible position. At the turn of the nineteenth century, the situation improved somewhat: specialised medical literature on ageing was published with increasing frequency; more students submitted dissertations in this field; medical professionals became more and more involved in the debates about old age as a social problem.[4] In 1909, a handbook of age-related diseases was published, written by renowned authors and edited by a Berlin professor of internal medicine.[5] With growing specialisation in the medical profession in general, the elderly were selected more frequently as objects for study, as was the case in the field of psychiatry.[6] The only 'Habilitation' (the mandatory second thesis in the career of a university professor) about an age-related topic written in the period between 1885 and 1914 was in psychiatry.[7]

Compared with the triumph of paediatrics, however, the various efforts to establish a distinct geriatric speciality in academic and practical medicine remained reluctant, isolated and for a long time without success. If one chooses to look at North America, one notes that although Ignaz Nascher proposed in 1909 the use of the term 'geriatrics' in direct analogous usage to 'paediatrics', a new speciality complete with the establishment of chairs, curricula and corresponding examinations was not created.[8]

In addition to the delayed professionalisation of geriatrics, if one uses medical dissertations in order to measure interest in ageing and age-related health problems, the results point to marginalisation throughout the nineteenth century and into the first decades of our century. A quantitative analysis of the situation in Germany produced the following results: the ratio of medical theses (mainly doctoral dissertations) devoted to geriatric topics in comparison with those devoted to paediatric topics was 1:19 in the decade before the First World War, 1:15 in the early 1930s, decreased to 1:11 in the years 1950 to 1955 and fell further to approximately 1:6 around 1980.[9]

While the relative attention to topics on ageing can generally be seen to increase over the period studied, indicators directly related to the place of ageing in the medical sciences actually lend the least support for my broader thesis. Even when one takes into consideration a recent interest in Alzheimer's disease, in geropsychiatry and neurobiology, it might be said that old age has found a place within the mainstream of health care issues, but it still cannot be said that old age has moved into the centre of medical science.

It is productive to ask with which representatives of the health care system the elderly came into contact, and how these contacts changed over the course of the period in question. The routine experiences of medical professionals must be drawn upon in this instance, barring the existence of the writings of well-documented and well-known authors. Three points of contact can be identified wherein medical professionals observed the ailments associated with advancing age. First, contact was made in institutions such as hospitals, hospices or old-age homes by staff physicians, many of whom became the earliest authors in the geriatric field. Second, Poor Law doctors in working-class areas also regularly treated the elderly, predominantly women, as widowed women formed a large portion of the poor in such neighbourhoods. And third, and as a result of the Workers' Pension Law passed in the Reichstag in 1889 and implemented in 1891, contact was established between physicians who conducted examinations in order to determine capacity or incapacity to work; the role of the physician as 'gate keeper' had previously been established in a similar manner by miners' unions, occupational pension funds, or under state employees' benefits. These institutional contexts will be taken up in the next section of this chapter, since in each of these instances the elderly were drawn into the parameters of the welfare state. Before addressing this issue specifically, however, I would like to emphasise exactly how distanced the medical profession remained from questions concerning the elderly, how marginal these questions were within the health care system, in the period before the First World War.

A statistical analysis of medical terminology associated with the ageing process from the eighteenth to the twentieth century is relevant in this instance. Death registries, tables charting disabilities in the workers' insurance, or statistical reports by Poor Law authorities, as well as more specialised medical literature, provide material for analysis. The results are striking. At exactly the same time in the second half of the nineteenth century when scientific advances affect the nomenclature identifying diseases and causes of death, that is when diagnoses become more sharply defined to relate ever more specific causes of death, a rise in reported causes of death attributed simply to 'age-related infirmity' (old age, senility) occurs in the population over 60 years of age. The frequency of this designation increases from the mid nineteenth century, falling off only in the early twentieth century. It is also significant to the relationship between the medical profession and both poor and working-class populations in the German empire to note that this designation is present not only in statistics about the poor, but also in documentation gathered by state welfare agencies. Even though the social insurance agencies repeatedly objected, on legal grounds, to the use of this designation as a 'natural' cause of death or disability, 'age-related infirmity' remained the standard usage well into the interwar period.[10]

The data that I collected in a case study on Cologne in the nineteenth century permit a more detailed analysis of the contacts between doctors and the elderly. In four years (1835, 1855, 1874, 1894) a representative sample of all deaths at age 60 and over was drawn from the particularly rich mortality registers of this city. For the decades of the 1830s and 1850s, a more comprehensive sample for all ages can serve for comparative purposes. From this database, one can extract, for example, the percentage of cases with a certificate on the cause of death and with a doctor present. The already high proportion in the early nineteenth century (about 75 per cent in 1835) and the increase up to 1894 (92 per cent) show that older people were not *per se* excluded from ordinary medical care. Older women had a marginally lower proportion of death certificates than men, but the difference is statistically insignificant and had disappeared by 1894. Additional information on the doctors who signed these certificates allows a multivariate analysis to be carried out on the relationship between different variables (age, sex, status, Poor Law doctor, no doctor, etc.) and the chance of the cause of death being diagnosed as 'old age' or 'senility'. The results clearly show that these medical concepts did not merely express neglect or absence of professional attention for marginal social groups. Although the cases treated by Poor Law doctors and those without treatment had a slightly higher chance of being labelled this way, in general non-specific terminology was universal and was found even in the highest social ranks. The older the deceased person, the higher the chance that his or her ailments were simply classified as age related (i.e. natural).

An overview of the changing importance of old age as observed by the medical profession, then, hardly follows a linear path from the margins to the centre of professional interest. A hesitating and slow movement from a position of neglect brought old-age concerns at least into the mainstream of attention. It can be speculated that the elderly have benefited less from the increased attention to geriatric health *per se* than from innovations made in other branches of health care which have since become standard treatment options, such as hip replacement or pacemaker technology.

## Integration into the welfare state: moving forces and agents

To explain the shifting importance of old age in the health system, it is necessary to disentangle the agents of change from the consequences of their actions. What happened to the elderly is embedded within a more broadly defined process of change. Even if one focuses on hospital treatment, as I will propose in the following, it should be possible to make a similar argument when outpatient treatment, prescriptions, and the provision of technical diagnoses and therapies are considered. Hospitals and their patients, however, have attracted considerable attention from medical and social historians in recent years so that generalisations about long-term trends are increasingly well supported.[11]

Hospitals themselves evolved rapidly in quality and increased in number from the end of the nineteenth century on. National statistics, available from 1877, for general hospitals in the German Reich inform us about this process. The availability of hospital beds grew from 1 per 379 inhabitants in 1880 to 1 per 110 in 1930; the efficiency of treatment increased, as is demonstrated by shorter stays among patients. As a result, more people benefited from hospital care: 135 per 10,000 inhabitants in 1880; 657 per 10,000 in 1930.[12] As one approaches the present day, the profile of patients benefiting from inpatient care becomes more and more representative of the profile of patients benefiting from the health care system overall.

The 'gate keepers' of hospital care during the nineteenth century, the agents that produced the old pattern governing age and gender profile, were: (1) local Poor Law administrations; (2) health insurance funds; (3) doctors; and (4) hospital administrations.[13] Confronted with such a 'supply side' of service providers, patients – segmented by class, gender, age and medical need – constituted an extremely heterogeneous 'demand side'. It is my belief that the 'pull' factors created by social policies and legislation should be supplemented in future research by 'push' factors such as the availability of family care for the elderly, the changing character of their morbidity, etc.[14]

The establishment of a national social insurance system in the 1880s in Germany had a profound impact on the entire health care system of the country. Bismarck's health insurance plan for workers had important forerunners in friendly societies and mandatory municipal schemes,[15] yet for those demographic groups which had been more or less excluded from medical services in the nineteenth century (children, housewives and the elderly), their inclusion in a system designed to benefit the worker was not guaranteed. This emerging welfare state still relied heavily on municipal welfare offices and the statutes of Poor Law medicine to care for neglected groups. Of these, mothers and infants began to be targeted regularly by welfare organisations at the beginning of this century, leaving the elderly largely without similar assistance. Before the integration of family members and pensioners into the national health insurance, their latent need, especially for inpatient care or pharmaceutical products, was not translated into an actual demand and active policy of coverage.

In Germany the law was amended in 1941 entitling social insurance pensioners to continuous health insurance benefits for a nominal contribution. In 1956 pensioners became automatic members of a health insurance designed specifically for them within the social security system, and finally in 1968 the law was again reformed to increase their coverage further.[16] In Britain, the introduction of the National Health Service in 1948 brought an even greater extension of social protection compared with Germany. In the

United States the elderly as well as the poor received specialised programmes with the introduction of Medicaid and Medicare in 1965.

## Utilisation of health services by age and gender

Decisive support for my thesis rests on the patterns of medical consumption, especially of inpatient hospital care, during the last 100 to 150 years. Three indicators are proposed to follow this change over time: (1) number of deaths in an institution per 100 deaths of same age and gender; (2) number of persons treated in hospital per 1,000 population of same age and gender; (3) health expenditures (especially by health insurers) by age and gender.

The first indicator, death in hospital, is historically the most readily available. For recent decades the usefulness of this indicator is limited, however, since the great majority of deaths today take place in an institutional setting with variations by age and gender determined mainly by the circumstances of death (e.g. accidents and suicides in young adult males). Nonetheless, the contrast of the present situation with historical data is striking. In the nineteenth and in the first third of the twentieth century, young and middle-aged adults, predominantly men, were the most frequent patients of general hospitals (see Figure 7.1). The inclusion of deaths which occurred in other types of institutions (asylums, prisons, old-age homes) raises the percentages for the entire period, but the general life-cycle pattern remains 'n'-shaped. An interregional comparison within Prussia reveals distinct stages of development: the more urbanised the region, the higher the proportion of infants and elderly who died in an institution.

Over the course of the twentieth century, the various marginalised groups, that is young children, adult women and the elderly, became more and more integrated into the system of health care. A striking example is the growing attention paid to neo-natal and infant care in hospital. In the city of Cologne in 1908, 15 per cent of all deaths under 1 year occurred in hospital compared with 33 per cent for all ages, in 1913 the ratio was 28 per cent to 42 per cent and by 1929 the institutionalisation of infant mortality had surpassed that of the general population, 54.6 per cent to approximately 50 per cent.[17]

When the second indicator is taken into account, treatment in hospital by age and gender, a profound shift in the utilisation of these medical services is apparent from an 'n'-shaped curve to a 'u'-shaped one. While in 1900 the distribution of persons treated in hospital in rural Prussia looks like the pattern of institutional death, the curve for men in Berlin already resembles the pattern found today in industrialised countries.

Obviously the data on treatment and death within institutions must be weighted with the length of stay and cost of treatment for the various age groups. It might very well be that even the markedly 'n'-shaped patterns of the nineteenth century might appear less dramatic in terms of cost expenditures. Although open to further study and amendment, the indicators presented here point to a fundamental transition from an *old pattern*

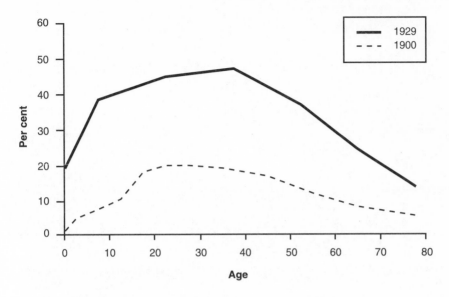

*Figure 7.1* Number of deaths in hospital per 100 deaths of same age, Prussia, 1900 and 1929
*Source*: Conrad, 'Zwischen Krankenhaus', p. 191.

(Figure 7.2), which dominated from the early nineteenth century until the Second World War, to a *new pattern* (Figure 7.3) which has taken shape since the 1950s. Owing to the interest of health insurers, the data for present-day Germany concern costs and not simply the incidence of treatments. Similar graphs, for example for short-term hospital treatments per 1,000 population in France, 1985–7, confirm the 'u'-shaped pattern.[18]

Of course, by concentrating on hospitalised patients a necessarily one-sided picture emerges. Those who did not or could not seek out stationary care determine the user profile of ambulatory care facilities. Although this remains a still vastly under-researched field, selected examination of indicators taken in a sample year, 1900, allows one to determine an age and gender profile for patients of Berlin and Hamburg Poor Law doctors (*Armenärtze*). Because of the particular status of Poor Law doctors, statistics gathered in this manner are evidence not only of the difference between ambulatory and stationary care, but also of that between a poor versus an insured population. Both sets of statistics complement one another, and result in an age and gender profile that is the reverse of the hospitalised population. In considering, for example, the proportion of the needy receiving medical care within the city, this figure approximates that obtained when analysing the distribution of sickness and death among this population: infants and the elderly form the highest percentile, the population between 16 and 50 years of age forms the lowest. Gender difference is also marked in the young adult population and higher age groups: in Hamburg, women over 25 were treated

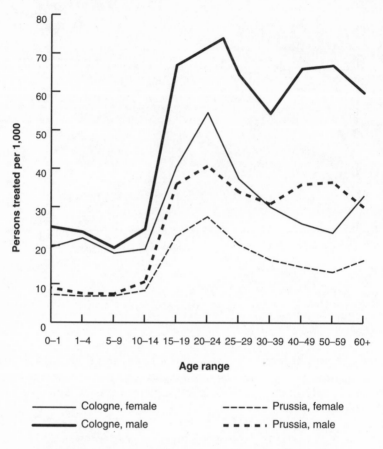

*Figure 7.2* Rate of persons treated in a general hospital per 1,000 population,
          Prussia and district of Cologne, 1900
*Source*: Conrad (1991), p. 192.

three times as often as men in the same age category by Poor Law doctors;
in Berlin twice as often. In the population over age 60 in Berlin, 8 per cent of
the men but over 14 per cent of the women were treated in the sample year;
in Hamburg in the population over 70, not quite 5 per cent of the men but
approximately 12 per cent of the women received some treatment. The age
and gender profile of the needy does not negate the picture previously
drawn, but in effect reveals the mirror image of the massive allocations of
resources to the young and middle-aged, mostly male adults, that we have
noted within the hospital and insured population.

    The third indicator, expenditures per capita as distributed over age and
gender groups, forms the core of today's assessments of the health care system.
Historically such data are rare; much more research is needed on the economic
side of health care in history. Expenditures or sick days per member are only

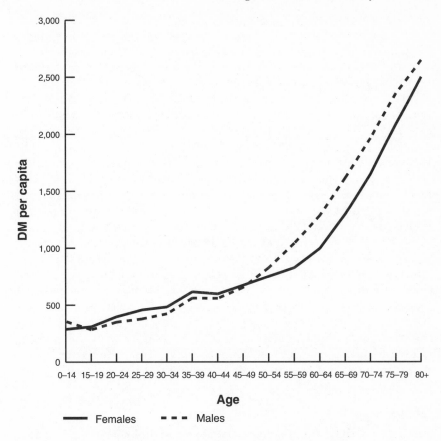

*Figure 7.3* Hospital expenditure in the German workers' health insurance system in 1991, by age and sex
*Source*: Jacobs *et al.* (1993), p. 21.

occasionally provided by friendly societies, health insurers or Poor Law administrations, if available at all. As a rule, such indicators increase in higher age groups, although here it is possible to observe 'healthy worker effects' over age 65 or 70 since people of ill health tend to exit the labour market with disability pensions. The working of self-selection in the labour market may also account for some notable gender differences. A large survey of insured workers in the city of Leipzig between 1887 and 1905 shows increasing sick days per member by age for men, but stable rates for women over age 40. Older men also had a higher risk than women of becoming ineligible for benefits because of length of sickness, a risk again closely correlated with increasing age.[19] Among industrial workers over the age of 50 or 60 a higher risk of accidents, only partly covered by health insurance, is also apparent.[20]

Based on internal acceptance and operation records, a medical dissertation concerning surgery patients at a Berlin hospital between the years 1923 and

1962 allows us to examine the user profile of the transitionary period between the old and the new pattern, between a youth-centred and an old-age-centred utilisation profile.[21] In analysing the age distribution of patients seeking care, its author underlines not only the increased use of clinical facilities but also the evident ageing of the general population, particularly notable in the case of Berlin. This double dynamic mirrors in its very specific localised examination of hospitalisation the general trend discerned within the health care system as a whole since the 1950s. The age distribution of patients in the Humboldt Hospital in Berlin's Reinickendorf section demonstrates a shift from a single peak among the population aged 21–30 years in the period 1923 to 1932, and within the population aged 21–40 years from 1933 to 1942, to a double peak in the population aged 11–30 years and in the population aged 51–70 years in the years leading up to 1962. Of added note is the increased incidence of operations administered to patients of advanced age: while in the period 1923 to 1932 only 1.6 per cent of all patients were over 70 years of age, in the period 1953 to 1962 the percentage rose to 15.5 per cent, as the overall population of the elderly over 70 years increased from 5.2 to 11.2 per cent. Thus, a disproportionate increase is evident in the hospitalised population of advanced age, specifically the population over age 70, when calculating age-specific hospitalisation rates taking Berlin's overall population in 1939 and 1961 as a base. In the 1950s and 1960s a distribution curve of utilisation of health care services emerges that identifies a peak at an early age (among 11 to 20 year olds) as well as at an advanced age (over 70 years of age).

**Towards a model of transition**

The structural shifts outlined above seem to me so profound and lasting that one can, in fact, speak of an entirely *new pattern*. In comparison with the late nineteenth century, two decisive developments have taken place: the age profile of hospital utilisation in particular, and probably health costs in general, has been inverted, and the discriminatory exclusion of women and small children from the health care system has largely been compensated. The former under-medicalisation of the elderly has been replaced by a double dynamic of longer lives and growing numbers on the one hand, and increased inclusion in, and demand on, the welfare state on the other. Based on the data gathered, I would go so far as to call this a transition in the health care system that parallels the demographic and epidemiological transitions in significance.[22] Such a model assists us in understanding the institutional and social framework that has shaped the way demographic change functions inside the modern welfare state. Like the secular demographic and epidemiological shifts, this fundamental transition has created challenges for medicine, social policy and ethics which still await response.

In the 1920s when health care specialists and welfare administrators first took note of these shifts they reacted with measured alarm to the potential financial and political consequences. Since the interwar years, the anxieties surrounding the 'greying' of industrial societies have accompanied most debates about pensions or health care. In the last twenty years, however, such discussions have developed a much broader scope. The social spending concerns of most western governments have, to the exclusion of other significant factors, set the tone for consideration of the role of ageing within a general framework of rising health care costs. In my view, the studies by many health care economists have missed the point slightly. While focusing exclusively on the effect of demographic ageing on rising demands for health care,[23] they have not taken into consideration the changing age profile of utilisation and expenditure. Thus, resulting interpretations based on a purely demographic factor, rather than on a nuanced one as I suggest, downplayed the impact of the ageing population,[24] and stressed instead technological progress, more generous benefits and extended coverage as the factors governing overall cost. From the historical evidence presented above a more dynamic, but also more dramatic, model emerges: the very age group that grows in relative weight in terms of population, that experiences higher life expectancies, but also exhibits the highest rate of morbidity, also has gained increasing and easier access to the core services provided by the health care system. This double dynamic of expansion as a group on the one hand, and greater inclusion in the welfare state on the other, is undoubtedly one of the powerful motors driving the post-war growth in the cost of health care. While in the late 1980s and 1990s, European countries (but not the United States) saw a rather stable percentage of GNP spent on health care, a similar combined dynamism of demographic and social factors might lead to a real cost explosion in the years when the baby-boomers will retire.

Some recent studies have demonstrated greater awareness of the changing utilisation pattern. In a 1989 French study it has been noted that between 1970 and 1980 the elderly in France showed higher increases in medical use and expenditure than any other age group, except the category of children under age 5.[25] Victor R. Fuchs has concluded in his 1993 study of health policy in the United States that the 'use of health care by the elderly has grown more rapidly than the rate of use by the population below age 65', noting further that 'for the period from 1965 to 1981, the differential trend on a per capita basis was 1.5 percent per annum, and for the period 1976 to 1981, it was 2.3 percent per annum'.[26] Especially in the United States the growing inclusion of the retired into the health care system also involved increased out-of-pocket expenditures and/or additional private insurance, apart from the fast-growing budgets of Medicare and Medicaid.

The shift of old age from the margins to the centre of the health care system involved both the participation and status of the elderly within society. Passively, the elderly as a group have experienced structural changes in demographic structures, labour markets, social policies and health technologies. But they and their relatives have, both as individuals and members of social groups, actively participated in making these changes work for them. Their increased inclusion into the welfare state and better access to medical services have deeply influenced their well-being and standard of life. While there are no doubt social and cultural costs to the benefits of 'medicalisation', most people would invariably agree that it has been a positive change.

## Notes

1 For nuanced historical approaches to the 'medicalisation' of ageing see Carole Haber, *Beyond Sixty-Five. The Dilemma of Old Age in America's Past*, New York, 1983, pp. 47–81; Hans-Joachim von Kondratowitz, 'The medicalization of old age: continuity and change in Germany from the 18th to the early 20th century', in M. Pelling and R. Smith (eds), *Life, Death, and the Elderly*, London, 1991, pp. 134–64; Henning Kirk, 'Geriatric medicine and the categorisation of old age – the historical linkage', *Ageing and Society*, 1992, vol. 12, pp. 483–97; Thomas R. Cole, *The Journey of Life. A Cultural History of Aging in America*, Cambridge, 1992, part 3; Patrice Bourdelais, *Le nouvel âge de la vieillesse: histoire du vieillissement de la population*, Paris, 1993, pp. 320–53.
2 See Bourdelais, *Le nouvel âge*, pp. 218–37, and Bourdelais' chapter in this volume.
3 See Christoph Conrad, 'Vom Rand in das Zentrum des Gesundheitssystems: alte Menschen im 19. und 20. Jahrhundert', *Medizin, Gesellschaft und Geschichte*, 1993, vol. 12, pp. 21–41; *idem, Vom Greis zum Rentner. Der Strukturwandel des Alters in Deutschland zwischen 1830 und 1930*, Göttingen, 1994.
4 Stefan Schmorrte, 'Alter und Medizin. Die Anfänge der Geriatrie in Deutschland', *Archiv für Sozialgeschichte*, 1990, vol. 30, pp. 15–41.
5 J. Schwalbe (ed.), *Lehrbuch der Greisenkrankheiten*, Stuttgart, 1909.
6 See the references in Conrad, 'Vom Rand', p. 38.
7 This post-doctoral study was carried out at the Hospice de Bicêtre, Paris (with Professor P. Marie) and at the psychiatric clinic of Munich University (with Professor A. Alzheimer): see Eugen von Malaigé, 'Studien über Wesen und Grundlagen seniler Gehstörungen', *Archiv für Psychiatrie*, 1909, vol. 46, no. 3.
8 Carole Haber, 'Geriatrics: a specialty in search of specialists', *Zeitschrift für Gerontologie*, 1984, vol. 17, pp. 26–31; David K. Carboni, *Geriatric Medicine in the United States and Great Britain*, London, 1982; for Germany, see Karl-Heinz Eulner, *Die Entwicklung der medizinischen Spezialfächer an den Universitäten des deutschen Sprachgebietes*, Stuttgart, 1970.
9 Included in my analysis under the concept 'old age' were the rubrics: age, old people, senile, disability, geriatric (and compounds); similarly under 'childhood' were included: children, infant/infancy, paediatric. The data were gathered from the various indexes of the register of German university publications. See Conrad, 'Vom Rand', pp. 25–6.
10 Christoph Conrad, 'La "sénilité" comme problème social: cause de décès, d'invalidité et de pauvreté (exemples allemands du XVIII$^e$ au XX$^e$ siècle)', *Annales de démographie historique*, 1985, pp. 39–51.
11 See Olivier Faure and Dominique Dessertine, *Populations hospitalisées dans la région lyonnaise aux XIXe et XXe siècles*, Lyon, 1991; Anders Brändström and Lars-Göran Tedebrand (eds), *Health and Social Change. Disease, Health and Public Care in the Sundsvall District 1750–1950*, Umeå, 1993; Alfons Labisch and Reinhard Spree (eds), *'Einem jeden Kranken in einem Hospitale sein eigenes Bett'. Zur Sozialgeschichte des Allgemeinen Krankenhauses in Deutschland im 19. Jahrhundert*, Frankfurt a. M., 1996; and the contributions in *Annales de démographie historique*, 1994; six articles on 'Vivre et mourir à l'hôpital', pp. 217–316.

12 *Bevölkerung und Wirtschaft, 1871–1972*, ed. Statistisches Bundesamt Wiesbaden, Stuttgart/Mainz, 1972, p. 125.
13 Reinhard Spree, 'Krankenhausentwicklung und Sozialpolitik in Deutschland während des 19. Jahrhunderts', *Historische Zeitschrift*, 1995, vol. 260, pp. 75–105.
14 For a discussion of these issues see Jon Hendricks (ed.), *Health and Health Care Utilization in Later Life*, New York, 1995.
15 Ibid.
16 Gerda Holz, *Die Alterslast – ein Gewinn für andere?*, vol. 1, Berlin, 1990, pp. 232ff.
17 Conrad, *Vom Greis zum Rentner*, p. 183.
18 Andrée Mizrachi and Arié Mizrachi, 'Les tendances à long terme de la consommation médicale', *Futuribles*, 1990, no. 147, p. 42.
19 Ingrid von Stumm, *Gesundheit, Arbeit und Geschlecht im Kaiserreich am Beispiel der Krankenstatistik der Leipziger Ortskrankenkasse, 1887–1905*, Frankfurt am Main, 1995, pp. 56–8.
20 Friedrich Prinzing, 'Die Erkrankungshäufigkeit nach Beruf und Alter', *Zeitschrift für die gesamte Staatswissenschaft*, 1902, vol. 58, pp. 432–58; G. A. Klein, *Die Deutsche Arbeiterversicherung. Sonderausstellung auf der internat. Hygieneausstellung Dresden 1911. Katalog*, Berlin, 1911, table 17.
21 Jürgen Radke, 'Über den Strukturwandel des chirurgischen Krankengutes eines mittleren städtischen Krankenhauses', Unpublished medical thesis, Free University of Berlin, 1965.
22 See, for example, John Landers, 'Introduction', in 'Historical epidemiology and the health transition', *Health Transition Review*, 1992, vol. 2, supplement, pp. 1–27; Simon Szreter, 'The idea of demographic transition and the study of fertility change: a critical intellectual history', *Population and Development Review*, 1993, vol. 17, pp. 659–701.
23 For instance, OECD, *Social Expenditure 1960–1990: Problems of Growth and Control*, Paris, 1985.
24 See, for example, Bert Rürup, 'Bevölkerungsentwicklung und soziale Sicherungssysteme. Prognosen und Optionen', in H.-U. Klose (ed.), *Altern hat Zukunft. Bevölkerungsentwicklung und dynamische Wirtschaft*, Opladen, 1993, pp. 280–1.
25 ILO, *From Pyramid to Pillar. Population Change and Social Security in Europe*, Geneva, 1989, pp. 135–9; Mizrachi and Mizrachi, 'Les tendances'.
26 Victor R. Fuchs, *The Future of Health Policy*, Cambridge, MA, 1993, p. 76.

# 8 Old age in the New World

## New Zealand's colonial welfare experiment

*David Thomson*

### Introduction

One hundred years ago 'the problem of the aged poor' attracted lively debate, and possible solutions swapped freely across national and oceanic boundaries. That burst of reforming has been well recognised by historians, but less closely considered have been the varying paths of western nations to their new turn-of-the-century ventures in provision for old age. These included a number of welfare experiments in the half century prior to the establishment of state old-age pensions, which were at least as radical as were their better-known successors, though in very different ways. One of them, which I shall call 'the New Zealand colonial welfare experiment', is our subject here.

New Zealand's experiences last century are intriguing in themselves, but have a wider resonance as well. For one thing, the introduction of tax-funded, non-contributory old-age pensions in 1898 was seen by many as a world-leading venture. That claim can of course be challenged, and others later overtook New Zealand in reforming boldness, but the country's early foray into state age pensions continues to earn it a place in comparative histories of the evolution of state welfare. It is worth considering the peculiar circumstances that led to these pension laws, and to which they were a reaction. For the path to state welfare, in New Zealand at least, was not what many have believed.

Second, New Zealand proved something of a test for nineteenth-century European and specifically British ideas about welfare, and the duties of individual, family and wider community. The colonists were firmly against public assistance of a Poor Law nature, or even the suggestion of an individual right to community support in any circumstances. That is, the settlers sought to live by the sternest of nineteenth-century strictures against public relief. What happened when those ideals were pushed hard?

Third, that experiment has a contemporary salience, as western societies fumble towards an 'enterprise state' or a 'stakeholder society' to replace the twentieth century's 'welfare state'. Many of the options being touted bear a remarkable resemblance to those advocated widely last century, and tested then in New Zealand. Again, the question of 'what happened' has considerable pertinence.

Beyond all that, New Zealand's experiment forms part of a more general 'frontier' issue. How did or do New Worlds differ from Old? And more particularly, how did pioneering in North America or Australasia last century affect the behaviours of British settlers, and what might this tell us in turn about the cultures from which they were drawn? New Zealand's settlers were overwhelmingly from Britain, and brought a mix of the habits, values, ideas and prejudices of the Victorian era.[1] But these would be acted out in new circumstances, including an odd frontier demography, absence of existing institutions and wide availability of land. This produced welfare policies that were clearly British derived, and yet distortions of those seen back home. The resulting colonial variants – for New Zealand cannot have been alone in this – were a vital ingredient in the welfare ferment of 100 years ago, though an element often hard to recognise.

The next section lays out the general nature of the welfare experiment, with its firm emphasis upon individual and family responsibility and the continuing refusal to give any right to public support. The remainder of the chapter is concerned with realities: what actually happens when a country pursues such goals? Our discussion focuses upon the elderly, though the patterns indicated were common to other groups as well, and upon their income rather than other possible needs.[2]

## The colonial welfare experiment

In many areas of life colonial governments were highly active – promoting immigration, distributing land, building infrastructure, running the railways and more. But in one area at least, that of providing support for the destitute, New Zealand pressed hard in another direction altogether. The legislative frame for this was erected very early on. It had many aspects – laws to secure property, promote savings, protect friendly societies and the like – but two were pivotal in setting New Zealand on its particular path. The first concerned family obligations, the second charitable aid.

In England, home to the majority of migrants, welfare rights and responsibilities were written into the Poor Laws dating back to the sixteenth century, and into court interpretations of these through the subsequent centuries. Yet while much of English law was carried over wholesale into New Zealand law, the Poor Laws were not. Instead, the colonists separated out the various objectives woven into the Poor Law, and fashioned their own distinctive garment from those threads.

The key measure, one of the first pieces of New Zealand law, was the Destitute Persons Ordinance of 1846, enacted by the non-elected Crown Colony government just six years after British authority was assumed, and when the settler population was a mere 7,000. In brief words borrowed from the famous Elizabethan Poor Law Act of 1601, the New Zealand ordinance stated that

> the father and grandfather, mother and grandmother, and the children of every destitute person, not able to support himself by his own labour, shall, being of sufficient ability, be liable to support every such destitute person in the manner hereinafter mentioned.[3]

But such borrowings are deceptive, for the intention was radically new. The English Act created a legal right of destitute persons to assistance from the local parish, that is from the collectivity beyond the family, and most of the lengthy parent statute was concerned with setting up the machinery for gathering rates to pay for this, appointing officers to administer the fund, empowering magistrates to enforce compliance and so on. Buried well down among the many clauses was the short statement taken by New Zealanders as their model, which placed some duties to assist the destitute upon a restricted range of kin – grandparents their grandchildren, parents their children, children their parents, and no more.

Moreover, court judgements in England through the centuries had circumscribed even these few apparent family obligations. In-laws were not to be counted; a woman's responsibilities ceased upon marriage; brother, sister or grandchild bore no legal obligations under any circumstances; payments of cash support alone could be ordered (not sharing of a home or provision of care); and the impoverished had no claim upon the general wealth of a liable relative, beyond just enough to lift him or her out of utter destitution. The definition of 'destitute' was also strict: the resourceless person had to be judged so by the Poor Law officers and given Poor Law relief in consequence, before any action against relatives could be contemplated. In effect, legal action was to be by the Poor Law officers, for reimbursement of the community by the relatives of some of the public expense already being met in supporting the destitute person. No one had a right to take direct legal action against anyone for his or her own maintenance.[4]

None of this entered colonial law. There was no mention in 1846 of a right to support by the community – there was to be no Poor Law. The sole right was to support by the specified near relatives, and whether or not the wider community might offer other assistance would be a separate, voluntary, charitable matter. In New Zealand, too, action was to be taken directly by one family member against another – no intermediary stood between. And the person who was not perhaps destitute, but who felt poor compared with a relative, could sue for a share of that wealth and magistrates could order support payments of up to 20 shillings per person per week, or the equivalent of a two to three days' labouring wages. Behind a seemingly innocent borrowing of familiar phrases lay a crucial inversion of individual and collective rights and duties.

This remained the legal position until century's end. The Destitute Persons Laws continued in force well into the twentieth century, but with the passing of the 1898 Old Age Pensions Act changes began, as a first group of needy persons were given an enforceable right to income support by non-relatives. And it was this break with the dominating principle of the past fifty years of settlement, more than any other matter, which so preoccupied the New Zealand legislators in their extremely lengthy debates about old-age pensions through the 1880s and 1890s.

The Destitute Persons Laws themselves were amended at various stages, with 1877, 1883, 1894, 1908 and 1910 seeing the more important revisions, and at each successive amendment the law of family obligation hardened. For example, the 1877 revision extended 'liable near relative' to include step-father, stepmother, and brother: a government proposal to include sister as well was judged too extreme then. Other clauses in 1877 allowed anyone to initiate an action for maintenance on behalf of anyone else; magistrates could now issue arrest warrants or order property seized in pursuit of money from a near relative; and relatives could from here on be judged in absentia.[5] An 1883 addition permitted imprisonment of those suspected of planning to abscond to Australia to avoid liabilities, and gave magistrates greater powers to examine under oath whomever they chose.[6]

An 1894 amendment made grandchildren liable near relatives, and extended the reach of maintenance orders in various further ways.[7] Nor did the extensions end there. In 1910 daughters and sisters were added to the list of liable near relatives, and the powers of enforcement given to the courts were once again enlarged: the Liberal government's Attorney-General had proposed making uncles and aunts, nieces and nephews liable as well, but this was not accepted. That law stayed in force until repealed by the Domestic Proceedings Act 1968, at which point all familial obligations were dropped, other than of husbands to support wives and of parents their minor children.

Little of this, which simply had no parallels back home, occasioned controversy in New Zealand. Parliamentary debate on these Acts was gener-ally brief, few objected to extending family obligations, and some always wanted to press things further. In 1910, for instance, the debate was unusu-ally full, and the justification given by Findlay of the Liberal government for yet more legislation was the standard one. Growing numbers of those whom he described variously as 'ne'er-do-wells', 'unfit', 'feebleminded' and the 'morally degenerate' were failing in their responsibilities to support them-selves or their relatives, and were leaving the costs to fall to the state. Bringing them to their obligations would save taxes, but more importantly was the state's duty, for it would teach valuable lessons:

> nothing makes a man a better citizen than bearing manfully his respon-sibilities. When men or women begin to turn their backs on social responsibility decline has already begun. If you can by some system

compel or induce people to bear their responsibilities properly, to that extent you are helping them to maintain their respectability and improve their character as citizens.[8]

The counterpart to these family maintenance laws was a 'system' of meagre public support, though there was little systematic about it and precious little law on the subject at any stage. Despite the best hopes of many a colonist, settlers did of course get sick, have accidents, desert wives, leave orphans, have babies out of wedlock, fail to find work or grow old, and family was often not present to help. That is, many of the realities of life which had brought the Poor Law into existence back home were repeated in the new colony, and yet the resolve not to respond with familiar forms of public assistance was very striking.

New Zealand colonial governments – there was a federal system of half a dozen and more tiny provincial governments from 1854 to 1876, a single national government thereafter – acted slowly, reluctantly, messily and minimally in this area. They refused to let the language of the Poor Law take hold: 'pauper', 'workhouse', 'poorhouse' and the like were not used. And they repeated endlessly a faith that charity would meet all needs not met by individuals and their relatives. The abiding goals would be voluntary assistance rather than compulsory support, minimal formality rather than statutory structures, charitable donation rather than tax funding, assistance to the individual rather than relief to whole groups, and rigid discrimination between the worthy and deserving and the unworthy and undeserving.

The outcome was charitable aid, the colonial alternative to a Poor Law. The term was borrowed from Australia, and both the charitable (not as of right) and the aid (help towards independence) were stressed. Under the loose rubric of charitable aid the provincial governments of the 1860s and 1870s built hospitals with outrelief departments, distributed food rations, paid rents, employed men on relief schemes, subsidised benevolent asylums, and ran female refuges. But there was nothing uniform about this, financing was drawn haphazardly from rates, customs dues, land grants, bequests, donations and public appeals, and few governments bothered to formalise any of it in their laws.

With the demise of the provinces in 1876 responsibility for charitable aid passed in theory to central government, in practice to a myriad of minute borough and county authorities, to benevolent trusts or even to individuals, with central government simply subsidising whatever arrangements were in place locally in 1876.[9] Parliamentarians debated several bills for the organising of charitable aid in the later 1870s, and the views of settlers were rehearsed at length. One group argued for some sort of a Poor Law, by which they meant giving citizens a statutory right to public assistance when destitute. William Rolleston of Canterbury, then in opposition but a long-time government minister, dismissed the claim that assistance could be left to charity and local initiative – the state to him had clear obligations to the poor:

> I think the time is coming when we shall look upon those members of the community who have been earning their bread by the sweat of their brow, when they fall into distress and have been unable to provide for their families – that we shall look upon them as persons who we are bound to provide for as a matter of duty, and not as a matter of charity.[10]

But more opposed the notion and insisted upon self-help, or charity where that failed. Donald Reid, another long-serving government minister, spoke for many of his fear that with a poor rate

> the class requiring assistance would begin to consider that they had a right to demand the money which was collected by means of the poor rate, whereas they ought rather to feel that any assistance they obtained was given as a charity.

His faith in charity, by contrast, was unbounded:

> I do not believe that there is a district in the colony where we could not find 50 philanthropic men who would be prepared to undertake the duty of raising sufficient funds to relieve the poor in their own locality.[11]

Not until 1885 was New Zealand's first national Act passed dealing with charitable aid, forty years behind the Destitute Persons Laws and long after the colonial government had entered vigorously upon state education, public works, personal insurance and a great deal more. Further, the 1885 Act was concerned solely with administration. Unusually, it lacked a preamble or any statement of principle, and failed to define charitable aid or even hint at the nature and purpose of this vague thing. No minimum standards of relief were set, firm central authority established, or procedures for distribution specified – charitable aid was to be, well, whatever local authorities understood it to be, or were already doing in its name. And crucially, no right to charitable aid was acknowledged.

There the law sat, well into the twentieth century. It was tinkered with on several occasions, but in all essentials it remained unaltered – local autonomy and variety, mixed public and private funding, no statements of principle or intent, and no rights to anything. The contrast is marked between the early and continuing clarity and force of legislation on the welfare obligations of individuals and families, and the late and reluctant law-making on non-family support.

This pushing of responsibility towards relatives had varied roots. A first cluster of influences were of course ideas and experiences drawn from home. The heated debates in both England and Scotland from the late eighteenth century on the advantages and drawbacks of a formal Poor Law were part of this. So were the cutbacks taking place from at least 1820 in relief activity, both north and south of the border, in consequence of a growing anti-Poor-Law mood. Another factor was the broader intellectual thrust across the nineteenth century towards individual enterprise, as exemplified in the writings of economists from Adam Smith on, or as popularised in the works of Samuel Smiles. Important, too, was the powerful crusade in England against Poor Law outdoor relief from the 1860s, which within twenty years had halved the proportions of the aged receiving Poor Law assistance. And perhaps most crucially of all, the migrants' cultural baggage contained heavy dollops of Victorian 'respectability'. This the colonists would cling to with a special intensity, perhaps because in the early decades of settlement, dominated by soldiering and gold fever, many feared the triumph of the very opposite. Hard work, thrift, sobriety, family, self-help and conformity would be valued particularly highly.

A number of things in the new land reinforced this mindset and enabled it to take firm root. One was the lack of established institutions – those of the Maori did not count in settler eyes. An example was the absence of ancient land laws, or ownership patterns passed down by history. Another was the local justices, and the class structures which gave them power. In England demands to cut poor relief were moderated through much of the nineteenth century by local gentry, operating as magistrates in petty sessions or on Boards of Guardians of the Poor, who still accepted a 'moral economy' which said that the labouring poor had a legitimate expectation of support, in old age or sickness in particular, in return for tolerating a very unequal social order. Such older institutions of restraint upon change and experiment were absent in the colony.

A second critical colonial condition was a peculiar demography. Most importantly, for several decades the elderly, major 'consumers' of public relief in any era, were simply absent. The settler population grew rapidly, from about 1,000 in 1840 to a quarter million by 1870, a half million ten years later, and 800,000 by the turn of the century. But the migrants were overwhelmingly young, and their fertility high. By 1870 still just one in 100 was aged 65 or more: in Britain the ratio was four or five in 100, or seven or eight in 100 in many rural areas, and had probably been higher still in earlier centuries.[12] During the 1880s and 1890s the colonial population aged rapidly, with numbers doubling each decade, to pass four in 100 of all persons by century's end, and this occasioned much anxiety about a feared loss of youthful New World energy. State old-age pensions were one outcome of this extraordinarily swift ageing, but for some decades before this strong views against public assistance and for family responsibility were cheap to hold – very few voters were old, or even saw the aged about, or had ageing parents by whom to feel burdened.

Colonial demography favoured the experiment in other ways as well. Nineteenth-century migrants were both self-selecting, and enticed, vetted and paid by government officials. Migrant assistance schemes were common, and a substantial minority of all arrivals came under their auspices. The poorest and sickest were left behind, and the new arrivals encountered a relatively benign physical environment, low population densities and high personal incomes by international standards. As a result expectation of life was the best in the world down to the First World War at least. The potential demand for support in sickness was going to be low, and so the colonial welfare experiment easy.

Women, too, were in short supply, few remained single, and illegitimate births were modest in number. Just one in twenty remained unmarried, compared with three or four in twenty in contemporary Britain, and lowered death rates should have meant reduced widowhood as well as strong chances for remarriage. Since women without husbands – whether widowed, deserted, unmarried and pregnant, or unmarried and underemployed – had long absorbed a second large chunk of all Poor Law spending, their relative absence in the colony would again have made the welfare experiment a ready option, for a time.

A further force in this direction was perhaps the migrants' place of origin. It appears, though it is a current matter of some debate among historians, that formal Poor Law assistance was for long much more widely available in some parts of England than in others – in the south rather than the north, in rural areas more than urban, in smaller centres ahead of large cities.[13] The districts from which the migrants were drawn are not well understood, but it appears that substantial fractions came from areas with relatively restrictive Poor Law traditions, including London, parts of the Midlands, the industrial north, and Scotland.

About one-quarter of the settlers came from north of the border, and their influence upon colonial society went beyond their mere numbers. The Poor Law of their Scottish background had long been a looser, more meagre affair than its English counterpart, and the New Zealand experiment, with its stress upon family, informality, neighbourly responsibility, and charity, clearly owed much to this tradition.[14] Even so, New Zealand departed from Scottish precedent in vital ways. Scotland did, after all, have Poor Law statutes to underpin public relief, and routine rates assessments and relief distributions to the aged and other needy persons across large chunks of the more affluent parts of the country. Further, Scottish relief was being criticised by a Royal Commission at the very time that New Zealand drew up its first Destitute Persons Laws, and the resulting 1845 amendment to the Scottish Poor Laws was designed to extend and expand public assistance: New Zealand chose not to draw upon this. In other words, Scottish migrants, like their English counterparts, took the chance offered by colony building to 'pick and mix' from among their traditions, and to press a few matters unusually hard.

The process of migrating aided the experiment in yet more ways. New Zealand settlers included few Utopian planners, or even those seeking religious or political freedom, but were overwhelmingly economic migrants, seeking to better themselves materially. Gaining an 'independence' or a 'competence' featured strongly in this, which usually meant to own land or at least a home, and to build small communities of hard-working, self-made, and mutually supporting families. The poor or those dependent on others were failures in this view, and had no place in the new Arcadia.

At least one more factor probably pushed New Zealand towards minimal public assistance – the nature of colonial society itself, about which there continues lively debate. One view, of long standing and still enjoying wide support, stresses that unusually close bonds of mutual support soon characterised the new communities. The counter view emphasises bondlessness or 'social atomisation', with large numbers of colonists being lonely, isolated, family-less, alienated and rather desperate people, who had little tying them to the new neighbours among whom migration had thrust them rather randomly.[15]

Both views may well have their place. A portion of newcomers soon settled, formed families if they did not bring them with them, and forged strong links with neighbours. Others, especially the large numbers of unmarried men, remained itinerant, unattached, and effectively non-participating. Mutual suspicions between these two colonial segments may have served once again to tilt welfare arrangements towards minimal formalisation of rights. Those who settled – the term 'settler' was usually reserved for this segment – would have enjoyed many sources of informal neighbourly support, and so perhaps a reluctance to create compulsory public welfare in addition. The 'atomised', by contrast, may well have experienced greater poverty, but would have been unable to call upon neighbourly goodwill and reciprocity. Nor would their more settled compatriots feel bound to tax themselves to assist what they saw as a dangerously shiftless element.

## The experiment in practice

This, then, was the experiment – to do what many political economists, Poor Law administrators, charity organisers and others called for at home but were hamstrung in achieving, and organise a society around self-help, individualism, family responsibility, and no rights to wider support. The experiment would at least begin under some unusually favourable conditions: how would it end? The brief answer is that New Zealanders tried hard to make their experiment work, and clung to it strongly well into the twentieth century, even though it was showing serious strains by the last years of the nineteenth century.

In what follows I explore this by asking: 'how did the elderly get by in such a world?' The aged are potentially the most vulnerable large group under a 'no public welfare' regime, and upon their ability or failure to marshal sufficient private resources might well hinge the success of just such an experiment, now as then. The discussion is under four broad headings, taken in no particular order of prominence – government support, thrift, charity, and self and family. Government action is discussed first, because this is crucial in understanding how the other forms of support would or would not develop.

### Government assistance

Central to the colonial experiment was active government. The settlers might abhor welfare upon an Old World, Poor Law model, but they did demand a high degree of government help in other ways: one was perhaps an essential quid pro quo for the other. John Ballance, the Liberal Premier in the early 1890s, spoke for a great many when describing his political philosophy as 'self help and state aid'. To the colonists there was no irony or inconsistency here: self-made, independent settlers would be a product of active government. Intervention to assist the aged prior to introducing state old-age pensions took a number of indirect forms, and was overwhelmingly male focused: very little was done for women, ageing or otherwise, who were assumed to be protected via their husbands or children.

### Cheap land

Distributing cheap or free land was undoubtedly the most significant of all colonial government 'welfare' measures, though it would not have been talked of in those terms. It underpinned the whole colonial welfare experiment, meant that large fractions of men and women arrived at old age with property holdings, and set New Zealand well apart from its British parent. Settlers craved land ownership, and government was expected to deliver on that dream, and when the ready supply of land gave out so the colonial welfare experiment ran into difficulties.

The basic patterns behind the land distribution were quite simple, though they came with infinite variations.[16] In the first step, land was acquired at minimal cost from the Maori, whose ownership of the whole of New Zealand was recognised in the Treaty of Waitangi in 1840. This meant that all land must be 'purchased' from Maori, and that the Crown would be the major vehicle for this buying and on-distributing to settlers.[17] Large blocks were acquired in the 1840s and 1850s at very little cost: in one well-known instance, Kemp's Purchase of the 20 million acre lower half of the South Island was completed in 1848 for £2,000. Fraud and deception in many dealings was and still is charged, and in the 1860s war and confiscation joined the means by which the Crown secured Maori land. Government purchase continued until about the First World War, and only halted as the stock of Maori or 'waste' land ran out.

This Crown estate was then passed to the eager settlers, while trying to balance the colonists' land lust, their lack of personal resources, the high expenses of land development, government demands for revenue, and an urge to counter land aggregation and favour close settlement by 'the small man'. Aid to prospective settlers took two broad forms. Public works provided roads, bridges and railways through new areas of settlement, making it possible for settlers to get to their allocated blocks, find wage work while beginning their first rough homes and clearing the land, and move goods in and later out. Public works also gave struggling settlers vital early local markets for their produce – timber for railway sleepers, food for large works gangs – and at least as important, gave capital appreciation on the land and so the chance to speculate in land and then move on. And second, governments devised a myriad of schemes to distribute Crown land at minimal cost to the first-comers. When New Zealand's land laws were consolidated in 1892, for example, fifty-two separate acts and ordinances and their associated regulations had to be repealed, so great had been the proliferation of provincial and national land schemes.

One early group of programmes involved free land for military settlers. From 1851 British servicemen retiring to New Zealand, often from India, could claim free land on a sliding scale – up to 400 acres for senior officers, down to 40 acres for privates. The scheme was extended in the 1860s to those who fought against the Maori in the New Zealand or Land Wars, and in all nearly 8,000 land grants were made at an average of 45 acres apiece. This number was not insignificant, when the total number of rural landholders by the early 1880s, for example, was about 35,000. Similar but much smaller free-grant schemes operated from time to time for civilians.

The larger land programmes involved disposal to civilian settlers, and a number of core principles soon emerged. Crown land would be dispersed in small parcels, and in general an individual could claim only one block during his (and occasionally her) lifetime. Prices would be set low, for the most part in the range 5*s*. to about 30*s*. an acre for rural land. Terms of repayment would be easy, and in return settlers must indeed settle the land – they were to reside on their blocks, and develop them at specified minimal annual rates. The aim was clear: close settlement by farming families, with the absentee land accumulator excluded.

These ideals soon led to some fairly standard procedures. The Crown was responsible for surveying a block for settlement, preparing access roads, and announcing the date, price and terms of purchase. The new owners would be chosen by ballot – pushing up prices by auction was not allowed – and could pay the set price as cash on the spot, but much more often would accept the government's deferred payment. Crown leasing rather than freeholding was also carried on throughout, though it was never popular with settlers other than as a cheap first step to eventual ownership. In the 1890s the government began lending money for land improvement, in addition to simply getting men and families onto the land. And with the Lands for Settlement Act, also of 1894, the Crown began compulsory repurchase of large private estates, for subdivision and resale to new settlers upon the standard balloting and deferred-payment terms.[18] Within thirty years some 625 estates of nearly 2 million acres in total had been repurchased for subdivision among about 9,000 new owners.

The result of all this, together with a lively private land market, was wide property ownership far beyond anything the colonists had known at home, and it formed the heart of the colonial welfare experiment. A unique 1882 listing of all freeholders provides our best evidence on this, giving for each property owner the name, district where living, and total acres and value of property held.[19] Around 71,000 individuals, about nine in every ten of them men, were named as owners, being split roughly equally between holders of urban and of rural property. They represented about one-half of all adult males, and at least 40 per cent of all male manual workers.[20]

Moreover, we must suspect that rates of ownership among older men were a good deal higher still. A large fraction of the population were still very recent arrivals, and would not yet have had time to 'settle' and acquire land, though they would do so in time. Large portions of all men, too, were still young and unmarried, and so not in the normal life stages for owning: one-third of adult men were still in their twenties, and 75 per cent of those were unmarried. And in addition to the 71,000 freeholders were some 10,000 Crown leaseholders, with significant property rights in their leases as well as expectations of likely future ownership. If around 50 per cent of all men over age 20 were owners, then substantial majorities of perhaps three-quarters and more of the middle-aged and elderly were likely to own. By 1900 the general ratio of owners to adults was still close to the 1882 level, though it almost certainly fell thereafter.

Many of course had real property of modest value, with 47 per cent of holdings valued at £250 or less, and properties of just £20 or so are recorded quite widely. Nevertheless, a number of things suggest that substantial properties were common among the working classes, and that even properties of small pounds' worth could still be of some substance.

For one thing, the numbers of men of manual occupations and with real property of £500 or more at once strikes the eye. So, too, do the substantial holdings of many of the women named. Further, these values refer only to real estate, and New Zealand's historian of wealth suggests both that these 1882 land valuations were unduly conservative, and that other property was substantial, especially for urban business and professional people.[21] And properties of even modest value were of a not-inconsequential nature, and to their ageing owners would have both 'income-saving' worth (because housing did not need to be rented) as well as some 'income-generating' capacity (because food could be grown, produce marketed, house space or acres rented, or land sold). There is no ready way of estimating the contemporary worth of colonial holdings, but several suggest themselves.

Real estate valued at £250, for instance, represented perhaps three to five years of annual adult male manual worker earnings, counting skilled and unskilled together, and perhaps twice as many years of female earnings – crude price-to-earnings ratios not unlike those of many urban areas in the present. The average value of all rural dwellings (excluding land) in the late 1880s was just £55, spread across one-roomed huts and twenty-roomed mansions alike. Farms of 100 acres or more, and all the residential and farm buildings upon them, were in general valued at £4–5 an acre. Smaller holdings, in the range 7–100 acres and generally closer to towns, had an average value of £350.[22] Unimproved Crown land sold in the 1880s for around 10s. an acre in the forested North Island, or £2 an acre in the open and more settled South: urban quarter-acre housing sections were sold by the Crown for £30–40 for the most part.[23] A government publication of 1875, which may have been putting a rather positive gloss on things, suggested that rough first bush homes could be erected for a very few pounds, a two-roomed wooden cottage in a town for £40 or £50, and a more substantial urban bungalow of four to six rooms for £150–200, 'lined, papered and fitted'.[24]

All this suggests that even holdings of a listed value of just £20 or £30 were likely not merely bare land, but would include a crude dwelling as well. Ageing persons with holdings of £250 or so – large fractions likely had much more – would own substantial bungalows in towns, or cottages on farms in the countryside. These represented personal resources unknown to the great bulk of their contemporaries back home, and are evidence that to a quite remarkable degree the colonial dream of owner independence was being realised, at least for the men reaching old age in the later nineteenth century. The signal role in this of government and of the 'luck' of being among the first migrants should not be forgotten.

## Managing the labour market

Less direct public assistance was given more widely via numerous government interventions in the colonial labour market, which the settlers expected because this was seen as promoting personal independence. None of it was directed specifically at the aged, but it would have aided them nevertheless, by boosting earnings prior to old age, by creating jobs for those approaching old age, or by easing competition for jobs from younger workers.[25]

A first intervention was control of immigration. Given where New Zealand lay and the rugged and forested lie of the land, migration was always going to be slow and expensive, and organisation and priming of it essential. This task fell quickly to government, and although much migration was always beyond control, regulation of inflows was soon being attempted to achieve demographic balance and a 'respectable' national character, and to protect jobs and wages for those already here. This last became an increasingly loud demand from the later 1870s in particular, as trade weakened, debt grew, and jobs vanished. Assisted migration schemes were stopped, and agents in Britain directed to discourage prospective new migrants, by politicians with a wary eye on the growing street protests of the unemployed.

A related and more successful protection for earnings came with public works, which have been touched upon already. In common with the other new settlements in Australia and North America, public schemes for building roads, railways, harbours and more were significant employers of labour in New Zealand through the century. This gave public works a key secondary function, as counters to unemployment, and during the last quarter of the century in particular they were run very deliberately to dampen jobless numbers and bolster wages and business in key regions. The numbers employed were never huge – a few thousand in many years, a peak of around 8,000 in the early twentieth century – but they did involve significant fractions of the more casualised manual worker populations, and the wages paid to them helped stabilise an erratic colonial labour market.

Beyond these large public works with their ostensible infrastructural rather than relief objectives lay a range of smaller, avowed relief work schemes. These were most often run by local government, were short term, and were funded by a mixture of general taxes, local rates, and special appeals. A few colonists expressed unease over the principles involved, for local relief work at stone-breaking or road-making on wages set according to family size sounded rather too much like the Old Poor Law back home. But the majority took another view: public assistance without a work requirement would be wrong, but providing work and so maintaining the 'independence' of a colonist was a legitimate and worthy function of government.

Tariff protection became another tool in the colonial government's battle to protect jobs and earnings, to prop up 'self-help', and so deflect the call for public assistance. New Zealand governments were never committed ideologically on the tariff question, though Free Trade and Protection labels were bandied about for a time in the 1880s. From early on tariff debates were quite openly about balancing the raising of government revenue (most came from customs duties), placating regional and sectoral interests, and boosting local industries and jobs. As government debt grew and employment weakened in the 1880s, the demands for protection of local manufacturing came more to the fore, and deliberate protection grew. In the 1877 customs duties revision the standard rate on imported manufactured goods was set at 10 per cent; in 1882 this was raised to 15 per cent, and in 1887 to 20 and 25 per cent.[26]

In the last years of the century several more levers were added. Employment in the public service expanded rapidly, often it was said as a means of absorbing surplus labour (and of rewarding the politically loyal). A network of official labour bureaux began from the 1870s and were consolidated in the 1890s, to spread information about jobs, put employers in touch with job seekers, or pay or lend fares to places of prospective work. And new labour laws from the 1890s had the unintended but lasting effect of establishing national minimum wages which soon covered a large fraction of all adult male manual workers. The central point is clear: governments committed to avoiding a Poor Law recognised a need to manage jobs in consequence.

### Government pensions

War pensions formed only a minor support for the colonial elderly, and there was nothing comparable with the massive veterans' programmes of the turn-of-the-century United States, for example, where large fractions of all elderly men collected a military pension. Through the last decades of the nineteenth century the Imperial government (i.e. British taxpayers) spent about £30,000 a year in New Zealand on war pensioners. By the early twentieth century this provided just over 1,000 pensions to perhaps 2 per cent of elderly men; earlier the proportions would have been lower, since the ex-soldiers were then not yet aged. The colonial government itself paid a mere handful of military pensions – it much preferred to compensate with grants of land earlier in life, and left it at that.

Colonial civil servants were superannuated under a mess of individual and small-group schemes, and the numbers were again never large. An 1888 list, for instance, names 114 men as sharing a total of £22,000.[27] A few other ex-servants were compensated in other ways, but not more than one or two in 100 aged men were collecting anything, and thereafter the proportions shrank as the elderly population swelled. Superannuated female civil servants were very rare indeed.

The big change came with the Old Age Pension Act of 1898, which created non-contributory pensions for the general citizenry past age 65. By 1900 pensions of 7s. a week (about one day's labouring wages) were being paid to the poorer one-third of elderly men and women, and interestingly, to much larger fractions of Maori. But this early 'generosity' soon slipped, and the proportions pensioned settled to 25–30 per cent through to the 1930s. The sums involved – £200,000 in 1900 – were many times greater than all public spending on charitable aid (let alone that to the aged only), but still small by comparison with payments on maturing life policies, or tiny beside the sums held in savings banks or in other forms of investment. In short, state old-age pensions were not a significant part of how the colonial elderly gained a living, because they came so late in the colonial era, and while they were very important in the long history of the twentieth-century welfare state, they probably played only a modest part in the overall 'income packaging' of the aged before about the Second World War.

### A minimal charitable aid

Charitable aid was a strikingly meagre affair throughout the colonial era. For example, by 1870 Canterbury province was renowned and widely denounced by many for its generosity in charitable aid. From the early 1860s Canterbury had a charitable aid officer to distribute relief, a government orphanage and a female refuge, and a public hospital and lunatic asylum – both important institutions of general relief in the absence of a poorhouse or the like. Rents were paid for destitute persons, children boarded out, food rations granted, and stone-breaking or tree-planting work provided on the 'Charitable Aid relief gang'.[28]

But a surviving relief list from 1870 – such things are extremely rare in New Zealand – indicates that even in notoriously 'profligate' Canterbury, charitable aid was on a very limited scale by any wider comparison.[29] Just one in 100 Canterbury adults were named on the 'permanent' relief list, when in contemporary England the proportion was many times greater. Not unexpectedly, females outnumbered males, with deserted wives or widows with children and the families of men in jail most prominent. Very little cash was given to anyone, and outdoor assistance was by way of rent payments to landlords, food or clothing rations, or wages for men at 2*s.* 6*d.* to 4*s.* a day on relief work. In short, the most spendthrift of provinces was doing what Poor Law opponents in Britain would demand throughout the century but very seldom achieve. It was giving help to few, aiding in kind when it did so, and imposing a work test where possible.

More records survive from the 1890s to confirm the limited scope of colonial charitable aid. In 1890, at a particularly low point for the colony in the global Long Depression, public spending on charitable aid was £75,000, or about 2*s.* 6*d.* a head, or the equivalent of three or so hours of the depressed wages of that year.[30] This was very small by English standards, even allowing for possible demographic differences. Early in the century annual per capita Poor Law spending in England and Wales had averaged 10*s.* to 12*s.*, and much more in southern and rural regions. It fell to a low national average of about 6*s.* following the New Poor Law reforms of 1834, and ranged around 7*s.* and 8*s.* through the rest of the century. Relative to per capita GNP estimates, about which there is of course some uncertainty, English Poor Law spending around 1890 was four to five times that of New Zealand.

A rapid bricks-and-mortar programme in the 1880s and 1890s was also redirecting the colony's limited charitable aid spending, again in line with the toughest anti-public-welfare thinking then being expressed in Britain and North America. Homes for the aged multiplied most notably, so that close to half of all recurrent or non-capital charitable aid spending was now on indoor relief. That balance was to tilt still further, to reach 65:35 by 1910, and so went way beyond anything achieved in this direction in England, outside of a few much discussed and unusual London unions.

The occasional extant relief listings from the 1890s make plain once again the decided colonial bent against public assistance, even to the aged. The best lists are from Otago, where the trustees of the Otago Benevolent Association (essentially public funded) ran the country's largest mixed, general poorhouse-like institution in Dunedin, as well as gave outdoor relief. Of the 285 inmates on 1 January 1898 (i.e. midsummer) 123 were men and nineteen women in their seventies or eighties, and a further seventy-four and fifteen in their sixties. They included just 0.8 per cent of men and 0.3 per cent of Otago women aged 55–64, or 3 per cent of men and 0.7 per cent of women aged 65–74. For men this was about half the comparable contemporary English rate, for women about one-quarter. Men in the Benevolent Institution past age 75 formed a more substantial 9 per cent of their Otago age group (on a par with the English rate), while for women past age 75 the rate was 2.4 per cent and half the English equivalent.[31]

Outdoor relief in Dunedin was even more restricted, relative to the English habit. Through the depressed 1890s there were about 400 'permanent' outdoor relief cases, and most of them were elderly. The 370 cases on the 1 January 1893 list, for example, included 3.2 per cent of all Otago men aged 65 or more (a further 4.1 per cent were in the Institution), and 3.9 per cent of women of that age (another 1.1 per cent were in the Institution).[32] The low overall proportions of aged women assisted are particularly striking, at one-fifth or less of the comparable English rate.

These relief lists do not note the aid given in each instance, but detailed personal case files make the patterns pretty clear.[33] Great stress was placed upon 'moral character'. Special attention was given to tracing, contacting and pressuring relatives or 'friends' to assist, as a precondition to granting any charitable aid. All, including the aged, were expected to earn part of their own maintenance, though this proved difficult to enforce in a slack labour market. Aid was granted for short periods, and reinvestigation of circumstances (especially of relatives) was frequent. And the amounts given were never a living allowance, but a contribution to be coupled with 'voluntary' support from the needy themselves, from family, neighbours and charities.

All this put end-of-century New Zealand well towards the 'dry' or Charity Organisation Society approved extreme in nineteenth-century thinking on poor relief. In this respect at least the colonial experiment was running on track: some public aid had been conceded, but even aged women, the group generally first in any country to be granted assistance, were getting very little by such means.

*Thrift*

In the colonial ethos thrift enjoyed a hallowed place. With a little help from government, and the spur of knowing there was no right to public assistance to fall back upon, so the thinking went, the settlers would work hard, live frugally, bond their families, think ahead, and save for assorted contingencies and for old age in particular. How far they did save remains unclear, but some aspects of colonial thrift can be traced.

The major form of thrift practised was probably the land owning which has been discussed already. Colonists saved in various other ways, but showed little interest in mutual associations, which were the main forms of saving among the mass of manual workers back home.[34] They chose instead highly individual forms of saving, over which each could retain close personal control.

Friendly societies, for example, expanded only slowly and too late to play any part in sustaining the colonial aged. The advantages to manual workers of belonging to the societies were lauded in New Zealand at least as loudly as in nineteenth-century Britain, laws along English lines to protect the societies were soon passed, and within a very few years of settlement both independent local societies and branches of the large international orders were forming in the colony. Yet a number of things make plain the irrelevance of the friendly societies to the colonial elderly.[35]

For one thing, few joined. By 1890, total friendly society memberships of all sorts were equivalent to one in seven of the adult male population, and by the 1920s peak a little below one in four. This was way below English ratios, which were perhaps one to two by the 1870s, and was well below Australian levels as well. The aged belonged at much lower rates still. The only published listing, for 1882, shows that while the membership rate at ages 15 to 40 was about 15 per 100 men, it fell off progressively at higher ages to be just one in 100 past age 65. And of those who joined, many dropped out within a year or two. This was good for society finances – young men left after paying contributions but claiming little. But it meant that the proportions of 'effective members', who would stay in long enough to gain the full protection which membership promised, were well below even the low official counts.

Further, the New Zealand societies were tiny and fiercely independent, so that the risk pooling offered to members was fragile and unreliable. The average lodge size in 1890 was seventy-five members, those with 200 or more were very unusual, and one-half of all societies had less than fifty members. This may have been good for conviviality, but dreadful as an insurance against adversity, especially in the expensive later years of life. Nor were the New Zealand societies much concerned with the aged. None provided pensions or the like in old age, although their British parents were beginning to do this. The only possibility for the old was extended sick pay, yet the amounts of this paid out shrank over time, just when the elderly population mushroomed. And over it all loomed the question of solvency. The vast majority of nineteenth-century societies, perhaps not surprisingly, were considered actuarially unsound by the Registrar and his independent valuers, in that lifetime promises to members outstripped potential income.

Other mutual associations were similarly irrelevant to the colonial aged. Trade unions were slow to develop among the scattered and individualistic migrants, were limited in ambition, stuck closely to fighting for immediate workplace benefits for current workers, and did not operate mutual benefit schemes for cover in sickness, unemployment or old age. Employer-sponsored benefit societies arose from the late 1880s, to reach about thirty in number and 5,400 members at the one, 1897, count.[36] This was about one-tenth of the low membership of friendly societies, and benefits were immediate ones to current employees alone – employer pension schemes were a development of the twentieth century in New Zealand. The only Old World mutual association to establish some firm hold in the colony was, perhaps predictably, the building society, which aided urban workers in particular into home ownership.

Life insurance was purchased much more readily than was membership taken up in a friendly society, but it probably came too late for the colonial aged, beyond an affluent minority. By the 1860s both British and Australian life companies were operating in the colony, with North American ones to follow, and in 1869 the New Zealand government created its own life office in competition with these. In 1890 New Zealanders held 181 'ordinary' life policies per 1,000 adults, and by 1920, 263 per 1,000, that is at twice the rate of friendly society membership. Nineteenth-century life policies were over-whelmingly for payment upon death, which meant that they were not a way of providing income for one's own later life, but a lump sum for a surviving spouse or heirs. From the end of the century the predominance changed swiftly to policies maturing at a set age in the saver's own life, with ages 50–65 being most common.[37]

'Ordinary' policies for the most part were for sums equivalent to half to one year of average earnings, and interestingly, that was the rough value they have held through this century as well. A further development of the last years of the nineteenth century was 'industrial' life insurance, or smaller policies aimed at the 'industrial' classes, with payments at maturity generally totalling just a few weeks of average earnings. By 1920 each 1,000 New Zealanders held 215 industrial life policies, in addition to their 263 ordinary ones. But even more than with ordinary policies, industrial ones came too late to play a part in providing income in a colonial old age.

Substantial sums were involved in life insurance pay-outs, but it is not clear who collected the money. In 1900, for instance, the life companies operating in New Zealand paid £317,000 on maturing policies, or the equiv-alent of eight times all sick pay paid by friendly societies, or four times total charitable aid spending (indoor and outdoor combined), or 1.6 times the cost of state old-age pensions. Most of it probably went to the ageing spouses or the children of the middle classes, with relatively little as yet finding its way to ageing men, or to the mass of the wage-worker popula-tion. And while the sums were large, life insurance was still small business in New Zealand by comparison with elsewhere – by the 1920s, for example, the Canadians held two times and US residents three times as many life policies per 1,000 population.

Cash savings were likely important to the colonial aged, though there are few good measures of these. Statistics of bank deposits were collected, but there is no knowing how much money migrants may have left behind in

Britain or Australia. The colonists also appear to have been surprisingly casual with substantial cash sums – or very wary of banks – and would carry them about as they moved or leave them with friends or landladies to be reclaimed later. Banks of issue, later known as the trading banks, were in operation from the 1840s, but through the nineteenth century charged substantially for their services, paid little or no interest on deposits, and were not relevant to 'the small saver'. Trustee banks to meet the small saver's needs appeared from the 1840s also, and a network of post office savings banks was in place from the 1860s.

By 1880 the colonists held 47,500 savings bank accounts, in a ratio of one to every five adults – about twice the ratio of friendly society membership, and ahead of the number of life policies.[38] The savings in these totalled £1.2 million, at an average £25 per account, or the equivalent of three or four months of full adult male wages. Thereafter bank savings were to grow very rapidly. They doubled across the 'depressed' 1880s, to £3.1 million in the savings banks alone – seven times the accumulated funds and forty-five times the annual income of friendly societies, or seven times the annual premiums paid into life policies, or forty times public expenditure on charitable aid, or forty-five times the total revenues of public hospitals. By 1900, after another decade of economic difficulty according to the conventional accounts, savings by small savers at trustee banks had more than doubled again, and there was now about one savings account to every two adults.

Little is known of who held these accounts, or what 'un-banked' cash people may have had, or what other property or investments savers may also have enjoyed. These could have been substantial, for sums in savings banks represented only a small portion of total investments in the colony: in 1900, along with the £6.1 million in savings banks there was £17 million on deposit in the trading banks, while £6.7 million was put into new land mortgages in that one year alone, much of it by individuals investing through local solicitors.

Nor do we know that savers saw their nest eggs as being for old age, or were willing to run them down when elderly: the twentieth-century elderly, in New Zealand as elsewhere, have proven very reluctant to 'spend down' their life savings, and there is little reason to think things very different a century ago. The sums held, too, would in a great many cases have been small relative to the costs of living through old age. The average New Zealand man or woman of 65 in 1890 could expect another twelve or more years of life: at a modest living cost of 10*s*. a week this could add up to £300 and more at the average, or a sum far beyond the cash reserves of most. Even so, cash savings in particular, and thrift in general, do appear to have formed a central part of the incomes of the colonial aged, in all likelihood to degrees not seen outside of the more comfortable middle classes back home.

### Charity

Nineteenth-century philanthropy has received some scholarly attention else-where but very little in New Zealand. The range of possible activities coming under this heading is extremely wide, and the following treats them in three loose groupings: formal, semi- or small formal, and informal.

### Formal charity

Formal, large-scale philanthropic endeavours such as grew strikingly in nineteenth-century Britain or North America did not flourish at all in the small colony. There were too few accumulations of wealth to be tapped, or urban middle classes to subscribe, or unmarried women to run the organisa-tions. A few small examples on the British model did appear – the Auckland and the Onehunga Ladies' Benevolent Societies dating from the 1850s are examples – but their resources were tiny, and they were soon heavily depen-dent upon government subsidy rather than private giving. Moreover, the aged did not appear among their favoured objects of charity, just as they did not in contemporary Britain. At the end of the century, as numbers of the aged doubled each decade, several homes for the aged were founded by church organisations, notably the Salvation Army and orders of the Roman Catholic Church. But the proportions of the elderly involved remained tiny, and the priorities of the more formal charities remained children and 'fallen women'.

### Semi-formal charity

What I have called semi- or small-formal charities were centred upon parish churches for the most part, and were much the more numerous type of charity organisation in the colony. For instance, the records from around 1890 for Dunedin, the most substantial and affluent of the colonial cities, mention a church-run female refuge and a Patients and Prisoners Aid Society, along with numerous small parish charities – a Dorcas Charity of Hanover Street Church, the 'Ladies of Knox Church', the Roman Catholic Charity, 'assistance from the Church of Christ', a 'Mornington Charity', the St Andrew's Charity, the Salvation Army, the Tabernacle Charity, and the Forbury Baptist Chapel Charity.[39] Other sources mention even less formal church assistance, drawn from weekly church-door collections.[40] But all make plain that the sums involved were minute, and once again that the elderly were not among the prime objects of this charity.

### Good neighbourliness

Good neighbourliness, or direct person-to-person help outside of the family, is perhaps the most difficult of all charities to weigh. Many insisted, in New

Zealand as in nineteenth-century Britain and elsewhere, that spontaneous neighbourly assistance has always been the most vital of charities, and that help to the poor by other poor was ubiquitous and crucial.

This may have been so in the colony. All sorts of records – letters, diaries, novels, charitable aid listings, newspapers, obituaries, evidence to official inquiries, old-age pension applications – point repeatedly to wide small-scale giving in many forms. Early arrivals would share housing with newcomers, and travellers in sparsely settled regions could expect a bed for a night. Food seems to have been shared on many occasions, with visitors, with sick neighbours, with the streams of moving men, women and children who characterised an early stage of colonisation. Farmers shared tasks and equipment, to avoid squandering scarce cash on paid labour or specialist machinery, to spread skills and combat loneliness. Money seems to have been 'given' or 'lent', surprisingly casually to late twentieth-century eyes, often to fairly passing acquaintances and with dubious prospects of repayment. 'Friends' chipped in, more or less voluntarily, with a shilling or so a week to top up meagre charitable aid rations. Women took in other's children, cleaned for a sick neighbour, or helped furnish a rough dwelling. Locals held whiparounds or 'passed the hat', thereby raising substantial sums for some particularly unfortunate individual or family, when a cottage was lost to fire perhaps, or a husband to floods. Special appeals, often organised by local newspapers, could bring in large amounts following an earthquake or bush fire which devastated a larger group. Perhaps even 'swagging' or 'going on the road' had elements of good neighbourliness to it, and was clearly important to numbers of older, single men. A powerful unwritten rural code binding larger farmers and their essential but very seasonal workforces said that tramping men could expect an evening meal, bed and breakfast gratis, before being either offered work for wages or asked to move on in search of it elsewhere.

There is no ready way to put scale to any of this, or to weigh its significance in one place or time against some other. I have the impression from years of reading in the nineteenth-century histories of Britain and New Zealand that such informal activity was more prevalent in the colony, though it is possible that this is an artefact of the types of records created: migrants, being separated from home and family, may simply have written more in consequence in describing their new lives to those back home, or in justifying the wrench and shock of it all to themselves as well as to others. But there are other reasons for speculating that more extensive informal non-family giving may have been a characteristic of the colony.

For one thing, a greater general affluence would have meant that the colonists more often had surpluses to share – they could act as others back home might not, even if holding common values. The presence among the colonists of substantial numbers of single men, with good earnings and minor family responsibilities, increased the uncommitted resources available for giving: 'passing the hat' in mining or forestry camps to assist an unfortunate colleague or his family could raise very substantial sums from ordinary workers, equivalent to a year or more of average wages.[41] Further, the colonists probably had greater need of this informal mutual assistance, which of course had strong elements of reciprocal expectation to it. The underdevelopment of more institutionalised assistance – friendly societies, trade unions, parish charities, philanthropic foundations, charitable aid – would push the settlers in this direction. So, too, might the rending of family ties that went with the long trip from Europe, or the frequent movements that were so typical of life once in the new colony.

On the other hand, we should also recognise likely limits to good neigh-bourliness. Constant mobility would hamper the forming of reciprocal trust. So, too, would divisions between settled and itinerant, respectable and rowdy, teetotal and drinking, all of which were evident in colonial communi-ties: mutual support might work informally within these subcommunities, but not so readily between them. The strong emphasis upon independence and self-reliance may also have put limits upon what colonists were willing to receive or give: taking charity, even from neighbours and equals, might threaten loss of self-respect and social position.

There remains, too, the question of the place of the aged in all this. The elderly were strikingly absent among the key targets for formal and semi-formal charity, and it does not follow that they must therefore have gained heavily from informal support. The scale of the long-run, relentless and substantial needs of the aged for income support are of another order alto-gether from those of younger persons in temporary misfortune, and good neighbourliness may well have been most readily suited to short-term, sudden or spectacular crises, where the possibilities of mutual reciprocity are more evident to all involved.

### Self and family

This brings us to perhaps the least assessable of all of the incomes of the aged. The task of weighing family assistance is fraught in every setting, but especially problematic in colonial New Zealand because of the non-avail-ability of key records. No census manuscripts survive, the destruction of all personal and household schedules then and still being required by law. The Registrar General's records of births, deaths and marriages are generally not open to social researchers. Wage books of large employers have not come to light, and neither friendly society nor trade union archives reveal much of employment histories. Our quest to unpick the 'income packaging' of the colonial elderly runs into serious difficulties at this point, and with that any attempt to weigh the 'success' of the colonial experiment. This is particularly frustrating with respect to aged women, who seem to be all but excluded from direct assistance via the more measurable means of income support – property holding, charitable aid, pensions – and who might in consequence loom large in the cloudier areas of informal and familial support.

Paid employment in later life is one such unfortunate area of darkness. Popular memory seems to hold that before this century few ever reached old age, or lived long into old age, and that continued employment rather than retirement characterised those last years. In other words, memory affirms the colonial experiment: in the absence of compulsory community support, the aged worked on.

New Zealand's scattered written records conspire to reinforce such a view. The regular population censuses, begun in the 1860s, were never designed to reveal work habits, rather than to locate everyone in some occupational and so social class category. The division used between 'breadwinner' and 'dependant' proves of no help at all, since a pensioner with no earned income or a child with part-time work would each be classed as a 'breadwinner', if some description of a job done, now or in the past, could be elicited. A question about unemployment entered the census in the 1890s but the results were not presented by age until the 1920s – and the original schedules have of course gone. Non-statistical records are similarly unhelpful. Because hard work and personal independence were valued so highly, all records – diaries, letters, obituaries and more – consciously or unconsciously stress work as the central feature of respectable life, at all ages, and to talk of retiring or taking it easy or enjoying some quiet years was dangerously close to a character slur. We must treat all discussions of work in later life with suspicion.

Much as with the issue of charity, there are good arguments both for and against the likelihood of extensive employment in later life. On the one hand, colonial society may have offered an unusual number of openings for the ageing. Most workplaces were tiny, and a large fraction of men were self-employed or parts of small contracting gangs: the large public works schemes, for example, were all run by the end of the century as small-gang contracts, with a group of men accepting a contract for a task, the profits and losses then falling to them. The wide ownership of property, including farm land, may also have created a less regimented workplace, in which ageing men and women could 'create' jobs for themselves on terms not available back home. The colonists, too, appear to have been unusually healthy for their time, and this may have made continued working into old age a more practical possibility for many than in other places.[42]

On the other hand, a number of things caution against the assumption that ancestors worked on and on. Research on the United States suggests substantial retirement among older men there late last century, when ownership of property and other savings had many similarities to those found in New Zealand: men retired when they could afford it, and perhaps one-third did so, most noticeably around or soon after age 60.[43] To judge from charitable aid casefiles, or applications for civil service and old-age pensions, a fair number of the colonial aged were not in good physical shape, but carried the scars of earlier accidents, illnesses or congenital deformities, as well as of more recent degenerative impairments, on a scale now hard to recall. Nor did the heavy, slogging nature of much colonial work in exposed conditions make for jobs well suited to the ageing, and Department of Labour inspectors in the 1890s spoke often of the decrepit aged men whom they saw and often helped to tramp the country in search of work, though few would be capable of holding a job if such should ever be found.

Moreover, for substantial portions of the last quarter of the century the colonial labour market was chronically oversupplied: unemployment among men was at 10 per cent and more in some estimates, and emigrants to Australia in search of work exceeded total immigration to New Zealand for several years. Given the nature of colonial labouring jobs, and the seemingly universal habit before the mid twentieth century of laying off older men first in any job shortage, it is hard to imagine that the colonial elderly were not being squeezed hard in the scramble for jobs and wages, and failing in that fight.[44] A unique and extraordinarily meticulous diary of one such colonial labouring man has come to light of late, and charts with numbing repetitiveness the losing battle to keep and hold jobs or to stop wages sliding as James Cox aged from his forties to his eighties.[45]

We come, finally, to the central issue of family, which lay at the heart of the colonial welfare experiment alongside land, working and saving to maintain an independence. Most New Zealanders accept unquestioningly that colonial society consisted of small, close, supportive communities and large, close, supportive families. Once again, there are arguments both for and against accepting this 'memory', together with a frustrating paucity of means by which to test the various plausible hypotheses. The problems with census and registration sources have already been mentioned. Equally limiting was the lack of interest on the part of past census takers in recording anything of familial or domestic arrangements, before the schedules were destroyed, and very few tables on this were published before the 1970s. Building genealogies is a thriving national pastime, but no co-ordination of the results has been attempted, and assessing the nature or scale of kin interactions has yet to catch the imaginations of family historians.

A number of things suggest that the colonial experiment may have worked as intended, with family support for the aged being unusually high. Several have been touched upon already – the general affluence of colonists, the absence of formal alternatives, the long lives lived by the colonial elderly. Our inability thus far to uncover significant sources of support for ageing women in particular might also point to this general conclusion. So do a number of more specific records, though some are open to conflicting interpretations.

Most pertinent here are the few surviving relief casefiles of charitable aid institutions, and even more the papers of the magistrates' courts which were responsible for enforcing the Destitute Persons Laws. The casefiles from Dunedin in the 1890s report routine, repeated and detailed investigation of relatives, as well as of a vaguer, wider group of 'friends', who were called to pledge ongoing support for the impoverished relief applicant, as a precondition to public assistance. My impression is that this vigour – and the contributions solicited – went beyond that seen outside of a very few, COS-dominated, districts in late century Britain, though this cannot be quantified.

The same is suggested by the court papers, which reveal that the statutory powers over relatives were employed frequently throughout the colonial era. Prosecution of men for deserting wives or minor children was common, just as it was in contemporary Britain, but more interesting here are the colonial cases involving aged persons. The Wellington court records from the 1890s illustrate a number of key features.[46]

First, maintenance cases were brought to court by a variety of persons – the elder her- or himself, but equally often by what look like other family members, perhaps daughters or sons who wanted their siblings made to share the burden of support. Second, successful prosecutions and the issuing of orders for maintenance often took several visits to court to secure, but did result in a court order in a majority of instances.

Third, the sums involved were paid weekly, direct to the elder, and involved much more than mere survival amounts. The smallest orders were for about 2*s.* a week, but were often for larger figures. In the early months of 1893, for instance, H. O., a traveller, was ordered to pay his father 5*s.* a week; J. W., a hairdresser, 5*s.* a week to his mother; and the four sons of E. O., a combined 20*s.* a week.

Fourth, maintenance orders remained in force for a good many years, though there is no record in which to trace this consistently. In 1891 T. C., a butcher, and E. C., a carrier, were each ordered to pay 6*s.* 8*d.* a week to their mother; five years later she consented by letter to the quashing of the orders. That same month in 1891 R. C., a plumber, was made to pay 5*s.* a week and his brother, J. C., 7*s.* 6*d.* a week to their mother; seven years later R. C. returned to court to get the order against him lowered to 2*s.* 6*d.*, in view of his reduced circumstances. In 1895 W. M. was ordered to pay 7*s.* 6*d.* a week to his father, the sum later being reduced to 5*s.*; in 1902 W. M. sought a further reduction, arguing that his father now received a 7*s.* a week old-age pension as well as 15*s.* a week from three other sons, but W. M.'s order to pay was not cancelled until 1906.

Fifth, magistrates proved ready to fine and imprison men who failed to meet their obligations to parents. In 1892 H. O. was ordered to pay 5*s.* a week to his father; four months later, now two months in arrears, he was sentenced to two months' imprisonment with hard labour, to take effect at once. More common was a suspended sentence, with a few weeks to clear the debt and avoid jail. In July 1895 T. C. was given one month's hard labour, held off for fourteen days, for neglecting to pay the 6*s.* 8*d.* a week due to his mother. That same month W. M. was sentenced to the same, but suspended for four days only, for falling down on the order of 5*s.* a week to his father.

A sixth feature is the small but persisting number of prosecutions of relatives other than sons. In December 1892 C. B. sought maintenance from her daughter, married to a farmer in the South Island, and 7*s*. 6*d*. a week was ordered. In 1893 J. M. and his wife brought a prosecution against their daughter M. S., perhaps a married woman of some means; the case was dismissed without explanation. In 1895 a man was brought to the court for being in arrears on an order to pay 2*s*. a week to his sister. That same year H. C. was made to pay his sister 2*s*. a week. In October two brothers G. were charged with failing to assist their sister, and 5*s*. a week was eventually ordered from each.

Seventh, the prosecution rate appeared to accelerate and the sums ordered to climb, after state old-age pensions were introduced. This reflects the strong determination, written into the new pension law, that family responsibility should remain a key support for the ageing. In 1905 in Wellington, for instance, an unknown number of earlier orders were still in force. In addition, during that year J. O. was ordered to pay 2*s*. 6*d*. a week to his father; A. B., a stock dealer, 7*s*. 6*d*. to his father; R. M., farmer, 10*s*. to his mother; W. D., labourer, 5*s*. to his mother; H. S., caretaker, 5*s*. to his mother; F. D. 2*s*. 6*d*. to his mother; W. S., driver, 15*s*. to his mother, G. P., hotel keeper, 10*s*. to his mother; and W. G., dairy farmer, 5*s*. a week to his mother.

All this had few if any parallels back home, and raises key questions of interpretation. Most importantly, were the few appearing in court being made to do what the majority did voluntarily, or did not do? I incline towards the former, for several reasons. Legal action on emotive issues such as this is unlikely to be successful, if pushed against strong popular opposition. The loud, bitter and prolonged debates surrounding the New Poor Law in England in the 1830s and 1840s gave good instances of this, and the anti-relief drive was reined in substantially in consequence. Yet there is very little evidence of any such general popular reaction against the maintenance laws in New Zealand.

Another interesting indication of broad support for familial financial responsibilities was the new war pension legislation of 1915. This included for the first time pensions for life to the parents of servicemen killed in action, on the grounds that recruitment would prove difficult, and parents reluctant to let their sons go, if the finances of the aged were not so secured. In other words, it was assumed that a son would already be or would have become a financial prop for his parents, and that his loss must therefore be compensated with money. Through the 1920s around 5,000 a year of these 'parent pensions' were paid, the number being about one-quarter the number of general old-age pensions. Since New Zealand governments did not lightly give out state cash without a work test, this again suggests a wide acceptance that sons were indeed significant financial contributors to ageing parents.

Nevertheless, there are also good grounds for caution in weighing the spread and scale of colonial familial support. A first was colonial demography, with a large fraction of migrants having left most or all of their rela-tives in other countries. Second, most colonial women may have had children, but not so all colonial men. The overwhelming majority of women in nineteenth-century New Zealand married, and median birth numbers for those marrying in the 1860s or 1870s were seven or eight.[47] Given the rela-tively good survival rates of colonial children, with three-quarters or so likely to reach adulthood, this should have meant that the majority of women reaching old age by the turn of the century would have several surviving children. But women reaching old age before this may well have had more truncated kin networks because of migration, and this could limit their potential supporters: those reaching old age later had smaller networks of young relatives because of falling fertility. This was still more true for the more numerous men reaching old age last century, one-third or more of whom may well have been unmarried or married but childless. The frequent and often long-distance moves which characterised much colonial life would also limit the proximity of older and younger relatives, and so perhaps the ability or the willingness to assist. No attempts have yet been made to simu-late the possible kin networks within this migrant colony.

A further reason for caution is the absence of evidence of family support in places where we might expect to find just such evidence. An example is the in-depth survey conducted under Toynbee's direction into the early twentieth-century childhoods of 108 now-aged Wellingtonians.[48] Not one of her forty or so 'middle-class' respondents recalled a grandparent sharing a home with them during childhood, and only 'several' of the more than sixty 'working-class' ones did so. This begs further questions about how many grandparents there actually were to go around – how many *could* have lived with a grandparent present, even in theory? – but it does warn against imag-ining that live-in elderly relatives were a normal part of colonial life.

This finding might imply no more than that families ordinarily assisted their elders by giving money or other assistance, not by sharing a home. But again, evidence of this happening is lacking. Toynbee's interviewees recalled very little of this. No middle-class respondents and only 'a few' working-class ones could recall any day-to-day aid between kin – most simply had no kin living close enough for such to happen. In just one of 108 interviews were aged grandparents recalled as being financially dependent upon a child, in that instance a widowed daughter in the 1920s, although a couple of others remembered unmarried children who stayed on living with parents to help them out. All this can raise doubts about the uses of childhood memory to explore such matters – perhaps children simply do not see what is going on. But despite expecting and so setting out to find strong evidence of close family ties in late colonial New Zealand, Toynbee could turn up little of it, rather against her own theories and sympathies.

Other interesting silences are 'heard' in several places. An early survey of working-class household income and expenditure was undertaken in 1893 by the new Department of Labour. There are many problems with the results, arising from the odd sample used, but the questions about expenditure put to all were detailed – and not one household mentioned any expenditure in support of aged or other relatives. This is not peculiar to New Zealand: contemporary surveys of household budgets by Booth, Rowntree, Bowley and others are equally silent on this matter. Colonial letters, diaries and the like surviving from 100 years ago also make little mention of money shared in support of the ageing, though they talk a great deal of kin interactions of other forms. And some records – early applications for old-age pensions are the striking instance – speak powerfully of great resentment at having to receive support from younger family members, and the immense emotional relief to relatives offered by the new state pension.

## A successful experiment?

What, then, of the experiment's 'success'? Some things clearly did not happen as many hoped or intended – mutual aid associations did not flourish, and formal philanthropy remained small, for example. But in other important respects key aims were met to a considerable degree. Wide property ownership was achieved, and other individual savings were built, to give substantial fractions an independence in later life. When state old-age pensions were introduced only one-third of the aged came below the personal income and assets levels to qualify, even though these might have appeared quite high to contemporary Britons: the full £18 a year or 7s. a week pension did not begin to abate until other income passed £34 a year or 13s. a week, or assets passed £250 net worth. Familial assistance to the aged was pushed hard, and may well have been substantial in a good number of instances, within the limits set by migration and demography. The apparent relative good health of the colonial elderly might point further to the experiment's general achievements.

However, it is less clear that the experiment could last, or provide ready models for other places and times. Peculiar conditions may have permitted, for a spell, the appearance of a society that had solved the perennial problem of how to maintain its aged. But by century's end those special conditions were passing fast, the experiment was being put to a more demanding test, serious strains soon showed, and the society moved swiftly to introduce rights to public assistance in later life.

A central peculiarity was of course the colonial demography. The settler population was to remain comparatively youthful by European standards throughout the twentieth century, but around 1900 the aged fractions came close for a time to the agedness of the Old World. This, combined with unusual longevity, multiplied very rapidly the demands for redistribution of income to the old. At the same time, fertility was falling swiftly, from the average seven or eight births per woman to about four to the marriages of 1900, and 2.5 to the marriages of the 1920s. The two processes magnified the perceived, potential and actual demands facing each of those offspring, and so put the experiment in family responsibility under added pressure. By the end of the century, too, substantial fractions of the adult population were for the first time New Zealand born, and so had their older relatives present in this country, rather than distant in Britain. Having been a rather remote and theoretical matter in earlier colonial decades, family responsibility for the old swiftly became an immediate and very practical matter for large numbers in the century's last years.

Wide property ownership, especially of more than just a dwelling, was also a passing colonial phenomenon, though our data on this are limited. In the 1880s around 50 per cent of all adult males and perhaps three-quarters of older men had held freehold property. By the First World War, when a question on home owning first entered the population census, about 35 per cent of adult men owned a home (no age breakdowns are available), while the numbers of owner–farmers were still much the same as in the later nineteenth century, even as the population had gone on expanding. This suggests both lowered rates of home ownership – they have since rebuilt past colonial levels – and a shrinking spread of 'income-generating' property. Savings in various other forms were growing around the turn of the century: life policies, for instance, reached a ratio of one to every four adults in 1900, one to two in the 1920s, and one to one around 1950. But it is not clear that private savings were mounting on a scale to replace dwindling property ownership or the rise in the elderly population. At least half of those life policies were industrial ones, for sums inconsequential beside the expenses of old age, and other savings such as through friendly societies or employee benefit schemes were still largely irrelevant to the elderly. The personal savings vital to sustaining the welfare experiment were not being put in place for the aged of the early twentieth century.

Changes in the job market may also have helped undermine the experiment, though this remains speculative. Many at century's end, in New Zealand as elsewhere, worried about a quickening, elder-penalising pace of work, although the evidence that this actually pushed the aged into unemployment is not convincing. Less open to doubt is the historical decline in self-employment, which used to be most prevalent in the later stages of working life. Ransom, Sutch and associates in the United States have highlighted important connections between self-employment, the building of savings, and the resources available to sustain retirement, and it is possible that the shrinking of both property ownership and self-employment led to new difficulties for ageing men (and their younger relatives) in both staying in and extricating themselves from the labour market.

Questions of 'success' also raise the matter of 'in whose eyes?' There is good evidence of considerable poverty among some of the colonial aged, alongside comfort and freedom for others: the experiment did not work well for all. It may also have been that the experiment worked better for ageing males than for ageing women, who would seem to have been forced to depend more upon family and charity than upon property and savings.

Anecdotal evidence of tension and bitterness within families also poses questions about 'success'. Forcing younger relatives to pay older ones could put all under great pressure, with elders resenting their dependence upon children and grandchildren, those children and grandchildren resenting the competition from elders for limited resources. Family dependence could also increase inequities within and between families, and leave much to the erratic play of chance, with individuals' life plans and opportunities determined heavily and perhaps unfairly by the chance that parents will die early or late, or of being one among many or few offspring. In an industrialising modern society, where the ethic of equality of opportunity was also strong, this high exposure to random family events may have become increasingly unacceptable. The new universal suffrage gave electors a means to voice their concerns.

When put to the test the colonial experiment revealed important limitations, and the introduction of state old-age pensions was an admission that in a New World some Old World realities would have to be acknowledged: substantial and long-living elderly populations require substantial public sharing of costs, across age, family and social groups. Experimenting once again now with enforced personal saving or greater familial responsibility for the old might possibly work differently – investment markets, among other things, are today much more sophisticated. But one historical experiment with these ideas, in circumstances at least initially rather favourable to their success, gives grounds for caution in searching too far down this road for the 'post-welfare state'.

## Notes

1 'Settler', 'colonist' and 'New Zealander' will here refer only to the non-Maori, European arrivals of the nineteenth century.
2 This essay draws upon a larger study: D. Thomson, *A World Without Welfare: New Zealand's Colonial Experiment*, Auckland, 1998.
3 Section 1, 10 Vic No. 9, in W. Badger, *Statutes of New Zealand*, Christchurch, 1892.
4 A fuller discussion of these legal issues appears in D. Thomson, ' "I am not my father's keeper": families and the elderly in nineteenth century England', *Law and History Review*, 1984, vol. 2, pp. 265–86.
5 41 Vic No. 44, *Statutes of New Zealand*, 1877.
6 47 Vic No. 26, *Statutes of New Zealand*, 1883.
7 58 Vic No. 22, *Statutes of New Zealand*, 1894.
8 *New Zealand Parliamentary Debates*, 8 September 1910, vol. 151, p. 436.
9 The best study of this is M. Tennant, *Paupers and Providers: Charitable Aid in New Zealand*, Wellington, 1989.
10 *New Zealand Parliamentary Debates*, 27 July 1877, vol. 24, p. 75.
11 Ibid., pp. 73–4.
12 The best estimates of the age balance before the era of the modern census are those in E. A. Wrigley and R. S. Schofield, *The Population History of England 1541–1871: A Reconstruction*, London, 1981, p. 216.
13 The argument that Poor Law assistance to the nineteenth-century English aged was extensive has been championed by the present author. For a summary state-

ment see D. Thomson, 'The welfare of the elderly in the past: a family or community responsibility?', in M. Pelling and R. M. Smith (eds), *Life, Death and the Elderly: Historical Perspectives*, London, 1991, pp. 194–221. Important questions about this have been raised, for example, in P. Thane, 'Old people and their families in the English past', in M. Daunton (ed.), *Charity, Self-interest and Welfare in the English Past*, London, 1996, pp.113–38.

14 Scottish Poor Law history is discussed in R. Mitchison, 'The Poor Law', in T. M. Devine and Rosalind Mitchison (eds), *People and Society in Scotland, I, 1760–1830*, Edinburgh, 1988, pp. 252–67, or R. A. Cage, *The Scottish Poor Law, 1745–1845*, Edinburgh, 1981. The Scottish statutes are examined in R. P. Lamond, *The Scottish Poor Laws: Their History, Policy and Operation*, revised edition, Glasgow, 1892.

15 The most provocative advocate of the 'atomisation' argument is M. Fairburn, 'Local community or atomised society? The social structure of nineteenth century New Zealand', *New Zealand Journal of History*, 1982, vol. 16, pp. 146–67. Recent champions of 'community' include R. Arnold, 'Community in rural Victorian New Zealand', *New Zealand Journal of History*, 1990, vol. 24, pp. 3–21.

16 The most comprehensive account of government land schemes remains W. Jourdain, *Land Legislation and Settlement in New Zealand*, Wellington, 1925.

17 The Treaty created 'Crown pre-emption', or the right of the Crown to be sole purchaser of Maori land, though Crown pre-emption was waived for thirty years from the mid 1860s.

18 In fact the powers of compulsion were hardly ever used, so keen were heavily indebted owners to sell to the Crown.

19 *A Return of the Freeholders of New Zealand*, Wellington, 1884. This was prepared by the Property Tax Office, from returns filed under the 1879 Property Tax Law. Its publication drew charges of invasion of privacy, and the exercise was never repeated. Through the next twenty-five years short statistical returns on ownership were published from time to time in *Appendices to the Journals of the House of Representatives*, that is the series close in nature to British Parliamentary Command Papers.

20 The *Return* has not yet received the critical attention it deserves. This discussion draws upon two studies of it: C. Toynbee, 'Class and social structure in nineteenth century New Zealand', *New Zealand Journal of History*, 1979, vol. 13, pp. 65–84, and M. Fairburn, *The Ideal Society and its Enemies: The Foundations of Modern New Zealand Society, 1850–1900*, Auckland, 1989, ch. 4.

21 M. Galt, 'Wealth and income in New Zealand, 1879–1939', Unpublished Ph.D. thesis in Economic History, Victoria University of Wellington, 1985.

22 Results of a Property Assessment, *Appendices to the Journals of the House of Representatives*, B-15, 1890.

23 Report on the Crown Lands Department for the year ending 31 March 1882, ibid., C-1, 1882.

24 *Official Handbook of New Zealand*, Wellington, 1875.

25 A useful recent survey of some of these interventions is J. Martin, 'Unemployment, government and the labour market in New Zealand, 1860–1890', *New Zealand Journal of History*, 1995, vol. 29, pp. 170–96.

26 G. Hawke, *The Making of New Zealand: An Economic History*, Cambridge, 1985, pp. 112–14.

27 List of Pensions Paid by the Colony, *Appendices to the Journals of the House of Representatives*, B-18, 1888.

28 Appropriations Ordinance, Canterbury Provincial Government, *Provincial Government Ordinances*, Session XXXIX, Christchurch, 1873.

29 Return of Persons Receiving Relief from the Provincial Government on 30 September 1870, Charitable Aid Depot, Paper No. 20 to Canterbury Provincial Government, Session XXXIV. Held at Canterbury Museum.
30 Calculated from data published annually by the government in *Statistics of New Zealand*.
31 Otago Benevolent Institution Inmates Book, 1898. Held in Otago Hospital Board Collection, Hocken Library, University of Otago.
32 Otago Benevolent Institution Outdoor Relief Book, 1893. Held in Otago Hospital Board Collection, Hocken Library, University of Otago. The English statistics are discussed in D. Thomson, 'From workhouse to nursing home: residential care of elderly people in England since 1840', *Ageing and Society*, 1983, vol. 3, pp. 43–70.
33 Otago Benevolent Institution Outdoor Relief Casebooks, 1889–1910. Otago Hospital Board Collection, Hocken Library, University of Otago.
34 The best study of working-class saving habits remains P. Johnson, *Saving and Spending: The Working-class Economy in Britain, 1870–1939*, Oxford, 1985.
35 The key sources here are the annual reports from the 1870s of the Registrar of Friendly Societies, which were published in the *Appendices to the Journals of the House of Representatives*.
36 Report and Evidence of the Royal Commission on Private Benefit Societies, ibid., H-2, 1897.
37 Data on life policies were published annually in the official annual *Statistics of New Zealand*.
38 Banking details also appear in *Statistics of New Zealand*.
39 These examples are taken from the Outdoor Relief Casefiles of the Otago Benevolent Institution, which record assistance already being received in other ways by applicants for charitable aid.
40 See, for example, the history of social work in Dunedin by the city's dominant Presbyterian Church: S. Rae, *From Relief to Social Work: A History of the Presbyterian Social Service Association, Otago, 1906–81*, Dunedin, 1981.
41 A recent study of North Island bush communities in the 1880s which gives instances of this type of giving is R. Arnold, *New Zealand's Burning: The Settlers' World in the mid 1880s*, Wellington, 1994.
42 This is so if we accept that lower death rates at higher ages is indicative of better general health at those ages. That has long been the conventional wisdom, but it is being challenged increasingly now, as late twentieth-century populations live longer but do not necessarily enjoy equally lengthening 'disability-free' years.
43 For example, R. L. Ransom and R. Sutch, 'The labor of older Americans: retirement of men on and off the job, 1870–1937', *Journal of Economic History*, 1986, vol. 46, pp. 1–30.
44 The first New Zealand tabulations of unemployment by age, from the censuses of the interwar years, showed a marked age gradient. In 1936, for instance, about 2 per cent of males aged 15–19 reported themselves as unemployed and seeking work, alongside 5–6 per cent of those in their twenties, 6–7 per cent in their thirties, 7–8 per cent in their forties, 11 per cent in their fifties, and 16 per cent past age 60. Duration of unemployment showed a parallel age gradient.
45 The diary is the subject of M. Fairburn, *Nearly Out of Heart and Hope*, Auckland, 1995.
46 Two sets of Wellington Magistrates' Court records form the basis of the following discussion: the Criminal Record Books, 1893–, forming class JC Wellington 1, and the Register of Orders for Maintenance under the Destitute Persons Acts, 1891–, forming class JC Wellington 6, both at National Archives of New Zealand, Wellington.

47 The source of this was a fertility census in 1911, much like the better-known British one of that year. The New Zealand results were published with disappointingly little detail, before forms were destroyed.
48 C. Toynbee, *Her Work and His, Kin and Community in New Zealand, 1900–1930*, Wellington, 1995.

# 9    The family lives of old people

*Pat Thane*

A persistent theme of western discourse over many centuries has been the conviction that younger people neglect their older relatives. This has been reinforced by the conviction of historians of the household and the family that, at least in north-western Europe, there has long been no cultural obligation upon younger to support older generations.[1] One historian has gone so far as to argue that historically it has been 'unEnglish behaviour to expect children to support parents';[2] older people who could not support themselves had to look to whatever poor relief system was available. This interpretation has been derived from the study of household listings which describe who shares a roof with whom and tell us much that is valuable about close relationships over many centuries. Of their nature, however, they can tell us very little about relationships between kin and others who do not share a home. This is a problem for those concerned about the history of intergenerational relationships, particularly in view of another interpretation which suggests that the culture of north-western Europe is characterised by close and supportive relationships between generations, which normally stop short of sharing a household – 'intimacy at a distance' as two sociologists have characterised it.[3] Unfortunately the evidence that this might have been so in the past is scanty and anecdotal.[4] It was no one's duty to collect systematic records of everyday, generally non-financial, reciprocity.

Only after the Second World War were there systematic studies of the relationships between old people and their families. This was partly due to the expansion and somewhat increased rigour of social survey research at this time. Awareness that close relationships existed between the generations even when they did not share a household, and that they were important both for the older and the younger people, initially emerged unexpectedly from surveys with other concerns. The surprise expressed by researchers indicates how widespread was the belief that old people were often and increasingly isolated. The conviction that this was so was particularly well established in medical and social work discourse, not surprisingly because health and social workers were most likely to encounter older people in difficulties. A different picture began to emerge when researchers looked at 'normal' old people in their homes and communities rather than focusing on those in contact with professionals.

The increasing marginalisation of older people had also become a taken-for-granted assumption of sociological theory, promoted in particular by Talcott Parsons' influential assertion that the increased geographical mobility of younger people in modern society left old people isolated.[5] This was not derived from empirical findings and, when investigated, turned out not to be the case, even in the United States, where the belief was born.[6] Of more lasting influence, and empirically equally dubious, is the assumption of economic theory that most voluntaristic transfers, including between generations, are abandoned in 'the great transformation' from pre-commercial to modern economies, being irrational, inefficient behaviour for naturally profit-maximising, self-interested humankind which is unconcerned about the welfare of others.[7]

## Old age in Wolverhampton

The first widely noticed British survey to stumble upon the importance of old people's family networks and the variety of exchanges within them was not primarily sociological but medical, conducted by J. H. Sheldon in 1945–7 for the Nuffield Foundation. This was one of a cluster of investigations into ageing established by the Foundation. Sheldon, Director of Medicine at The Royal Hospital, Wolverhampton, investigated the health of a representative sample of old people living at home in Wolverhampton. It was a pioneering attempt to assess the health of 'normal' old people in order to expand the currently limited understanding of 'normal' ageing.

Sheldon soon discovered the 'surprising fact' that

> contact with old people in their homes immediately brings to light the fact that the family is of fundamental importance. This is best seen by the extent to which old people who are ostensibly living alone . . . are in actual fact by no means living alone, but are in close and regular contact with their children.[8]

In over 20 per cent of the sample

> the old people had relatives living so close that the limitations imposed by architecture were resolved by family affection – in times of ease each household more or less going its own way, in times of stress functioning together as one unit.[9]

Contact between generations took a variety of forms. Sheldon described, among others:

A man aged 72 – a widower – lives by himself. A married daughter lives some fifty yards away with an entrance through the garden. Subject does his own housework, but the daughter does his shopping and brings him a hot meal every day, while he goes to the daughter on Sundays. Subject is very lonely, but prefers this arrangement. It preserves his independence and prevents him having to spend the whole day in a house full of small children.

A widow aged 70 lives by herself. She habitually spends the day with a married daughter living in the same street and helps to look after the grandchildren, which she greatly enjoys and at which she is very useful. She only uses her own home for bed and breakfast. In case of illness, of either the subject or the daughter, each would look after the other.

In the sample 53 per cent of widowers and 51 per cent of widows lived alone but with children close by. Sheldon judged that for 40 per cent of the sample their 'happiness and domestic efficiency was dependent on the accessibility of their children or other relatives . . . each family is independent in health and co-operative in illness'. 'It is clear that the decision of a widowed subject to live alone is dependent, in half the cases, on the fact that relatives – usually children – are living close at hand.'[10]

Living 'near' was defined by Sheldon as 'a distance within which a hot meal could be carried from one house to another without needing re-heating' – or not more than five minutes' walking distance. He found that many meals were carried to and from the houses of older people, or daughters regularly cooked at and/or cleaned the parental home.[11] On this definition 30 per cent of the sample had relatives living 'near'. Many more had children living beyond this narrow range with whom they were in constant contact. For example:

A woman aged 64 is very lonely, living by herself after the recent death of her husband. She has four sons who come regularly to see her and a granddaughter aged 16 comes regularly to sleep. Subject wishes to continue living by herself and says the granddaughter's company makes all the difference.[12]

In nine cases married daughters 'had to make regular journeys of considerable extent in order to assist their parents to run their houses'. All of these had tried to move closer but had been unsuccessful owing to the shortage of housing following the war.

Sheldon concluded that 'the whole question of the part played in the economy of old people's households by their children living in other houses is one of great importance and merits a full-dress study', and that health and welfare policy should in future take it into account.[13]

A number of older people had no close relatives, living near or far.

Sheldon noted that 'where there are no family ties, these tend to be replaced by friendships formed earlier in life' – as when two women of the same occupation such as nursing or teaching set up home together when they retire. He also found that, in the mid twentieth as in earlier centuries, old people held on to their independence for as long as they were able:

> The majority of old people are responsible for their own domestic care and they consistently make every effort to maintain this state of affairs, so that the percentage of women doing their own housework unaided remains at a steady figure up to the period 75–9 years of age . . . more old people are looking after themselves than are dependent on others [but] those in the older groups inevitably become increasingly dependent on the younger generation, especially the daughter.

He was convinced that 'There is little doubt that up to the age of seventy-five at least, women give the community more than they take in the matter of domestic responsibility.'[14] When unmarried children lived with parents, forms of reciprocity varied: 'another common mode of existence is that of the daughter in employment who is looked after by her parents during the week, but does the housework over the weekend'.[15] The stress on reciprocity and the contribution of old people to the care of others, in place of the stereotype of passive dependency, was to become another major theme of post-war research.

Sheldon estimated that about 7 per cent of old people were struggling to maintain independence when they were physically incapable of it. But his main conclusion was that it was misleading to treat households as discrete units:

> It should again be emphasised that to regard old people in their homes as a series of individual experiences is to miss the point of their mode of life in the community. The family is clearly the unit in the majority of instances.[16]

Only a few old people 'withdraw into a solitary existence'.[17] And

> while a considerable number of old people may ostensibly be living alone and would be so classified in the census, their children may be living sufficiently close for the two families to function as one where necessary, so that the phrase 'living alone' is not a true description of the state of affairs.

The old people in Sheldon's sample lived in a variety of arrangements. Widowhood might prompt a move to live with married children, usually a daughter, though more commonly and at earlier ages for widowers than widows. Widows had a greater variety of opportunities for independent living, such as taking in boarders or sharing a household with another woman. Fourteen of them kept shops, six single-handed. These women 'were all of vigorous mentality – one woman of eighty ran a small mixed shop entirely alone, in addition to looking after herself and said it was the contact with people in the shop that kept her alive'.[18]

Sheldon was eager to convey the positive picture of normal old age which emerged so surprisingly to him from the survey, in contrast with his twenty years' experience in medical practice. In consequence he may have underestimated the tensions in family relationships. Nevertheless he usefully challenged firmly established stereotypes and pointed to a world of intergenerational reciprocity which was real, whatever its – surely immensely varied – emotional content. He commented that 'old age undoubtedly places great strains on the younger generation, but that is only part of the picture, and it is well to remember the debt owed by the community to the domestic work done by the older woman'.[19] Eight of the sample (1.67 per cent) were cared for by younger relatives, usually daughters, who had given up paid work to look after them. This was often possible only because other siblings worked to provide the family income, but 'she then undergoes a particular hardship by becoming dependent on others for pocket money'.[20] Alternatively when the household could not afford to lose her income:

> a daughter may by having to remain at work, become almost a slave – at work all day, and doing the housework or nursing that may be required in the early mornings and evenings. No less than 43 per cent of the younger generation concerned in the care of old people were in employment and there were instances of severe hardship in this group.[21]

Married daughters could carry no less strain:

> A woman aged 62 who was a member of the sample, is a tower of physical strength, keeping home for her husband and daughter and does everything including the washing and mangling. She also has the care of an aged mother (aged 89) who is bedridden after a fall downstairs. She has looked after her for 24 years and for the last eight years has had no break. She says she is dying to have a fortnight by the sea with her husband, but the domestic ties make this totally impossible.[22]

On the other hand, ten old women were bringing up grandchildren, often also in considerable hardship.

Sheldon was surprised by the number of men – 35 per cent of the sample – who 'assisted' with housework:

> the usual feature is for the man to make the morning cup of tea, light the fire and do the washing up. He frequently makes himself responsible for the heavy work in the house – such as scrubbing and cleaning,

getting the coal in etc. The shopping is usually done by the woman, if her health is sufficiently good, but several men were encountered who made a speciality of shopping, doing it for several households. The cooking is done by the women in most cases but not all – some of the men being particularly skilled and enjoying it. . . . Almost every division of labour was found, but except where the woman was physically incapable the man was virtually never trusted to make the beds.[23]

## Family and kinship in east London

Peter Willmott and Michael Young's sociological study of Bethnal Green in east London in the mid-1950s made a wider impact than Sheldon's and established, at least in academic circles, awareness that active family networks were still important in modern societies, though like Sheldon they made this discovery by accident, in a study primarily focused on housing policy. This revealed that a high proportion of adults lived close to their parents, though daughters lived closer than sons. A significant proportion lived with parents for a time after marriage, more often daughters and more often youngest than older daughters. As in Wolverhampton, most older people asserted that living physically nearby, but independently of, close relatives was the ideal relationship.

Willmott and Young described, often in tones of surprise, a world of closely interconnected family exchange. For example, Mr and Mrs Banton took over Mrs Banton's grandfather's private tenancy when he went into a home, when her mother 'had a word' with the rent collector. He had been looked after by an aunt living nearby until her house was 'cleared' by the Council and she was moved to an estate outside London. Mrs Banton's mother lived nearby and Mrs Banton went round several times a day to see her and to fetch her shopping. Her mother was less active than when she was younger but could still look after the grandchildren when the need arose.[24] Mothers could find their children homes in the neighbourhood through their knowledge of local movements and of how to negotiate moves. With increasing Council control of the property market such arrangements were becoming more difficult.

Willmott and Young commented:

> These accounts put a new light on the ordinary idea of the household. People live together – they are considered to be in the same household. But what if they spend a good part of the day and eat (or at least drink tea) regularly in someone else's household? The households are then to some extent merged . . . the daily lives of many women are not confined to the places where they sleep; they are spread over two or more households, in each of which they regularly spend part of their time.[25]

They described a community in which links between the generations were strong, though two adult generations rarely lived in the same household except sometimes for short periods following marriage or at the very end of the older people's lives. Families centred upon 'Mum'. There was constant exchange of visits and services which official social services sometimes complemented but did not replace. Mothers helped out when children were born to their daughters, cared for children while their mothers worked. There were close relationships between grandchildren and grandparents.

In the 1950s many people moved from overcrowding and poor housing in Bethnal Green to suburban council housing estates. The central purpose of Willmott and Young's study was to investigate the effects of such moves. They surveyed Bethnal Greeners' moves to 'Greenleigh', less than twenty miles away on a direct underground line. Some of the migrants brought their relatives to join them. One man explained how his mother had moved after them. His 13-year-old daughter went in twice a week:

> she clears the place and runs errands. All the children go round there and help. And I help with the gardening and I decorated her house. My father came down too and my brother Tom has moved to Greenleigh as well.[26]

After the move most migrants saw less of relatives and less help was exchanged, for example in sickness and childbirth, owing to distance and cost of travel, but over time more relatives moved to be together. Increasingly telephones were installed, to keep in touch. Families adjusted to changed circumstances.

Willmott and Young were surprised to find the extended family alive and well in inner London. In their rather stilted study they treated it as a survival from the hard times of the past, destined for extinction as prosperity brought into being what they believed was the modern norm of the nuclear household headed by companionate parents, as predicted by sociological theory. Nevertheless their interpretation of family life in Bethnal Green was positive, even nostalgic. They accepted their subjects' accounts very much at face value presenting Bethnal Green as a model urban village in which there was remarkably little strife, in contrast to the conflicts vividly evident in accounts of Bethnal Green in earlier[27] and later[28] decades.

## The family lives of old people

Old people and their families were not the main concern of Willmott and Young's study though they emerged prominently in it. They were central to a companion study by Peter Townsend. This was funded by the Nuffield Foundation and designed to establish whether Sheldon's and other comparable[29] findings about the family relationships of old people could be replicated.[30]

Townsend also found that old people in Bethnal Green often chose to live alone after widowhood. They wanted to be independent, to remain in their homes for as long as they could. They expressed fears – as old people long had[31] – of the conflict that might arise if they lived with younger people. As various old people told him: 'It's nice to be near, but not too near.' 'You need a private place.' 'It's right to be independent.' They had good reason to prefer independence. The report of the committee chaired by Rowntree for the Nuffield Foundation suggested that old people dependent upon others were sometimes inadequately fed. Resources were not necessarily equally distributed within households.[32]

Townsend found that sometimes two generations shared a house, but kept separate households, though the women might spend a lot of time together during the day. As the older generation aged the households might increasingly merge. As in Wolverhampton, most old couples and singles living alone received help from and gave help to relatives. Townsend, like Sheldon, stressed reciprocity between generations in contrast to the stereotype of old people as dependent objects of care. Among many examples he found:

Mrs Hopkins, a widow in her early sixties, lived alone in a new council flat. She did most of her own shopping, cooking, cleaning and washing, although she had some help with the errands from one of her daughters-in-law, a grandson and one of her two sons, all of whom lived in an adjoining borough. In the day she looked after a grandson aged six, and at midday her son came for a meal and so did her other son's wife. She charged them 2s each for the meal. 'I wouldn't trouble to cook for myself. That's why I like them coming.' She spent her weekends with one or other of her sons.[33]

A woman and her married daughters living nearby were able to organise domestic work and care of the children in such a way that each of them was able to maintain a part-time job. The grandmother went off to work as an office cleaner at 6 in the morning, returning home at 10 a.m. She then had the care of the grandchildren while two married daughters went out to work, one as a waitress, one as a part-time newspaper wrapper. The daughters did her shopping on their way home from work.[34]

Such relationships were complex. Townsend noted that

part of the strength of family relationships comes from individuals receiving and returning services. Some old people can no longer reciprocate the services performed for them and this seems to make them less willing to accept help and their relatives sometimes less willing to give it. Among infirm people it was noticeable that a few getting least help were not in a position to give anything in exchange.[35]

Townsend, like Sheldon and Willmott and Young, concluded that

> It was wrong to consider the domestic affairs of the elderly in terms of
> the bricks and mortar of a structurally separate home as much for those
> living alone as for those living with relatives of two or three
> generations.[36]

Financial transfers were most common where the generations shared a
household, but 'many old people had financial help from children living
elsewhere and the day-to-day provision of meals and care of grandchildren
led to many exchanges of money and goods in kind'. Of Townsend's sample
of old people 61 per cent depended upon or were assisted by regular contributions from relatives. If regular help in kind was included the proportion
rose to 75 per cent. Financial transactions were of three main kinds: money
paid by children or other relatives for their board in the household; cash or
gifts from relatives living elsewhere, usually children; payments in money or
kind for services performed by old people, such as provision of meals for
married children or care of grandchildren. The value of the cash transactions must have been much less than the real value of services exchanged.

The old people treated such transactions as a matter of course. 'It would
be their duty, just like we did for our parents', one person put it. She and her
husband received between 10 shillings and a pound a week from their children, and emphasised that this would increase if needed. Gifts were usually
small – between 2 shillings and sixpence and 10 shillings – irregular and
given for a purpose: they might pay for costly necessities, like boots, or luxu-
ries like holidays. Sons were more likely than daughters to give money. They
often had easier access to ready cash though it may also suggest a less close
relationship with parents.[37] Those who received nothing generally had no
close relatives or the relatives were themselves too poor to assist.[38]

Such transactions could be difficult to identify, partly because they were
such a taken-for-granted feature of family relationships:

> A widow at first said she had no help from her children. 'I'd sooner go
> without than ask. They shouldn't need to be asked should they?' A son
> lived outside London and a daughter in the next street. It turned out she
> had just spent a month at her son's home, at his expense, and apart from
> staying with him from time to time in the year he had helped her buy
> clothing and linen recently. It also turned out her daughter's husband
> had artificial legs and lived for frequent spells on sickness benefit[39]

and so could not help her. Transfers within the families of older people were
more complex than Townsend was able to scrutinise, but he concluded that
'principles by which household budgets of elderly people are normally
collected and evaluated may require re-examination'.[40] They could indeed be
complex. One widow

lived with her two married daughters and had a housekeeping allowance from one of them, while the eldest contributed to the rent. . . . The youngest daughter's allowance was roughly £4 for herself, her husband and child, and in addition she paid her mother between 10s and £1 for looking after the child. Sometimes the widow had a meal with her eldest daughter. A nephew was given a bed in the house four nights of the week and the nephew's mother paid 10s in addition to the sum he paid for meals. Two married sons living nearby gave the widow a few shillings each week and she had meals in their homes at week-ends. She quoted instances of one or the other in the family paying for an oil-stove, a dress and club subscriptions.[41]

Such transactions were important in the economies of many old people – though how important for how many remained unclear. The system of means-testing for state benefits was an incentive for old people to be reticent about them, as the Poor Law had long been. The extent of poverty in retirement, which Townsend also documented,[42] meant that the need for support from relatives was real. When wives received gifts they would not necessarily tell their husbands, just as they were themselves mostly ignorant of their husbands' earnings when at work.[43] But when he retired generally the wife controlled the pension and doled out his pocket-money.

The family relationships which Townsend described were similar to those uncovered by Willmott and Young. Again Mum was the central figure and grandmothers, especially, often had close relationships with grandchildren and were closely involved in their upbringing. Sometimes grandchildren would stay with them full or part-time, for company, for assistance or to relieve pressure on the parental family. One small boy told Townsend: 'I've got two homes. I live with my Nan and go upstairs to my Mummy to sleep.'

Many of the older people were in their late fifties or sixties when their youngest child reached marriageable age; most children lived with their parents until marriage. After marriage, relationships with children varied. Daughters who married men of higher social status tended to see less of their parents, though sons who rose in status saw as much of their parents as other sons. Very few of the old people in Bethnal Green lost contact with all of their children.

Of Townsend's sample (of 203 people, two-thirds of them women) 58 per cent were members of three-generation families and saw relatives of the other generations every day or almost every day. More distant relatives provided a support system which might be called upon in emergencies, as were neighbours, though unless neighbours happened also to be relatives they were less important than relatives in old people's lives. Very few old people were isolated. Those who described themselves as lonely Townsend believed were likely to be 'desolated' owing to the loss of a loved close relative, rather than isolated.[44]

Some had no living relatives or had lost touch with them. Townsend examined the recent records of a local geriatric hospital and of east Londoners who had died in LCC Homes and concluded that

> Old people who make claims on the institutional and domiciliary services of the state seem to form a very unrepresentative group. More live alone, are unmarried, childless or have sons not daughters or are separated from the daughters they have.[45]

The Bethnal Green survey suggested that between 5 and 10 per cent of the sample would have required institutional care but for help from relatives or friends. Other older people lived with less struggle with a lesser degree of support from others: 6 per cent had their cleaning done by local authority home-helps, 43 per cent by relatives and friends. Much the same was true of other services. Townsend concluded that social services should integrate into their thinking recognition of the regularity and importance of family reciprocity and support family networks rather than, as they did, treat them as a reason why no service was required. Services could not substitute for the family and generally neither older people nor their relatives wanted them to, but they could complement family support and reduce the strain of interdependence for both generations. He found little hard evidence of neglect on the part of old people's children despite the fears that were still frequently expressed.[46] He commented:

> Doctors, social workers and others who express such fears may sometimes forget that they are in danger of generalising from an extremely untypical sub-section of the population or from a few extreme examples known personally . . . and the fact that these fears have been expressed by one generation after another inclines one to be sceptical.[47]

Townsend traced the relationships and tensions within families[48] with far greater subtlety than Willmott and Young. He did not believe that he was observing family forms which were declining archaisms in the modern world, but saw families as flexible institutions adaptive to a variety of environments. Townsend's more detailed, warmer and more empathetic study was more alert to the nuances and conflicts of family life and the complex motivation of exchange among relatives than those of Willmott and Young. He concluded that still 'the three generation extended family . . . provides the normal environment for old people'. No other ties were so important to them.

What had changed since the beginning of the twentieth century, compared with the centuries before, was that more old people lived alone and fewer lived as boarders in the homes of non-relatives. With greater prosperity more could maintain their own households. The proportions living with married children had increased somewhat, probably due to higher survival rates at older ages. Fewer older people had unmarried children living at home. Women now completed their families at earlier ages and parents in their sixties were less likely to have teenage children. Average marriage ages had fallen and a higher proportion of the population was married than fifty years earlier, so fewer unmarried children remained with their parents. Relationships with married children had become increasingly important for the rising numbers of older people.

## Family and class in a London suburb

Sheldon had interviewed a cross-class sample of old people in Wolverhampton, whereas the Bethnal Green samples were exclusively working class. Willmott and Young believed that the path of change towards more 'modern' family relationships might be more evident in a middle-class environment. In 1959 they embarked on a study of 'Family and Class in a London Suburb', in Woodford, to the north-east of London. Again they were surprised by what they found.

In Woodford compared with Bethnal Green parents and adult children more rarely lived in the same borough and fewer still within five minutes' walk. Many younger people had moved away from their parents' neighbourhood to better homes or jobs. Older people took this for granted. Yet still 30 per cent of younger married people had seen their mothers in the twenty-four hours before their interviews (compared with 43 per cent in Bethnal Green), 33 per cent within the previous week (31 per cent in Bethnal Green); 37 per cent had not seen her for longer (26 per cent in Bethnal Green). Contact between the generations was not negligible, but in view of the distances there was less casual 'dropping in' in Woodford than in Bethnal Green.

The proportion of unmarried children living with pensioner parents was almost identical to that in Bethnal Green: 23 per cent of married children shared a dwelling with parents (21 per cent in Bethnal Green), 17 per cent lived within five minutes (32 per cent), 22 per cent within the same borough (11 per cent). Younger people in Woodford were more likely to possess cars and/or easily to afford public transport. Close proximity was less intimately related to regular contact than for the poorer people of Bethnal Green. Willmott and Young were 'surprised' that the similarities between the two boroughs were more notable than the differences.

Although many older people in Woodford lived far away from *most* of their children they were likely to live close to at least *one* of them, and the likelihood that this was so increased with age, consequent on removal by one or other generation. The similarities between the boroughs were greater at higher ages. As they aged parents were visited more and were more likely to share a home with married children, often following widowhood or illness. It was harder than in Bethnal Green for the two generations to find homes close by, owing not least to the income and class gap, and the more mobile population meant that the older people were less likely to be long-established residents. Often they moved from elsewhere to live with children and the unfamiliarity of the neighbourhood could cause problems. In consequence Willmott and Young saw many of these old people as relatively deprived compared with Bethnal Greeners, despite the relative prosperity of their surroundings.

Some families did, however, function much like those of Bethnal Green:

> Mr Randall, a retired surveyor, also belongs to an extended family. His day as he described it himself in his diary, is very much mixed up with his daughter's. He visits her home constantly. 'Bicycled up to my daughter Joan. I usually go to lunch with her when my sister is at work. She was in the middle of cooking dinner so I went to the baker's for bread and two tins of food for the cat. Up the Green I ran into my friend Arthur and had a chat. Said cheerio and went back to my daughter. She was still getting dinner ready and as there was no-one to talk to I went into the lounge and strummed on the piano.'

He had lunch with his daughter, son-in-law and grandson, and then listened to a Chopin recording with his grandson.[49]

Willmott and Young found that still in Woodford 'among the older parents it is the minority who do not belong to some kind of continuing family group, whether in the one house or spread over several'.[50] They discovered:

> In ill-health, infirmity or widowhood the aged people are, by and large, cared for by their children. Asked what use she made of various social services, Mrs Broadbent said, 'It's unnecessary when you've got children isn't it?' Kinship may mean less in the suburb at other stages in life, but in old age, when the need arises, the family is once more the main source of support. The old felt they could call on their children, the children that they should respond, 'When they've brought you up' said Mr Burgess 'you feel you've got a certain amount of moral obligation to them.' This sense of filial duty was as strong in one district as another.[51]

What about people without children? The researchers discovered from a special analysis of the 1951 census returns that only a minority (21 per cent) of these lived alone: 53 per cent shared a household with relatives, 26 per cent with friends. Twenty-five unmarried people lived with siblings. One household of two sisters and a brother, all never married, had lived together all their lives. Other single people lived with nieces, cousins, friends. Six lived alone, but had good contact with others. Willmott and Young commented: 'In fact one of the striking things in Woodford as in the East End is how single people generally make up for the absence of other relationships by seeing more of their brothers and sisters.'[52] Only one single person and three childless, widowed people in the sample had no relatives or friends. On

Townsend's rough and ready definition of 'isolation' – three or less contacts in a day – 11 per cent of older people in Woodford were isolated compared with 10 per cent in Bethnal Green. Widowhood and infirmity could cause isolation and depression anywhere.

There were differences between Woodford and Bethnal Green. Retired middle-class men in Woodford had more common interests with their wives and closer contact with their children than the working-class men in Bethnal Green. Older people gave less help to younger people than in Bethnal Green, but they received as much.[53] There were close links between mothers and daughters, but mother was less dominating in Woodford.

Willmott and Young concluded:

> Most people are not solitary. Old people without children are on the whole no more isolated or neglected than those with them. The main reason is that the family, as adaptable in the suburbs as in the city, is efficient at providing substitutes for the missing parts. . . . Almost everybody succeeds, somehow or other, in surrounding himself with a family or its atmosphere . . . why people need a family of some kind, especially in later life is obvious. What is less obvious is why the relatives who are thus sought after should respond. Often, of course, the arrangement is of mutual benefit – the spinster sisters or friends both need each other. Where this is not so, the relatives . . . seem to feel a sense of obligation, perhaps weaker than that of children to their parents, but at least akin to it. Mr Loder's niece, with whom he lives, confides 'He's an awful nuisance sometimes, but I can't turn him out can I? After all he's father's brother and there's no-one else he could go to.'[54]

But the Woodford study did not dissuade Willmott and Young of their conviction that reciprocity beyond the nuclear core of the family was bound for the dustbin of history.[55]

## The national picture

Research on old people and their families continued to pour out. In 1959 Peter Townsend published a review of thirty-three surveys of old age in Great Britain conducted between 1945 and 1958. These included his own, but not those of Sheldon, Willmott and Young and others which were not primarily social surveys of old people.[56] The surveys were scattered through the British Isles and were mainly, though not exclusively, urban. They were of variable scope and methodological quality, but they agreed strikingly on two things: the strength of family ties and the 'isolation and deplorable condition of a small minority who do not seem to be contacted by any welfare services'.[57] Townsend concluded:

The fact is that the large majority of people in Great Britain lead a reasonably secure life within their families . . . most old people have children living nearby even when they live alone e.g. seventy-four per cent of those in a Nottinghamshire town, eighty-seven per cent of those with children in Andover, eighty-five per cent of retired men in Aberdeen had a child in the city; eighty-nine per cent in a rural district in Anglesey had at least one child in the same dwelling or parish. The contacts are generally close.[58]

Only 8 per cent of a Liverpool sample had no 'regular' contact with family; 92 per cent in two districts of Nottinghamshire were regularly visited daily or weekly by relatives. These and subsequent surveys indicated that perhaps two-thirds of older people had a reasonable degree of security within their families, receiving help with their everyday chores when needed, as well as in emergencies. Half the remainder were likely to impose a severe strain upon their families; the other half were isolated.[59]

Between 1961 and 1964 a series of comparable cross-national surveys of people over 65 were carried out in the United States, Britain and Denmark.[60] The British national survey, conducted by Townsend and Dorothy Wedderburn (which interviewed 4,000 older people, alongside smaller studies of old people in institutions and of those living alone), found, yet again, that old people preferred to live in their own homes and could long continue to do so, given adequate support for themselves and their families; but that publicly funded support services, such as home-helps, district nurses, mobile chiropodists, were still inadequate. Townsend and Wedderburn concluded that 'the relationship between the family and the welfare state is much more subtle than has been implied'.[61] They were not alternatives, as current sociological orthodoxy suggested, but complemented one another. Services provided what families could not, such as specialist medical care, and assisted families to care for dependent older people. The survey also confirmed the reciprocal nature of transfers and how often help was transferred downwards as well as upwards through the generations.

Townsend and Wedderburn found that income from the state, in the form of pensions and/or National Assistance, was the most important source of income of old people. Only 2 per cent revealed financial help from relatives.[62] Much more help was in kind: 'gifts of food, clothing and help with holidays, outings and so on . . . this survey has confirmed that such help is extensive'; 60 per cent of old women and one-third of couples living alone were receiving help of this kind which was worth 'upwards of two or three shillings a week' (the single person's retirement pension at this time was £2 a week). Assistance when the generations lived together was harder to calculate.[63]

In a complementary study, Jeremy Tunstall studied 538 older people, living alone in four areas: the London suburb of Harrow; the medium-sized southern town of Northampton; Oldham, a northern town of equivalent size; and rural south Norfolk. The book opened with a gloomy reinforcement of popular stereotypes:

> Old people are eight times more likely to live alone than are people aged under 65. About 1,300,000 people aged 65 and over in Britain today live alone. A larger number, about 1,600,000, in reply to a question will say they are lonely (a quarter of these being 'often' lonely). About a million old people in Britain are socially isolated.[64]

Tunstall also pointed out that about 5,000,000 were not.

In describing old people who were largely isolated Tunstall perhaps gave too little weight to the effects both of poverty and of individual personality in limiting their social contacts. One man whose work in the cotton industry had been his life had been made to retire at age 76 when his employers discovered his age. He would have liked to continue going to the working-men's club, but 'wherever you go, you need the money. . . . I'd be made welcome; people would buy me drinks. How would you feel about that if you couldn't buy them back?' He had a daughter across the road with whom he spent an evening a week, and his son and grandchildren visited him every Saturday morning. They were willing to shop for him, but he feared they would spend too much. The interview conveys the effects of poverty on his social relationships and the loss of status he experienced when unable to reciprocate, and also a bad-tempered tone – perhaps the result of his new hardship, perhaps a longer-established barrier between himself and others – which itself might have distanced him from close contacts, including with his children, who nonetheless continued to see him frequently.[65] By contrast an outgoing and better-off woman, a retired college lecturer, who had no contact with relatives, had recently moved to a village where she knew no one, but had already made friends and had wide interests.[66]

Nonetheless, Tunstall's study was more psychologically aware than others. He speculated as to how far isolation in later life was connected with personality patterns established in earlier years, and how much with specific crises of later life due to retirement, bereavement and disability: 'old age is for each person who reaches it a new experience . . . ageing people have to learn the social role of the old person'; how they performed that role was influenced by their life histories.[67] Old age, he argued, should be studied in the context of the individual life cycle, for 'patterns of ageing stretch far back into the individual's past', influenced by whether they had siblings or children, by their occupations, income and intellectual resources,[68] rather than in terms of currently fashionable generalised theories such as that of 'disengagement'. Like Sheldon almost twenty years before, Tunstall complained that the pattern of 'normal' social development in old age was still not defined, not least because individual experiences were very variable, more so than those of other phases of the life course.[69]

The 'overwhelming majority' of old people in Tunstall's sample said they preferred to live alone, though Tunstall wondered how often this was putting a brave face on a situation over which they had little control.[70] Nevertheless he concluded that

> the popular preference, given reasonable health, is to maintain regular contact with children, siblings or others, without imposing upon them or becoming too dependent upon them. Other things being equal, many (or even most) widowed or single old people prefer to live alone while maintaining close ties with relatives outside the household. However, other things often are not equal.[71]

An older person might face a choice between living with a daughter or rarely seeing her because of distance; ill health might bring incapacity.

In Britain in the 1960s, Tunstall concluded, 'there is no automatic respect paid to old people, but the most respected and powerful people in our society are often quite elderly'.[72] He found no clear social class differences in relations between the generations: 'On the present evidence pictures of the working class as either callously neglecting all its elderly parents or cosily integrating them into three-generation households are equally without foundation.'[73] He found the highest proportion of old people living alone in inner London, the lowest in the London suburbs, a pattern replicated in other conurbations. Living alone for old people was commonest where it was common for all age groups. 'Extreme isolation' was greatest in rural south Norfolk which contained 25 per cent of old people in the sample but 50 per cent of all isolates. The sample was too small to provide an explanation but 'the evidence points away from any comfortable conclusions about the true sociability of rural life'.[74] 'The popular idea of old people being more alone in urban centres than in rural areas is without foundation.'[75] Loneliness did not only afflict those who lived alone: 27 per cent of the 'often lonely' were married and lived with their partners, though frequently in a state of conflict or with a partner in poor health. Women who lived alone were less likely to be 'lonely' than men.

Like other researchers Tunstall called for social services to support families, noting that a number of local authorities would not provide a home-help if the old person had a daughter in the local authority area. He argued that social services should also make an effort to discover what old people wanted and provide choices. For example,

> an old woman whose arthritis prevents her from cooking should be able to choose between having mobile meals delivered or having her home help cook them or being transported to a club or Centre to eat the meals there, or a combination of the three.[76]

Clubs could help overcome isolation, but those specifically for old people were slightly less attractive to his sample than clubs and associations unrestricted by age.[77]

Later studies reinforced all of these findings. Karn's survey in the early 1970s of retirement to the seaside found exceptionally large numbers of older people living in seaside resorts.[78] In 1971 people of pensionable age made up 44 per cent of the population of Bexhill, 39 per cent in Clacton and 33 per cent in Eastbourne compared with a national percentage of 16.[79] Those who retired to the seaside came disproportionately from the higher social classes, mostly moved as couples and were more likely than average to have no surviving children. Those with children lived at a greater distance from them than in other studies: for example, retirees to the Sussex coast often had children in London whence they had migrated. However, they still saw them regularly and there were strong reasons to suppose that many old people returned to live near their children as they aged, in particular following widowhood; or sometimes children moved to them. The pattern was similar to that of Woodford. Some older people appeared to be experiencing in retirement a period of happy independence of family ties before greater dependence upon them became necessary.[80]

A different type of source, Elizabeth Roberts' oral history of women and their families in three Lancashire towns between 1940 and 1970, confirmed the findings of the contemporary surveys of southern communities. Despite changes affecting families over the post-war period, more striking was continuity with the findings of Roberts' earlier study of the same towns from 1890 to 1940:[81] 'It is always important to remember that much help from kin was not only dependent upon relations living in the same house, much assistance being rendered by members of the family living nearby.'[82] For example, when Mrs Brayshaw was growing up in the 1950s and 1960s:

> We had relatives living next door, my mother's cousin and her husband. My grandmother and her sister lived next door but one. When I was a small child I remember having two breakfasts most days. I used to have one at home then shuffle off next door.

The combined efforts of this family enabled the grandmother to stay in her own home. She moved in with her daughter only in the last year of her life.[83]

In the late 1950s Mrs Kennedy's mother became unable to look after herself. Her daughter had no room in her small house, so she went to live with her son in the next street.

> So when they went to work, she used to come round to me all day and then go back to them when she had had her tea. That was for about eighteen months before she died. She was no trouble at all. The boys used to play with her and if I wanted to go to the shops she would look after them for me.[84]

In 1970 Mrs Owen had lived in the same house since 1940. Her mother and an aunt still lived nearby, her daughter and family across the road. She and her daughter spent much of the day together when Mrs Owen was not visiting her own mother, whom she saw on most days: 'I always used to say I was going home.' Her mother-in-law, who had become blind, lived nearby and was more likely to visit the Owens than was Mrs Owen's mother.

Roberts found some decline in co-residence over time but that this 'does not necessarily imply any lowering of standards of care for relatives nor a loosening of the bonds of kinship'. But the emotional relationships involved were not simple; some respondents expressed irritation with and even resentment of relatives, but these feelings did not necessarily lead to abandonment of long-established norms regarding obligations to help kin.[85] The motives expressed were a mixture of love, duty, affection, obligation and self-interest (such as the desire to inherit property). More often care for old people was simply taken for granted: 'Relatives were cared for because it was assumed that that was what one did.' Ties with neighbours seemed to be weakening, but not those with kin: 'Blood is thicker than water' remained an important axiom. Sometimes a sense of obligation was reinforced by fear of gossip and social disapproval if relatives were thought to be neglected.[86]

Grandmothers were not always loving partners in the family network of reciprocity. One woman recalled how her parents lived for most of their marriage with her father's tyrannical mother who dominated him and would not allow them to leave, despite his wife's unhappiness. The older woman refused to look after her granddaughter 'because she said it was my mother's place to stay at home and do the cooking and cleaning and not to go out to work'.[87] Other grandmothers were too busy with their own lives to have time to care for grandchildren.[88]

Another woman was living in a bedsitter with her husband and new baby in 1948 when her mother's cousin offered her a house at a low rent if she would care for the relative's blind mother. This arrangement lasted sixteen years. The old woman was very difficult. The house had only two bedrooms and soon another child was born. The younger people felt that they could not put the old woman in a home, because the house belonged to her daughter, nor could they leave and abandon her; 'I wouldn't have done that. You see we had been brought up to look after one another.'[89] Roberts concluded:

> Clearly those in our study did not give help to just anyone claiming kinship . . . the most usual help was given up and down a straight genealogical line of grandparents, parents and children. While it is clear that respondents were aware of rules and obligations governing their relations with kin, it is much less apparent that they consciously assessed the various considerations . . . as with their forebears, respondents appeared to possess norms which had been internalised . . . [and] generally acted towards kin because 'it was the thing to do'.[90]

Only a small minority had few contacts with relatives owing to quarrels or migration.

Roberts, like Willmott, Young and Townsend, studied settled and secure if not necessarily prosperous neighbourhoods. Coates and Silburn's study of the very poor 'slum' district of St Ann's in Nottingham in the mid 1960s found that much lower proportions of people had relatives nearby. Everyone who could afford to moved away. When they studied a more comfortable Nottingham council estate the pattern was similar to that in Bethnal Green.[91]

## Interpreting family relationships

A group of anthropologists, led by Raymond Firth, studied 'Families and their Relatives' in two middle-class districts of north London, Highgate and the anonymised interwar housing estate 'Greenbanks'. They produced a more subtle analysis of intergenerational relationships within families than that achieved by most of the sociologists.[92] They found that the 'standard view', an 'ideal norm', was that families 'ought to stick together', but such sentiments were stronger for immediate than for more distant relatives. The sense of responsibility for 'elderly relatives' was especially strongly expressed:

> It has various constituents, ranging from actual monetary help or advice on financial problems, to performance of small manual services, visiting, entertainment and the provision of a place to live. . . . Undoubtedly to many people one of the most important obligations is that of visiting, of 'seeing something' of the relative. Most people have a kind of 'model' of social existence. There is a tacit assumption that it is necessary to maintain some social relationships in order to keep going as a fully functioning personality. . . . The notion here is that a person exists through his own activities primarily while he remains able-bodied, but that he sometimes continues to be socially effective as he grows older increasingly through the efforts that others make on his behalf.[93]

Mrs Maskell expressed especially clearly 'the general norms of obligation to kin':

> I was brought up very strongly by my mother that everyone should be independent and able to look after themselves. But I've changed my views on the subject. . . . Just looking at people, and how nasty it was to look at people who had no-one in particular to look after them in any way. . . . Relatives shouldn't do anything unless they want to . . . but if a situation arises then they should cope with it to some degree. . . . Unless they like them (their kin) I feel they have only duties towards them, in times of trouble I think. And then I think they have very strong duties

towards them because it is very unpleasant and very difficult, in times of difficulty, to get outsiders to cope at all.[94]

Others more clearly expressed these obligations to older relatives as unpleasurable though inescapable burdens, in particular when parents had themselves been unsupportive of their children. 'Questions about duty to parents (and other very close kin) could usually be answered spontaneously' as those about more distant kin could not.[95]

> One woman said she believed that people had a duty to look after their mothers and that this was the strongest kinship obligation. She herself had never felt any obligation towards her father, who was a 'strange man' and 'never there'. She believed that fathers who had fulfilled their obligations to their children ought to be looked after when they got old, but not otherwise.

The researchers found that:

> Another type of response is the development of a sense of guilt in response of inadequate fulfilment of obligation (or of what is regarded as inadequate). One woman expressed a strong sense of obligation towards older relatives, but worried that she found her mother-in-law 'dull and trying' (a view confirmed by the field worker who met her) with no common interests. Her husband also found his mother 'slow and conventional and generally rather uninteresting'. Yet despite all this he saw his mother every week as he knew how much it meant to her; and his wife also saw her frequently. But clearly the wife felt that she could do more, and that she had to justify why she was not doing it. Her husband and her friends said that if one did not get on with relatives one should not visit because neither side would enjoy it. She agreed 'but I do feel that if my mother-in-law needed anything I would do it . . . what people do for relatives is very dependent on their circumstances anyway. . . . I suppose you *might* feel that because they're relatives you should keep on seeing them, but I find it very tedious to have to see people when there's nothing in common with them.' Others resented that they carried out their obligations to older relatives whereas other family members did not.[96]

For 85 per cent of their samples in the two districts 'relations between these parents and their sons or daughters were good or reasonably equitable'. In the remainder 'relations were described as bad, or non-existent; or there was dislike by the married son or daughter for the parent without this necessarily being reciprocated or even understood'.[97] The study concluded:

A central point of all this is that instead of dealing with conventional stereotypes of 'mother-love', 'Mum', 'father-figures' or whatever, our evidence shows a set of highly complex patterns of relationship between married adults and their parents. Fathers and mothers are people formerly in the domestic circle for whom on the whole there is a very great deal of affection, admiration and respect, and willingness to commit much time and energy in gratifying their wishes. At the same time, while it is recognised that they have a prior right to make demands, such demands may be resented, even while being fulfilled . . . some demands may be regarded as excessive, as blackmail, employing as instruments those emotional ties which are felt to be properly a free, not enforced, tribute to affection and gratitude. Yet very rarely is there sufficient explosion of resentment to lead to complete breakdown of social relationship between married son or daughter and parent. The upshot is often a kind of elaborate strategy of relations, in which there is much manipulation of personal wants and resources against the background of admitted social obligation.[98]

## Family and kinship in the 1980s and 1990s

A government-sponsored national survey of 'the elderly at home' in 1976 reinforced the picture of generally supportive family networks.[99] There were, however, fewer surveys of kinship in the 1970s. They increased in the 1980s in the context of revived concern about the ageing of the population and growing poverty. Thompson, Itzin and Abenstern found in south London

> that patterns of family care have not changed over the past fifty years. Both then and now many children look after their elderly parents and today, as in the past, the work which this care involves falls largely to women.[100]

They gave up the older people to institutions only when they needed care beyond the capacity of the family. Even when a father who had deserted his wife and daughters when they were young turned up expecting his daughters to care for him at the end of his life, 'bitter and reluctant, they nevertheless took him on and he lived with them – one after the other – until he died'.[101] The older generation also had expected the last living parent or parent-in-law to live with them for the last few years of their lives, even if this meant sharing a bedroom with the older person or giving up the front parlour for their bedroom.

But here as elsewhere the older people were more often 'fit and active – offering support to their children and grandchildren rather than the other way around'.[102] They had close relationships with children but moved to live with them with the greatest reluctance, however willing their children to give them a home. One woman said:

Charles wants me to go, he's had a room built for me. Our Norman has had a room built for me, but I'm not giving my little home up and that's what upsets them. They think I shouldn't be on my own now. But I'm not giving up my home for nobody.[103]

A study in Sheffield in the mid 1980s addressed the increasing fears that the growing numbers of middle-aged women in the paid workforce would rob old people of their accustomed carers. Such apprehensions overlooked how throughout history women had combined the care of older people with both paid work and heavier domestic work, with larger families and less convenient homes. The Sheffield study revealed the lengths to which married women went to care for elderly relatives and keep them in the community, despite the demands of their immediate families and of paid work, as they always had.[104] Elizabeth Roberts made the same discovery in Lancashire.[105]

The Sheffield researchers also stressed something probably understated in other studies, that 'family care can be among the very best and the very worst experiences that human beings can devise for one another . . . within families it is possible for people to experience the most damaging and emotionally destructive relationships'.[106] By 1989 another researcher could comment:

It is now generally accepted that most care, help and support in old age comes from informal sources. An image of the family as an available and responsible source of support has gradually replaced an earlier stereotype of the fragmented modern family in industrial societies as unavailable and unconcerned with the plight of its older generations.[107]

By this time it was equally generally accepted that old people gave as well as received help;[108] and that when families needed support from social services because an elderly relative had become burdensome, it was unlikely to be forthcoming. Still, for local authorities the availability of family care was a reason to withhold services. Nor were services adequate for the minority without families, who still had a higher probability of entering residential care. Middle-class family networks were more widely dispersed than working-class ones but also less constrained by distance owing to readier access to transport and telephones. Older middle-class people also turned more readily to friends for support. Working-class people were slower to seek help outside the family.

A comparison in 1990 of samples of old people in central Liverpool (where they were mainly working class) and in rural North Wales (where a high proportion were middle class, and had often moved there on retirement) found that a high proportion of the Liverpudlians had lived for many years (at least thirty) in their neighbourhood and had strong family and other local ties. In North Wales the mainly Welsh-speaking, mainly working-class, long-settled inhabitants were closer in pattern to the Liverpool sample than to the middle-class incomers. This challenged the continuing image of the city as less supportive than the countryside and of Liverpool in particular as an area of social disruption.[109]

The inadequacy of support services for families led in the 1980s to a literature of concern about 'carers', generally portrayed as single women whose lives were seriously constrained by looking after aged parents .The problem was real, as it long had been, for a minority of women.[110] Such writing, however, tended to objectify 'old people' as objects of care and to fuel alarm about the inevitability of a period of serious dependency at the end of life.[111] Out of understandable concern for seriously disadvantaged and under-supported carers, it risked understating the extent to which 'caring' could be pleasing and fulfilling.[112] It also underestimated the amount of 'caring' performed by men, especially for their spouses. An analysis drawn from the General Household Survey (GHS) of Britain 1985 found that about one adult in seven (about 6 million people) provided unpaid care and one in five households contained a carer; 3 per cent of the population (1.4 million) devoted at least twenty hours a week to caring;[113] 2 per cent of female and 2 per cent of male adults cared for someone sick, handicapped or aged in their household; 10 per cent of women and 7 per cent of men gave 'some regular service or help' to a sick, handicapped or older relative, friend or neighbour who did not live with them. 'Service' could include gardening or shopping; it was provided mainly for spouses, parents or to a lesser extent parents-in-law. Half of all caring was for a parent or, less frequently, a parent-in-law. Co-resident care averaged fifty-three hours a week, non-resident care nine hours, mainly because older people living with younger relatives were generally more infirm and in need of care. Gender differences in the provision of care were negligible.[114]

Not all carers were 'young'. People over 65 provided 35 per cent of caring for others above that age – a conservative estimate since the GHS excluded from its survey 'normal' domestic activities performed by women (only) for others.[115] By the 1990s more people were living to be very old, into their eighties, and also becoming dependent, if at all, at later ages. In consequence their children might themselves be past retirement when the older generation needed more support, all the more probably in view of the declining age of retirement.[116] About 20 per cent of all people over 60 were caring for people who were older still.

It continued to be clear that old people 'do not give up their independence easily'; 'with few exceptions they are reluctant subjects in caring and dependency ... elderly people desire, often more than anything else, the preservation of their independence'.[117] Indeed there was evidence that many old people preferred state services, when they were adequate and responsive, and even preferred residential care, when it was comfortable and supportive, to feeling that they burdened their children, though they would opt for it only when they were incapable of living in their own homes.[118] Reciprocity was more important in family than in professional care. When old people could no longer give to family members as well as receiving they resisted dependence upon them.[119]

Fears continued that the further increase in the numbers of married women in paid work, together with changing household patterns, would, at last, destroy family cohesion and reciprocity. The British Social Attitudes survey showed a fall between the mid 1980s and the mid 1990s in the frequency with which married women in full-time work visited their mothers. But still almost 50 per cent of those who did not share a household with their mothers visited her at least once a week. It was not clear whether frequency of contact increased with the increasing age and disability of the mother as earlier surveys had shown. There was every sign that, as they had always done, women maintained their supportive role as well as their paid work, often at considerable physical and emotional cost to themselves and still with exiguous support from social services. This was as true of women who expressed support for feminist goals of equal opportunities in the workplace as of those who did not.[120] Still, about 60 per cent of older people lived within one hour's journey of at least one close relative, one-quarter to one-third within fifteen minutes, and contact was frequent.[121]

If not women's paid work, then divorce and the increasing flexibility of partnership and household arrangements were expected to diminish the family contacts of older people. Not, of course, that loss of a spouse is an historically new experience; throughout time widowhood had broken up families.[122] And research indicated that divorce could strengthen intergenerational family ties, as lateral ties with partners weakened. After divorce or separation people, especially women, often moved closer to parents, for mutual support. Remarriage and the formation of step-relationships could increase rather than diminish family resources.[123]

The changing ethnic population of much of the British Isles and the different cultural expectations of the family of various immigrant groups and their descendants complicate analysis of change over time. By the 1990s Britain, especially in the cities, was a profoundly different, more multicultural, society than it had ever been. The white working-class Bethnal Green of the 1950s (about 8 per cent composed of descendants of East European Jewish migrants of the period before 1914[124]) had become in the 1990s Tower Hamlets with a substantial population of residents of Bangladeshi and other overseas origins. Wolverhampton was a 'white' town when Sheldon investigated it in the 1940s. By the 1990s it had a substantial population of Caribbean and Asian origin and Woodford was home to many affluent British Asians. Family support and reciprocity was at least as strong in these cultural groups of immigrant origin, though sometimes in forms different from British tradition, for example expectations about sharing homes with elders differed.

Cross-national studies, time and again, found that family reciprocity was the norm in developed and less developed countries, showed no sign of diminishing as a correlate of economic development and was everywhere a major component of the care of old people: 70 per cent of old people in the world in the 1980s relied exclusively on family support for social security.[125] In advanced countries younger people rarely supported elders with cash, certainly they gave vastly less than they received, but they reciprocated equally massively in the form of care.[126] In a sample of developed countries, including the United States, Japan, West Germany and Sweden, more old people were living alone, but close contact with relatives was not diminishing. In Sweden at least it was increasing as the technology of communication improved.[127] Increased prosperity and modern technology enabled family relationships to adapt to changed circumstances: the microwave oven made it easier to provide meals for a dependent older person; motor vehicles, air transport, telephones, e-mail eased regular contact and response to emergencies over long distances. The fact of contact between the generations changed little over time. The content of relationships may have changed and the time devoted to them on the part of both younger and the older people, who also often led fuller lives than in previous generations.

Researchers were impressed by 'the pervasiveness of family integration everywhere. Children not only maintain communication with their aged parents . . . but provide [them] with concrete care and services. These services are regular and important for the survival of older people.'[128] They found no strong relationship between the level of formal welfare services and informal family services. Contrary to what had long been suggested by critics of state welfare, a strong welfare state did not 'crowd out' family care. Levels of family support were higher in West Germany, where welfare services were strong, than in the United States where they were weaker. The United States and Britain, with different state welfare traditions, had similar levels of family support.[129] In Britain official policy continued, as it had since the 1950s[130] and indeed through the whole history of the Poor Law, to assume that formal services were ancillary and complementary to those of the family. In the mid 1980s it was estimated that unpaid family services were saving the social services budget around £24 billion a year when the cost of personal social services was about £3.4 billion. Based on local authority pay rates (£7 per hour in 1989) the market value of caring provide by unpaid carers was £39.1 billion in 1992, or about 7.5 per cent of national income in that year; 83 per cent of this was spent on caring for older people. In total this was almost four times as much as joint public and private expenditure for long-term care and about as much as the total spent on the National Health Service.[131] Family support for older people is not a negligible feature of the welfare state.

## Conclusion

A mass of evidence showed with striking consistency between 1945 and the mid 1990s that it was extremely rare for families to provide the *whole* support of older people – and with the coming of universal pensions they did not need to. They did provide a very great deal when it was needed, most often in the form of services, and this support was vital to the well-being of very many old people, often the only buffer between them and an institution. Of course most older people needed little or no more assistance than did younger people, often less, and still less did they need 'care'. Very many of them gave at least as much support as they received.

Yet family ties could constrain as well as support older people. Younger relatives' stereotypes of their capacities might cast them in dependent roles, restraining independence and adventurousness. Nevertheless, even at the latest ages some older people were independent and adventurous, but unavoidably some were frail. It is unnecessary to romanticise relations between the generations to acknowledge that for most people they remained close and that giving support, though not necessarily love, or even liking, to older relatives when it was needed was customary in the late twentieth century, part of the taken-for-granted way of life, which most people assumed was age-old custom.

With good reason. Relations between older people and their relatives in Britain in the distant past are elusive, but there are reasons to assume that they were close. It is improbable that researchers in the late twentieth century were detecting something quite new, in a period in which, in principle, older people had a greater capacity to live independently of family than in earlier times. More probably researchers were belatedly noting the continued centrality of reciprocity to human relationships even in the most 'developed' societies and the persistent underestimation by social science theorists of the importance of non-monetary, non-market transfers in such societies.[132] The essentially short-term time horizon of most work in the social sciences impedes the capacity of the social sciences to analyse change, or continuity. In relation to the study of the family and intergenerational relationships at least it encourages excessive generalisation about the extent and implications of any specific aspect of change. In the recent past household and family structures, patterns of paid work, technology and modes of communication have undergone widespread changes in the developed world. They have not, as is widely assumed, been accompanied by equally widespread changes in intergenerational relationships within families. Long-run historical studies suggest that the relationship between structure and culture, between economic and technological change and affective human relationships, is more complex than social science theory conventionally assumes.

Ancient complementary structures of public and private welfare survived into the welfare state, facilitated rather than being destroyed by greater prosperity and ease of communications. The private exchanges that take place within the family, rather than being attenuated remnants which progress had passed by, are integral to the structures and functions of state welfare institutions.

# Notes

1  P. Laslett and R. Wall (eds), *Household and Family in Past Time*, Cambridge, 1972.
2  D. Thomson, 'The welfare of the elderly in the past: a family or community responsibility?', in M. Pelling and R. Smith (eds), *Life, Death and the Elderly: Historical Perspectives*, London, 1991, p. 198.
3  L. Rosenmayr and E. Kockeis, 'Proposition for a sociological theory of aging and the family', *International Social Science Journal*, 1963, vol. 3, pp. 418–19.
4  Discussed in Pat Thane, 'Old people and their families in the English past', in M. Daunton (ed.), *Charity, Self-interest and Welfare in the English Past*, London, 1996 , pp. 113–38 .
5  Talcott Parsons, *Essays in Sociological Theory*, New York, 1954.
6  E. Shanas and M. B. Sussman (eds), *Family, Bureaucracy and the Elderly*, Durham, NC, 1977.
7  A. Offer, 'Between the gift and the market: the economy of regard', *Economic History Review*, 1997, vol. 50, pp. 450–76.
8  J. H. Sheldon, *The Social Medicine of Old Age*, Oxford, 1948, p.140.
9  Ibid., p.152.
10  Ibid., p. 154.
11  Ibid., p. 150.
12  Ibid., p. 156.
13  Ibid.
14  Ibid., p. 141.
15  Ibid., p. 159.
16  Ibid., p. 142.
17  Ibid., p. 148.
18  Ibid., p. 150.
19  Ibid., p. 157.
20  Ibid., p. 160.
21  Ibid.
22  Ibid., p. 25.
23  Ibid., p. 158.
24  M. Young and P. Willmott, *Family and Kinship in East London*, Harmondsworth, 1957, pp. 37–8.
25  Ibid., p. 47.
26  Ibid., p. 125.
27  Ellen Ross, *Love and Toil. Motherhood in Outcast London*, Oxford, 1993; Raphael Samuel, *East-end Underworld. Chapters in the Life of Arthur Harding*, London, 1981; Anna Davin, *Growing Up Poor. Home, School and Street in London, 1870–1914*, London, 1996.
28  Jocelyn Cornwell, *Hard-Earned Lives*, London, 1984.
29  National Council of Social Service, *Over Seventy*, London, 1954; G. F. Adams and G. A. Cheeseman, *Old People in Northern Ireland*, Belfast, 1951.
30  P. Townsend, *The Family Life of Old People*, London, 1957.
31  P. Thane, *Old Age: Continuity and Change in English History*, Oxford, 1999.
32  Nuffield Foundation, *Old People: Report of a Survey Committee on the Problems of Ageing and the Care of Old People*, Oxford, 1947, p. 30.
33  Ibid., p. 45.
34  Ibid., p. 150.
35  Ibid., p. 56.
36  Ibid., p. 46.
37  Offer, 'Economy of regard', p. 454.
38  Townsend, *Family Life*, pp. 64–6.

39  Ibid., p. 66.
40  Ibid., p. 67.
41  Ibid.
42  Ibid., pp. 154ff.
43  Ibid., p. 222.
44  Ibid., p. 182.
45  This was confirmed by his later study of old people in institutions: P. Townsend, *The Last Refuge*, London, 1964.
46  Laslett and Wall, *Household and Family*.
47  Townsend, *Family Life*, p. 202.
48  Ibid., for example pp. 220–8.
49  P. Willmott and M. Young, *Family and Class in a London Suburb*, London, 1960, pp. 48–9.
50  Ibid., p. 49.
51  Ibid., p. 50.
52  Ibid., p. 53.
53  Ibid., p. 71.
54  Ibid., p. 58.
55  This argument was further developed in M. Young and P. Willmott, *The Symmetrical Family. A Study of Work and Leisure in the London Region*, London, 1973, which pays remarkably little attention to family relationships beyond the nuclear core.
56  P. Townsend, 'Surveys of old age in Great Britain, 1945–1958', *Bulletin of the World Health Organization*, Geneva, 1959, no. 21, pp. 583–91.
57  Ibid., p. 586.
58  Ibid., pp. 586–7.
59  Ibid., p. 587; C. Rosser and C. C. Harris, *The Family and Social Change*, London, 1965.
60  P. Townsend and D. Wedderburn, *The Aged in the Welfare State*, London, 1965, p.6; Shanas and Sussman, *Family, Bureaucracy and the Elderly*.
61  Townsend and Wedderburn, *The Aged*, p. 34.
62  Ibid., p. 97.
63  Ibid., p.102.
64  J. Tunstall, *Old and Alone*, London, 1966, p.1.
65  Ibid., pp. 26–7.
66  Ibid., p. 36.
67  Ibid., p. 233.
68  Ibid., p. 268.
69  Ibid., p. 240.
70  Ibid., p. 55.
71  Ibid., pp. 56–7.
72  Ibid., p. 256.
73  Ibid., p. 53.
74  Ibid., p. 83.
75  Ibid., p.108. The Nuffield Foundation Report made the same finding. See Nuffield Foundation, *Old People*, p. 53.
76  Tunstall, *Old and Alone*, p. 296.
77  Ibid., p. 297.
78  V. Karn, *Retiring to the Seaside*, London, 1977.
79  Ibid., p. 14.
80  Ibid., p. 75.
81  Elizabeth Roberts, *A Woman's Place. An Oral History of Working Class Women, 1890–1940*, Oxford, 1984.

82 Elizabeth Roberts, *Women and Families. An Oral History 1940–1970*, Oxford, 1995, p. 175.
83 Ibid., p.191.
84 Ibid.
85 Ibid., p. 175.
86 Ibid., p. 180.
87 Ibid., p. 181.
88 Ibid., p. 188.
89 Ibid., p. 185.
90 Ibid., p. 197.
91 K. Coates and R. Silburn, *Poverty: The Forgotten Englishmen*, Harmondsworth, 1970.
92 Raymond Firth, Jane Hybert and Anthony Forge, *Families and their Relatives. Kinship in a Middle Class Sector of London*, London, 1969, pp.102–3.
93 Ibid., pp. 102–3, 105–6.
94 Ibid., p. 106.
95 Ibid., p. 109.
96 Ibid., pp. 109–11.
97 Ibid., p. 400.
98 Ibid., pp. 406–7.
99 A. Hunt, *The Elderly at Home*, London, 1978.
100 P. Thompson, C. Itzin and M. Abenstern, *I Don't Feel Old*, Oxford, 1990, p. 208.
101 Ibid., p. 209.
102 Ibid., p. 210.
103 Ibid.
104 H. Qureshi and A. Walker, 'Caring for elderly people: the family and the state', in C. Phillipson and A. Walker (eds), *Ageing and Social Policy. A Critical Assessment*, Aldershot, 1986.
105 Roberts, *Women and Families*, p. 176.
106 Qureshi and Walker 'Caring for elderly people', p. 117.
107 G. Claire Wenger, 'Support networks in old age: constructing a typology', in Margot Jeffreys (ed.), *Growing Old in the Twentieth Century*, London, 1989, p. 166. See also G. C. Wenger, *The Supportive Network: Coping with Old Age*, London, 1984.
108 Wenger, 'Support networks', pp. 167–8.
109 G. Claire Wenger, 'A comparison of urban with rural support networks: Liverpool and North Wales', *Ageing and Society*, 1995, vol. 15, pp. 59–82.
110 J. Lewis and B. Meredith, *Daughters Who Care: Daughters Caring for Mothers at Home*, London, 1988; J. Finch and D. Groves (eds), *A Labour of Love: Women, Work and Caring*, London, 1983.
111 S. Arber and J. Ginn, *Gender and Later Life*, London, 1991, p.130.
112 Scott A. Bass (ed.), *Older and Active. How Americans over 55 are Contributing to Society*, New Haven, CT, and London, 1995.
113 Offer, 'Economy of regard', p. 462; H. Green, *Informal Carers*, General Household Survey 1985, series GN5, no.15, suppl. A, London, 1988.
114 Arber and Ginn, *Gender*, pp. 131–4.
115 Ibid., p.135.
116 M. Kohli *et al.* (eds), *Time for Retirement: Comparative Studies of Early Exit from the Labour Force*, Cambridge, 1991.
117 H. Qureshi and A. Walker, *The Caring Relationship*, London, 1989, pp.18–19; Arber and Ginn, *Gender*, pp.18–19.
118 A. Sixsmith, 'Independence and home in later life', in C. Phillipson *et al.* (eds), *Dependency and Interdependency in Old Age*, London, 1986, pp. 338–47.

119 J. Finch, *Family Obligations and Social Change*, Cambridge, 1989; Arber and Ginn, *Gender*, pp. 140–3.
120 ESRC Seminar on Household and Population Change, London, 1997. Paper by J. Bornat *et al.*
121 Ibid. Paper by E. Grundy and M. Murphy.
122 M. Anderson, 'The emergence of the modern life cycle in Britain', *Social History*, 1985, vol 10.
123 K. Wachter, 'Kinship resources for the elderly', *Philosophical Transactions of the Royal Society of London, Series B*, 1997, vol. 352, pp. 1811–18.
124 Young and Willmott, *Family and Kinship*, p. 13.
125 Offer, 'Economy of regard', pp. 461–2; World Bank, *Averting the Old Age Crisis*, New York, 1994, p. 49.
126 Ibid., p. 462; table 2.3, p. 63.
127 M. Rein and D. Salzman, 'Social integration, participation and exchange in five industrial countries', in Scott A. Bass (ed.), *Older and Active. How Americans over 55 are Contributing to Society*, New Haven, CT, and London, 1995, pp. 237–62.
128 Ibid.
129 Ibid.
130 Townsend, *Family Life*.
131 Offer, 'Economy of regard', p. 462.
132 Ibid.

# 10 Parallel histories of retirement in modern Britain

*Paul Johnson*

## Introduction

Over the course of the twentieth century planned and anticipated retirement from employment has evolved in Britain from being an exceptional experience for a minority of privileged workers to being the commonplace experience of the majority. In 1901 over 60 per cent of males aged 65 and above were recorded in the census as being active in the labour force; today fewer than one in ten of this age group are still in paid work.[1] At the end of Victoria's reign only civil servants and the long-term employees of railway companies and a few other paternalistic employers qualified for an occupational pension, while the state provided nothing other than Poor Law relief to the destitute. Today half the workforce is enrolled in an occupational pension scheme, and virtually everyone is entitled to a state pension.[2] At the turn of the century less than half of all 20 year olds could expect to survive to age 65; today average life expectancy at age 20 is well over 70 years for men, and higher for women.[3] These massive changes to income, work and life chances at older ages have created a social group – variously referred to as pensioners, retirees and senior citizens – which is distinct in size, economic capacity, civil status and expectations, from the collectivity of older persons a century ago.

Yet it would be wrong to think of this twentieth-century historical transformation in the activity and status of older people as a simple tale of progress, of 'whig' history writ large. The historian's eye can as easily locate depressing stories of continued pain as of progressive achievement. Take the case of poverty. Just over 100 years ago the British parliament received a report from a Royal Commission that had been appointed to investigate the economic and social circumstances of the aged poor. The Commission concluded that although the great majority of working people were 'fairly provident, fairly thrifty, fairly industrious and fairly temperate' throughout their working lives, well over a third of them became abjectly poor in old age and had to rely on Poor Law financial assistance to prevent absolute destitution.[4] Almost a century later, in 1992, the second national report on the United Kingdom for the European Commission Observatory on Ageing and

Older People noted that 30 per cent of all pensioners had incomes at or below the national poverty level, and that the elderly constituted a large proportion of the 'socially excluded'.[5] To be sure, conceptions of poverty have changed enormously over the intervening years, but this constancy in the proportion of older people living below some socially acceptable standard is a profoundly depressing outcome after decades of social reform and welfare state expansion

Can these different representations of a century of ageing and retirement in Britain be reconciled? Not if the aim is to produce a master narrative of the history of retirement. Even at the level of social process, retirement is too complex a phenomenon, and too contestable a concept, to permit the uncontentious unfolding of a unique history. If interest shifts from social process to individual experience, then the array of evidence and interpretation widens further. Perhaps a key to this complexity lies in the language used today to identify older people. 'Pensioner', 'retiree', 'senior citizen': these three terms are often used interchangeably, but they refer to quite different underlying concepts of income source, employment status and citizenship, and they relate to quite distinct historical phenomena and historical narratives. Only by separating out these different terms, by examining their different but parallel histories, can we discern the reasons for the development of opposing interpretations of the history of old age in the twentieth century. The historical polarities can be extreme: massive economic advance for older people or continued poverty; release from wage slavery or forced exclusion from the labour market; tremendous gains in terms of social and civic status or increased marginalisation and social exclusion. This chapter examines the diversity of historical interpretation of old age in the twentieth century by looking at the evolution of retirement in Britain not as a single historical process, but as a number of overlapping and interacting histories which have produced complex and often unintended outcomes. It sketches the outlines of three of these histories of retirement: retirement as a history of public policy, retirement as a history of economic and labour market change, and retirement as a history of evolving perceptions of the life course. The purpose is not to privilege one type of evidence or interpretation above another, but to illustrate the interconnectedness of parallel accounts of the same phenomenon.

## Retirement and public policy

In 1908 the British government introduced a national non-contributory old-age pension for all citizens of good character aged 70 years and above, whose annual income was less than £21. This pioneering piece of legislation was the first time that central government had acknowledged and assumed direct responsibility for the financial welfare of British people in old age, and it has, therefore, been seen as a 'tentative and halting step' along a path towards the comprehensive 'cradle to grave' welfare state established after the Second World War.[6] The expansion of public financial provision for old age and retirement has involved incremental extension of coverage to an ever larger proportion of the population, and on an ever more comprehensive basis. In 1925 a contributory National Insurance pension payable to manual workers at age 65 was grafted onto the original non-contributory scheme. In 1940 the eligibility age for female pensioners was reduced from 65 to 60. In 1948 this contributory insurance pension was extended, as part of the Beveridge social insurance system, to include all citizens, not just manual workers. In 1959 graduated contributions were introduced for higher earners, who in return received a higher state pension, and in 1975 a supplementary state earnings-related pension scheme (SERPS) was launched to provide additional income in old age to workers who were not members of an employer pension scheme.

Simultaneous with this widening public involvement in pension provision has come a significant increase in the size of the older population. The combination of policy extension and demographic change has increased the proportion of the population eligible for pensions from little more than 3 per cent of the total before the First World War to almost 20 per cent today, and public expenditure on pensions has grown to become the largest single item in the government's budget (see Table 10.1).

This twentieth-century expansion of public pension coverage and expenditure is a phenomenon common to most advanced industrial economies, and many explanations for such a widespread trend embody some element of a general thesis about 'modernisation'. An early attempt by Wilensky to develop a comparative analysis of social security systems identified the 'logic of industrialism' as a key explanatory factor, with the old-age pension being a more or less automatic response to the increasing functional redundancy of older workers brought about by the technological imperatives of industrialisation.[7] Other authors have stressed pensions as an arena of political conflict between broad class interests, with policy advance reflecting periods of electoral success by parties of the left,[8] or as an arena of narrow

*Table 10.1* State pension payments in the UK, 1910–93

| | Pension payments (£m) | Payments as a percentage of | | UK population over pension age (%) |
|---|---|---|---|---|
| | | GNP | Government expenditure | |
| 1910 | 10 | 0.4 | 4.3 | 3.1 |
| 1930 | 54 | 1.2 | 5.0 | 9.6 |
| 1950 | 305 | 2.6 | 7.8 | 13.4 |
| 1970 | 1,896 | 4.3 | 11.3 | 16.1 |
| 1993 | 31,500 | 5.2 | 13.0 | 18.7 |

*Sources*: Johnson and Falkingham, 1988, p. 141; Department of Social Security, 1993, pp. 6–10.

economic interest-group conflict, with policy advance reflecting the shifting political alliances formed within and across class lines by fluctuating 'actuarial factions'.[9] A more conspiratorial interpretation has been offered by neo-Marxists who have identified public spending on pensions as a direct mechanism of state control or co-option of (surplus) labour.[10] Given the wide variation between countries in the form, finance and operation of their public pension systems it is perhaps not surprising that these grand explanatory frameworks have been found wanting when put to an empirical test.[11] Yet this unconvincing relationship between grand theory and perceived policy development is not readily resolved by narrowing the focus from comparative analyses to a unique national case. The historical record of pension policy in twentieth-century Britain reveals a complex set of motives and a number of equivocal policy outcomes.

Historians have identified many causal factors behind the initial 1908 pension – political pressures from organised labour, an attempt by the predominantly middle-class Liberal party to win working-class votes, an evolving ideology of state intervention for the public good, and a conscious attempt by capitalists to shift some of the costs of the reproduction of labour from themselves to the state.[12] Each of these interpretations is valid, but none of them alone is convincing in explaining why this first piece of pension legislation was introduced. For the thirty years before the introduction of the 1908 Old Age Pension Act there was an ongoing debate about the need for a public pension, its mode of finance, who should be eligible and at what level it should be paid.[13] The breadth of ideas aired, opinions advanced and positions taken means that there is no shortage of alternative historical readings. Much depends on whether greater weight is placed on the influence of long-term economic and social forces or that of short-term political expediency.

Simple explanations also fail to account for the course of subsequent pension system development. The Conservative party was responsible for introducing insurance pensions in 1925 and graduated pensions in 1959, the Labour party for extending pension coverage beyond the manual working population in 1948, and for inaugurating the supplementary SERPS pension in 1975, although over this legislation there was conspicuous all-party support.[14] However, neither party has ever made pension policy a major campaign issue in the run-up to a general election, nor has the trade union movement prioritised pension issues over more overtly employment-related concerns. In the post-war period politicians have found pension policy easy to promise, but hard to deliver. In the late 1950s a Labour party study group chaired by Richard Crossman developed a radical proposal for a comprehensive national superannuation scheme, but it was shelved during the 1964–70 Labour government.[15] The Conservative government in the 1990s indicated that it would radically reform the state pension, but no proposals were forthcoming until two months before the party was voted out of office in May 1997. The Labour opposition throughout the 1980s promised to restore cuts made in 1980 to the basic state pension, but this pledge was dropped before the 1997 election campaign. When looking at the political record of pensions policy in Britain since 1908, it is clear that pensioners have consistently been viewed by all main political parties as worthy of legislative attention and deserving of public financial support. Yet the proportion of pensioners deemed to be living in or on the margins of poverty remains around the 30 per cent level. How can the often repeated political intentions to deliver a 'fair deal for pensioners' have remained so divorced from the public policy realities for such a long period?

The answer lies not (just) in the latent venality of politicians, but in the practical constraints of public policy financial expediency. Although the 1908 pension was the first incursion of central government into the field of old-age income support, local government had long been supporting the infirm and penurious elderly through the Poor Law. By the end of the nineteenth century the Poor Law provided pensions in fact, if not in name, to the majority of people who survived to 70 years of age.[16] The 1908 legislation transferred much of the cost of this income support from local rate-payers (i.e. property owners) to the national exchequer, and part of this cost was immediately switched back onto manual workers through an increase in excise duties on alcohol and tobacco.[17] The extension of pensions to people aged 65 to 70 in 1925 was based entirely on an insurance model, with pensioners earning their entitlements through contributions made by themselves and their employers, because the non-contributory basis of the initial old-age pension was considered too expensive to develop. In these early incursions into the provision of public pensions, politicians were well aware that they could not, for electoral reasons, afford to give pensioners a blank cheque.

Beveridge was also concerned about the cost of pensions. He recognised that 'the problem of the nature and extent of the provision to be made for old age is the most important, and in some ways the most difficult, of all the problems of social security' because of the growing number of older people and the very high cost involved in providing them all with a pension income.[18] He proposed an insurance model of old-age pensions based on actuarial principles and an accumulating fund, and a transition period of twenty years so that the capital value of the fund could be built up. However, administrative and political pragmatism quickly undermined this idea. An accumulating fund of idle assets was too much of a luxury for governments facing unmatchable popular demands for higher public expenditure, while taking twenty years to raise pension payments to the same level as other social security benefits was an electorally unsustainable policy. Pensions were paid at the 'full' rate from the inauguration of the post-war social security system in 1948, and the idea of an accumulating fund had been abandoned and public pensions converted to a pay-as-you-go basis by the end of the 1950s.[19] This change in the financial basis of the public pension system to a complete reliance on workers' national insurance contributions established exactly what Beveridge had attempted to avoid – a direct trade-off between the income of pensioners and the contributions of workers. In this competition, the interests of workers – well organised, vocal and electorally dominant – were always likely to dominate the interests of pensioners, even if the public debate was seldom posed in these starkly confrontational terms.

In the mid 1980s, however, public discussion of pension policy was explicitly cast in terms of a zero-sum trade-off between workers and pensioners. The Conservative government's proposals for the reform of social security focused heavily on the projected future cost of the public pension, particularly the supplementary SERPS pension.[20] Although motivated to some degree by an ideological desire to reduce the scope and cost of the welfare state, the proposal to abolish SERPS was also in part a response to independent estimates that the long-run cost would be far higher than originally intended.[21] A compromise decision was taken to reduce the level of public pension benefits in order to allow personal tax rates to fall (or to prevent them rising) and to encourage private provision for old age. The fiscal incentives and blandishments after 1988 to take out private pensions, whether heeded or not, could have no impact in the short run on pensioner incomes, since new pension contracts take three or four decades to mature. The inevitable result of the 1980s pension reforms was to make current pensioners worse-off in order to reduce the tax liability on future workers. New Labour, with its economically nonsensical commitment to abide by the previous government's spending plans, has automatically aligned itself to what is now a deeply entrenched element of post-war public policy – of favouring the interests of workers and taxpayers above those of poorer pensioners.

It is clear that throughout the twentieth century financial considerations have been a consistent impediment to the scope of public old-age income support. When the Royal Commission investigated the condition of the aged poor in the 1890s their financial need was plain for all to see, and there was widespread agreement that some form of public support for the elderly was morally justified. What delayed government action was the cost – in 1895 the Royal Commission balked at the financial burden on property and industrial enterprise that would be imposed by tax-financed pensions.[22] It was concern over cost that constrained Beveridge's ambitions for pensions after the Second World War, and the enormous fiscal implications of raising the real value of pensions in a universal pay-as-you-go public pension system continue to undermine calls for more generous pensions. The twentieth-century history of public policy towards retirement and pensions in Britain is, therefore, curiously polarised. On the one hand there is the story of popular and successful institutional innovation which has led to the comprehensive incorporation of older people within the welfare state in a role as 'pensioners', and to the allocation of a large share of public revenue to this group via the state pension. On the other hand there is a consistent history of cross-party inability or unwillingness ever to provide adequate resources to meet expectations or to provide a pension income above a low subsistence level.

## Retirement and the labour market

The failure to raise the average level of public pensions in Britain towards the level achieved in the last decade by most other European countries has partly been a matter of choice – electors and governments have preferred lower taxes to higher pensions. But enduringly low public pensions are in part the result of an autonomous but parallel history of changing labour market conditions which have greatly extended the demand for public income support in old age. In the 1880s almost 75 per cent of men aged 65 and above were in some form of employment. Over the past century retirement has shifted from being an exception to being the norm; by 1951 only 31 per cent of men in this age group were in work, a figure which had fallen to a mere 8 per cent by 1991. This secular decline in labour force participation rates for older men and rise in retirement is in part a consequence of increasing public provision of income in old age, but it has a more complex history.

Most of the fall in participation rates between 1881 and 1921 was a result of sectoral shifts in the economy. In Britain, as in other countries, employment opportunities for older workers were much higher in agriculture than in industry or commerce, and the contraction of the agricultural sector from the late nineteenth century had a disproportionate impact on the participation rates of older men.[23] In the interwar period, however, there was an unambiguous decline in participation rates for men over 65, irrespective of changes in the sectoral composition of the workforce. In theory this could have been a result of the payment of insurance-based pensions from 1928 to manual workers aged 65 and above who had made an appropriate number of National Insurance contributions, though in practice there is no evidence that the 65–9 age group contributed disproportionately to the rising retirement rate in the period.[24] This is perhaps not surprising when the level of the pension is taken into account. Paid at the rate of 10*s*. per week, it was an income that stood well below contemporary estimates of the poverty line. The maximum public pension income for a single- and for a two-person household stood at just 56 per cent and 86 per cent respectively of Rowntree's estimate of the appropriate minimum poverty line income.[25]

Far from older workers being lured from the labour force by the attraction of high public pensions, they instead appear increasingly to have been forced out by the policy of employers. Analysis of a survey conducted in London in 1931 of almost 27,000 working-class households indicates that the labour market options for older workers were severely constrained. In a flexible labour market the older worker would be able to 'trade down' by moving to a less demanding, lower-paid job over time. In fact there turns out to be no negative gradient between age and the wage rate for men over 60 in the London labour market in 1931.[26] This indicates older workers had either to maintain labour effort and productivity at the same rate as younger workers or to withdraw from work entirely.

In fact even if these older men were able and willing to maintain their effort and productivity, this was no guarantee that they would keep their jobs. Unemployment in the interwar period was particularly concentrated among older industrial workers; employers and trade unions conspired to preserve jobs for younger workers with family responsibilities. As if this age bias were not enough, age discrimination was widely advocated as a potentially beneficial workplace practice. Ernest Bevin was just one of a number of socialists who advocated the use of the public pension system to promote higher levels of retirement in order to create more employment opportunities for the young.[27]

Labour shortage during the Second World War temporarily reversed the downward trend in employment among older men, although the introduction in 1948 of a public pension that was conditional on retirement from full-time employment must have had some negative impact on participation. More important in accounting for the collapse of employment at higher ages over the last five decades are two other factors: the desire of many employers to replace older staff with younger workers, and the accumulation by many older workers of sufficient savings to allow them to give up full-time work.

Age discrimination in the workplace is certainly not a creation of the post-war period. In the 1890s trade unionists were arguing that older men were finding it increasingly difficult to retain their jobs because of growing levels of workplace stress, and in recognition of this fact several craft unions established independent superannuation funds in the last decades of the nineteenth century.[28] Yet since the 1960s employers have become increasingly youth oriented in their hiring policy, so that many jobs are now effectively barred to applicants over 40 or 45. The problem for the older worker is not that he (or, in the expanded female labour market of the post-war period, she) suffers a much higher risk of becoming unemployed, but rather that, once out of work, the older person finds it much more difficult to re-enter.[29] The discriminatory recruitment policies are in part determined by economics, since in the seniority wage systems operated by many large employers, remuneration is positively related to age, and therefore for any given task an older employee costs more than a younger one. But ageism in the workplace is also the result of deep-seated, but quite erroneous, beliefs that the productivity of workers declines after age 40. Detailed laboratory and workplace tests of capacity reveal that, for the great majority of manual and non-manual tasks, there is on average no appreciable age-related decrement in performance for people until they reach their mid 60s.[30] Nevertheless, age discrimination has acted to push older workers out of employment, and at increasingly young ages. In 1961, 97 per cent of British men aged 55–9 and 91 per cent of those aged 60–4 were active in the labour force; by 1991 these rates had fallen to 77 and 53 per cent respectively.

This negative account of the declining fortunes of older workers over the course of the twentieth century is not, however, the only way of viewing the history of labour force participation. Not all older people may wish to work, and over time more of them have been able to choose to leave the workforce because they have accumulated sufficient pension entitlements through their occupational pension schemes. About 5 per cent of workers were enrolled in occupational pension schemes around 1900, rising to 13 per cent in 1936, 35 per cent in 1956, and 53 per cent in 1967, since when coverage has stabilised at around half the total workforce.[31] However, the time lag between joining an occupational pension scheme and receiving benefits means that it was not until 1985 that the proportion of pensioners in receipt of an occupational pension crept above 50 per cent, up from 34 per cent in 1970.[32]

Whether older workers have been pushed unwillingly into retirement or have deliberately sought to exchange work for leisure is technically very difficult to determine. A quantitative assessment of retirement and early retirement since the 1950s finds that in the main people have been pushed at age 65 (few companies permit employees to stay on after this age) but that at earlier ages the retirement decision has owed much more to individual choice which is itself a function of (poor) health and (good) pension savings.[33] This is consistent with studies from the 1980s which find that the early retired can be divided into two groups: the 'poor' who had few assets or pension rights and who had been driven into premature retirement by bad health, and the 'non-poor' who had chosen to give up work early in order to enjoy well-financed leisure.[34]

Some idea of the relative importance of these push and pull factors, and how this may have changed over time, can be gleaned from Table 10.2, which shows how the composition of pensioner incomes has changed over the past sixty years. The share of social security benefits in average pensioner income has risen over time from more than 40 to over 50 per cent. However, even as early as 1929–31 state benefits were the dominant source of pensioner income, and it seems implausible that the relatively small increase in their proportionate share since then could account for the massive fall in participation rates. Income from savings and investments has remained stable, but the contribution of occupational pensions has increased significantly. Comparing 1993 with 1929–31, private sources of non-employment income in retirement (from pensions and investments) have doubled their relative share. At the same time, employment income has changed over sixty years from being a major to a minor source of pensioner income. This illustrates just how important the history of twentieth century labour market evolution has been to the status and income of older people. It also demonstrates why the enormous expansion of public income support for older people has failed to achieve the expected improvement in pensioners' relative incomes. The rise in public provision has done no more than compensate for the loss

*Table 10.2* Main components of pensioner incomes (percentages)

|         | Earnings | State benefits | Occupational pension | Investment income |
|---------|----------|----------------|----------------------|-------------------|
| 1929–31 | 35       | 44             | 5                    | 14                |
| 1951    | 27       | 42             | 15                   | 15                |
| 1961    | 22       | 48             | 16                   | 15                |
| 1971    | 18       | 48             | 21                   | 10                |
| 1981    | 10       | 59             | 21                   | 10                |
| 1993    | 6        | 56             | 23                   | 16                |

*Sources*: Johnson, 1989, p. 70; Disney *et al.*, 1995, p.17.

of employment income. As the welfare state has expanded, so more demands have been placed on it by autonomous changes in the economy and the labour market; the achievements have consistently fallen short of the ever-widening objectives. Meanwhile the proportion of people entering retirement with substantial assets and large occupational pension entitlements has increased, and this has created a gap, ever more visible, between rich and poor retirees.

The twentieth-century history of retirees is a history of changing fortunes. At the beginning of the century to be old and out of work was synonymous with being poor for all but a very small minority of middle- and upper-class people. Today for a growing proportion (though still a minority) of retirees the end of work heralds not poverty and economic dependency but instead a new life-course stage of active and well-resourced leisure. A key determinant of fortune in old age is now the individual's earlier labour force history. If this is a history of continuous employment in a pensionable job at average or above average wages, then retirement is likely to be financially secure. But if the previous work history involved long earnings gaps, or part-time work, or below average pay and a non-pensionable job, then retirement will almost inevitably be a time of reduced financial capacity and dependency on public welfare. The type of work you do now determines the type of retirement you live. Twentieth-century labour market changes have enormously improved the retirement experience of many people – the 'core' workers in well-paid, stable jobs – but have done little to enhance living conditions in old age for 'peripheral' workers. It is this group who comprise today's impoverished retirees, unable to obtain employment, but unable to survive on their meagre assets.

## Retirement and perceptions of the life course

As well as being an element of public policy intervention and labour market change, the history of retirement has also been an important part of the reconceptualisation of the life course that has occurred in the twentieth century. People's expectations of retirement, how they plan for it and experience it, have altered enormously over the past 100 years. One very simple reason for this is that most people can now expect not only to survive into retirement, but to do so in good health for well over a decade. Retirement has, therefore, changed from being a residual phase of life, experienced by a minority, to being a normal part of the life course, of equal or longer duration than childhood and adolescence.

With this demographic change has come a revolution in personal expectations. During the interwar depression the novelist J. B. Priestley described the life course of the workers of Bradford as 'a brief childhood at one end and a few sinking weary years at the other end, and between them these five solid decades of work: that is their record'.[35] This negative view of old age was widely held, and with good reason. Retirement appeared to the outside observer as a postscript to working life, a brief and insignificant interlude between the end of economic activity and the end of physical existence. How it was viewed by older people themselves is much more difficult to determine. As Thane has noted in the previous chapter, the majority of social investigations of older people in the post-1945 period problematised the elderly because of their perceived social or economic dependency. This was equally true for earlier periods, when official interest focused on the demands that the dependent aged poor might place on public authorities. Since investigators were primed to address the problems of old age it is little wonder that they conspicuously failed to ask questions about capacity and achievement. And, as noted in Chapter 1, since there are few diaries or autobiographies for the pre-1945 period that give more than passing treatment to the experience of ageing and the condition of being a retiree or pensioner, it is difficult, perhaps impossible, to discover how people negotiated their own ageing. Did they see the later part of their life course as just 'a few sinking weary years', or did it provide opportunities for personal fulfilment?

If the historical record is almost silent on this question, then we might draw inferences from more recent experience. Rising life expectancy, better health and, for some at least, significantly higher real incomes, have made retirement into something positive; a new chapter rather than a postscript. Instead of using the word 'retired', with all its negative connotations of economic redundancy, older people in Britain increasingly use the term 'third age' to describe their phase of the life course, and 'senior citizen' to describe their status. To quote Peter Laslett, the leading advocate of this reconceptualisation of the lifecourse, 'First comes an era of dependence, socialisation, immaturity and education; second an era of independence, maturity and responsibility, of earning and saving; third an era of personal fulfilment.'[36] Personal fulfilment involves older people taking a much more active role in political affairs, being more assertive in their demands for equal access to employment opportunities, and being central rather than marginal to the social activities of civil society. Instead of a monochrome old age of general dependency and poverty there is opportunity for colourful, active diversity.

Popular images of retirement have also become much more diverse and fragmented, reflecting the enormous diversity of capacity and experience amongst older people. Stories of impoverished pensioners dying of hypothermia in unheated apartments vie with accounts of thousands of British retirees who retreat to the warmer climes of Spain and Florida for the winter. For each media tale of hardship in old age there is one of wayward abandon – the bungee-jumping octogenarian, the parachuting granny. But these are, of course, no more than images, views from without. They give little indication of whether the experience of old age has changed from within, from the perspective of the ageing individual. The cultural history of old age in twentieth-century Britain has yet to be written, and the paucity of source material on the mass of working-class elderly means that any future account will at best be partial. Instead we can look to contemporary studies. Paul Thompson has used the methodology of the oral historian to investigate the experience of old age in the 1980s among a cross-section of older women and men.[37] The central finding of this sympathetic and evocative study is summed up in the title: *I Don't Feel Old*. For Thompson's respondents, old age was some 'other', to which they did not belong. They certainly did not regard themselves as being in a liminal state between a meaningful world of work and the oblivion of death. For these people retirement had its own challenges, achievements and disappointments, just like other phases of life – childhood, adolescence, marriage, parenthood.

## Conclusion

For the historian of old age in twentieth century Britain, the sentiments of Thompson's respondents raise important questions about how different historical readings might be reconciled. The history of pensions and public policy looks at political and administrative processes and outcomes. These embody formal age thresholds that designate the old – the pensioners – to be different from the rest of society. As Bourdelais shows in Chapter 6 above, the age thresholds are themselves often inherited relics of earlier public policies, and their functional relevance may decline over time, but they remain powerful forces in structuring political discourse and civic relationships. The history of retirement and the labour market looks at the economic behaviour of workers and employers. This behaviour interacts with formal and informal age thresholds to produce a socially unique group – retirees – who no longer expect, or are expected, to work. Both these histories, which emphasise division and difference between pensioners/retirees and the rest of society, sit uneasily with the self-perception of old people in modern Britain who do not see themselves as a group apart, who do not see physical age as a personally meaningful social identifier. The historian's task is to determine how far the views of Thompson's respondents echo the attitudes of many past generations of older people, and how far they are the product of a specific 1980s conjuncture of public policy evolution, economic change and social development.

We can begin to think about how this task might be approached by turning back to the three criteria proposed in Chapter 1 for examining the long-run history of old age and ageing – well-being, participation and status. These criteria are reflected in the parallel histories of public policy, the labour market, and perceptions of the life course, and are manifested in the terms pensioner, retiree and senior citizen or 'third-ager'. How much is status a function of, or at least conditioned by, well-being and participation? As Smith makes clear in Chapter 4, an income in old age was available for many older people in Britain well before the introduction of statutory old-age pensions in 1908. But this was an income provided by the Poor Law, and so was only ever available to people who were abjectly poor and who were prepared to undergo intensive investigation into their personal circumstances and to forego their civic rights (paupers were automatically disfranchised). Public policy towards pensions in the twentieth century has had the effect of incorporating all elderly people into the polity – there is now no formal discrimination against people drawing a public pension. Indeed quite the reverse – pensioner status brings additional entitlements such as subsidised public transport. In this respect, therefore, the development of public pension structures and the construction of absolute entitlements to an old-age pension has significantly enhanced the status of older people.

In terms of participation, the development of occupational pension systems has extended to the masses what was once the privilege of a few property owners – the ability to command an income even when not engaged in wage labour. The decline in the share of earnings in pensioner income shown in Table 10.2 is indicative of a general weakening of the historic association between work and income. It is part of a more fundamental restructuring of the value system of modern society, a restructuring which has seen consumption and consumerism challenge production and the world of work as the indicator by which social standing is measured. This change permits retirees today to define themselves not by what they do or produce, but by where they travel, how they spend their time, with whom they associate. Today's retiree has no need to be the self-defined redundant ex-worker.

Public policy and the labour market are necessarily powerful forces which structure the environment in which older people live and give meaning to their lives. Without twentieth-century developments in pensions policy and retirement behaviour, and the consequences of these changes for the well-being, participation and status of older people, it is unlikely that the high expectations of many of today's retirees for self-fulfilment and personal development could be attained. This is not to say that the 1990s is a 'golden age' for old age; as noted above, the historical record is contentious, and many older people are still poor and socially excluded. But many are not, and their command over resources and their political and social standing appear to have been unmatched in past societies except among a very small and privileged elite. This suggests to me that the history of old age in the twentieth century is best seen in modernist rather than post-modernist terms. In a key post-modernist text, Bauman characterises the post-modern project as a 'universal dismantling of power supported structures' which privileges mood and experience, 'everyday life', over systems.[38] But as the history of retirement and old age in twentieth century Britain shows, mood and experience have been fundamentally influenced by systems; self-perceptions in old age are strongly affected by the command over time and financial resources provided by formal retirement and public and private pensions. To ignore the self-perceptions, as many historians have done in the past, is to produce a one-sided story of institutional change. But to ignore the institutional systems is to produce a decontextualised story of individual experience in which dynamic development over time is ignored.

# Notes

1　Paul Johnson, 'The employment and retirement of older men in England and Wales, 1881–1981', *Economic History Review*, 1994, vol. 47, pp. 112–13.

2　Leslie Hannah, *Inventing Retirement*, Cambridge, 1986.

3　M. Anderson, 'The impact on the family relationships of the elderly of changes since Victorian times in government income maintenance provisions', in E. Shanas and M. B. Sussman (eds), *Family, Bureaucracy and the Elderly*, Durham, NC, 1977, pp. 36–59.

4　*Royal Commission on the Aged Poor*, PP 1895, vol. XIV, p. xv.

5　Alan Walker, 'Social and economic policies and older people in the UK', mimeo, University of Sheffield, 1992, p. 64.

6　A. I. Ogus, 'Great Britain', in P. A. Kohler and H. F. Zacher (eds), *The Evolution of Social Insurance, 1881–1981*, London, 1982, pp. 178–9.

7　H. Wilensky, *The Welfare State and Equality: Structural and Ideological Roots of Public Expenditures*, Berkeley, CA, 1975.

8　W. Korpi, *The Democratic Class Struggle*, London, 1983; G. Esping-Andersen, *The Three Worlds of Welfare Capitalism*, Cambridge, 1990.

9　Peter Baldwin, *The Politics of Social Solidarity: Class Bases of the European Welfare State 1875–1975*, Cambridge, 1990.

10　Ian Gough, *The Political Economy of the Welfare State*, London, 1979; C. Offe, *Contradictions of the Welfare State*, Cambridge, MA, 1984.

11　John B. Williamson and Fred C. Pampel, *Old-Age Security in Comparative Perspective*, Oxford, 1993.

12　E. P. Hennock, *British Social Reform and German Precedents. The Case of Social Insurance 1880–1914*, Oxford, 1987; Michael Freeden, *The New Liberalism*, Oxford, 1978; J. R. Hay, *The Origins of the Liberal Welfare Reforms, 1906–1914*, London, 1975.

13　Pat Thane, 'Non-contributory versus insurance pensions, 1878–1908', in Pat Thane (ed.), *The Origins of British Social Policy*, London, 1978, pp. 84–106.

14　E. Shragge, *Pensions Policy in Britain*, London, 1984; R. Lowe, *The Welfare State in Britain since 1945*, Basingstoke, 1993.

15　Helen Fawcett, 'The Beveridge strait-jacket: policy formation and the problem of poverty in old age', *Contemporary British History*, 1996, vol. 10, pp. 20–42.

16 David Thomson, 'The decline of social welfare: falling state support for the elderly since early Victorian times', *Ageing and Society*, 1984, vol. 4, pp. 451–82.
17 Bruce Murray, *The People's Budget, 1909/10*, Oxford, 1980.
18 *Social Insurance and Allied Services* (The Beveridge Report), Cmd. 6404, London, 1942, p. 90.
19 Paul Johnson and Jane Falkingham, *Ageing and Economic Welfare*, London, 1992, pp. 125–6.
20 Department of Health and Social Security, *Reform of Social Security*, Cmnd 9517, London, 1985.
21 R. Hemming and J. Kay, 'The costs of the State Earnings Related Pension Scheme', *Economic Journal*, 1982, vol. 92, pp. 300–19.
22 *Royal Commission on the Aged Poor*, p. lxix.
23 Johnson, 'The employment and retirement of older men', p. 116.
24 Ibid., p. 123.
25 B. S. Rowntree, *Poverty and Progress. A Second Social Survey of York*, London, 1941, p. 502.
26 Dudley Baines and Paul Johnson, 'The labour force participation and economic well-being of older men in London, 1929–31', Working Paper in Economic History 37/97, London School of Economics, September 1997.
27 John Macnicol and Andrew Blaikie, 'The politics of retirement, 1908–1948', in Margot Jefferys (ed.), *Growing Old in the Twentieth Century*, London, 1989, p. 31.
28 See Alfred Jephcott's evidence to the *Royal Commission on the Aged Poor*, especially q. 14571. For details on trade union superannuation schemes see K. Fukasawa, 'Voluntary provision for old age by trade unions in Britain before the coming of the welfare state', Unpublished Ph.D. thesis, University of London, 1996.
29 Frank Laczko and Chris Phillipson, *Changing Work and Retirement*, Buckingham, 1991, ch. 3.
30 Peter Warr, 'Age and employment', in M. Dunnette *et al.* (eds), *Handbook of Industrial and Organisational Psychology*, vol, 4, Palo Alto, CA, 1992.
31 Hannah, *Inventing Retirement*, pp. 40, 125.
32 A. Dawson and G. Evans, 'Pensioners' incomes and expenditure, 1970–1985', *Employment Gazette*, 1987, May, pp. 243–52.
33 Paul Johnson, 'The labour force participation of older men in Britain, 1951–81', *Work, Employment and Society*, 1989, vol 3, pp. 351–68.
34 F. Laczko, A. Dale, S. Arber and N. Gilbert, 'Early retirement in a period of high unemployment', *Journal of Social Policy*, 1988, vol. 17, pp. 313–33.
35 J. B. Priestley, *English Journey*, London, 1934, p. 194.
36 Peter Laslett, *A Fresh Map of Life: The Emergence of the Third Age*, London, 1989, p. 4.
37 Paul Thompson, Catherine Itzin and Michelle Abenstern, *I Don't Feel Old*, Oxford, 1990.
38 Z. Bauman, *Intimations of Postmodernity*, London, 1992, p. ix.

# Bibliography

*A Return of the Freeholders of New Zealand*, Wellington, 1884.

*Acta Sanctorum*, ed. the Bollandist Fathers, Paris, 1863.

Adams, G. F. and Cheeseman, G. A., *Old People in Northern Ireland*, Belfast, 1951.

ADH, 'Vivre et mourir à l'hôpital' (6 articles), in *Annales de démographie historique*, 1994, pp. 217–316.

Aegidius Romanus [Giles of Rome], *De regimine principum*, Rome, 1607.

Alberti, Leon Battista, *I libri della famiglia: The Family in Renaissance Florence*, trans. R. M. Watkins, Columbia, SC, 1969.

Albertus Magnus [Albert the Great], *De aetate sive de juventute et senectute*, in *Parva naturalia*, in *Opera omnia*, ed. A. Borgent, vol. 9, Paris, 1890.

Anderson, M., 'The impact on the family relationships of the elderly of changes since Victorian times in government income maintenance provisions', in E. Shanas and M. B. Sussman (eds), *Family, Bureaucracy and the Elderly*, Durham, NC, 1977, pp. 36–59.

Anderson, M., 'The emergence of the modern life cycle in Britain', *Social History*, 1985, vol. 10.

*Annales de démographie historique* (1985): *Vieillir autrefois*.

*Annales de démographie historique* (1991): *Grand-Parents, Aïeux*.

*Annales S. Iustinae Patavini*, ed. G. H. Pertz, in *M.G.H. Script*, vol.19, Hannover, 1886; reprint Stuttgart, 1963, pp. 149–93.

Arber, S. and Ginn, J., *Gender and Later Life*, London, 1991.

Ariès, P., *L'Enfant et la vie familiale sous l'Ancien Régime*, Paris, 1960.

Ariès, P., *Centuries of Childhood*, New York, 1962.

Ariès, P., *The Hour of Our Death*, New York, 1981.

Aristotle, *Ethica nicomachea*, in *The Basic Works of Aristotle*, ed. R. Mckeon, New York, 1968.

Aristotle, *Rhetorica*, in *The Basic Works of Aristotle*, ed. R. Mckeon, New York, 1968.

Arnaldus de Villanova, *De regimine sanitatis*, in *Opera omnia*, Basel, 1585.

Arnold, R., 'Community in rural Victorian New Zealand', *New Zealand Journal of History*, 1990, vol. 24, pp. 3–21.

Arnold, R., *New Zealand's Burning: The Settlers' World in the mid 1880s*, Wellington, 1994.

Aron, Raymond, *Dimensions de la conscience historique*, Paris, 1964.

Audirac, Pierre-Alain, 'Les personnes âgées, de la vie de famille à l'isolement', *Economie et statistiques*, 1985, no. 175, March, pp. 46–8.

Augustine, St, *Retractiones*, ed. A. Mutzenbecher, *CCSL*, 1984, vol. 57, Turnhout.

Bacon, Roger, *De retardatione accidentium senectutis cum aliis opusculis de rebus medicinalibus*, ed. A. G. Little and E. Withington, Oxford, 1928.

Bacon, Roger, *Opus majus*, trans. R. B. Burke, Philadelphia, 1928.

Bacon, Roger, *Opus majus*, ed. J. H. Bridge, Frankfurt, 1964.

Badger, W., *Statutes of New Zealand*, Christchurch, 1892.

Baines, D. and Johnson, P., 'The labour force participation and economic well-being of older men in London, 1929–31', Working Paper in Economic History 37/97, London School of Economics, September 1997.

Baldwin, P., *The Politics of Social Solidarity: Class Bases of the European Welfare State 1875–1975*, Cambridge, 1990.

Barker-Read, M., 'The treatment of the aged poor in five selected west Kent parishes from settlement to Speenhamland (1662–1797)', Unpublished Ph.D. thesis, Open University, 1988.

Bartholomaeus Anglicus, *Liber de proprietatibus rerum*, Strasbourg, 1505.

Bartholomaeus Anglicus, *On the Properties of Things: John Trevisa's Translation of Bartholomaeus Anglicus' De proprietatibus rerum*, ed. M. C. Seymour, Oxford, 1975.

Bass, Scott A. (ed.), *Older and Active. How Americans over 55 are Contributing to Society*, New Haven, CT, and London, 1995.

Bauman, Z., *Intimations of Postmodernity*, London, 1992.

Bernard de Gordon, *De conservatione vitae humanae seu de regimine sanitatis*, Leipzig, 1570.

Bernard of Clairvaux, *De moribus et officio episcoporum*, Epist. 42, *PL*, vol. 182, cols 810–34.

Bernardino de Sienne, *De calamitatibus et miseriis vitae humanae et maxime senectutis*, Ser. 16 in *Opera omnia*, vol. 7, pp. 243–62, ed. the Fathers of the Collegium S. Bonaventurae, Florence, 1959.

Berthorius, Petrus, *Dictionarium*, in *Opera omnia*, Cologne, 1730.

Bertillon, Jacques, 'Parallélisme des mouvements de population dans les différents pays d'Europe', *Journal de la Société de Statistique de Paris*, 1904, no. 10, October, pp. 345–8.

Bertillon, Jacques, 'De la dépopulation de la France', *Journal de la Société de Statistique de Paris*, 1895, no. 12, December, pp. 410–38.

*Bevölkerung und Wirtschaft 1871–1972*, ed. Statistisches Bundesamt Wiesbaden, Stuttgart/Mainz, 1972.

Bois, J.-P., *Les vieux: de Montaigne aux premières retraites*, Paris, 1989.

Borscheid, P., *Geschichte des Alters 16.–18. Jahrhundert*, Münster, 1987.

Boulton, J., 'Going on the parish: the parish pension and its meaning in the London suburbs, 1640–1724', in T. Hitchcock *et al.* (eds), *Chronicling Poverty: The Voices and Strategies of the English Poor, 1640–1840*, London, 1997, pp. 19–46.

Bourdelais, P., *Le nouvel âge de la vieillesse: histoire du vieillissement de la population*, Paris, 1993.

Boverat, Fernand, *Le vieillissement de la population*, Paris, 1946.

Brändström, A. and Tedebrand, L.-G. (eds), *Health and Social Change. Disease, Health and Public Care in the Sundsvall District 1750–1950*, Umeå, 1993.

Brody, B. A. (ed.), *Suicide and Euthanasia*, Dordrecht, 1989.

Bromyard, John, *Summa praedicantium*, 2 vols, Antwerp, 1614.

'Bureaux and bureaucrats: literature and social theory', in *L'Esprit Créateur*, 1994, vol. 34.

Burrow, J. A., *The Ages of Man: A Study in Medieval Writing and Thought*, Oxford, 1986.

Cage, R. A., *The Scottish Poor Law, 1745–1845*, Edinburgh, 1981.

Caldwell, J. C., *A Theory of Fertility Decline*, London, 1982.

Carboni, D. K., *Geriatric Medicine in the United States and Great Britain*, London, 1982.

Carrick, P., *Medical Ethics in Antiquity*, Dordrecht, 1985.

Carruthers, M., *The Book of Memory: A Study of Memory in Medieval Culture*, Cambridge, 1993.

Chandler, D. S., *Social Assistance and Bureaucratic Politics: The Montepíos of Colonial Mexico, 1767–1821*, Albuquerque, NM, 1991.

Clark, E., 'The quest for security in medieval England', in M. M. Sheehan (ed.), *Aging and the Aged in Medieval Europe*, Toronto, 1990, pp. 189–200.

Coates, K. and Silburn, R., *Poverty: The Forgotten Englishmen*, Harmondsworth, 1970.

Cole, T. R., *The Journey of Life. A Cultural History of Aging in America*, Cambridge, 1992.

Conrad, C., 'La "sénilité" comme problème social: cause de décès, d'invalidité, et de pauvreté (exemples allemands du XVIII^e au XX^e siècle)', *Annales de démographie historique*, 1985, pp. 39–51.

Conrad, C., 'Zwischen Krankenhaus und Pflegeheim: Anstaltsfürsorge für ältere Menschen am Beispiel Köln, 1900–1933', in J. Reulecke *et al.* (eds), *Stadt und Gesundheit. Zum Wandel von 'Volksgesundheit' und kommunaler Gesundheitspolitik im 19. und frühen 20. Jahrhundert*, Stuttgart, 1991, pp. 187–202.

Conrad, C., 'Vom Rand in das Zentrum des Gesundheitssystems: alte Menschen im 19. und 20. Jahrhundert', *Medizin, Gesellschaft und Geschichte*, 1993, vol. 12, pp. 21–41.

Conrad, C., *Vom Greis zum Rentner: Der Strukturwandel des Alters in Deutschland zwischen 1830 und 1930*, Göttingen, 1994.

Conrad, C. and von Kondratowitz, H.-J. (eds), *Zur Kulturgeschichte des Alterns/Toward a Cultural History of Aging*, Berlin, 1993.

Cornwell, J., *Hard-Earned Lives*, London, 1984.

Dante Alighieri, *Convivio*, in *Le opere di Dante*, ed. M. Barbi, Florence, 1921.

Darrow, M., *Revolution in the House*, Princeton, NJ, 1989.

Daunton, M. (ed.), *Charity, Self-interest and Welfare in the English Past*, London, 1996.

Davin, A., *Growing Up Poor. Home, School and Street in London, 1870–1914*, London, 1996.

Davison, L., Hitchcock, T., Keirn, T. and Shoemaker, R. B. (eds), *Still the Grumbling Hive: The Response to Social and Economic Problems in England 1689–1750*, Stroud, 1992.

Dawson, A. and Evans, G., 'Pensioners' incomes and expenditure, 1970–1985', *Employment Gazette*, 1987, May, pp. 243–52.

Deguileville, Guillaume de, *Le pèlerinage de la vie humaine*, ed. J. J. Stürzinger, London, 1893.

Department of Health and Social Security, *Reform of Social Security*, Cmnd 9517, London, 1985.

Department of Social Security, *The Future of Social Security*, London, 1993.

Deschamps, Eustache, *Oeuvres complètes*, 11 vols, ed. le Marquis de Queux de Saint-Hilaire, Paris, 1878–1903.

de Wildt, A. and van der Ham, W., *Tijd van Leven: Ouder worden in Nederland vroeger en nu*, Amsterdam, 1993.

Dinh Quang-Chi and Labat, Jean-Claude, *Projection de population totale pour la France, 1985–2040*, Les Collections de l'INSEE, Series D, no. 113, Paris, 1987.

Disney, R., Johnson, P. and Stears, G., *Pensions in the UK: Current Situation, Trends, and Policy Options*, London, 1995.

Dobson, E., Review of Richardson, *Old Age*, in *Antiquity*, 1934, vol. 8, pp. 365–6.

Duby, G., 'Dans la France du nord-ouest au XIIᵉ siècle: les jeunes dans la société aristocratique', *Annales ESC*, 1964, vol. 19, pp. 839–43.

Duchêne, J. and Wunsch, G., 'Les tables de mortalité limite: quand la biologie vient au secours du démographe', in M. Loriaux *et al.* (eds), *Populations âgées et révolution grise*, Brussels, 1990, pp. 321–32.

Dumons, B., 'Les retraites sous la troisième république: Lyon et sa région (1880–1914). Population, modes de vie et comportements', Université de Lyon 2, 1990.

Dupâquier, J. (ed.), *Marriage and Remarriage in Populations of the Past*, London, 1981.

Eckhart, Meister, *Sermones*, in *Die deutschen und lateinischen Werke*, vol. 4, ed. E. Benz *et al.*, Stuttgart, 1956.

Eden, Sir F. M., *The State of the Poor*, 3 vols, London, 1797.

Ehmer, J., *Sozialgeschichte des Alters*, Frankfurt, 1990.

Engelbert of Admont, *Liber de causis longevitatis hominum ante diluvium*, in *Thesaurus anecdotorum novissimus*, ed. J. Pertz, Augsburg, 1721, vol. 1, cols 439–502.

Esping-Andersen, G., *The Three Worlds of Welfare Capitalism*, Cambridge, 1990.

Eulner, K.-H., *Die Entwicklung der medizinischen Spezialfächer an den Universitäten des deutschen Sprachgebietes*, Stuttgart, 1970.

Evans, R. J., *In Defence of History*, London, 1997.

Fairburn, M., 'Local community or atomised society? The social structure of nineteenth century New Zealand', *New Zealand Journal of History*, 1982, vol. 16, pp. 146–67.

Fairburn, M., *The Ideal Society and its Enemies: The Foundations of Modern New Zealand Society, 1850–1900*, Auckland, 1989.

Fairburn, M., *Nearly Out of Heart and Hope*, Auckland, 1995.

Falkner, T. M., *The Poetics of Old Age in Greek Epic, Lyric and Tragedy*, London, 1995.

Falkner, T. M. and de Luce, J. (eds), *Old Age in Greek and Latin Literature*, New York, 1989.

Faure, O. and Dessertine, D., *Populations hospitalisées dans la région lyonnaise aux XIXᵉ et XXᵉ siècles*, Lyon, 1991.

Fawcett, H., 'The Beveridge strait-jacket: policy formation and the problem of poverty in old age', *Contemporary British History*, 1996, vol. 10, pp. 20–42.

Featherstone, M. and Hepworth, M., 'The mask of ageing and the postmodern life-course', in M. Featherstone *et al.* (eds), *The Body*, London, 1991.

Febvre, Lucien, 'Vers une autre histoire', *Revue de métaphysique et de morale*, 1949, pp. 237–40.

Feller, E., 'Agents et retraités des transports parisiens: trajectoires individuelles et changement social dans l'entre-deux-guerres', *Mémoires et Documents*, Vincennes, 1994.

Finch, J., *Family Obligations and Social Change*, Cambridge, 1989.

Finch, J. and Groves, D. (eds), *A Labour of Love: Women, Work and Caring*, London, 1983.

Finlay, R., 'The Venetian Republic as a gerontocracy: age and politics in the Renaissance', *Journal of Medieval and Renaissance Studies*, 1978, vol. 8, pp. 157–78.

Finley, M., 'The elderly in classical antiquity', *Greece and Rome*, 1981, vol. 28, pp. 156–71; reprinted in *Ageing and Society*, 1984, vol. 4, pp. 391–408.

Firth, R., Hybert, J. and Forge, A., *Families and their Relatives. Kinship in a Middle Class Sector of London*, London, 1969.

Francis, W. (ed.), *The Book of Vices and Virtues: A Fourteenth-Century Translation of the 'Somme le roi' of Lorens d'Orléans*, London, 1942.

Freeden, M., *The New Liberalism*, Oxford, 1978.

Frossard, Michel, 'Editorial', *Prévenir. Cahiers d'étude et de réflexion édités par la coopérative d'édition de la vie mutualiste*, 1987, no. 15, pp. 3–6.

Fuchs, V. R., *The Future of Health Policy*, Cambridge, MA, 1993.

Fukasawa, K., 'Voluntary provision for old age by trade unions in Britain before the coming of the welfare state', Unpublished Ph.D. thesis, University of London, 1996.

Gagé, J., 'Classes d'âge, rites et vêtements de passage dans l'ancien Latium', *Cahiers internationaux de sociologie*, 1958, vol. 24, pp. 34–64.

Gaillard, Michel *et al.*, 'La consommation en soins de santé des personnes de plus de 60 ans en 1982', *Carnets statistiques*, 1983, no. 6, December, pp. 80–2.

Galt, M., 'Wealth and income in New Zealand, 1879–1939', Unpublished Ph.D. thesis in Economic History, Victoria University of Wellington, 1985.

Gaymu, Joëlle, 'Les populations âgées au recensement de 1982', *Population*, 1985, no. 4–5.

Gerson, Jean, *A un vieillard*, in *Oeuvres complètes*, vol. 2, ed. Mgr. Glorieux, Paris, 1960.

Gilbert, C., 'When did a man in the renaissance grow old?', *Studies in the Renaissance*, 1967, vol. 14, pp. 7–32.

Giraldus Cambrensis [Gerald of Wales], *Gemma ecclesiastica*, ed. J. Brewer, Rolls Series, vol. 21, London, 1862.

Glascock, A. P. and Feinman, S. L., 'Social asset or social burden: treatment of the aged in non-industrial societies', in C. L. Fry (ed.), *Dimensions: Aging, Culture and Health*, New York, 1981.

Gough, I., *The Political Economy of the Welfare State*, London, 1979.

Green, H., *Informal Carers*, General Household Survey 1985, series GN5, no.15, suppl. A, London, 1988.

Guillemard, A.-M., *La retraite: une mort sociale*, Paris, 1973.

Guillemard, A.-M., *La vieillesse et l'Etat*, Paris, 1980.

Guillemard, A.-M., *Le déclin du social: Formation et crise des politiques de la vieillesse*, Paris, 1986.

Guillemard, A.-M., Légaré, J. and Ansart, P. (eds), *Entre travail, retraite et vieillesse: Le grand écart*, Paris, 1995.

Gutton, J.-P., *Naissance du vieillard: Essai sur l'histoire des rapports entre les vieillards et la société en France*, Paris, 1988.

Haber, C., *Beyond Sixty-Five. The Dilemma of Old Age in America's Past*, New York, 1983.

Haber, C., 'Geriatrics: a specialty in search of specialists', *Zeitschrift für Gerontologie*, 1984, vol. 17, pp. 26–31.

Hannah, L., *Inventing Retirement*, Cambridge, 1986.

Hawke, G., *The Making of New Zealand: An Economic History*, Cambridge, 1985.

Hay, J. R., *The Origins of the Liberal Welfare Reforms, 1906–1914*, London, 1975.

Hemming, R. and Kay, J., 'The costs of the State Earnings Related Pension Scheme', *Economic Journal*, 1982, vol. 92, pp. 300–19.

Henderson, J. and Wall, R. (eds), *Poor Women and Children in the European Past*, London, 1994.

Hendricks, J. (ed.), *Health and Health Care Utilization in Later Life*, New York, 1995.

Hennock, E. P., *British Social Reform and German Precedents. The Case of Social Insurance 1880–1914*, Oxford, 1987.

Herlihy, D., 'Age, property and career in medieval society', in M. M. Sheehan (ed.), *Aging and the Aged in Medieval Europe*, Toronto, 1990, pp. 143–58.

Herlihy, D. and Klapisch, Ch., *Les Toscans et leurs familles. Étude du Catasto florentin de 1427*, Paris, 1978.

Hill, C., *Liberty Against the Law*, Harmondsworth, 1997.

Hindle, G. B., *Provision for the Relief of the Poor in Manchester, 1754–1826*, Cheetham Society, Manchester, 1975.

Hitchcock, T., 'Paupers and preachers: the SPCK and the parochial workhouse movement', in L. Davison *et al.* (eds), *Still the Grumbling Hive: The Response to Social and Economic Problems in England 1689–1750*, Stroud, 1992, pp. 145–66.

Hitchcock, T., King, P. and Sharpe, P. (eds), *Chronicling Poverty: The Voices and Strategies of the English Poor, 1640–1840*, London, 1997.

Hollingsworth, T. H., 'A demographic study of the British ducal families', *Population Studies*, 1957, vol. 11, pp. 4–26.

Holz, G., *Die Alterslast – ein Gewinn für andere?*, vol. I, Berlin, 1990.

Honorius Augustodunensis [Honorius of Autun], *De philosophia mundi libri quattuor*, *PL*, vol. 172, pp. 39–102.

Hugonot, Robert and Laurence, *Atlas du vieillissement*, Toulouse, 1988.

Hunt, A., *The Elderly at Home*, London, 1978.

Hunt, E. H., 'Paupers and pensioners, past and present', *Ageing and Society*, 1989, vol. 9, pp. 407–30.

ILO, *From Pyramid to Pillar. Population Change and Social Security in Europe*, Geneva, 1989.

Innes, J., 'The "mixed economy of welfare" in early modern England: assessments of the options from Hale to Malthus', in M. Daunton (ed.), *Charity, Self-interest and Welfare in the English Past*, London, 1996, pp. 139–80.

Innocent III, *Lotharii cardinalis (Innocenti III) De miseria humanae conditionis*, ed. M. Maccarrone, Lugano, 1955.

Jacobs, K., Kniesche, A. and Reschke, P., *Ausgabenprofile nach Alter und Geschlecht in der gesetzlichen Krankenversicherung*, Berlin, 1993.

Jacobs, K., Kohli, M. and Rein, M., 'The evolution of early exit: a comparative analysis of labor force participation patterns', in M. Kohli *et al.* (eds), *Time for Retirement*, Cambridge, 1991, pp. 36–66.

Jacquart, D. and Thomasset, C., *Sexuality and Medicine in the Middle Ages*, trans. M. Adamson, Oxford, 1988.

John of Salisbury, *Policraticus*, 2 vols, ed. C. C. J. Webb, Oxford, 1909; reprint Frankfurt, 1965.

Johnson, P., *Saving and Spending: The Working-class Economy in Britain, 1870–1939*, Oxford, 1985.

Johnson, P., 'The labour force participation of older men in Britain, 1951–81', *Work, Employment and Society*, 1989, vol. 3, pp. 351–68.

Johnson, P., 'The employment and retirement of older men in England and Wales, 1881–1981', *Economic History Review*, 1994, vol. 47, pp. 106–28.

Johnson, P. and Falkingham, J., 'Intergenerational transfers and public expenditure on the elderly in modern Britain', *Ageing and Society*, 1988, vol. 8, pp. 129–46.

Johnson, P. and Falkingham, J., *Ageing and Economic Welfare*, London, 1992.

Jourdain, W., *Land Legislation and Settlement in New Zealand*, Wellington, 1925.

Joyce, P., *Democratic Subjects*, Cambridge, 1994.

Kaminsky, M. (ed.), *The Uses of Reminiscence: New Ways of Working with Older Adults*, New York, 1984.

Karn, V., *Retiring to the Seaside*, London, 1977.

Kelley, D. R., *Historians and the Law in Postrevolutionary France*, Princeton, NJ, 1984.

Kertzer, D. I. and Laslett, P. (eds), *Aging in the Past: Demography, Society and Old Age*, Berkeley, CA, and London, 1995.

Kertzer, D. I. and Schaie, W. K. (eds), *Age Structuring in Comparative Perspective*, Hillsdale, NJ, 1989.

King, S. A., 'Poor relief and English economic development reappraised', *Economic History Review*, 1997, vol. 50, pp. 360–8.

King, S. A., 'Reconstructing lives: the poor, the Poor Law, and welfare in Calverley, 1650–1820', *Social History*, 1997, vol. 22, pp. 318–38.

Kirk, H., 'Geriatric medicine and the categorisation of old age – the historical linkage', *Ageing and Society*, 1992, vol. 12, pp. 483–97.

Klapisch, Ch., 'Fiscalité et démographie en Toscane (1427–1430)', *Annales ESC*, 1969, vol. 24, pp. 1313–37.

Klapisch, Ch., ' "A uno pane e uno vino": the rural Tuscan family at the beginning of the fifteenth century', in *Women, Family and Ritual in Renaissance Italy*, Chicago, 1985, pp. 36–67.

Klassen, S., 'Aging gracefully in the eighteenth century: a study of elderly women in old regime Toulouse', Ph.D. thesis, Syracuse University.

Klein, G. A., *Die Deutsche Arbeiterversicherung. Sonderausstellung auf der internat. Hygieneausstellung Dresden 1911. Katalog*, Berlin, 1911.

Kohli, M., 'The world we forgot: a historical review of the life course', in V. W. Marshall (ed.), *Later Life: The Social Psychology of Ageing*, Beverly Hills, CA, 1986, pp. 271–303.

Kohli, M., 'Ageing as a challenge for sociological theory', *Ageing and Society*, 1988, vol. 8, pp. 367–94.

Kohli, M., Rein, M., Guillemard, A.-M. and van Gunsteren, H. (eds), *Time for Retirement: Comparative Studies of Early Exit from the Labour Force*, Cambridge, 1991.

Kondratowitz, H.-J. von, 'The medicalization of old age: continuity and change in Germany from the 18th to the early 20th century', in M. Pelling and R. M. Smith (eds), *Life, Death, and the Elderly*, London, 1991, pp. 134–64.

Korpi, W., *The Democratic Class Struggle*, London, 1983.

Koven, S. and Michel, S. (eds), *Mothers of a New World: Maternalist Politics and the Origins of Welfare States*, New York, 1993.

Labisch, A. and Spree, R. (eds), *'Einem jeden Kranken in einem Hospitale sein eigenes Bett'. Zur Sozialgeschichte des Allgemeinen Krankenhauses in Deutschland im 19. Jahrhundert*, Frankfurt am Main, 1996.

Laczko, F. and Phillipson, C., *Changing Work and Retirement*, Buckingham, 1991.

Laczko, F., Dale, A., Arber, S. and Gilbert, N., 'Early retirement in a period of high unemployment', *Journal of Social Policy*, 1988, vol. 17, pp. 313–33.

Lamond, R. P., *The Scottish Poor Laws: Their History, Policy and Operation*, revised edition, Glasgow, 1892.

Landers, J., 'Introduction', in 'Historical epidemiology and the health transition', *Health Transition Review*, 1992, vol. 2, suppl., pp. 1–27.

Laroque Report, *Commission d'étude des problèmes de la vieillesse*, Paris, 1962.

Laslett, P., 'Family, kinship and collectivity as systems of support in preindustrial Europe: a consideration of the "nuclear hardship" hypothesis', *Continuity and Change*, 1988, vol. 3, pp. 153–75.

Laslett, P., *A Fresh Map of Life: The Emergence of the Third Age*, London, 1989.

Laslett, P., 'Necessary knowledge: age and aging in the societies of the past', in D. I. Kertzer and P. Laslett (eds), *Aging in the Past: Demography, Society and Old Age*, Berkeley, CA, and London, 1995.

Laslett, P. and Wall, R. (eds), *Household and Family in Past Time*, Cambridge, 1972.

Latini, Brunetto, *Li livres dou trésor*, ed. F. J. Carmody, Berkeley, CA, 1948.

Lauwers, M., 'La mort et le corps des saints: La scène de la mort dans les *vitae* du Moyen Age', *Le Moyen Age*, 1988, vol. 94, pp. 21–50.

Lawn, B. (ed.), *The Prose Salernitan Questions*, Oxford, 1979.

Le Bras, H., 'Parents, grands-parents, bisaieux', *Population*, 1973, no.1, pp. 9–38.

Le Bras, H., 'Evolution des liens de famille au cours de l'existence, une comparaison entre la France actuelle et la France du XVIIIe siècle', *Les âges de la vie*, vol. 1, Travaux et documents (INED), no. 96, Paris, 1982, pp. 27–45.

Leonard, E. M., *The Early History of English Poor Relief*, Cambridge, 1900.

Le Roy Ladurie, E., *Les paysans de Languedoc*, 2 vols, Paris, 1966.

Le Roy Ladurie, E., *Montaillou. Village occitan de 1294–1324*, Paris, 1975.

Lewis, J. and Meredith, B., *Daughters Who Care: Daughters Caring for Mothers at Home*, London, 1988.

Lindert, P., 'Poor relief before the welfare ·state: Britain versus the continent, 1780–1880', mimeo, University of California, Davis, October 1997.

Loraux, N., ''Ηβη et ἀνδρεία: deux versions de la mort du combattant athénien', *Ancient Society*, 1975, vol. 6, pp. 1–31.

Loriaux, Michel, 'Il sera une fois . . . La révolution grise, jeux et enjeux autour d'une profonde mutation sociétale', in M. Loriaux *et al.* (eds), *Populations âgées et révolution grise*, Brussels, 1990.

Lowe, R., *The Welfare State in Britain since 1945*, Basingstoke, 1993.

Macnicol, J. and Blaikie, A., 'The politics of retirement, 1908–1948', in Margot Jefferys (ed.), *Growing Old in the Twentieth Century*, London, 1989, pp. 21–42.

Malaigé, E. von, 'Studien über Wesen und Grundlagen seniler Gehstörungen', *Archiv für Psychiatrie*, 1909, vol. 46, no. 3.

Martin, J., 'Unemployment, government and the labour market in New Zealand, 1860–1890', *New Zealand Journal of History*, 1995, vol. 29, pp. 170–96.

Maslowski, Jacqueline and Paillat, Paul, *III, Les ruraux âgés non agricoles*, Travaux et documents (INED), no. 68, Paris, 1976.

Minois, G., *History of Old Age*, Chicago, 1989.

Mitchison, R., 'The Poor Law', in T. M. Devine and Rosalind Mitchison (eds), *People and Society in Scotland, I, 1760–1830*, Edinburgh, 1988, pp. 252–67.

Mitterauer, M. and Sieder, R., *The European Family. Patriarchy to Partnership from the Middle Ages to the Present*, trans. K. Oosterveen and M. Hörzinger, Oxford, 1982.

Mizrachi, A. and Mizrachi, A., 'Les tendances à long terme de la consommation médicale', *Futuribles*, 1990, no. 147, pp. 33–54.

Moreau, Alain, 'Les personnes âgées à travers le système statistique', *Solidarité santé. Etudes statistiques*, 1987, no. 6, pp. 59–72.

Murray, B., *The People's Budget, 1909/10*, Oxford, 1980.

National Council of Social Service, *Over Seventy*, London, 1954.

Neufville, J. and Vogüé, A. (eds and trans), *La règle de Saint Benoit*, 6 vols, Paris, 1972.

*New Zealand Parliamentary Debates*, Wellington, various dates.

Newman-Brown, W., 'The receipt of poor relief and family situation, Aldenham, Hertfordshire, 1630–1690', in R. M. Smith (ed.), *Land, Kinship and Life-Cycle*, Cambridge, 1984, pp. 123–43.

Nuffield Foundation, *Old People: Report of a Survey Committee on the Problems of Ageing and the Care of Old People*, Oxford, 1947.

OECD, *Social Expenditure, 1960–1990: Problems of Growth and Control*, Paris, 1985.

Offe, C., *Contradictions of the Welfare State*, Cambridge, MA, 1984.

Offer, A., 'Between the gift and the market: the economy of regard', *Economic History Review*, 1997, vol. 50, pp. 450–76.

*Official Handbook of New Zealand*, Wellington, 1875.

Ogus, A. I., 'Great Britain', in P. A. Kohler and H. F. Zacher (eds), *The Evolution of Social Insurance, 1881–1981*, London, 1982, pp. 150–264.

Orme, N., 'The medieval almshouse for the clergy: Clyst Gabriel Hospital near Exeter', *Journal of Ecclesiastical History*, 1988, vol. 39, pp. 1–15.

Orme, N., 'Suffering of the clergy: illness and old age in Exeter diocese 1300–1540', in M. Pelling and R. M. Smith (eds), *Life, Death and the Elderly: Historical Perspectives*, London, 1991, pp. 62–73.

Ottaway, S., ' "The decline of life": aspects of aging in eighteenth-century England', Unpublished Ph.D. thesis, Brown University, 1997.

Otter, W. 'Memoir of Robert Malthus', published with 2nd edn of *Principles of Political Economy*, London, 1816.

Paris, Matthew, *Chronica majora*, ed. H. R. Luard, Rolls Series 25 (57), London, 1877.

Parkin, T. G., 'Age and the aged in Roman society: demographic, social, and legal aspects', Unpublished D.Phil. dissertation, University of Oxford, 1992.

Parkin, T. G., *Demography and Roman Society*, Baltimore, MD, and London, 1992.

Parkin, T. G., 'Out of sight, out of mind: elderly members of the Roman *familia*', in B. Rawson and P. R. C. Weaver (eds), *The Roman Family in Italy: Status, Sentiment, Space*, Oxford, 1997.

Parsons, T., *Essays in Sociological Theory*, New York, 1954.

Pedersen, S., *Family, Dependence, and the Origins of the Welfare State: Britain and France, 1914–1945*, Cambridge, 1993.

Pelling, M. and Smith, R. M. (eds), *Life, Death and the Elderly: Historical Perspectives*, London, 1991.

Pertile, A., *Storia del diritto italiano della caduca dell'Impero Romano alla codificazione*, Turin, 1892–1902.

Petrarca, Francesco, *Phisick against Fortune*, trans. Thomas Twyn, London, 1579.

Petrarca, Francesco, *De remediis utriusque fortune*, Rotterdam, 1649.

Philibert, M., 'Le statut de la personne âgée dans les sociétés antiques et préindustrielles', *Sociologie et sociétés*, 1984, vol. 16.2, pp. 15–27.

Philippe de Navarre, *Les quatre âges de l'homme*, ed. M. de Fréville, Paris, 1888.

Phillipson, C., *Capitalism and the Construction of Old Age*, London, 1982.

Pitrou, A., 'A l'ombre des grands-parents', *Autrement*, 1975, no. 3, pp. 104–22.

Plakans, A., 'Stepping down in former times: a comparative assessment of "retirement" in traditional Europe', in D. I. Kertzer and W. K. Schaie (eds), *Age Structuring in Comparative Perspective*, Hillsdale, NJ, 1989, pp. 175–95.

Pollet, G., 'Les retraites en France, 1880–1914: la naissance d'une politique sociale', Université de Lyon 2, 1990.

*Population par sexe, âge et état matrimonial de 1851 à 1962*, INSEE, Paris, 1968, no. 10.

Pouchelle, M. Ch., *The Body and Surgery in the Middle Ages*, trans. R. Morris, Oxford, 1990.

Powell, J. G. F. (ed.), *Cicero, Cato Maior de Senectute*, Cambridge, 1988.

Priestley, J. B., *English Journey*, London, 1934.

Prinzing, F., 'Die Erkrankungshäufigkeit nach Beruf und Alter', *Zeitschrift für die gesamte Staatswissenschaft*, 1902, vol. 58, pp. 432–58.

Qureshi, H. and Walker, A., 'Caring for elderly people: the family and the state', in C. Phillipson and A. Walker (eds), *Ageing and Social Policy. A Critical Assessment*, Aldershot, 1986.

Qureshi, H. and Walker, A., *The Caring Relationship*, London, 1989.

Radke, J., 'Über den Strukturwandel des chirurgischen Krankengutes eines mittleren städtischen Krankenhauses', Unpublished medical thesis, Free University of Berlin, 1965.

Rae, S., *From Relief to Social Work: A History of the Presbyterian Social Service Association, Otago, 1906–81*, Dunedin, 1981.

Ransom, R. L. and Sutch, R., 'The labor of older Americans: retirement of men on and off the job, 1870–1937', *Journal of Economic History*, 1986, vol. 46, pp. 1–30.

Rapetti, L. N. (ed.), *Li livres de jostice et de plet*, Paris, 1850.

*Regulae communis Ianuae anno 1363*, in *Historiae patriae monumenta*, vol.18, ed. C. Desimondi *et al.*, Turin, 1901.

Rein, M. and Salzman, D., 'Social integration, participation and exchange in five industrial countries', in Scott A. Bass (ed.), *Older and Active. How Americans over 55 are Contributing to Society*, New Haven, CT, and London, 1995, pp. 237–62.

Richardson, B. E., *Old Age among the Ancient Greeks. The Greek Portrayal of Old Age in Literature, Art, and Inscriptions, with a study of the Duration of Life among the Ancient Greeks on the basis of Inscriptional Evidence*, Baltimore, MD, 1933.

Roberts, E., *A Woman's Place. An Oral History of Working Class Women, 1890–1940*, Oxford, 1984.

Roberts, E., *Women and Families. An Oral History 1940–1970*, Oxford, 1995.

Robine, Jean-Marie, 'Bilan de santé des populations âgées: mortalité; dépendance et espérance de vie en bonne santé', in *Les institutions sanitaires et sociales face au vieillissement*, Ecole nationale de santé publique, Rennes, September 1988.

Rosenmayr, L. and Kockeis, E., 'Proposition for a sociological theory of aging and the family', *International Social Science Journal*, 1963, vol. 3, pp. 410–26.

Rosenthal, J. T., 'Medieval longevity and the secular peerage 1350–1500', *Population Studies*, 1973, vol. 27, pp. 287–93.

Rosenthal, J. T., 'Retirement and the life cycle in fifteenth-century England', in M. M. Sheehan (ed.), *Aging and the Aged in Medieval Europe*, Toronto, 1990, pp. 173–88.

Ross, E., *Love and Toil. Motherhood in Outcast London*, Oxford, 1993.

Rosser, C. and Harris, C. C., *The Family and Social Change*, London, 1965.

Roussel, Louis, *La famille après le mariage des enfants. Etude des relations entre générations*, Travaux et documents (INED), no. 78, Paris, 1976.

Rowntree, B. S., *Poverty and Progress. A Second Social Survey of York*, London, 1941.

*Royal Commission on the Aged Poor*, PP. 1895, XIV.

Rufinus, *Summa decretorum de Magister Rufinus*, ed. H. Singer, Aalen, 1963.

Rürup, B., 'Bevölkerungsentwicklung und soziale Sicherungssysteme. Prognosen und Optionen', in H.-U. Klose (ed.), *Altern hat Zukunft. Bevölkerungsentwicklung und dynamische Wirtschaft*, Opladen, 1993, pp. 258–85.

Russell, John, *The Boke of Nurture*, ed. F. J. Furnivall, London, 1867.

Samuel, R., *East-end Underworld. Chapters in the Life of Arthur Harding*, London, 1981 .

Sauvy, Alfred, 'La population française jusqu'en 1956, essai de prévision démographique', *Journal de la Société de Statistique de Paris*, 1928, no. 12, December, and 1929, no. 1, January.

Schmid, W., Review of Richardson, *Old Age*, in *Gnomon*, 1934, vol. 10, pp. 529–32.

Schmorrte, S., 'Alter und Medizin. Die Anfänge der Geriatrie in Deutschland', *Archiv für Sozialgeschichte*, 1990, vol. 30, pp. 15–41.

Schwalbe, J. (ed.), *Lehrbuch der Greisenkrankheiten*, Stuttgart, 1909.

Sears, E., *The Ages of Man: Medieval Interpretations of the Life Cycle*, Princeton, NJ, 1986.

Sen, A., *Inequality Reexamined*, Oxford, 1992.

Shahar, S., *Childhood in the Middle Ages*, London, 1990.

Shahar, S., 'Who were the old in the Middle Ages?', *Social History of Medicine*, 1993, vol. 6, pp. 313–41.

Shanas, E. and Sussman, M. B. (eds), *Family, Bureaucracy and the Elderly*, Durham, NC, 1977.

Sharpe, P., 'Gender-specific demographic adjustment to changing economic circumstances: Colyton 1538–1837', Unpublished Ph.D. thesis, University of Cambridge, 1988.

Sheldon, J. H., *The Social Medicine of Old Age*, Oxford, 1948.

Shragge, E., *Pensions Policy in Britain*, London, 1984.

Siegel, J. S., 'On the demography of aging', *Demography*, 1980, vol. 17, pp. 345–64.

Simmons, L. W., *The Role of the Aged in Primitive Society*, New Haven, CT, 1945.

Simmons, L. W., 'Aging in pre-industrial societies', in C. Tibbits (ed.), *Handbook of Social Gerontology: Societal Aspects of Aging*, Chicago, 1960.

Sixsmith, A., 'Independence and home in later life', in C. Phillipson *et al.* (eds), *Dependency and Interdependency in Old Age*, London, 1986, pp. 338–47.

Slack, P., *Poverty and Social Policy in Tudor and Stuart England*, London, 1988.

Slack, P., *The English Poor Law 1531–1782*, London, 1990.

Smith, J., 'The computer simulation of kin sets and kin counts', in J. Bongaarts *et al.* (eds), *Family Demography: Methods and Their Applications*, Oxford, 1987, pp. 249–66.

Smith, R. M. (ed.), *Land. Kinship and Life-Cycle*, Cambridge, 1984.

Smith, R. M., 'The structured dependency of the elderly as a recent development: some sceptical historical thoughts', *Ageing and Society*, 1984, vol. 4, pp. 409–28.

Smith, R. M., 'Welfare and the management of demographic uncertainty', in M. Keynes *et al.* (eds), *The Political Economy of Health and Welfare*, London, 1988, pp. 108–35.

Smith, R. M., 'The manorial court and the elderly tenant in late medieval England', in M. Pelling and R. M. Smith (eds), *Life, Death and the Elderly: Historical Perspectives*, London, 1991, pp. 39–61.

Smith, R. M., 'Les influences exogènes sur le "frein préventif" en Angleterre 1600–1750', in A. Blum *et al.* (eds), *Modèles de démographie historique*, Paris, 1992, pp. 173–91.

Smith, R. M., 'Charity, self-interest and welfare: reflections from demographic and family history', in M. Daunton (ed.), *Charity, Self-interest and Welfare in the English Past*, London, 1996, pp 23–49.

Snell, K. D. M., *Annals of the Labouring Poor: Social Change and Agrarian England 1600–1900*, Cambridge, 1985.

*Social Insurance and Allied Services* (The Beveridge Report), Cmd. 6404, London, 1942.

Sokoll, T., 'The pauper household: small and simple? The evidence from listings of inhabitants and pauper lists in early modern England reassessed', *Ethnologia Europaea*, 1987, vol. 17, pp. 21–33.

Sokoll, T., *Household and Family Among the Poor: The Case of Two Essex Communities in the Late Eighteenth and Early Nineteenth Centuries*, Bochum, 1992.

Sokoll, T., 'The household position of elderly widows in poverty. Evidence from two Essex communities in the Late eighteenth century', in J. Henderson and R. Wall (eds), *Poor Women and Children in the European Past*, London, 1994, pp. 207–24.

Sokoll, T., 'Old age in poverty: the record of Essex pauper letters, 1780–1834', in T. Hitchcock *et al.* (eds), *Chronicling Poverty: The Voices and Strategies of the English Poor, 1640–1840*, London, 1997, pp. 127–54.

Solar, P., 'Poor relief and English economic development before the industrial revolution', *Economic History Review*, 1995, vol. 48, pp. 1–22.

Solar, P., 'Poor relief and English economic development: a renewed plea for comparative history', *Economic History Review*, 1997, vol. 50, pp. 369–74.

Sorensen, A., 'Old age, retirement, and inheritance', in D. I. Kertzer and W. K. Schaie (eds), *Age Structuring in Comparative Perspective*, Hillsdale, NJ, 1989, pp. 197–213.

Spree, R., 'Krankenhausentwicklung und Sozialpolitik in Deutschland während des 19. Jahrhunderts', *Historische Zeitschrift*, 1995, vol. 260, pp. 75–105.

Stahmer, H. M., 'The aged in two ancient oral cultures: the ancient Hebrews and Homeric Greece', in S. F. Spicker *et al.* (eds), *Aging and the Elderly: Humanistic Perspectives in Gerontology*, Atlantic Highlands, NJ, 1978.

Stavenuiter, M., Bijsterveld, K. and Jansens, S. (eds), *Lange levens, stille getuigen: Oudre vrouwen in het verleden*, Zuthpen, 1995.

Stearns, P., *Old Age in European Society*, London, 1977.

Stearns, P. N., 'Review article', *History and Theory*, 1991, vol. 30, pp. 261–70.

Steiwer, N., 'Le personnage du vieillard dans le discours littéraire au XIXème siècle', Maîtrise d'histoire, Université de Paris, 1990.

Stone, L., *The Family, Sex and Marriage in England 1500–1800*, London, 1977.

Stumm, I. von, *Gesundheit, Arbeit und Geschlecht im Kaiserreich am Beispiel der Krankenstatistik der Leipziger Ortskrankenkasse, 1887–1905*, Frankfurt am Main, 1995.

Suder, W. (ed.), *Geras. Old Age in Greco-Roman Antiquity: A Classified Bibliography*, Wroclaw, 1991.

Sullerot Report, 'La situation démographique de la France et ses implications économiques et sociales: bilan et perspectives', *Journal Officiel*, 1978, no. 15, pp. 803–38.

Szreter, S., 'The idea of demographic transition and the study of fertility change: a critical intellectual history', *Population and Development Review*, 1993, vol. 17, pp. 659–701.

Tennant, M., *Paupers and Providers: Charitable Aid in New Zealand*, Wellington, 1989.

Thane, P., 'Non-contributory versus insurance pensions, 1878–1908', in Pat Thane (ed.), *The Origins of British Social Policy*, London, 1978, pp. 84–106.

Thane, P., 'Old age in English history', in C. Conrad and H.-J. von Kondratowitz (eds), *Zur Kulturgeschichte des Alterns*, Berlin, 1993, pp. 17–37.

Thane, P., 'The cultural history of old age', *Australian Cultural History*, 1995, vol. 14, pp. 23–9.

Thane, P., 'Old people and their families in the English past', in M. Daunton (ed.), *Charity, Self-interest and Welfare in the English Past*, London, 1996, pp. 113–38.

Thane, P., *Old Age: Continuity and Change in English History*, Oxford, 1999.

Thomas Aquinas, St, *Summa theologiae*, ed. and trans. The Fathers of Blackfriars, London, 1974.

Thompson, E. P., *The Making of the English Working Class*, London, 1963.

Thompson, P., Itzin, C. and Abenstern, M., *I Don't Feel Old*, Oxford, 1990.

Thomson, D., 'Provision for the elderly in England, 1830–1908', Unpublished Ph.D. thesis, University of Cambridge, 1980.

Thomson, D., 'From workhouse to nursing home: residential care of elderly people in England since 1840', *Ageing and Society*, 1983, vol. 3, pp. 43–70.

Thomson, D., ' "I am not my father's keeper": families and the elderly in nineteenth century England', *Law and History Review*, 1984, vol. 2, pp. 265–86.

Thomson, D., 'The decline of social welfare: falling state support for the elderly since early Victorian times', *Ageing and Society*, 1984, vol. 4, pp. 451–82.

Thomson, D., 'The welfare of the elderly in the past: a family or community responsibility?', in M. Pelling and R. M. Smith (eds), *Life, Death and the Elderly: Historical Perspectives*, London, 1991, pp. 194–221.

Thomson, D., *A World Without Welfare: New Zealand's Colonial Welfare Experiment*, Auckland, 1998.

Thuillier, G., *Les pensions de retraite des fonctionnaires au XIXème siècle*, Paris, 1994.

Tomkins, A., 'The experience of urban poverty: a comparison of Oxford and Shrewsbury, 1740–70', Unpublished D.Phil. thesis, University of Oxford, 1994.

Townsend, P., *The Family Life of Old People*, London, 1957.

Townsend, P., 'Surveys of old age in Great Britain, 1945–1958', *Bulletin of the World Health Organization*, Geneva, 1959, no. 21, pp. 583–91.

Townsend, P., *The Last Refuge*, London, 1964.

Townsend, P. and Wedderburn, D., *The Aged in the Welfare State*, London, 1965.

Toynbee, C., 'Class and social structure in nineteenth century New Zealand', *New Zealand Journal of History*, 1979, vol. 13, pp. 65–84.

Toynbee, C., *Her Work and His, Kin and Community in New Zealand, 1900–1930*, Wellington, 1995.

Troyansky, D. G., *Old Age in the Old Regime: Image and Experience in Eighteenth-Century France*, Ithaca, NY, 1989.

Troyansky, D. G., 'Old age, retirement, and the social contract in 18th- and 19th-century France', in C. Conrad and H.-J. von Kondratowitz (eds), *Zur Kulturgeschichte des Alterns*, 1993, pp. 77–95.

Troyansky, D. G., ' "I was Wife and Mother". French widows present themselves to the Ministry of Justice in the early nineteenth century', in M. Stavenuiter *et al.* (eds), *Lange levens, stille getuigen: Oudre vrouwen in het verleden*, Zuthpen, 1995, pp. 118–32.

Troyansky, D. G., 'Retraite, vieillesse, et contrat social: l'exemple des juges de la Haute-Vienne sous la Restauration', in A.-M. Guillemard *et al.* (eds), *Entre travail, retraite et vieillesse*, 1995, pp. 85–101.

Troyansky, D. G., 'Progress report: the history of old age in the western world', *Ageing and Society*, 1996, vol. 16, pp. 233–43.

Tunstall, J., *Old and Alone*, London, 1966.

Vallin, Jacques and Meslé, France, *Les causes de décès en France de 1925 à 1978*, Travaux et documents (INED), no. 115, Paris, 1988.

van Hooff, A. J. L., *From Autothanasia to Suicide: Self-Killing in Classical Antiquity*, London, 1990.

Van Kley, D. (ed.), *The French Idea of Freedom: The Old Regime and the Declaration of Rights of 1789*, Stanford, CA, 1994.

'Vieillissements', *Prévenir. Cahiers d'étude et de réflexion édités par la coopérative d'édition de la vie mutualiste*, 1987, no. 15, pp. 3–6.

Villehardouin, Geoffroi de, *La conquête de Constantinople*, ed. E. Faral, Paris, 1961.

Vincent de Beauvais, *Bibliotheca mundi seu speculum quadruplex: naturale, doctrinale, morale, historiale*, Douai, 1624.

Vinovskis, M., 'Stepping down in former times: the view from colonial and 19th-century America', in D. I. Kertzer and W. K. Schaie (eds), *Age Structuring in Comparative Perspective*, Hillsdale, NJ, 1989, pp. 215–25.

Wachter, K. W., 'Kinship resources for the elderly', *Philosophical Transactions of the Royal Society of London, Series B*, 1997, vol. 352, pp. 1811–18.

Walafrid Strabo, *Glossa ordinaria, PL*, vol.113.

Wales, T., 'Poverty, poor relief and the life-cycle: some evidence from seventeenth-century Norfolk', in R. M. Smith (ed.), *Land, Kinship and Life-Cycle*, Cambridge, 1984, pp. 351–404.

Walker, A., 'Social and economic policies and older people in the UK', mimeo, University of Sheffield, 1992.

Walker Bynum, C., *Holy Feast and Holy Fast: The Religious Significance of Food to Medieval Women*, Berkeley, CA, 1987.

Wall, R., 'Elderly persons and members of their households in England and Wales from preindustrial times to the present', in D. I. Kertzer and P. Laslett (eds), *Aging in the Past: Demography, Society and Old Age*, London, 1995, pp. 81–106.

Warr, P., 'Age and employment', in M. Dunnette *et al.* (eds), *Handbook of Industrial and Organisational Psychology*, vol. 4, Palo Alto, CA, 1992.

Warren, D. I., *Helping Networks: How People Cope with Problems in the Urban Community*, Notre Dame, IN, 1981.

Wear, A., 'Caring for the sick poor in St. Bartholomew's Exchange, 1580–1676', *Medical History*, 1991, suppl. no. 11, pp. 41–60.

Wenger, G. C., *The Supportive Network: Coping with Old Age*, London, 1984.

Wenger, G. C., 'Support networks in old age: constructing a typology', in M. Jeffreys (ed.), *Growing Old in the Twentieth Century*, London, 1989, pp. 166–85.

Wenger, G. C., 'A comparison of urban with rural support networks: Liverpool and North Wales', *Ageing and Society*, 1995, vol. 15, pp. 59–82.

Wiedemann, T., *Adults and Children in the Roman Empire*, London, 1989.

Wilensky, H., *The Welfare State and Equality: Structural and Ideological Roots of Public Expenditures*, Berkeley, CA, 1975.

Williamson, J. and Pampel, F., *Old-Age Security in Comparative Perspective*, Oxford, 1993.

Willmott, P. and Young, M., *Family and Class in a London Suburb*, London, 1960.

Woloch, I., *The New Regime: Transformations of the French Civic Order, 1789–1820s*, New York. 1994.

World Bank, *Averting the Old Age Crisis*, New York, 1994.

Wrigley, E. A. and Schofield, R. S., *The Population History of England 1541–1871: A Reconstruction*, London, 1981.

Wrigley, E. A., Davies, R. S., Oeppen, J. E. and Schofield, R. S., *English Population History from Family Reconstitutions 1580–1837*, Cambridge, 1997.

Young, M. and Willmott, P., *Family and Kinship in East London*, Harmondsworth, 1957.

Young, M. and Willmott, P., *The Symmetrical Family. A Study of Work and Leisure in the London Region*, London, 1973.

Zerbi, Gabriele, *Gerontocomia*, in *On the Care of the Aged and Maximianus' Elegies on Old Age and Love*, trans. L. R. Lind, Philadelphia, 1988.

# Index

———